B[illegible]G A SUCCESSFUL ARTIST

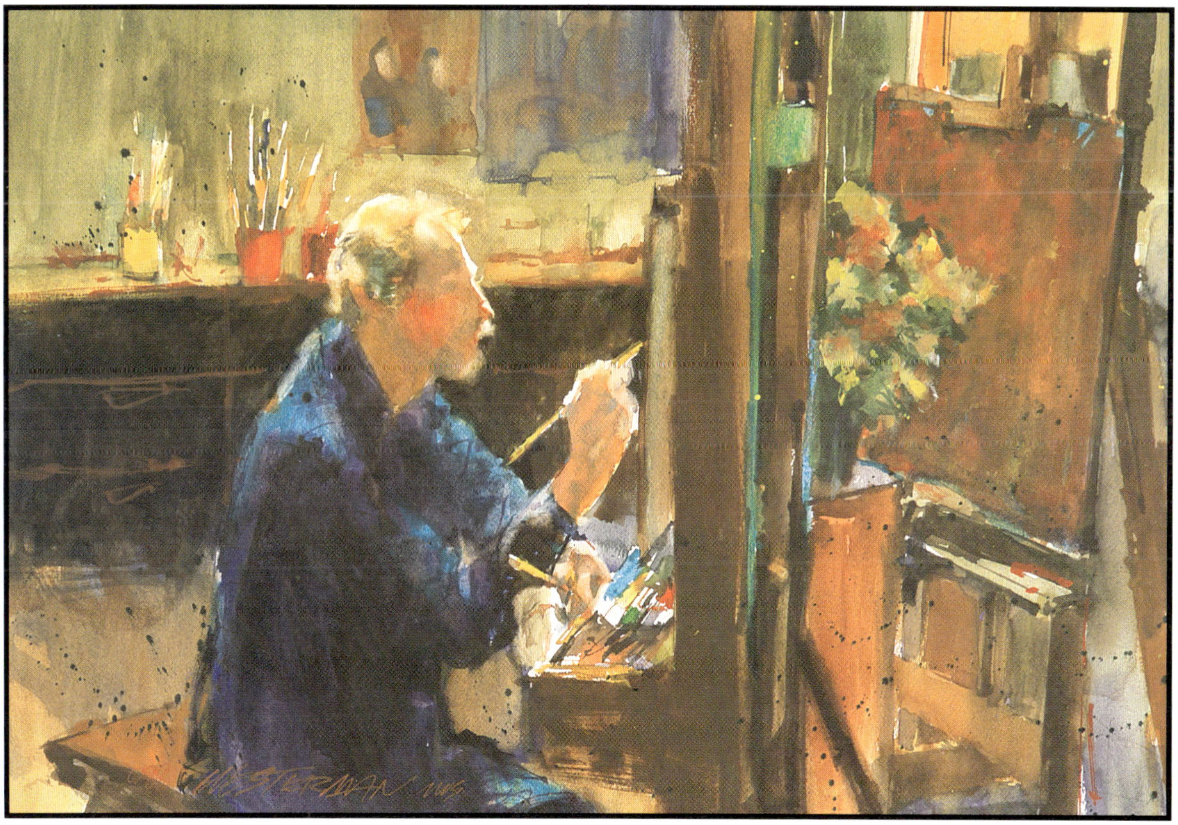

LEWIS LEHRMAN

NORTH LIGHT BOOKS
CINCINNATI, OHIO

ACKNOWLEDGMENTS

THE AUTHOR WOULD LIKE TO THANK THE following people, without whose particular contributions this book would never have been written:

My wife, Lola, for her all-important support; Gerry Metz, who was the first to allow me to rummage through his personal life as I evolved my concepts; Don Holden, for his enthusiasm and encouragement; Robert A. (Bob) Lehrman and Alan Howard, my literary role models; Greg Albert and Rachel Wolf, my North Light editors, for their assistance; and, of course, all those artists who so willingly opened their personal lives and thoughts to me.

 Published by North Light Books, an imprint of F&W Publications, Inc., 1507 Dana Avenue, Cincinnati, Ohio 45207; (800) 289-0963. First paperback printing 1996.

Other fine North Light Books are available at your local bookstore, art supply store or direct from the publisher.

00 99 98 97 96 5 4 3 2 1

Library of Congress Cataloging-in-Publication Data

Lehrman, Lewis Barrett
Becoming a successful artist / Lewis Barrett Lehrman. — 1st ed.
p. cm.
Includes index.
ISBN 0-89134-742-9
1. Artists—United States—Interviews. 2. Success—United States—Psychological aspects. 3. Art, American—Catalogs. 4. Art, Modern—20th century—United States—Catalogs. I. Title.
N6512.L43 1992
700′.92—dc20 91-43473
CIP

Thanks to each artist for permission to use interviews and art.

Edited by Rachel Wolf
Designed by Sandy Conopeotis

DEDICATION

THIS BOOK IS DEDICATED, FIRST, TO those artists who showed me the passion that bridges the chasm between dreamer and doer; and second, to you who read their stories, with the hope that you may find within yourself the passion to realize your dreams, whatever they may be.

ABOUT THE AUTHOR

LEWIS BARRETT LEHRMAN, IS A PROFESSIONAL watercolorist, teacher and author, whose books *Becoming a Successful Artist* (originally published in 1992 under the name *Being An Artist*), *Energize Your Paintings with Color* (1993), *Freshen Your Paintings with New Ideas* (1994), and *Oil Painting: The Workshop Experience* (1995) are published by North Light.

Becoming a Successful Artist came about as a way to answer Lehrman's own questions about art as a career, and he shares the insights and advice of these twenty-one professionals in this book.

Lehrman came to fine art following three decades in commercial art and illustration. He received his education at Carnegie Institute of Technology in Pittsburgh, PA, at Pratt Institute in Brooklyn, NY, and through numerous workshops and classes. A continuing watercolor instructor at The Scottsdale (AZ) Artists' School and elsewhere, his work is currently on exhibit at Vanier & Roberts Fine Arts, in Scottsdale, AZ.

Together with his wife, Lola, the Lehrmans reside in Scottsdale, AZ.

TABLE OF CONTENTS

INTRODUCTION

If anyone ever dreamed of being an artist, I did. It had been in the back of my mind since childhood. But it had always been just that—a dream, never to be taken seriously.

The parental warning, "Do you want to starve in a garrett?" rang in my ears, and I took the safer, more conventional route, establishng a freelance commercial art business in 1958. I met and married Lola in 1961, and together we did all the conventional things: suburban house, children, and all the rest.

By the mid-eighties, Lola and I were both involved in what had grown to become a complex, difficult and exhausting business with demanding deadlines, endless headaches, and a fifteen-employee payroll.

A spare-time painter, I still dreamed of someday being a full-time professional. People liked my watercolors and occasionally bought them. But the pressures of business devoured nearly every waking moment, and the four to six paintings I could find the time and the energy to do each year, usually on vacation trips, left me little opportunity for improvement or growth.

"If I had two years free of the pressures of business," I often said (somewhat naively, as it turned out), "I could be a professional."

Well, thanks to a timely inheritance, that opportunity came in 1984, and Lola and I decided to take it. We closed our business, sold our house and most of the stuff in it, and purchased a lovely two-hundred-year-old village colonial with a barn in the Berkshires of western Massachusetts. What followed was a year and a half of planning and renovation of both home and barn. In 1986, the main floor of our barn opened for business as The Gallery At Mill River. The upper floor became my wonderful, light-filled studio.

I was finally able to get down to full-time painting.

In the winter of 1987 we discovered Scottsdale, Arizona, with its delightful climate, its wonderful art school and its world of professional artists and galleries, and until 1993, when we sold our Massachusetts home and made Arizona our permanent residence, we made the annual round trip between the two.

There, and at home, I began to meet more and more professionals: artists who support themselves through their art. In the Berkshires, there were those whose work we exhibited, plus the artist friends we had come to know over the years. In Arizona, I met many more professionals, and, in getting to know them, began to learn about their backgrounds.

Their stories had never been told. When I began to realize the wealth of experience these artists represent, and how much being able to tap into this resource would mean to artists everywhere, I decided I would have to put their stories down on paper for all to read.

Until I began the project, I had little understanding of the complexity of the career I was attempting, little knowledge of the commitment it demanded, and even less of an idea of how best to pursue it. How valuable a book like this would have been for me along the way! Two years! Hah!

I interviewed as many different kinds of painters as I could. The questions I asked were based on what I, an aspiring professional, wanted to know, as well as what I thought you, the reader, might ask: How did you get where you are? Where is your career headed? How do you approach your work? What advice can you offer? What are your feelings about art in general?

My interviews took me from New England to the Southwest, from Florida to Alaska. I spoke with artists at the pinnacle of their careers, and artists still treading the risky pathways. The experiences and expectations they share are as varied as their artistic approaches. The fabric of art, I have learned, is rich and complex. Within it one finds common threads, and threads that are unique.

Quite incidentally—and totally unexpectedly—putting this book together had an extraordinary effect upon my own work. I had gone into the project worried that writing would take away too much of my painting time. So, arising early each day, I devoted from seven to ten o'clock to the book. By the time I was ready to head for my studio each day, I could hardly wait to get at my painting, so supercharged was I with creative energies and insights absorbed from the stories I was working on. Ideas flowed, and a whole new direction began to emerge in my own painting. In the first five months of 1991, when the bulk of my editing was done, I logged in as many successful paintings as I had completed in all of 1990!

The words of the stories that appear here are the artists' own, with as little tinkering as I could manage. I carefully refrained from editorializing, drawing conclusions, or otherwise attempting to direct the reader's attention to one artist's unassailable way of doing things versus another's. There are contradictions enough to go around. One could hardly expect to get agreement on such a personal subject from so many artists.

The culling of my many interviews (accomplished with my editors, Greg Albert and Rachel Wolf) to the twenty that appear here involved difficult choices. Each that survived the selection process is strong, brimming with hard-won experience. They are full of the kinds of illuminating insights and invaluable advice that any artist (and even the nonartist) can value and put to immediate use.

As the third party to each of these twenty conversations, you are invited to get to know these artists through their stories. Draw your impressions not only from what they say, but from what they leave unsaid. Everyone has to make choices—there are many paths not taken. Whether you use these stories to measure your own life's pathways, or use them as a source of new directions, approaches and insights, I think you will emerge enriched and moved by what you have read.

NITA ENGLE
It's Not the Arrival, It's the Journey

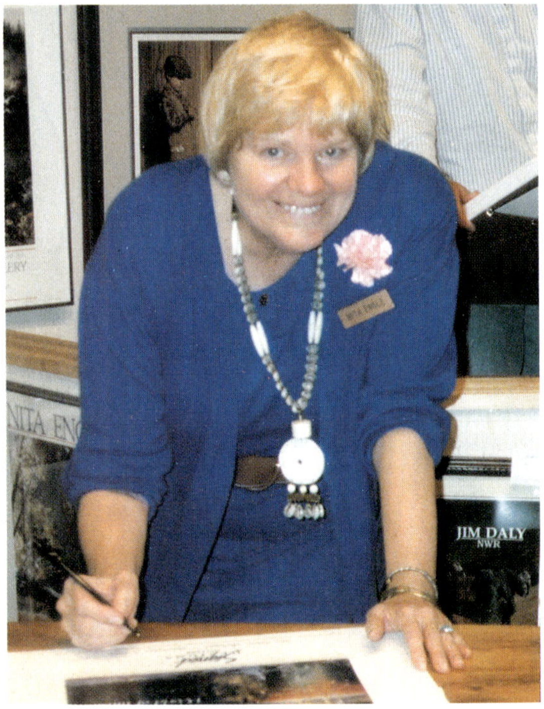

Nita Engle signing some of her popular prints.
Photo courtesy of Mill Pond Press.

I CAME AWAY FROM MY INTERVIEW WITH NITA ENGLE IMPRESSED WITH the sheer energy level of this talented painter. Responding to a question or comment, she would spill out her thoughts in rapid-fire succession, tripping over them as she strived to express them simultaneously. Her mind raced ahead as she anticipated the way our interview was headed, yet never lost track of the question that started her conceptual cascade.

I had finally connected with Nita at her home in Marquette, Michigan, a small town on the Lake Superior shore of the Upper Peninsula. At the edge of the northern wilderness, the scenery is beautiful, the winters long and *very* cold. Here, in the place she has loved and known since childhood, she hikes the woodlands, fly-casts in the Yellow Dog River, canoes the lakes, and absorbs the sights and sounds of the wilderness she paints so evocatively.

It seems that Nita's life moves as rapidly as her thoughts. Her many engagements and exhibitions around the country—and now around the world—leave her little time to cope with the painful back injury, which, it turns out, was the reason I'd had difficulty getting in touch with her. My desperate postcard eventually brought a return call, and the rest was easy.

How did you hurt your back?

I was walking in the woods, and stepped in a hole, and really twisted . . . plus, a whole lifetime of bending over a drawing board for fifteen hours a day.

Have you really been bending over a drawing board for that many years?

From the time I graduated from art school. I was in Chicago. The Artists' Guild there was very helpful . . . sort of an artists' employment agency. They sent me to a wallpaper firm, where I worked for a couple of years.

Designing wallpaper?

You know when you select a wallpaper pattern but you want it in different colors? They had apprentice artists doing all those colorings. I'd start out with thirteen hundred to choose from, and mix from there. It was a terrific background in color. But I got bored after a while, and wanted to move on. So I worked for a newspaper chain, doing layouts and paste-ups. Minor jobs—you know—on the way up. I had a goal, kind of, when I started out, to be self-employed as fast as I could.

As a commercial artist?

A graphic designer. I was really just painting on the side. I knew it was almost impossible to go from art school to making a living at painting. I worked my way through art school, had about three jobs at a time. I knew I'd have to go either into education, or into advertising design. I chose design.

Finally I got a job at a Chicago ad agency as a layout artist . . . then worked my way up. I was an art director and graphic designer for about nine years with this firm, which kept enlarging, merging, taking on new business.

What about being self-employed?

From the time I became art director, I was more or less my own boss. I would bill the agency and they would bill the client. I was called the art director, but I was essentially freelancing. I had a lot of freedom. Toward the end, I was farming mostly everything out to other freelancers, and going home to paint. It's important to develop your own time as fast as you can.

Was art always a passion?

Some of my first memories, at three or four, were my coloring books. They were like magic for me. I'd get up in the middle of the night to color . . . couldn't wait till morning! And I drew my way through school . . . did a lot of cartooning . . . traded cartoons for homework assignments. The first art prize I ever won was in eighth grade, at the county fair, for a painting. I was art editor of the yearbook . . . active in the arts club . . . whatever was going on. My parents were totally supportive.

I went through the Marquette public school system, Northern Michigan University for a year, and then to art school. I came back here only about ten years ago. I've lived all around . . . Chicago, New York, San Francisco, England.

Where did you go to art school?

Chicago Art Institute for four years, then a year at Roosevelt University in Chicago.

But about making the transition to painting. . . . I was living in Old Town in Chicago, right in the middle of the Old Town Art Fair. Most towns have an art fair. You're familiar with these. Well, we lived right in the middle of it, and it was crazy not to be part of it. So that's really how I got my start.

Anyway, I started to sell through the Art Fair, and gradually I started to make more money at painting than at freelancing, so I was

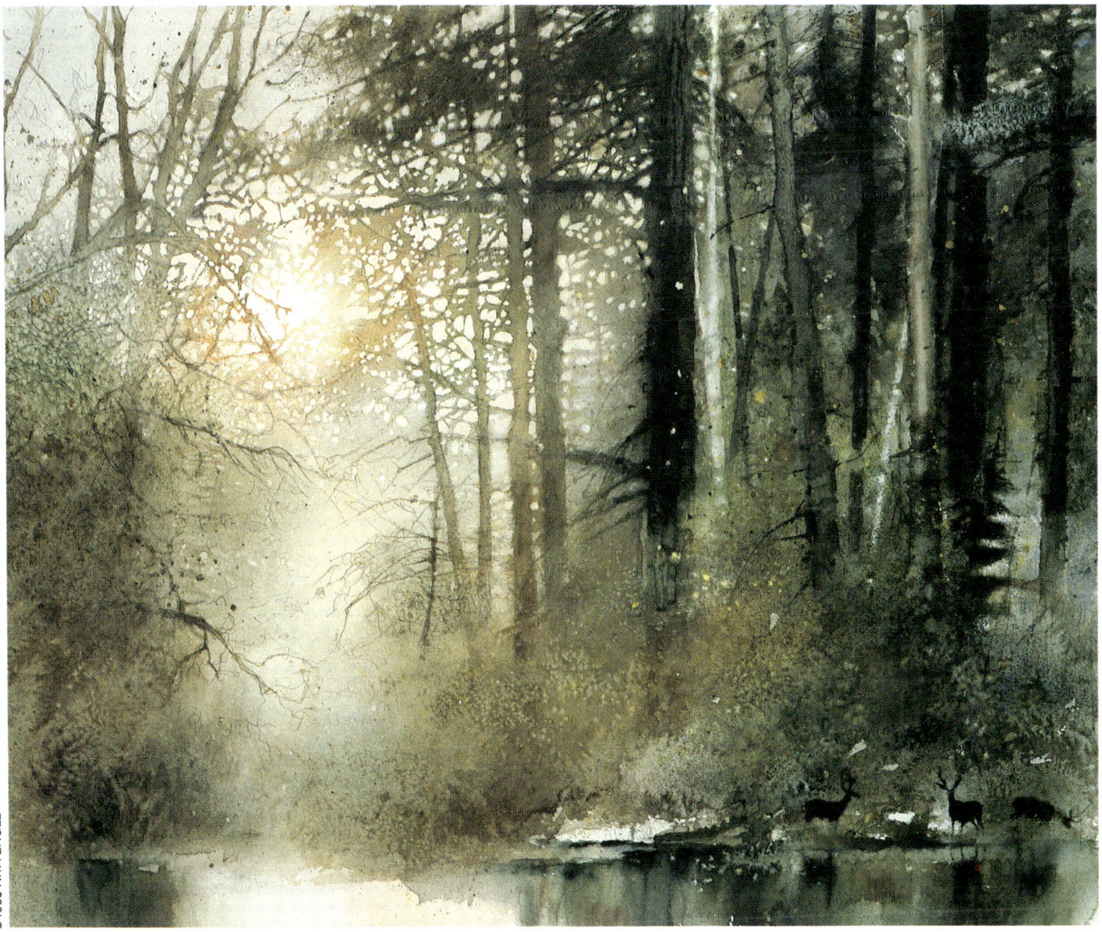

FOREST POOL
1987
WATERCOLOR
30″ × 22″
PRIVATE COLLECTION
PUBLISHED AS A LIMITED EDITION PRINT BY MILL POND PRESS INC.

A forest pool seems to me to be the very essence of wilderness country. There is a sense of timlessness. The greatest challenge here was trying to paint the great silence.
COURTESY OF THE ARTIST AND MILL POND PRESS, VENICE FL 34292-3505

Home Port
Watercolor
22" × 15"
Private Collection

My problem here was to make these lights intense and glowing, and to keep the white boats looking white. Boats and lights were masked. After two graduated dark washes, the mask was peeled. When I finally put a dark wash on the boats—eureka! All the wharf lights went on!

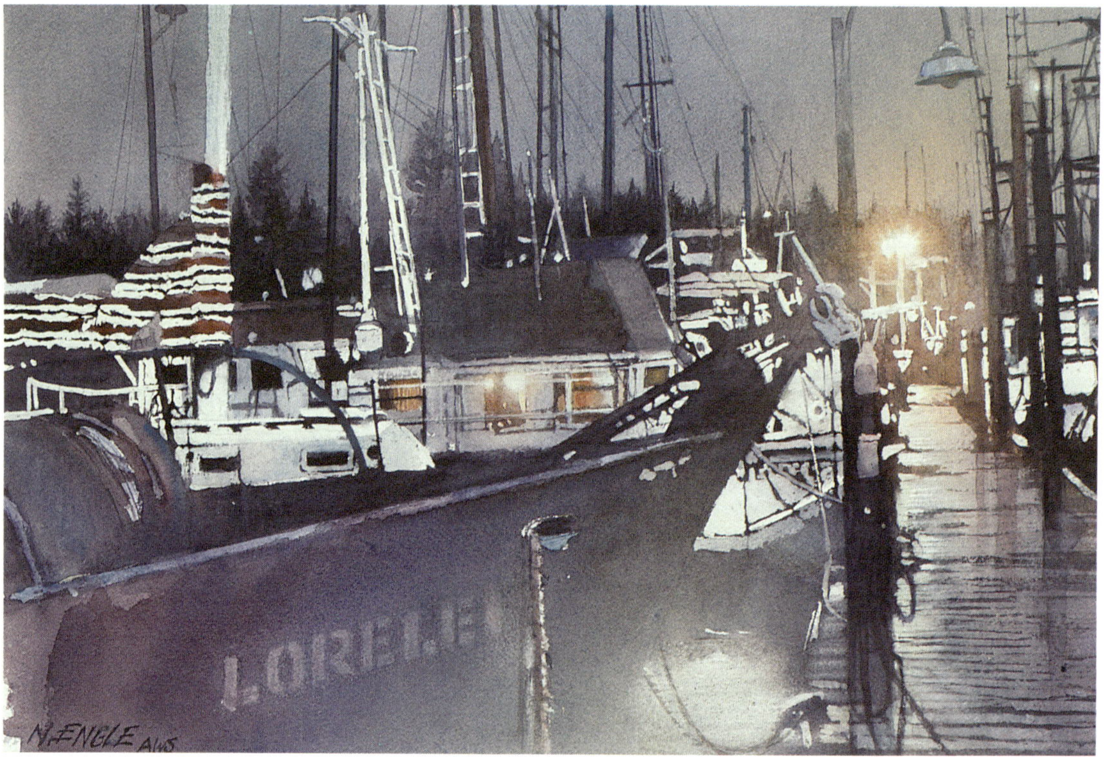

able to leave the agency without any great trauma (though I took a couple of accounts with me when I left, as kind of a safety net).

It's a long way, though, from the local art fair to the national recognition you enjoy today. How did that begin to happen?

It started when I began to enter the national shows. This is what I tell all my students when I do my workshops. You can enter local shows and win the gold medal of honor, and nothing will ever happen to your career. You'll just have the medal. But if you enter the national shows, just getting hung will make things happen.

The first painting I had in the American Watercolor Society show in New York was seen by the *Reader's Digest* people, they asked me to do illustrations for them. I immediately had seventeen million people seeing my work!

I tell my students, it's really important to keep entering national shows. It's just as important as, if you're a writer, to keep sending manuscripts to publishers.

I had no idea it could be such a door opener.

I'll tell you. A.W.S. is like getting a PhD!

You know, there are people in New York whose job it is to find new artists. They go to all these shows to find fresh talent. And lots of art directors with a particular story to illustrate, it might just hit them that this painter would be perfect for the assignment. I thought *Reader's Digest* would be a one-shot deal, but I worked steadily for them for about ten years, not only for the magazine (I always had assignments), but for condensed books, special books and foreign editions. I began getting letters from all over the world. Terrific exposure.

I was one of the few painters they had who were doing illustration in transparent watercolor, because most illustrators work in opaques and acrylics. And one thing led to another. The *Digest* would enter my work in the Society of Illustrators show in New York, which puts out a catalog of the show each year that art directors all over the country see. That's how I got a *Playboy* assignment. Mill Pond Press, my publisher, first saw my work in *Reader's Digest* and contacted me. They have dealers all across the country.

I think it was all the exposure from A.W.S., and *Readers Digest* and Mill Pond Press, that led to my articles in *American Artist*. I was Artist Of The Year and Cover Artist in November of

1984. Because of that (the article said that I gave workshops), I started getting invitations from everywhere to teach.

You were already teaching?

I began when I moved back to Marquette. After the first winter here, I started phoning all those southern places that had written to me, telling them yes, I would do workshops.

Anything to get out of the cold!

The power was off for eight days that winter. No heat, no light, no water. Nothing! They were rescuing people with helicopters! So now I spend a lot of time in the winter teaching workshops in warmer climates.

I've been all over. It would probably be easier to tell you the states I *haven't* been in. Now I'm doing international workshops, too. Last year I taught a painting safari in Africa. There will be a story about it in the watercolor supplement of *American Artist*. It was the experience of my life!

Tell me a little about your work with Mill Pond Press.

They've printed maybe forty-five of my pieces. Limited editions of 950 each. They've enabled me to really have time enough to experiment and grow as a painter. You know, when you sell a painting to somebody, one on one, you're making about a dime an hour, especially if you're slow at doing it.

Are you a slow painter?

I'm fast while it's going on and the paint is wet, but it might take a few weeks or a month or a year of thinking and experimenting before it's finished. I usually have about thirty paintings going at once. When I run into problems, I put them away and don't try to solve them right away. And one may be drying while I work on another. And I'm always into new projects. So I've got a whole lot of things going on at once.

Also, I hate to finish paintings, love to start them. You're going to ask me, "How long does it take you to finish a painting?" Right? My answer to that is, "As long as I've got!" If I've got a *Reader's Digest* deadline, I can finish a painting in a week or two. If I've got a year, it'll take a year. It'll take however long I've got. Because there's always something more I want to do.

And along with that is, "How do you know when a painting is finished?" The way I know is, there's no longer any place on it that irritates me. You know how you see something hanging that you've sold? And you want to snatch it down and take it away because you weren't done with it? Some paintings are an irritation from beginning to end. I tell you, half my work is taking away—rather than putting on—the paint. I call it my rewrite process.

The first part is really when about 90 percent of the paper is covered. It's throwing paint, and doing all kinds of techniques I've invented. Very loose. Very wild. Water running everywhere. After that's finished, there's the process of making it all come together into a painting.

Some people can dash off a perfect paragraph and never take out any words. Others

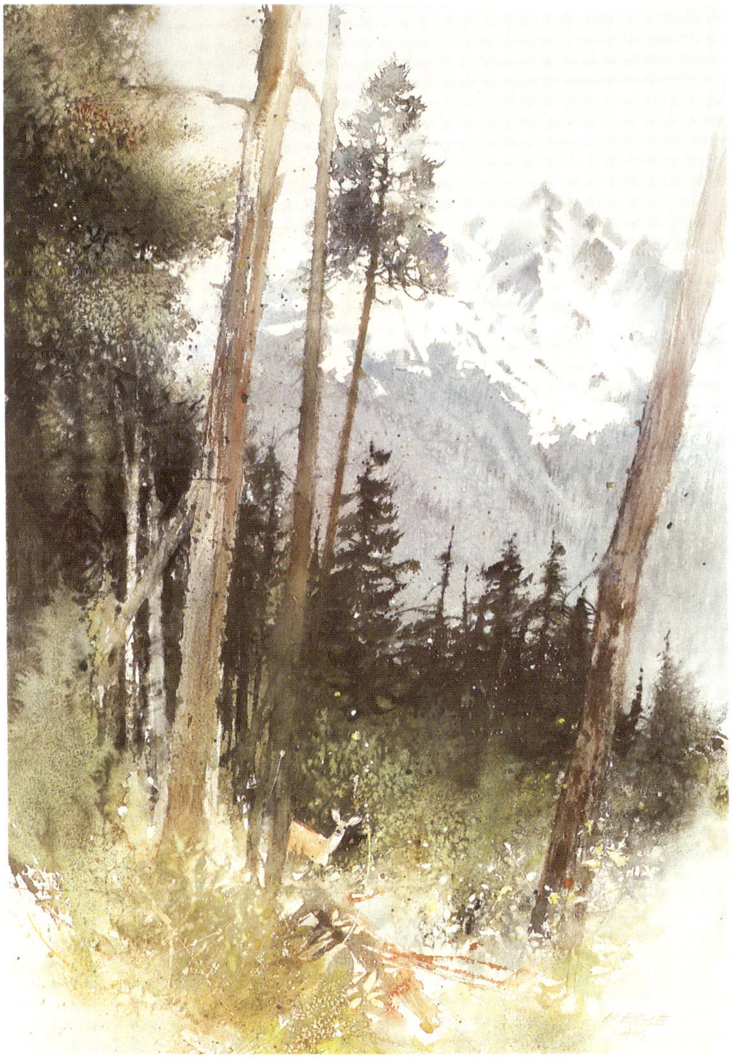

HIGH COUNTRY
WATERCOLOR
22″ × 30″
COLLECTION OF
READER'S DIGEST

A very satisfying painting, with many elements I find attractive. Textures of foliage and tree trunks, the pine trees I love, and above all, the contrasts that are so essential in painting. I tried to recreate my feeling of being overwhelmed by the magnificence of the natural world.

have to edit and edit. It's the same with painting. After I get all the paint on, I begin to eliminate everything that's unnecessary—scrubbing out, lifting, sharpening, taking out all the nonessential things. Everything that's left, at the end, has to be there. All the thinking that goes on with my work takes a long time. With a publisher, I do it once and get 950 in return. And the royalties keep coming in.

Do you paint every day?

I work all the time. In the morning, when I'm fresh, I work on color and on great big beginnings. I have classical music, or nothing, playing, because all my attention is on the painting. Later in the day, when the light starts to go, and after dinner, I work on detail and design. That's when I sit down and put on my glasses, and switch on a mystery story on the TV that my mind doesn't have to be involved with, while I'm doing this little pick, pick, pick detail.

If I'm painting a daisy field, for instance, I do a whole lot of wild texture for the field. That's morning work. After it's dry, maybe in the latter part of the day, I paint a few well-defined daisies in the foreground, and your eye reads the rest of it as a daisy field.

In other words, I'm making textures. I've invented many ways of doing that. I know what texture I'm after. Unlike a lot of painters who start by doing anything and then finding something in it, I really know from the beginning what I'm doing.

I call this way of painting "illusionism," because I'm creating an illusion of what's there. Impressionism is really your impression of what you're looking at. But my way is to add great detail, then take most of it away, to give the illusion. In other words, it's based on fact. I never make up things. I just make them into a painting. Usually, when I'm wandering around outdoors with camera and sketchbook, I'm getting facts for incorporation into a painting.

Do you paint on location?

Despite the weather, and the bugs, and all that, I do love it, and wish I could do more of it. But that's really a luxury now. All my techniques, and all that, are in the studio, so that's where most of the work gets done.

In the course of your career, has there been a role model in your life?

All along there have been people who've helped,

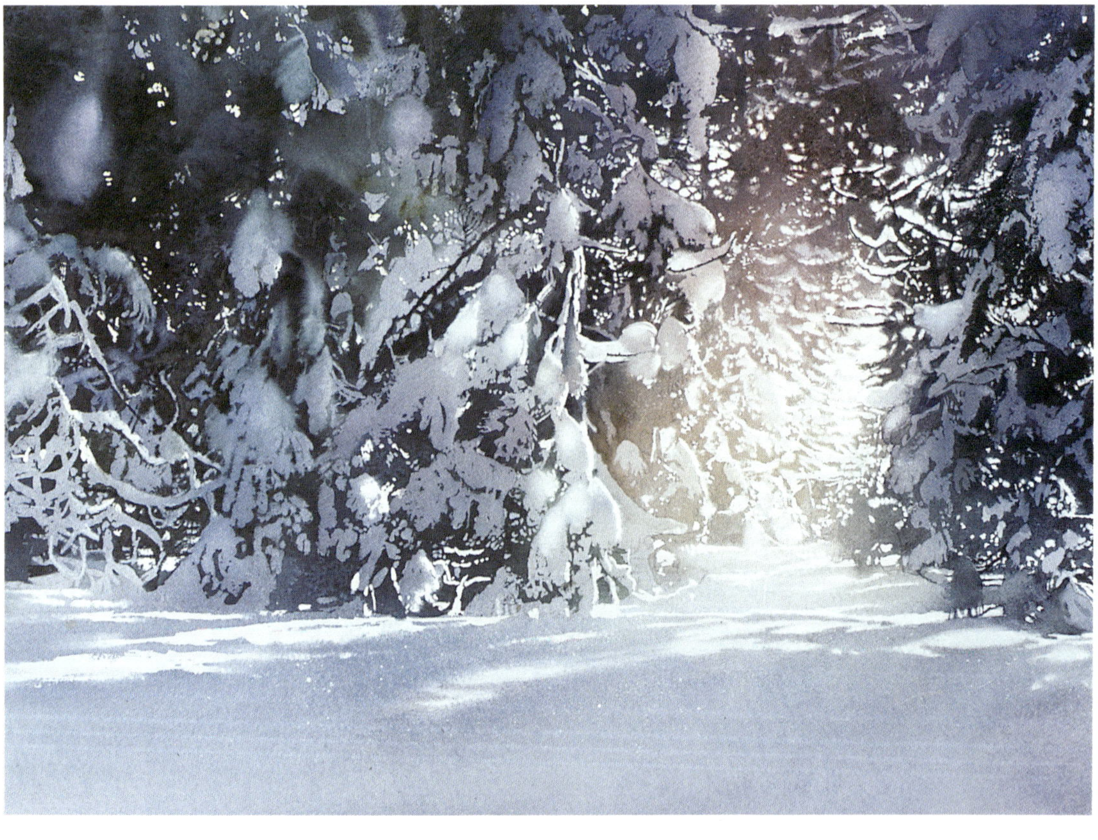

New Snow
Watercolor
30″ × 22″
Collection of
Dr. and Mrs. D.
Elzinga

This dazzling scene, and its profusion of detail, seemed at first impossible to paint. I have developed my methods by attempting to solve such problems as this. It is, in reality, illusion. And that is why I call my work "illusionism."

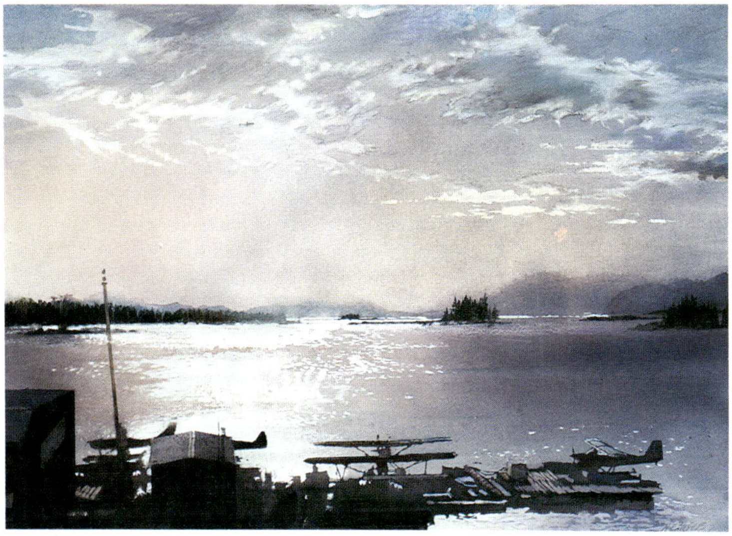

Into the Sun
Watercolor
30″ × 22″
Private Collection

I am most happy in my work when I am exploring ways to paint light. I decided to make the foreground almost a silhouette to emphasize "into the sun." After I'd finished, I decided the clouds needed a silver lining, so I lifted out the paint with my electric eraser.

but not a major figure. My hero in painting was J.M.W. Turner, the English painter [1775-1851]. I laughed when I read one thing about him: They'd be hanging his show, and he would still be running around with his paints, working on them right up to the opening!

Do you do that too?

There must be a reason why I'm racing to the airport every time with the paint still wet, to meet a deadline. Not just once in a while. Every time! It's not that I let it go till the last minute. I'm painting on it all the time, but there's always more to see, or do, or take off.

Why do you think some artists make it as professionals, while others end up dropping out?

I think that's entirely dependent on the paintings themselves. There are many people—some pretty well known—whose publicity is way ahead of their painting. I've always believed in letting my painting lead the way. If your painting is good, doors can be opened for you. It has a lot to do with your paintings' acceptance, plus your own determination and motivation.

You're talking about two different things: talent and perseverance.

I don't believe there's any such thing as talent, except for geniuses like Mozart. I think it's a desire to do it that starts when you're about four years old—whether to play ball, or the violin, or make art. Then, just by doing it all the time, you get very good at it . . . better than anyone else who *hasn't* been working at it. Perseverance—just working at it—is 90 percent of it.

People say, "I want to be an artist." Or even worse, "I want to be a *famous* artist." That has nothing to do with reality. The wording should be, "I want to *do* art!" Not, "I want to be a painter," but, "I want to paint!" One is wanting the persona. The other is actually being in love with the work. And in the end, that is the only thing that matters. I'll never get enough painting in. I'll never get my fill. I've got material for three hundred years! A constant challenge. It's exciting to me every time I do it!

Let's talk about that excitement and how it comes through in an artist's work. Why is it that some work seems to come alive on the wall, while other work just sits there, virtually invisible?

I have a really strong opinion about that. In fact, let me tie that in with the shows I judge all across the country.

To specifically answer your question (and this is really the second of the four points that I look for), this "life," as you put it, is the easiest to get into your painting. The only thing you have to do is to *love* your subject—what you're doing. And it happens. Never paint anything you're not absolutely excited about. I mean, if you're bored with it, everybody else will be, too. So I've given prizes where maybe the technique wasn't so good, almost primitive. But it had this "heart," I call it, this life to it. Because the painter loved what he was doing.

Now, of course, I have to hear your other three criteria.

Number one: Most important, the very first thing I look for, that I think every judge looks for, as the slides go flashing by, is shape: Design, composition. . . .

Number two is "heart."

Third is some kind of unusual perspective. I think that's more important than the drawing, when you're in a competition. It isn't necessary for enjoying a painting, but it is for judging. I totally ignore things like the golden mean. I like the excitement of the more dramatic viewpoint, I guess, because I was a graphic designer. And an unusual perspective stands out.

Finally, subject matter is important in a

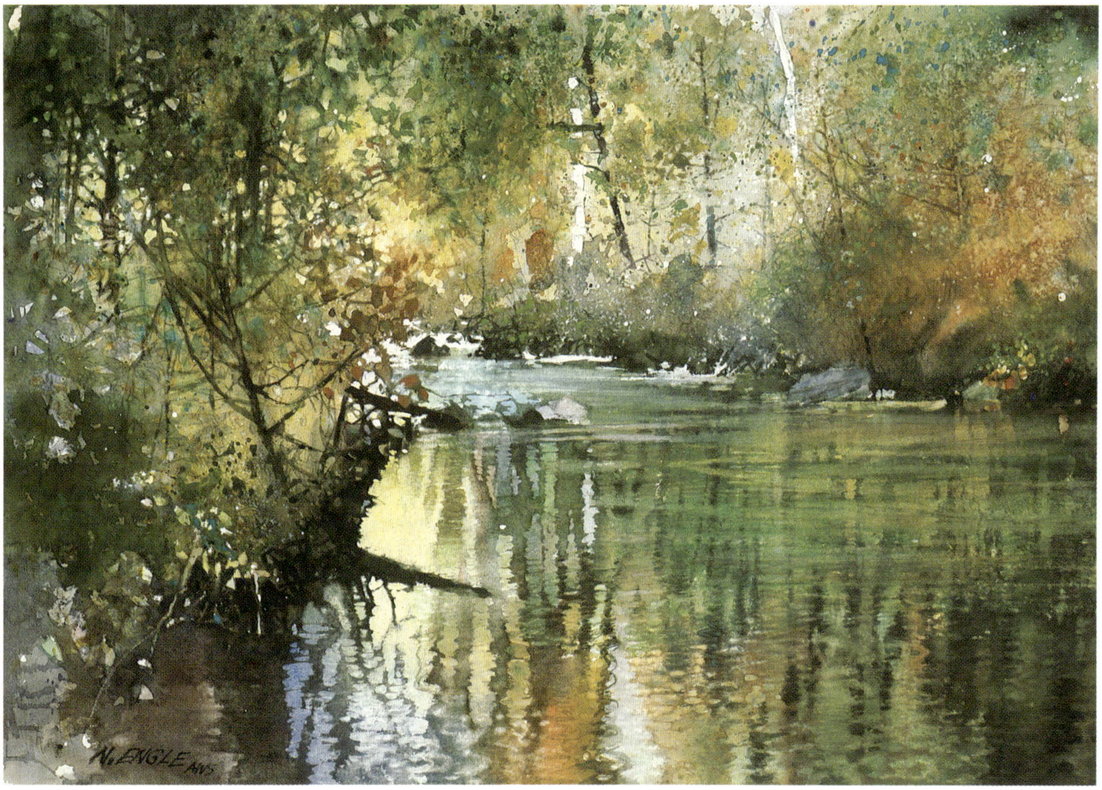

©1983 NITA ENGLE

Summer River
Watercolor
30″ × 22″
Private Collection
Published as a limited edition print by Mill Pond Press Inc.

One hot summer day I was fishing in this stream when I heard splashing upstream. Before I could move, I saw, coming around the bend on his hind legs, a bear, fishing or just splashing. I never found out. I was gone—leaving fifty feet of line wrapped around every bush and tree along the way. That day I decided to stay inside, and I painted this watercolor.
Courtesy of the artist and Mill Pond Press, Venice FL 34292-3505

competition, because there are fads. If you're on the jury, you may let in the first eight or ten still lifes with fruit jars and doilies, but after that you can't let in any more. Even if a stupendous one comes up later on, you'll have to reject it, because you really can't go back and remove the others, and you're trying to put together a well-rounded show. So what I'm trying to say is, be true to yourself. Don't try to second-guess the judges, just paint what you want.

What advice would you offer to artists who would like to live by their work?

Paint all the time. As much as you can. Study design! Experiment! And make a place where you don't have to put your stuff away. Studio space is absolutely essential; otherwise you won't have the desire. You have to have the desire. That's number one. My God, it's like running a business for yourself. You work ten times harder—much harder than if you have a job somewhere.

Enter national shows, no matter how many times you get rejected. Now, I'm not saying *not* to enter local things. They're important too. You become used to competition, which is really important to making you grow as an artist.

How about attending workshops?

It's good to learn the tools of the trade first, but after that, you have to develop them, and make them your own. . . . You have to have some unique thing that other people don't have. The way you find this is by working all the time and not repeating yourself, by trying things that will make you more creative. Explore. Experiment.

Read something—a descriptive passage of a novel, say—and illustrate it. Give yourself a deadline. I found my creativity by having assignments from publishers. The challenge made me think a whole different way.

But at what point should someone quit a job to try and make a go of art?

I don't know if there's any way you could just baldly quit a job and hope to make a living painting. I did it gradually.

I used to think the artist should try to get an art-related job, but maybe not. I know a painter who said he used it all up, and he'd rather drive a truck or dig a ditch, and then paint later. But you can't have a job that makes you so worn out that you don't work.

The ideal might be, when you're selling a few paintings, winning a few prizes, to get a part-time job. I really don't advocate quitting cold. I know people who are doing it, but there seems to be a great mass of really good painters working their way up in the galleries. Making it with the galleries is a long, slow way for a watercolorist.

Being published is a really good path to success. Maybe I'm advocating this because that's how I did it, but that's all I really know for sure: how I did it.

What's your definition of success?

Hmm. I feel like I should have great words of wisdom here. One of the things is never quite being able to paint the painting that satisfies you. It keeps you coming back for the next one. I guess what I'm really saying is, it's the doing of it that's success. It's not the arrival, it's the journey. It's doing what you really love to do, what you'd do whether you got paid for it or not. And watching your growth and getting more command of your work.

This sounds so clichéd: doing what you love to do, for a living. And making a living at it . . . that's a bonus. But to be a success, professionally, you have to become known, too. It's fun to win. It's fun to be recognized. I don't want to put that down. I guess there are many forms of success.

When are you going to do a book?

I've had a contract on my desk for a couple of years. But my friends warned me not to sign it until I'm ready to give my life to it, and I'm not there yet.

Have you seen the PBS program about my work? It's a half-hour program that was all over the country for a while. It's called *Nita Engle in Michigan*. (1985, Mill Pond Press, 310 Center Court, Venice FL, 34292. VHS, 30 min.) I was impressed with the crew that made it, and I might do my own instructional video one day.

Any final thoughts?

If I think of anything brilliant, I'll call you.

BLUE POOL
WATERCOLOR
22″ × 15″
COLLECTION OF
JUDGE AND MRS.
EDWARD QUINELL

This brook is all the more a valued treasure because it is in the back country, and such a struggle to get to, through bogs and over logs in low country, climbing rocks in high country. Lovely wilderness. My choice was a time of brilliant colors and intense sky, all reflected in this blue pool.

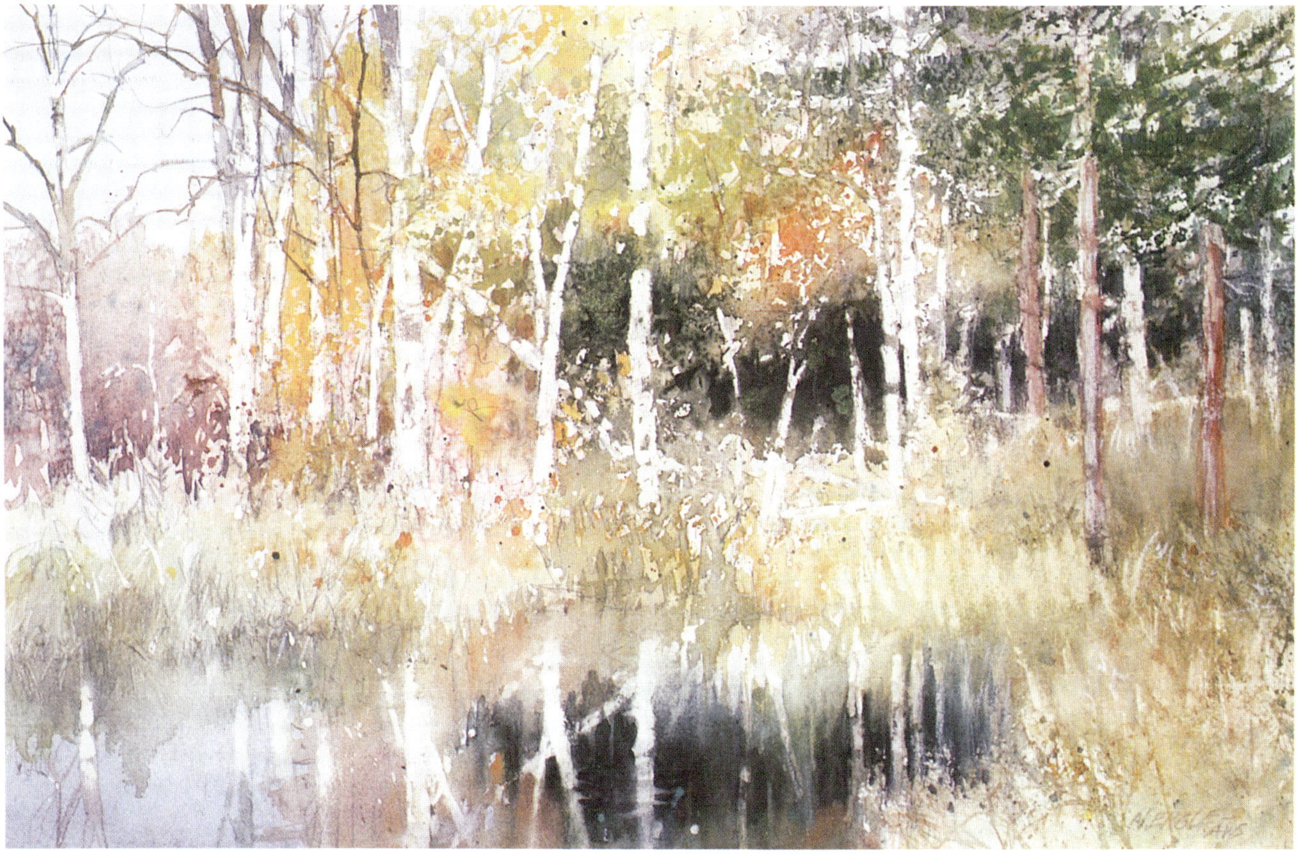

HARLEY BROWN

The Harder You Work, the Luckier You Get

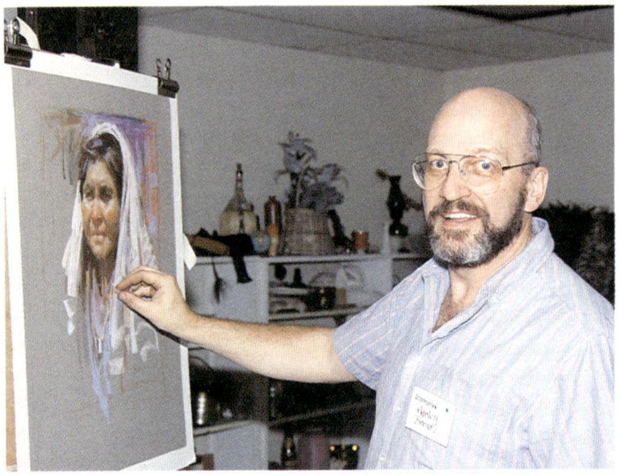

I caught Harley Brown at a demo during his Scottsdale Artists' School workshop. Photo by Lew Lehrman.

I'VE KNOWN HARLEY BROWN SINCE 1988, THE YEAR THAT MY WIFE, LOLA, was enrolled in his pastel portraiture workshop at the Scottsdale Artists' School. The sounds of the class, including (believe it or not), tap dancing, singing, keyboard music, laughter, plus Harley's unmistakable voice above the din, filtered through the door to the next room, where I was enrolled in another, more sedate class.

It is impossible not to be drawn into the fun and excitement that seem to surround Harley, who is fanatically devoted not only to his art, but to the imperative of communicating everything he knows about it in the space of a week.

It would be easy to pigeonhole Harley as totally obsessed with pastel portraiture, but that would miss his essence entirely. He is, in truth, a sensitive, caring, complete person whose genius (yes, genius), tenacity and faith have guided him through adversities that would have flattened most of us. Today, even as his work achieves the recognition it deserves, Harley is growing, evolving, and exploring his art in new ways. His joy of life and his love for people come through strongly.

We met for our interview one evening in Scottsdale after a grueling workshop day, and though exhausted (as was he) and battling an oncoming cold, I was swept along by his incredible energy. We continued long into the night, for one of my longest, and most electric, interviews.

At one point I asked him to speak directly to the aspiring professional:

I know how desperately terrible it is to try to get into the art world. Really tough. My suggestion is that the easiest thing to do is give up. Just quit. But, if you're determined, and you really want to make it, just know that virtually everybody else is going to give up. That leaves the road clear for you.

Was giving up ever an option you considered?

Despite everything, I have to tell you that not for one minute, not for one second, did I ever give up hope. I just had faith that eventually things would get better. Maybe not today, and maybe not next week. But someday. As an artist, you must never let go of that faith in yourself, that you're going to get better, and that things will get better.

When did you first realize that you wanted to be an artist?

From the very beginning. It's not as if I decided "I want to be an artist." It was always art.

My dad was an artist, a cartoonist with the local papers back in Moose Jaw, Saskatchewan. At the age of seven he was showing me the dynamics of art—like perspective, and light and shadow—that most people don't learn until their twenties.

When I was in eighth grade, a kid sold me an Andrew Loomis book for twenty-five cents: *Figure Drawing for All It's Worth.* That started me off, and it has influenced me to this day.

Luckily, I always had good art teachers. I had absolutely the worst marks in the history of the school, could never figure out chemistry, trigonometry, physics.

I made it through high school—barely—and went to work for a window display com-

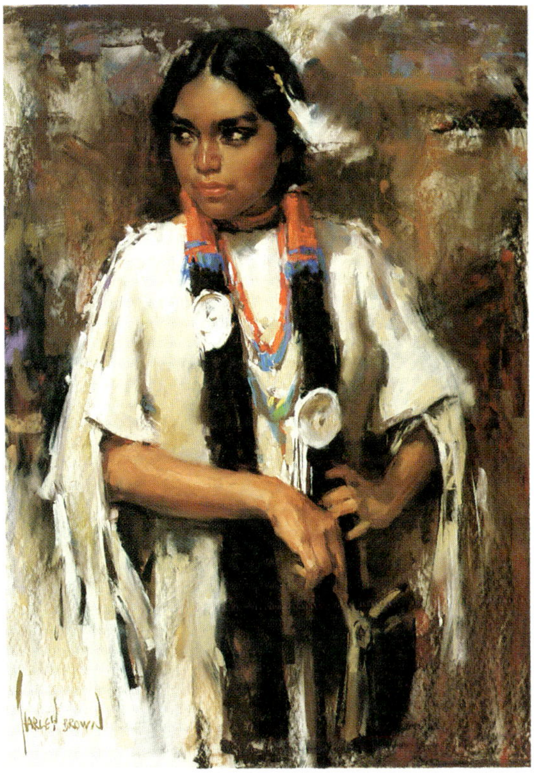

Kootenai Dancer
1987
Pastel
16″ × 20″
Private Collection

This painting was done with a certain amount of brevity. The feeling of exuberance somehow made my arm and hand move quickly around the paper. Note the background, pushed and pulled around her figure. I wanted it dark, yet vital, not obscuring her importance.

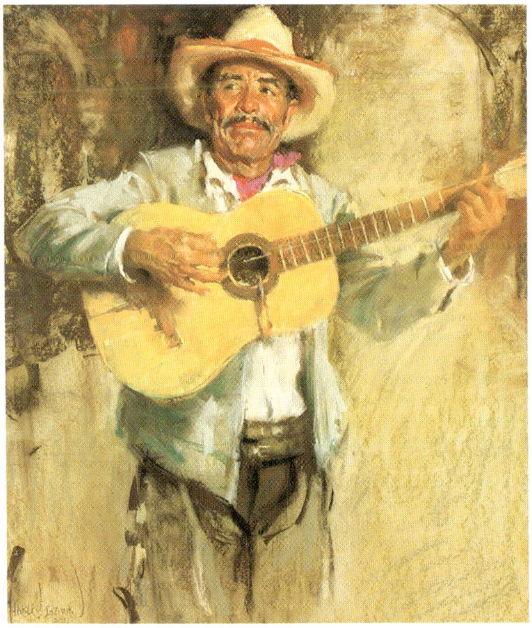

San Miguel Musician
1987
Pastel
27″ × 18″
Collection of Harvey and Rica Spivak

This gentleman followed me around that town for most of a day, chatting and singing songs. For the longest time I wasn't conscious of what a terrific subject he'd be. We had the greatest time! He and his guitar, nature and man-made objects, complementing each other.

pany. I remember my dad saying to me, "Do you want to work for other people for the rest of your life, or do you want to take a great big chance? If you want to be an artist, don't just talk about it. We'll support you." I owe him for that. The very next day I took time off and enrolled in the Alberta College of Art. It was a wonderful, free feeling, to be "following my bliss." I started in the fall, and went for the next three years, until they kicked me out.

Really, why?

I didn't toe the mark. They pushed abstract, and I started to get disgusted. I was drawing realistic figures, which they said was the lowest form of art. And they convinced me. I got very despondent, started partying and drinking, until finally, one day, the head guy said, "I admire your spunk, Brown, but you're *out*!" I remember walking out the door with little teardrops in my eyes. It was a terrible moment. I was a failure.

It really jarred me. Made me face the fact that I'd been just a bit of a jackass. So I borrowed ten bucks from my dad, went down to city hall, got a peddler's license, and went door to door, selling portraits for a dollar apiece. And I went to bars, doing portraits for fifty cents apiece.

Nobody wanted my stuff. I went to thirty doors before I got my first dollar sale. I remember overhearing my dad in the kitchen: "Let's give him another two weeks, and then he's got to get a legitimate job." And I went at it doubly hard, knocking on doors, having them slammed in my face.

And finally, it started to work. The first customer, the second, the third. Word of mouth. I raised my prices to three dollars, then five dollars. Eventually started to make a little money. I began doing portraits at the Hadassah bazaars, and at the Calgary Stampede.

Still living at home?

Well, I had met a wonderful lady, through a friend, and we were going together. One night she said, "Let's get married." I was about 23, and went from my parents' place to our marriage bed, which was a mattress on the floor of an attic apartment, for fifty dollars a month. It was day-to-day living.

I had no future, no prospects. She was amazing. More than supportive, as were her parents. They just loved me, and the fact that I was an artist. And things just started swelling, bit by bit.

Meantime, I was sticking my portraits in any store that would take them, at twenty-five dollars apiece. Restaurants, Kresge's, any place. Not one of them sold. I had dealers walk me out to the street, set my art down on the sidewalk, and tell me never to contact them again.

You must be in the Guinness Book of World Records *for rejection! How did you survive that?*

Once or twice is bad enough. But when it's dozens of times . . . your stomach is in a knot. You're depressed, you're choked up. There's just one thing you cannot let go of: that faith in yourself. I can relate entirely to the people out there who are trying to make it as artists.

But the wonderful thing is, if you *really* want it badly enough, I guarantee 100 percent you will make it. Not 99 percent! If you want it bad enough, you *will* get there!

Anyway, in the midst of all this struggle, we decided to go off to England. Sold everything, enrolled in Camberwell School Of Art. It was a thrilling time in our life, the two of us with our six-month-old baby. All our friends were poor. We'd sit up all night and philosophize about art, over Whatney's Ale and chips.

You finally returned to Canada?

After about two years.

Back in Calgary, I was desperate to get my work into some galleries. So I went to the library and got phone books for Houston, Dallas and so forth. Sent photos of my work, and got a few replies. One was from Ann Hagood at The Gallery at Shoal Creek. She phoned me and said, "I like your work. Start sending some." And I did.

Then one day, driving through Montana, I stopped at the State Historical Society, in Helena, and met Bob Morgan. I handed him my photos and said, "I don't suppose you'd ever want to show my pictures, would you?" How's that for salesmanship? He looked at them and said, "Not only would I like to show them, but I want to have a one-man show for you next summer. Can you get seventy pictures together?" I did, and they all sold that next summer, 1971. I've seen Bob many times since then, and anything he wants from me, he can have. He made the difference in my life.

Suddenly I was being taken seriously.

All this alternating between poverty and semi-poverty, did it affect your marriage?

Poverty was easy. From the day we married, I didn't want my wife to work. Maybe it was false pride, but the husband was the guy who made the living. It was hand to mouth. We'd need money for food, so I'd go down to the bar and maybe sell ten portraits, make five dollars.

You've got to be lucky enough to marry a real supportive person. They've got to be behind you, no matter what, and art is the ultimate challenge. Not only are you not making any money, but you can be impossible to live with when things are not going right.

During all that time, had you ever worked at anything aside from art?

Never! Never did I get a "legitimate" job. I was determined never to get one. The biggest mistake is to get a legitimate job! You start to get wages, and then you say, "As soon as I'm able to get on my feet as an artist, I'll quit." Never happens. You've almost got to be like a kid thrown in the middle of the lake to learn to swim. You've got to be thrown in the middle of the art world to learn to survive as an artist!

If you're young, and just out of art school, *don't* get a job. Start right out as an artist. Go door to door like I did . . . to bars and restaurants. Beg people to buy your stuff. Shove it down their throats. Don't take a job. Ever.

But what about people who come upon this later in life, already committed to spouse, family, mortgage? What then?

In a way it's deceivingly simple, and in a way it's deceivingly complex. You have to decide how badly you want it. It has to be *beyond* a burning desire. The simple part is making the choice. After you've said, "Yes, I'm going to do it," then the complex part comes in.

You have to set yourself a cut-off date, and stick to it. Sit down with your spouse, or by yourself, and be like iron. "Okay, two years." Or, "A year from July third." Whatever. Write it down. Take that time to set your finances straight. Sell this off. Work extra hours.

You've got to see yourself as having one life to live. You've got to say, "I have just so many years ahead of me, where I'm healthy and can pound the pavement, and go through the hell that it is to be a struggling artist." If you wait too long, you won't have the energy.

It's even harder for women, isn't it?

I've seen many in my classes. They feel shortchanged. They've had to take care of the kids, emotionally support the old man, run the house. Now they're fifty, and they're allowed to go out and pursue their skills. They're mad, and I don't blame them. It's unfair, but that's the way the world works. Nevertheless, many of them make up for lost time, and you would not believe how tenacious they are.

I can tell how tremendously you enjoy your classes. They're really an experience!

It's exciting, to communicate an idea and see it connect. I was just talking to an artist about negative space. She said, "I've been waiting to hear that all my life!" Without sounding corny, it just thrilled me! I really feel I owe it to others to pass on the little bit of knowledge I've gained in my lifetime. There should be no secrets in art.

Do you still participate in workshops?

Absolutely, and I always will. I want to hear what these people have to say. I tell them, "I want you to be tough with me!"

Bob Lougheed was tough on me the first time I showed him some of my work. I asked for his critique, and I thought he was going to praise me. Instead, he pointed out my weaknesses, my bad habits. It hurt me bad. Real bad. But I came back for more. I couldn't wait to get more.

How can an artist find a mentor or role model like Bob Lougheed?

Look around for artists you admire. Write them. Bug them. Don't be a nuisance, but be assertive. Send stuff. They'll probably not return it. Send more. Be friendly. Let them know you mean business. If you're wimpy about it, they'll know you're not serious. Beg for a critique. If you can convince them how deadly serious you are, you may get them to help you.

And look for schools. There are still a handful of wonderful places that don't allow room for "artiness." Just good, solid, hard-nosed, back-breaking drawing and painting.

"Artiness?"

I believe in representational painting, because I am very humbled by nature, and nature has its

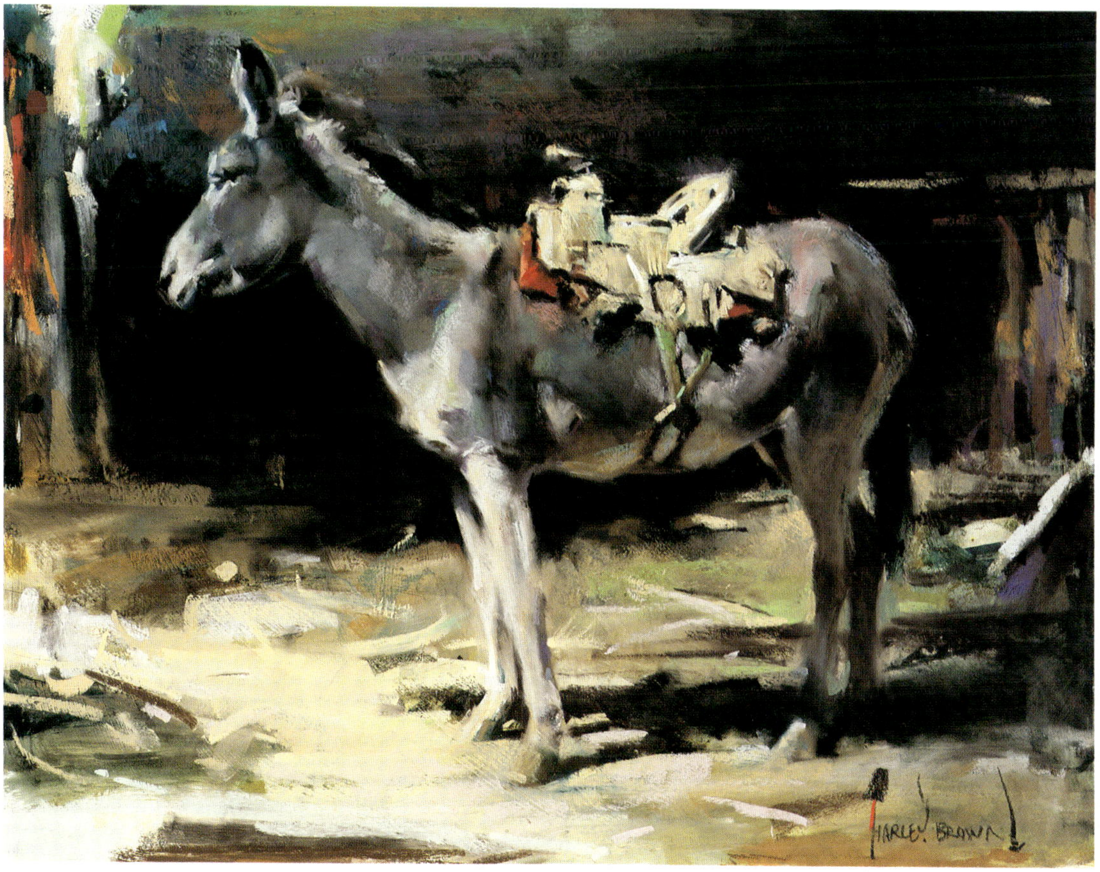

BURRO NO. 2
1989
PASTEL
18″ × 14″
COLLECTION OF
DR. RICHARD AND
GLENDA TOLL

This burro seems to have his attention elsewhere. He's alert and wants to know what's what. I enjoyed juxtaposing the natural (him) with the man-made (his saddle). They quite complement each other. My admiration for these ubiquitous beasts of burden lends impetus for drawing them.

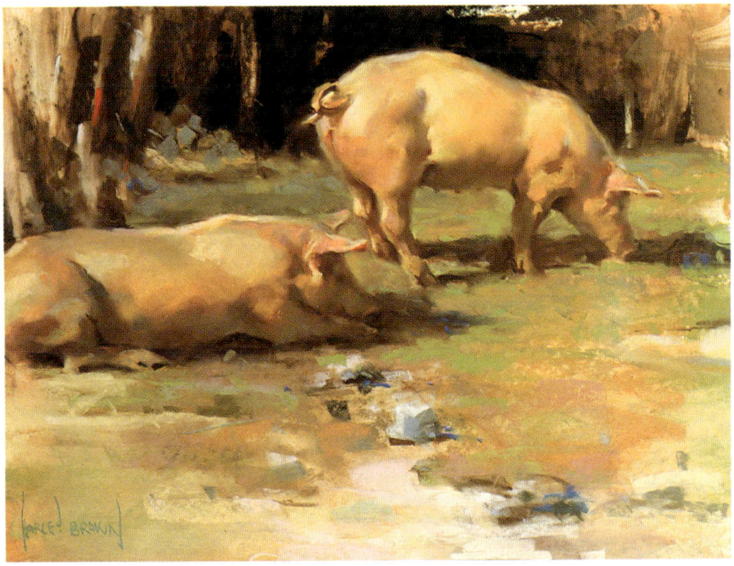

Lazy Afternoon
1989
Pastel
13″ × 18″
Collection of the Artist

This painting is my salute to pigs. In the academic sense, I don't know pig anatomy any more than the average guy. But unlike the average guy, I continue to train my powers of observation. As an artist, you should begin to acquire a certain feeling of the "rightness" of what you draw.

own abstract forms. I've come to see abstract art, in itself, as a very surface thing. You can fall in love with nature. With abstraction I find that you only fall in love with yourself.

Let's get back to how you began to make it with the galleries.

It was building up. I began to meet some of the greats. John Clymer, Tom Lovell, Clark Hulings, Bettina Steinke, whom I'd hero-worshipped since I was a kid of twelve. That's when I first met Bob Lougheed.

Then, one day, my wife collapsed and went into a coma. She was hospitalized, and very slowly, over a two-year period, died. We had two children, eight and five. We had just moved into a house, and I had to take over.

I was going through a very bad period, not earning anything. And knowing that she was never going to recover, I started drinking heavily. Going to bed with a bottle of Old Grandad on the pillow beside me. It was my pal.

Every once in a while, I'd do something and send it off to the galleries. Creditors were after me, and I was getting drunk every night, waking up with that awful anxiety every morning, thinking I was a total failure.

Not long after my wife died, Bob Morgan called and offered me another show in Helena. Somehow, I got the work together and the show was a success. But I was so drunk at the opening, I didn't even know I was there!

The very next morning, I remember, I got a bottle of cheap bourbon and filled a glass. I said, to anyone who wanted to hear me—which was nobody—"This is the last drink of my life." And it was.

When did you meet your present wife, Carol?

Not long afterward. She started to put a semblance of family life back into my world. Things began to get better. I don't think Carol would mind my saying this, because she has said it herself. She has probably resigned herself to the fact that she is number two. I am married to art. Art is number one.

But Carol has been wonderfully supportive at every turn. She handles the business end. She talks with dealers and patrons. Her critiques of my work are amazingly insightful for a non-artist. And she keeps me honest in my approach. Her love is very important to me.

I remember your statement I heard through that classroom door, "If you wanted something simple, you should have taken up brain surgery!"

I have to credit that to Hal Reid, and I think he got it from somebody else. These great artists, the Donald Teagues, the Tom Lovells, they all say the same thing: "There's no easy route."

You take your art very seriously, don't you?

I take my art completely seriously. But not myself. That's how I can take falls easily, and bounce right back. Take yourself too seriously, and you'll crack. It may take time, but you'll finally break apart.

Do you paint every day?

Matter of fact, I do. An artist has to promise himself that not a day can go by that he does not put something to paper or canvas. Maybe a spouse is subservient to the art of the artist, but the artist is in many ways subservient to his craft.

Do you think of yourself today as successful?

If you had asked me five or ten years ago, I'd have probably related it to prestige, and money, and standing . . . all those things. That's not how I would feel today—though perhaps that may be the result of having gotten some of those things.

Today, success to me is how I feel about what I'm doing.

Has luck been a factor?

I'd be lying if I denied it. If Bob Lougheed hadn't seen my work, or if I hadn't happened into Bob Morgan's place that day. . . . But if it hadn't been that, it would have been something else. I think if an artist has wonderful work, all the doors in the world will open for that person. Honest, convincing work. Not cute, clever, sellable stuff. Someone once said, "The harder you work, the luckier you get."

What do you think makes a work of art "wonderful"?

First of all, it's very important that an artist know the principles of art, the way a musician knows the principles of music. On top of that, there's conviction. It rarely fails: If an artist puts real conviction and excitement in a painting, somebody will see it, and get that same feeling.

More and more, I do things that just appeal to me. If they sell, okay. I'll keep doing what people expect from me because they keep me in food. But in the meantime I'll do these others that give me a thrill simply because I want to do them, and for no other reason, and these are invariably the ones that people get excited about.

JOE
1991
PASTEL
19″ × 15″
PRIVATE COLLECTION

I love the play of light on the human head. A strong light, properly placed, can make any face worth painting. It's Joe. No extras, no background, no hands. Enough intrigue to satisfy me. The drawing's strength is its simplicity.

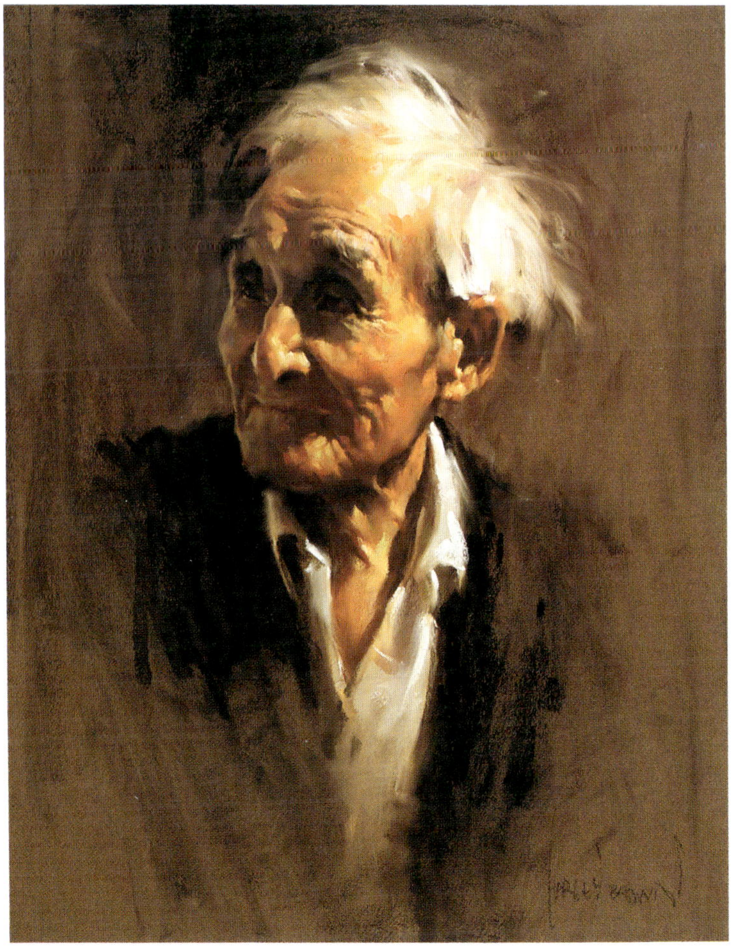

Let's talk about artists in general. Why do you think so few artists make it?

Some people are blessed with a little talent. Others are blessed with tenacity and they're never going to give up. I know many artists, tenacious but lacking talent, and they will only hit a certain level. The ones with talent and no tenacity will end up at an even lower level. Talent with tenacity is, of course, the ultimate. But if I were to have just one, I'd want tenacity. I think talent is very overrated.

How can an artist take that first step on the path to an art career?

Many great people who have changed their lives have done it in little bites. Lincoln once said, "The only reason I can cope with the future is that it happens *only* one day at a time."

Let me give you an example. I am very much a creature of habit. I plod along, at my pace, and never do anything out of the ordinary. But on the eve of my fiftieth birthday, I made a deal with myself. I'd start to change my life . . . *slightly*. From that day on, I promised myself that every day I would do one thing—even a minor thing—a little differently. Slowly I've begun to break down the conservatism in myself. And before long, that started to show up in my art. New subjects. New techniques.

If I can pass anything along, it's this: Secretly say to yourself that you're going to change the norm. Do something just a little different *tonight*. Something else tomorrow. You'll find that those small changes will start to graduate into big changes. And when you want to do those monumentally different things, they'll be a lot easier, and you'll be able to handle them.

JACK FLYNN
Don't Give Up

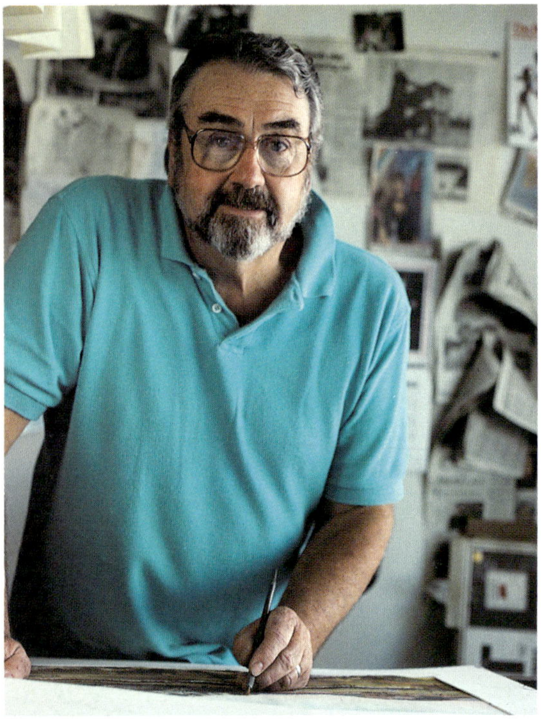

Jack Flynn at work.

I FIRST MET JACK FLYNN IN 1985. WE HAD RECENTLY MOVED TO THE BERKshires, and I'd heard that there was an ongoing watercolor class at the Berkshire Museum in Pittsfield, Massachusetts. Jack was teaching it to an enthusiastic classroom full of painters, many of whom had studied with him for years.

For the next few years, Monday morning with Jack was the jump-start for my week. His demos, his assistance, his enthusiasm, and his great good humor carried us along with a minimum of verbal communication. For, you see, Jack has been deaf since birth, and because he has never heard the spoken word, he cannot speak clearly. Nevertheless, with paintbrush and paper, by example and written word, through generosity and warmth, Jack has no communication problems whatsoever.

I interviewed Jack through the mail. I sent written questions to him. He returned taped responses that were communicated through his wife, Donna. For that reason, the words of this interview, though phrased as I believe Jack would have spoken them, are really the combined effort of both Jack and Donna.

Jack, please give me some background, for the readers, about your deafness.

I was born in 1927, and have been deaf from birth. Not totally, because I can hear loud noises, like sirens and motorcycles, which always startle me. (My mother had German measles when she was pregnant, and that was the cause.) I've gone to many specialists over the years, but there was nothing anyone could do.

But at the same time, I don't really consider my hearing a handicap. I've learned to live with it, and it has never been a problem in our lives, nor the children's or grandchildren's.

I drive, and have done so since I was young. Though I have been told that I could have a "handicapped" sticker for my car, I've always refused. There's nothing wrong with my legs! I do everything on my own, and if I have trouble communicating, there's always pencil and paper.

Tell me about your early days, and about how you became involved with art.

When I was about nine or ten, our next-door neighbor, an older boy named Jack Lucey, would come to my house. We were good friends, and he'd show me how to draw everything. I wasn't a natural artist, but I loved to read comic books, and I thought it would be fun to draw cartoons. So I copied them.

I was eight years old before I started school. My mother had met a teacher in Pittsfield, who told her about the Clarke School for the Deaf. But it was in Northampton, Massachusetts. My father didn't want me to go. He didn't want me to leave home, I guess, because he wouldn't be able to see me very often. But my mother pushed me. She was a very strong woman, and I owe her a lot. In the end, my father was happy that I had gone to the Clarke School.

Tell me about the school. Did you like it?

It was great. I played basketball, soccer and baseball there, and I did well. I came home for Christmas, and for the summer, but that was about all. I stayed at the Clarke School until 1945, when I returned home and entered Pittsfield High School as a sophomore. I hated it there. Hated school. I quit when I was a senior because I thought I could make it in the world of art. I looked around for a job, but could not find anything, so I went back to school, to catch up and graduate. I was twenty-one when I graduated, in 1948, and was embarrassed about that. After graduation, I went to the Butera School of Fine Art in Boston and graduated from there in 1951.

How did you find out about that school?

My high-school principal, Mr. Roy Strout, and my art teacher, Thomas Curtin, helped me. Mr. Strout's son had gone to Rhode Island School of Design. (An article about the late Thomas Curtin appeared in the January, 1991 *American Artist Magazine*.)

Did you find a job in art after graduation?

It was very difficult. I had no luck for a long time, and took odd jobs in Boston to earn a little income. Finally I got a job at a silk-screen studio, doing layout, paste-ups, copies and odd jobs. I stayed there for almost a year.

What happened?

My boss said I was valuable, but when I asked for a raise, she refused. So I said good-bye and went home to Pittsfield.

My father was manager, at the time, of an A&P in Pittsfield, and I asked him for a job. I worked at the supermarket for about ten years, taking time off whenever I could, mainly during the first four or five years, to drive to Boston or New York City, or elsewhere, to look for a job in art. I had no luck.

After my father retired, I continued to work for the new manager, until I injured my back very badly in 1964. It was this event, and the double-disc surgery I had to undergo, that forced me to change the direction of my life.

My mother accepted my injury, and the extra burden my convalescence placed on her, as God's will. She believed it was all part of the divine plan.

Finally, two months after my surgery, the first day out of my cast, my doctor ordered me

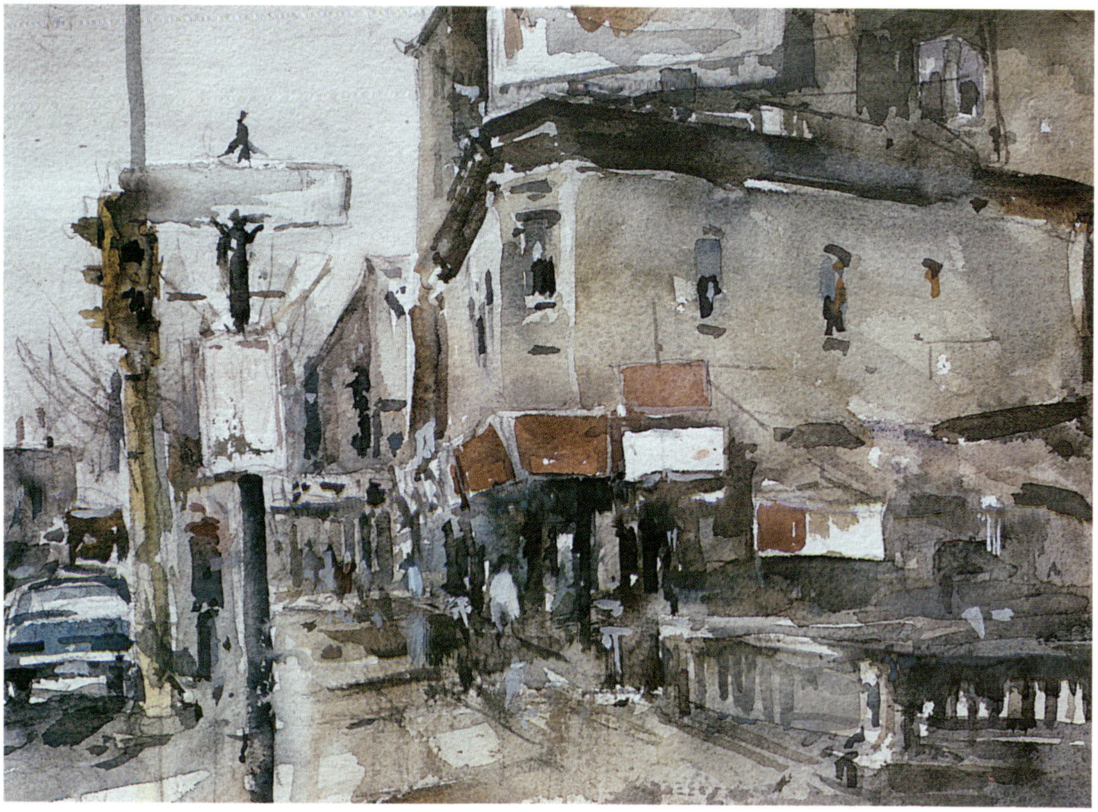

EAGLE STREET NEWSSTAND AT CORNER
1980
WATERCOLOR
15″ × 11″
COLLECTION OF MR. AND MRS. BRUCE CONNORS, PITTSFIELD, MA

I've always loved to paint cityscapes, but only in moody weather. This newsstand has been on this corner since I was a boy, and is probably the oldest one left in downtown Pittsfield. The scene was a difficult challenge, but all the details and reflections excited me.

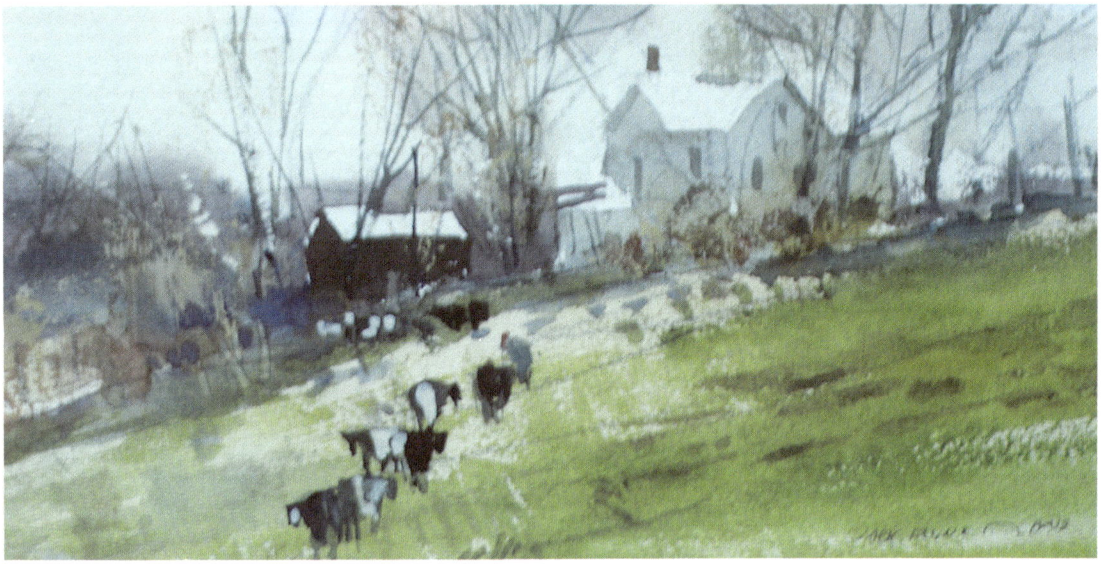

About Time for Milking
1989
Watercolor
15″ × 11″
Collection of the artist

I painted this scene on location in western Pennsylvania during a visit to Donna's family. My location paintings are usually quarter-sheet or smaller, to give me time to paint several scenes, and to capture the light before it changes. This one took about a half hour to complete.

to get out of bed, and told me that I was never again to lift heavy things (like supermarket stock). He was a tough doctor.

There I was, bored, with no job and with nothing to do. My mother suggested that I do something, draw something, so I started drawing again. Maybe that back operation was a blessing. It got me back into the art field. I think there is a reason for everything that happens.

While I recuperated, I met an artist-teacher from Pittsfield by the name of William H. Schultz. He ran an art school in nearby Lenox. For the next three or four years, I traveled to his studio every day and worked around the school. I took oil and pastel painting lessons from him, and we became good friends.

One time, as he was heading off to do a demo, he asked me to take over his class. I didn't think I could do it, because I was deaf. After that, he began having me teach in front of his classes. Bill would leave and I would have to take over. These were not handicapped students, and I was scared to death! But I did them.

Bill loved to read about art. He was my mentor. Not only did he teach me about painting, he taught me how to teach. In return, I worked around the school, cleaning up and so forth.

Were you working in watercolor then?

No. I had asked Bill if he could teach me watercolor, but it was not a medium that interested him. He did only oils and pastels.

We would go out to paint together all the time, in the Berkshires, or Vermont. And he was a very patient man. I, in turn, have learned to be very patient with the people who study with me.

Bill and I were both bachelors, both free. One day in late summer, he called me (through my mother). "Is Jack busy? Ask him if he'd like to drive over to Rockport [Massachusetts] overnight with me." Rockport was a well-known arts community, but I had never even heard of it! In fact, I knew nothing at all of fine art. I only knew about commercial art.

"Where's Rockport?" I asked.

"It's north of Boston," he replied. So we went there.

I was very impressed with Rockport. There was an art show going on, and all the artists and art instructors were there. It was a perfect town.

Walking down the street, we passed Don Stone's gallery. I remembered having read about him in a magazine somewhere, so I went in and introduced myself. I had looked through Rockport on that initial visit, and had found other teachers, but Don Stone's work was what I liked. It was beautiful. I asked if he would teach me watercolor, and he said yes. So I signed up for his week-long workshop. He gave me a list of supplies to buy, and I went to the art supply store right there in Rockport and bought brushes, paints and paper (spending less than twenty-five dollars for all of it, as I remember) and returned, ready to learn.

Don's demonstrations were terrific. I knew

nothing, and he made it look so simple! He had a workshop at his studio every week, all summer. I was so impressed that I signed up and studied with him for the next three years.

Rockport is a four-hour drive from Pittsfield. Did you move there?

I would simply get up every Tuesday morning and drive the two-hundred-odd miles to Rockport to attend his workshop. And after class I'd drive back home and spend the evening helping at Bill's school. I hated the drive, but I loved the art more!

Today I feel that watercolor belongs to me, and I owe it to Don Stone. And to Bill Schultz.

One summer day, when I had completed three years with Don Stone, Bill asked me to teach a watercolor class at his school, but I refused. I thought that people would be uncomfortable with me because I was deaf. That's what I thought, but I was wrong.

When did you finally teach your own class?

While I was at Bill Schultz's school, I met one of his students named Jeanne Johns. Jeanne's husband had found an old barn nearby, and he was going to take it down and move it to Lenox. I helped him take it apart, piece by piece, and rebuild it so his wife could have a gallery in it. Jeanne asked me to do a watercolor class there in the rebuilt barn, which was called The Loft Gallery. I did, and that was my first steady teaching job. It meant I was now working at least one day a week.

Well, in 1974, my wife Donna and I got married, so I had to get a full-time job. I wanted so much to paint watercolor that Donna asked Bill Schultz for names of places in the area where I might be able to teach. He came up with a number of names, and Donna wrote to all of them. I began to book classes. First, two days a week at the Berkshire Museum. Then another at the library in Winted, Connecticut.

By the time I got my classes going, I found I was working four days and several evenings a week. For the fifth day, I set up private classes in my home, and outdoor workshops. In between I still found time to paint. Donna had contacted a number of galleries, and many of them had responded. Gradually I began to have galleries ask to show my work.

Tell me about your American Watercolor Society membership.

I had learned about A.W.S. from Don Stone and the other Rockport artists. They suggested I try

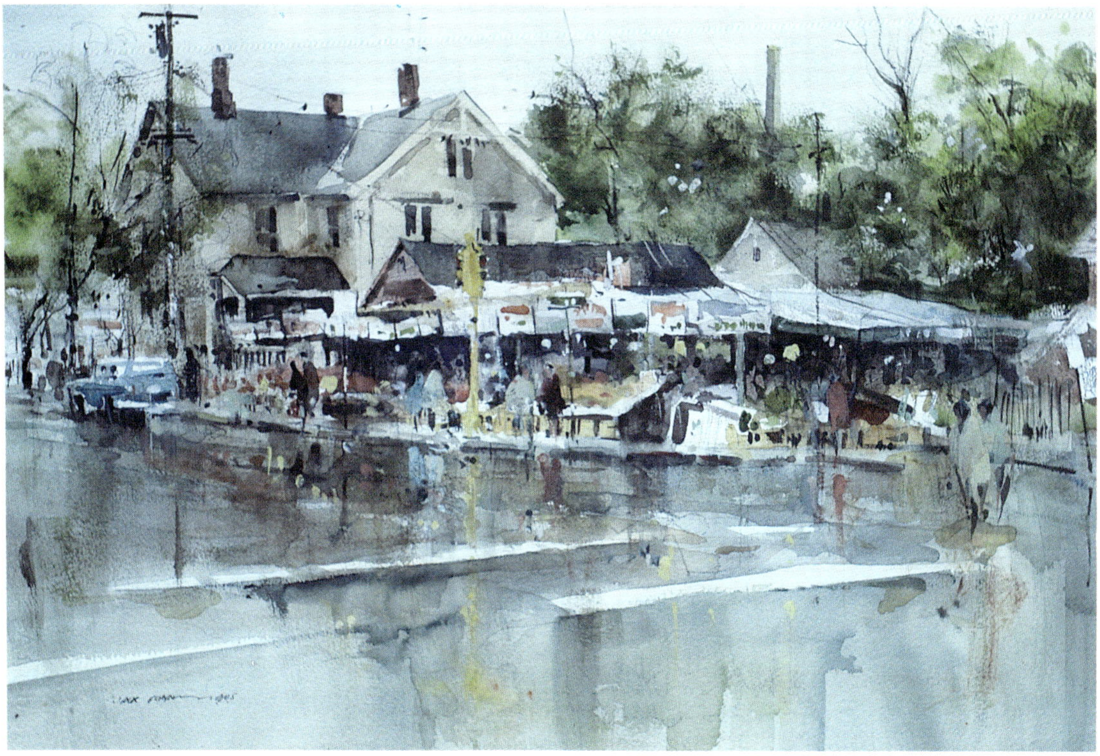

FRUIT MARKET ON TYLER STREET
1985
WATERCOLOR
22″ × 15″
COLLECTION OF MARGARET HALL, PITTSFIELD, MA

Times change, and scenes come and go. This well-known Pittsfield market still exists, but all the signs and things are gone. When we lived in Pittsfield, Donna always bought her produce here. Seeing it on a rainy day, I was impressed with its mood and the jumble of signs and color.

for it, so I did. At that time, in order to become a signature member, you had to be accepted for the A.W.S. annual exhibit three years out of five. The first year I entered, my painting was accepted. The second and third years it wasn't. Then the fourth year it was.

I remember that all-important fifth year. I had entered a painting, and came home to find the notification envelope in the mail. I told Donna to open it, but she wouldn't. I wouldn't open it either. We stood there, wondering how to get into this letter, until Donna called our young son over and said, "Open this up and tell us whether it's good news or bad news."

He read the letter, looked at us dead-pan, and said, "Oh, golly." We were crestfallen, but he was just pulling our leg. I was accepted that year, and became a signature member of A.W.S.

In a way, that was the kickoff of my career. With that recognition, I found it easier to get into the galleries, and to fill my workshop classes.

How did you set prices on your work in the beginning?

Initially, I had the galleries set the prices, and I have stayed with that. Of course the prices do go up over time, but the gallery owners are basically the people who set my prices for me.

After a while, my work was getting around even more than I realized.

I remember one Halloween when we were living in Pittsfield. I had taken the children out trick-or-treating, and at this one house, the man invited us in and struck up a conversation with my kids. I looked around and saw that the walls were full of my paintings! I didn't know what to say. Finally, I said, "They're beautiful!" "Yes, they are," the man said. "I am a Jack Flynn collector. All I do is collect Flynn paintings. I can't get enough of them!"

Well, I wasn't going to say anything, but children, you know, never shut up. My son said, "This is Jack Flynn, the artist!" It was so funny. They tell me my face turned bright red.

Between my painting, my classes, and my workshops, I was really busy full time, doing what I most enjoyed. I kept that up until 1989, when I turned sixty-two, and decided it was time to become a full-time painter.

Were you tired of teaching?

Not at all. Even though I am now a full-time painter, I will never completely retire from teaching. I still teach a few workshops each year, and even return to the Berkshires to teach now and then. But when I reached sixty-two, Donna told me that was it. No more heavy teaching. The driving was hard, the long trips and the bad weather had gotten to be too much. I have great memories of my classes. I loved doing them.

When I announced my retirement to Virginia Beach, there was no end of farewell parties for me. I still have, and will always have, many friends back in the Berkshires.

Now that you have the time to do so, do you paint every day?

Almost every day. I'm not a nine-to-five person. I paint when the urge hits, usually six or seven days a week. I paint at my leisure, sometimes in the morning, sometimes in the evening. I also like to work outdoors in the yard, and go to the beach in the summer. But when we go, I always have my camera and my sketchbook.

I have a bicycle, and I ride it all over town. I love to walk, too. But basically, I am a studio artist, because I would rather be alone while I am at work. For fun and relaxation, and not for serious work, I enjoy painting outdoors.

Cityscapes and people are my favorite subjects. I love to do those rainy, dark autumn and winter scenes. I love reflections. There's a lot of feeling in them for me. I like the light of early morning and late afternoon, the atmosphere and the long shadows. Bright days are just too pretty.

Today, my income comes from selling my work, doing the occasional workshop, and collecting on my Social Security.

Aside from painting, what else occupies your interests these days?

One of my loves is books. My library is filled with books on art, and on my other interests: The Civil War, The Revolutionary War, and World Wars I and II. I'm at the library at least two days a week. I love to go there, and to visit galleries, museums and historical places. But my first love is art. Watercolor, of course. And American impressionism.

That really goes all the way back to my days in high school, and it reminds me of something that happened a number of years ago. Over the years, I had lost touch with Thomas Curtin, the high-school art teacher who had helped me so much. He had left the area, and nobody knew where he had gone.

One weekend Donna and I were visiting friends in Vermont, and they took us into a little gallery to meet this elderly artist who they said was "just the nicest guy you'd ever want to meet." Lo and behold, it was Mr. Curtin! He was a wonderful artist. He had painted with Andrew Wyeth, and with Philip Jamison, but he didn't think that was any big deal at all.

When I wasn't near, Donna said she would like to buy one of his paintings for me. He said he had never sold a painting before, and that he'd consider it and get in touch with her, which he did. The painting Donna selected was an oil painting I had admired, and she brought it home with the signature still wet. It was a complete surprise, and I was overjoyed. I stayed in touch with Mr. Curtin until he passed away a few years ago. And his painting is one of my most prized possessions to this day.

Jack, you've come up the hard way in a difficult business. What do you think made you succeed where so many others have given up?

Being an artist is a very difficult way to make a living, and a difficult way to work. I feel I have been very lucky. But it is also true that artists fail because they do not work hard enough. Many artists feel that if they cannot make it in a couple of years, it is not worth the struggle. It took me a long time to get where I am, and I made it simply because I didn't give up.

I'm always pleased to hear that my former students are doing well with their art. Some have their own galleries now, and some teach watercolor, too. And yet there are many artists and watercolorists out there who are terrific, and never get the recognition or the reputation.

What advice would you give to artists who would like to live by their art?

Just this: Don't give up.

In 1988, Donna and I went to my fortieth high school reunion, the first I had ever attended. Almost half the 449 people who had graduated were there. Of all the graduates, only nine had accomplished what they said they wanted to do in our 1948 yearbook. I was one of them. My yearbook entry read:

"Ambition: To be a professional artist.
Jack be nimble, Jack be smart,
Draw a picture and show your art."

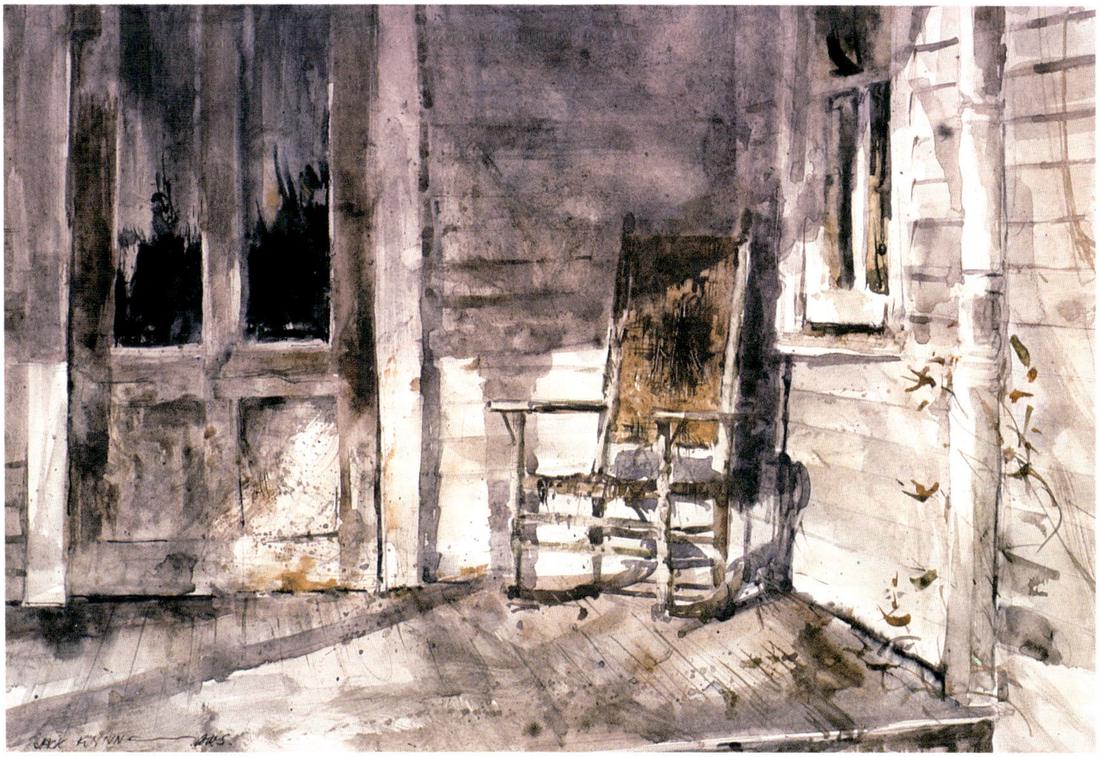

The Abandoned Chair
© 1975
Watercolor
22″ × 15″
Collection of the artist

I spotted this beautiful, quiet, worn-out old chair during an outdoor painting trip. It was late afternoon, and the long sunset shadows gave me a sad feeling. . . . Maybe the old man who had sat in his favorite chair had passed away.

GARY ERNEST SMITH
Know Your Strengths

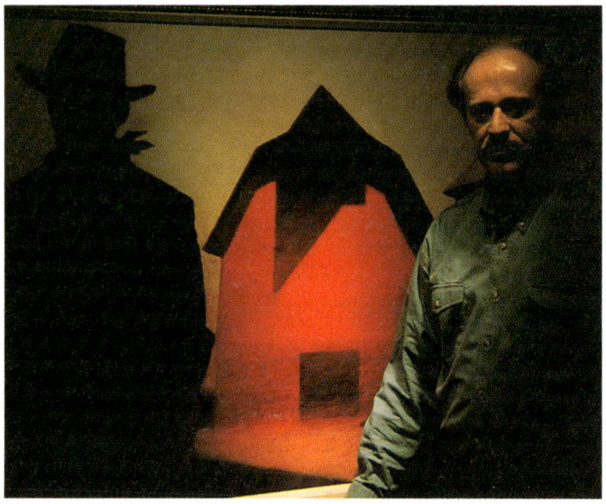

Gary Ernest Smith at the opening of his 1991 exhibit at Overland Trail Gallery in Scottsdale, Arizona. Photo by Lew Lehrman.

FOR THE PAST SEVERAL YEARS, I HAVE ATTENDED GARY ERNEST SMITH'S openings at the Overland Trail Gallery in Scottsdale, Arizona. His large, richly painted canvases line the walls, radiating the heat of farm country summers as they vividly portray the dust, the sweat, the pathos, the deepest feelings of rural life.

Amazingly, most, if not all, of the fifty-plus paintings on the walls at each year's show are already sold, at prices as high as $35,000 apiece!

I met with Gary at the gallery a few days after the opening of his 1991 exhibit. We sat and talked at a desk on the gallery floor, with the day's activity swirling around us, pausing in our conversation occasionally so that he could greet a visiting collector.

Seems to me, Gary, that you've realized every artist's dream: Recognition. Success. How did you pull it off?

In 1983, I was finally having some success as a regional artist in Utah, and was about to start looking for representation out of state, to expand my market. But just as I was ready to make that decision, a man walked into my studio with a proposition. Now, I'd had people say they wanted to represent me before, and I was always skeptical. Generally they just want to take your work on consignment and try to sell it for you and take a percentage. But this man walked in, paid me cash for fifteen of my paintings, and said, "I'm serious about this. I want to represent you!"

Sounds pretty serious to me.

That man was Ray Johnson, from Overland Trail Galleries in Scottsdale. He said, "I will stabilize your life. I will give you an income every month. You forget about the money. Just paint, and I will buy everything you do." He took my work and started promoting it and selling it. In time he came up with the exclusive arrangement we've had ever since.

That's absolutely amazing!

I should say so. It happens so seldom in life that you find someone who not only believes in you, but has the ability—and the financial backing—to take you to the top.

Today, my work is selling as fast as I can produce it. He's not taking a chance anymore, and neither am I. His job is to go out and find the clients, build the market, and build my reputation. He creates all the advertising, does all the promotion. My job is to produce the best art I possibly can.

Well, we both know that overnight success stories don't just happen. What led up to this fantastic break?

To start with, I grew up on a farm in a little town called Baker, in eastern Oregon. I lived about eighteen years of my life there. Never had any introduction to art until I was older. But I could draw well. By the time I got into junior high and high school, I was doing better drawings than my teachers. Of course, I had no idea then of what being an artist meant, and no particular direction as to an area to pursue, although painting sounded interesting.

At that age, was being a painter even a thought?

Absolutely. Of course, that was pure idealism. Because the reality was that artists only existed in books. You didn't make a living doing that sort of thing.

What contact did you have with the art world to even know about those things?

I used to spend summers with my aunt on the Oregon coast. She would have professional artists come in and teach workshops. My first experience with professionals was with those artist-teachers. It was one of those instructors who told me, "If you're going to make it in art, you first have to find a way to make a living, because you can't make a living painting." So I set my course to get a master's degree in art education. I'd teach to support my painting habit.

Where did you go to school?

I started at Eastern Oregon College in LeGrand, but transferred to Brigham Young University in Provo, Utah, where I received my master's degree in art.

After a tour in the service during the Vietnam war, I committed myself to a three-year teaching stint (although I felt that I wanted to paint rather than teach).

How did you make the transition from teacher to painter?

It was difficult. I was married at the time, and we had a child. I had to decide where my time was best spent: whether to teach and pursue a minor art career, or go for it full time. I opted for full time, even though I realized that I'd have to go out and create my own market.

What do you mean by creating a market?

To try to fit yourself into an existing market is rather short-lived. You can do it, and a lot of artists do. Take the Western market, for instance. Many artists see the market there, and they may be inclined toward that market anyway. The problem is, if you don't establish your own identity, your own subject matter, your own style and your own way of doing things, your career can be rather short-lived.

Too many young artists make the mistake of compromising in the beginning. "I've got to

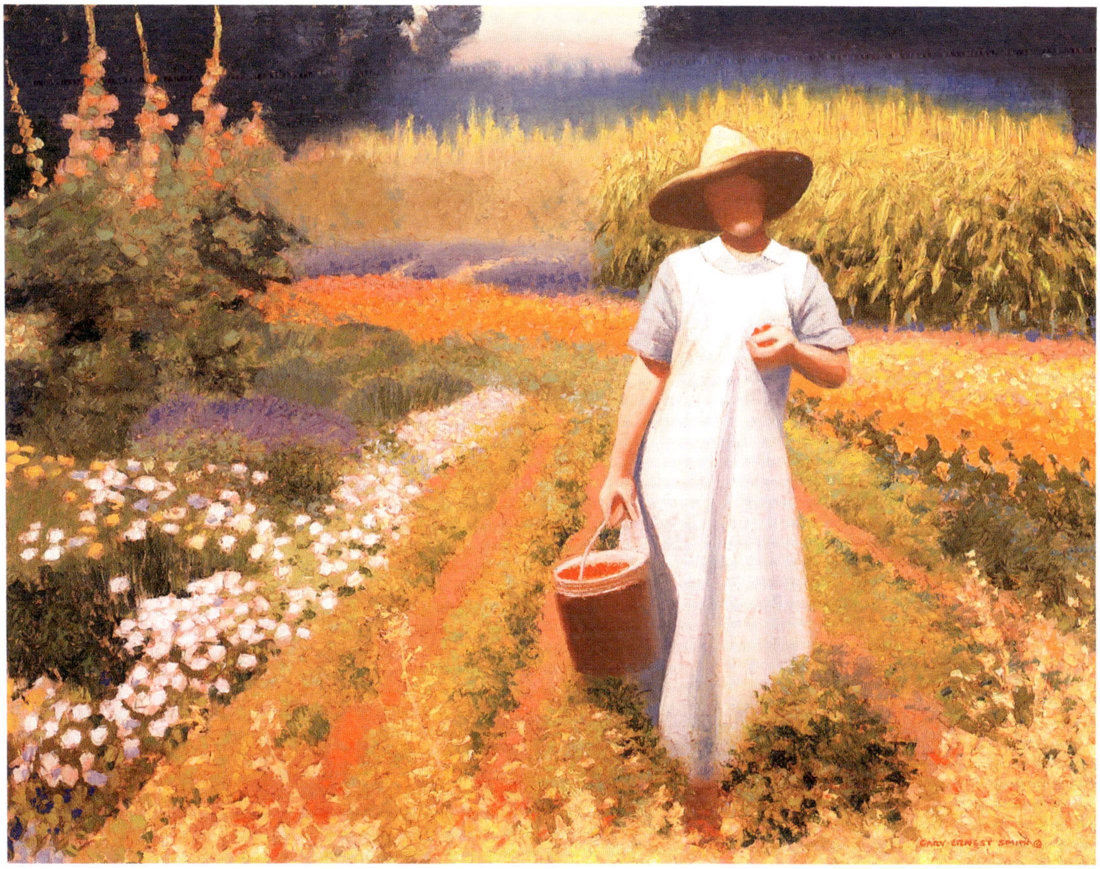

WOMAN IN A GARDEN
1989
OIL ON CANVAS
48″ × 36″
PRIVATE COLLECTION

Gardens allow me to play with color, light and values in a way my other paintings don't. Gardens represent to me a positive effort in life, which results in beauty. Aesthetically, they challenge me to organize color and form in a way that only a garden can.

PHOTOS OF ART IN THIS CHAPTER ARE BY BILL MCLEMORE, SCOTTSDALE, ARIZONA

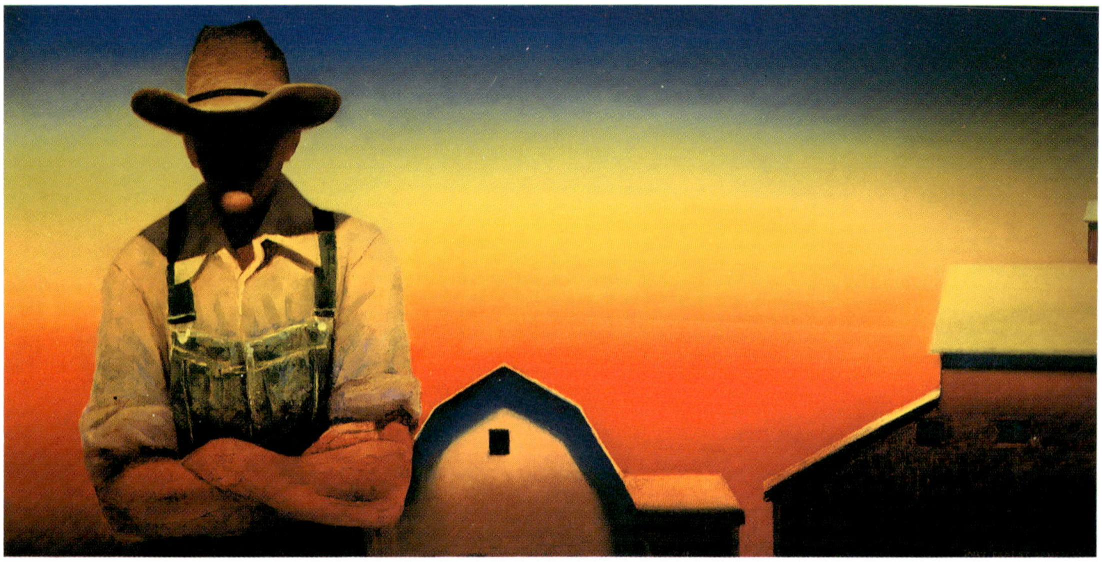

Farmer at Sunset
1990
Oil on canvas
48″ × 24″
Private Collection

Often I like to reduce things to simple forms. I put them in a dramatic setting with strong color and value, creating strong moods. I like the long horizontal, which creates a feeling of peace and tranquility, coupled with a bit of mystery.

make a living, so I'll paint this because I know there's a market for it." Then they get trapped in it.

Well, you had to make a living. How did you do it?

I created jobs. I'd go out and find new businesses—banks, public buildings, whatever I could. I kept very close contact with architects and interior designers, and worked with them. When they had an interior job, the walls would always be one of their main considerations. What would they put on them? I'd go out and find some historical event that had happened there, and do a lot of research and preparation. I'd make sketches for a mural and present them. Maybe one in five of my presentations ever got completed. So that meant I had to be out there all the time, hustling, to find opportunities.

How did your marriage fare through all of this?

Fortunately, my wife has the creative spirit, too. She's a professional musician, and she was willing to take the risk with me. She knew I was obsessed by this thing called painting, and that I probably had little choice but to follow it. Judy was supportive, but there certainly were those insecure times, not having any commissions, not having anything going, just enough money to buy gas to go look around. And usually, right when it was the worst, a painting would sell, or a commission would come through.

After a while, I was able to time my commissions so the money would be there when we needed it. It was never smooth, but at least it had a semblance of order that allowed me to produce.

Eventually I was able to do pretty well, doing all kinds of things. Portraits and landscapes, too. But I still felt unfulfilled. Yes, I wanted to make a living, but I had higher goals. There was something inside of me that I'd never had the opportunity to explore. By 1980, I had pretty well exhausted my tolerance for painting for others.

But let me back up a little. I had studied art in the sixties, when they told us that realism wasn't the way to go. I came to realize that abstract art, even though it had its place, was not where I belonged. And that's part of what every artist eventually comes to: "Who am I? What do I have to say? How do I find it?"

I certainly had explored those questions for a long time, and finally determined that to "make it" (and we all determine for ourselves what that means), I'd have to set my own goals. I had no idea if I would ever succeed, but I set my course high, and then tried to figure out how to get there.

The result of all this soul-searching was that one day in 1980 I just abandoned all my commercial work, cut off all my commissions. Stopped one day and said, "That's it. I'm forty years old, and half of my life is behind me. Now I want to do what I want to do!" I cut off literally $60,000 worth of commissions. But I knew that

Bringing Water
1990
Oil on canvas
48″ × 36″
Private Collection

In this painting I created the feeling of brilliant heat on a clear summer day, as the workers stack straw. We look at it today and see the dignity in the work, evocative of a time when people knew who they were, and directly reaped the rewards of their efforts.

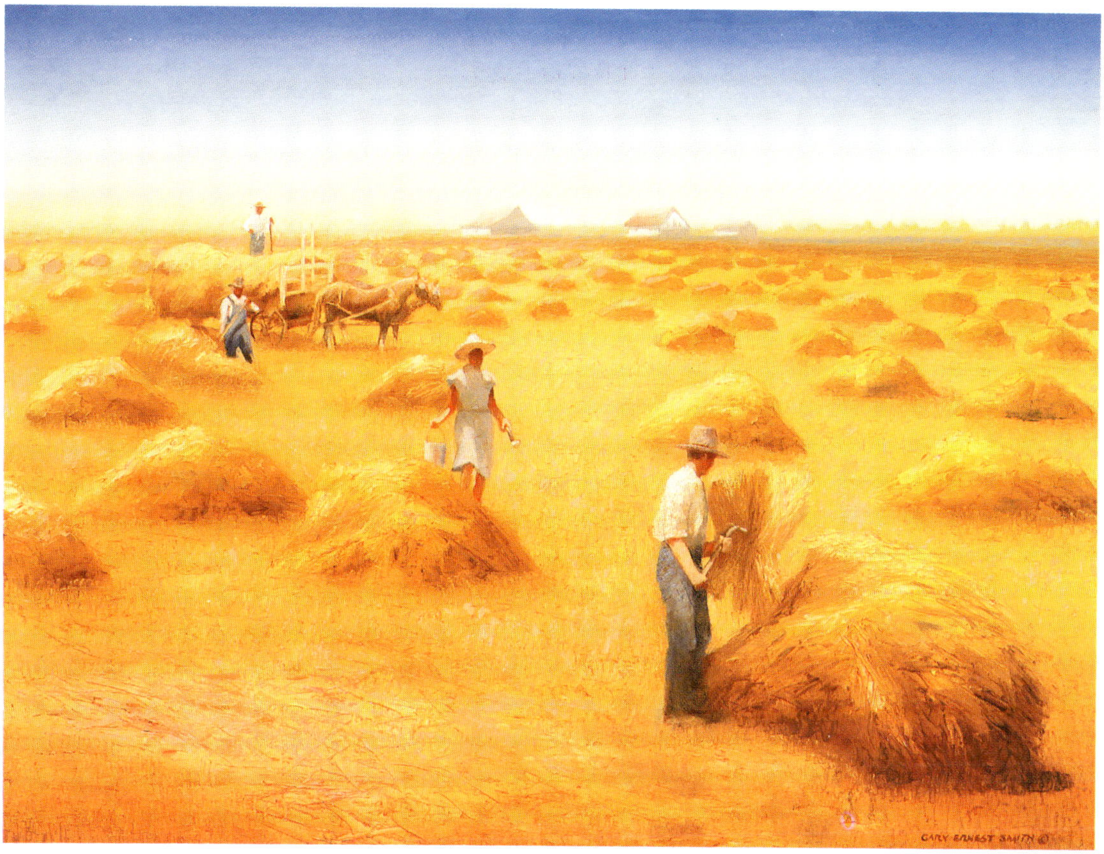

if I didn't make that decision right then, I'd end up being trapped again.

How did you plan to support your family?

I went to the bank and took a second mortgage on my home, to provide money for living expenses.

And started painting?

Not right away. I decided that if I was going to make this happen, I had first to discover who I was. I went back to the home in Oregon where I had grown up, and spent several weeks roaming the countryside, searching my soul. I was haunted by imagery in my head that I could not paint. Finally it began to manifest itself, and crystallize.

It dawned on me that there was something very important about my background, and my roots in the Oregon farm country. The only artist I knew of who had ever explored that experience was Grant Wood, whose "American Gothic" has become a cultural icon. I see my paintings as icons, too. Symbolic of the time and the period I remember as a boy, and the people I grew up with. I try to make my figures anonymous because they represent types rather than individuals. And because of that, a certain universality comes through.

I came home and began to experiment. My semiabstract murals were a take-off point, and I began to incorporate that approach into some of the scenes I remembered. It was a slow process, discovering something in one painting that worked, and later something else in another.

And it was about then I abandoned my paintbrush. Back in about 1975, I had become frustrated with the brush. It would never give me exactly what I was looking for. I started experimenting with the palette knife. I studied artists like Roualt, and other post-impressionists who used the knife. Their works didn't look like palette knife paintings, so I started exploring: painting, glazing, scraping, cutting, stomping—whatever it took to get the effects I was looking for. Gradually it developed, and I found I liked the look.

How long was it before you started showing your work?

For almost two years I just worked hard and didn't sell anything. We lived on the house money, which was really scary. Because at the end of that, what do you do?

I first showed my new work in 1982, at a gallery in Salt Lake City. My show was a sell-out! That gave me enough to pay back the loan, and provide a take-off point for my next era. What I did then was establish a relationship with a bank. They gave me a line of credit I could draw on, up to a certain amount. If I sold a painting that month and didn't need it, I could either pay back on it, or borrow less.

Not many bankers would do that for an artist.

It was a unique situation. I paid back every cent, though, and it really did free up my time. For a number of years, then, I showed my work through two local galleries, and between them, I was able to keep afloat. They took almost everything I produced.

In 1983, Ray Johnson walked in. And that's the story of my life.

Eight years later, it looks like you've reached your goals: Unique vision. Recognition. Financial success. Where do you go from here?

The money is only short term. That is, if the only thing sustaining me is that I am getting good prices, I am probably going to have a short-lived career. My art, in the end, has got to be what sustains it. Promotion will only get me to a certain point. The art has to stand the test of time. The next step is to start getting the attention of the art world. It's important to get recognition from the Eastern critics, who can be very tough, as it is from those in the West. To do that we're establishing traveling museum exhibitions. We selected about thirty paintings, which have been purchased by a group of four investors, as the nucleus of the museum show that is now traveling around the country. The museums have been a goal. My next goal will be to get into the better museums, and then into museum collections.

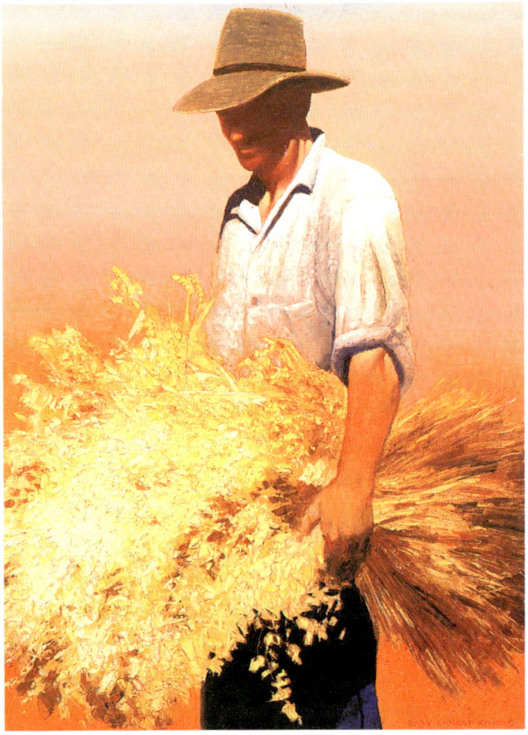

MAN WITH WHEAT BUNDLE
1990
OIL ON CANVAS
36″ × 48″
PRIVATE COLLECTION

To me, there is nothing more simple or universal than a man standing with the fruits of his labor, in this case a wheat bundle. We need to feel that, as human beings, our efforts have consequence in this life.

Let's talk about your approach to your work.

I grew up on a farm, with the very strong work patterns that established, and I've always had a real strong work ethic. I guess I brought those things with me.

My work habits are based around eight to twelve hours or more every day. Sometimes Saturdays, occasionally Sundays. I have maybe twenty paintings going at once, all in various stages.

My paintings are processes: underpainting (and letting that dry) and glazing (and letting *that* dry) and painting, and so on.

I don't want this to be an intellectual pursuit. I want it to be an emotional one, and I choose my colors to reach people on an emotional level. I try to express certain feelings with my use of color, even though I may not totally understand those feelings myself.

After I've roughed in a composition on my canvas, the shapes, and the basic color pattern, I do something that's a bit unique. I'll turn on talk radio, or something like that, to absolutely free my mind of thought, and let it respond intuitively to color. I just let the painting go wherever it will.

I know my strengths: color and shape. And I've learned how to use them effectively, to express the emotional quality I want.

Let's talk about the artists out there. Why do you think some of them will make it, and not others?

One of the biggest problems I've seen with young artists (having been one once) is that they're either very talented and unmotivated, or

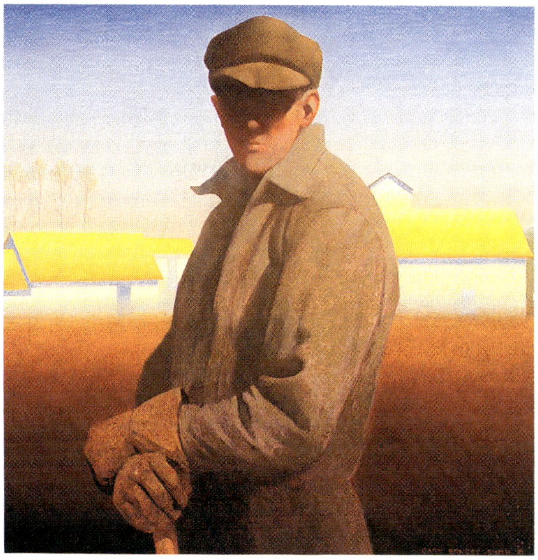

BOY WITH YELLOW ROOFS
1990
OIL ON CANVAS
48″ × 48″
PRIVATE COLLECTION

This anonymous working boy is in some ways a self-portrait. The figure is turned in a way so as to engage or confront the viewer. The rewards of the rural lifestyle are in finding contentment with yourself, with those closest to you, and with nature—hard work tempering the steel.

very motivated and untalented. Very seldom do you find that combination, that obsession, that it takes to weather the storm.

When I talk about talent, I'm not necessarily referring to how well they paint, because that can be learned. I'm talking about conceptualization. Taking unique ideas and doing something different with them than anyone has ever done before.

I've observed that there are really only three factors that will take an artist beyond just making a living. First, is having a work ethic. If an artist doesn't produce a lot of work, he won't ever reach his potential, because you grow through your production. Second is having a unique vision. And third is the right marketing. An artist today can't go very far without the correct marketing.

But what would you say to the artist who's not going to find a Ray Johnson?

First, build up a good body of work. Be competent in what you do. If your work is fragmented, going off in many directions, then you're not ready to make that statement. Fragmentation is confusing to galleries and clients. I went through that. Many styles, many subjects, until they ultimately began to crystallize.

Your work has to mature, and you have to have a vision of what you want to do. Only experience and time will give you the insight. So I'd say, don't be too hasty. Let it grow and mature naturally.

Picasso said he never even arrived at maturity in his work, never found his personal style, until he was sixty.

It's okay to be fragmented in the beginning. You can't say, "I want to paint like this because it sells." That's short-lived. You've got to say, "I know there's something in me that's important to me. I'm going to work like crazy to find it!" And that can take ten, fifteen, twenty years. There are no easy answers. Some people arrive a little sooner, some a little later.

You need a strong belief in yourself and what you're doing. That's number one. Then you've got to convince somebody else of it. If it's true, then that somebody else will see it. In the meantime, just keep producing, honing your techniques, making sure your work is good, and keeping on course, doing what you want to do.

What is it, do you think, that makes some art "wonderful," and other art just ordinary?

Too many artists spend too much time in art school. It's said that you take five years to get through it and ten years to forget it. A college education doesn't make an artist. It gives you tools. What you do with them is up to you.

Art is not just a series of techniques on a canvas. Art is an expression of an idea, and technique is nothing more than the vehicle that gets you to that expression. Whatever techniques you concoct to get to that expression become the part of your work that's unique.

Do any of your children plan to follow in your footsteps?

All four of my children are creative. My studio is at home so they've grown up around my work.

Have any of them said they are going to be artists?

Oh yes, the two boys want to.

And what do you tell them?

I say, "Great!" Perhaps, now, if they decide on an art career, I can provide a vehicle for them to get there quicker than I did.

But I want them to know it's not just a matter of sitting down and painting, and selling it. They've only seen the success. They don't remember the struggle. I just want my children to sense the struggle in it.

JUNE ALLARD BERTÉ
Make an Investment in Yourself

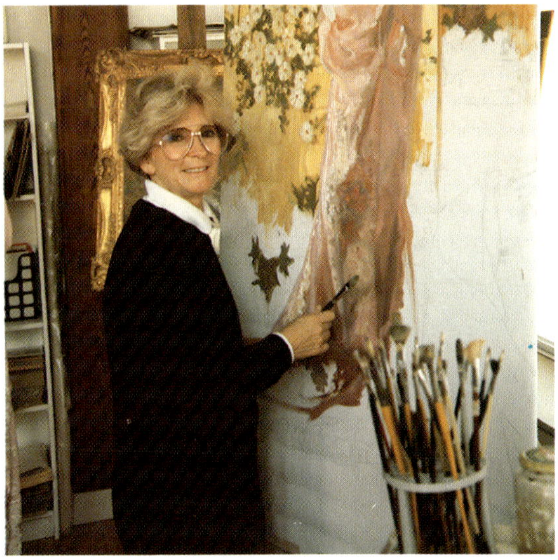

June Berté in her Springfield, Massachusetts studio, working on a six-by-six tri-fold screen. Photo by Lew Lehrman.

THERE IS AN AURA OF QUIET INTENSITY ABOUT JUNE ALLARD BERTÉ THAT tells you whatever she decides to do, she will do thoroughly, and well. Thus it is not surprising, to people who know her, how far she has come in such a relatively short time. Though not yet at the pinnacle of her success as an artist, she is unquestionably on the way. I find it exciting to watch the process taking place, and even to be a small part of it.

I was introduced to June by my wife, Lola, with whom she took a workshop class at The Scottsdale Artists' School. We both loved June's work, and subsequently decided to represent her through our own gallery. Later we met her husband, Ray, and began to know something of their story.

June and Ray have not had an easy time of it. Ray, a college professor, has fought his way through numerous bouts with cancer, while still managing to maintain his teaching career. June was incredibly busy with her own hectic freelance fashion illustration endeavors. At the same time, they were raising their family together—running their home, and doing all those things that families do.

Then, one winter weekend in 1980 . . .

It was a Sunday. We have friends who had been buying paintings from a watercolorist in Vermont, and the four of us had driven up there. It was snowing, and the artist invited us in. There he was, inside his beautiful studio, just painting. And his wife came in and said, "Neil, when you're finished with your guests, I have lunch for you." All his needs were taken care of. I was so impressed with this. He'd take his binoculars and look out at the ski trail, and if it wasn't too crowded, he'd ski! That's the way he lived.

I was so taken aback. You have to know that, until that point, I'd lived life on a merry-go-round with my commercial art, but I had grown dissatisfied with it. I'd lost my pleasure in it, constantly meeting the needs of art directors, running to New York, taking care of other accounts here in Springfield. Supermom at home. The kids still in high school.

Ray was continuing to battle his cancer. Good years, followed by bad years. We just never knew. When you're told five different times that you have just months to live, it wreaks tremendous havoc internally.

And I was feeling the urgency of time. My mother had died that year, and I had come into contact with my own mortality. Now I was the elder. Those thoughts do reach you. . . .

Anyway, that day in Vermont, I left the studio and waited in the car while my friends bought their painting. I was so moved, all I could do was sob all the way home. I couldn't talk. I couldn't even explain why I was crying. I can't even tell you now. Maybe they were tears for all the lost years. Or tears of joy, because I had finally seen what it was I wanted to do.

I thought it out for the next few days, and decided that I would take my commercial art funds and channel them toward self. That day in Vermont . . . in the snow . . . I think of it as

The Enchantress
1989
Oil on canvas
24″ × 30″
Collection of
Mr. and Mrs.
Robert Flynn,
Boston, MA

This painting was a joy for me to compose and execute. I chose to keep it painterly because of my immediate affinity for the child. She reminded me of a Flemish painting. Painting the whites in her outfit was a breakthrough for me, using complementary colors to show the white.

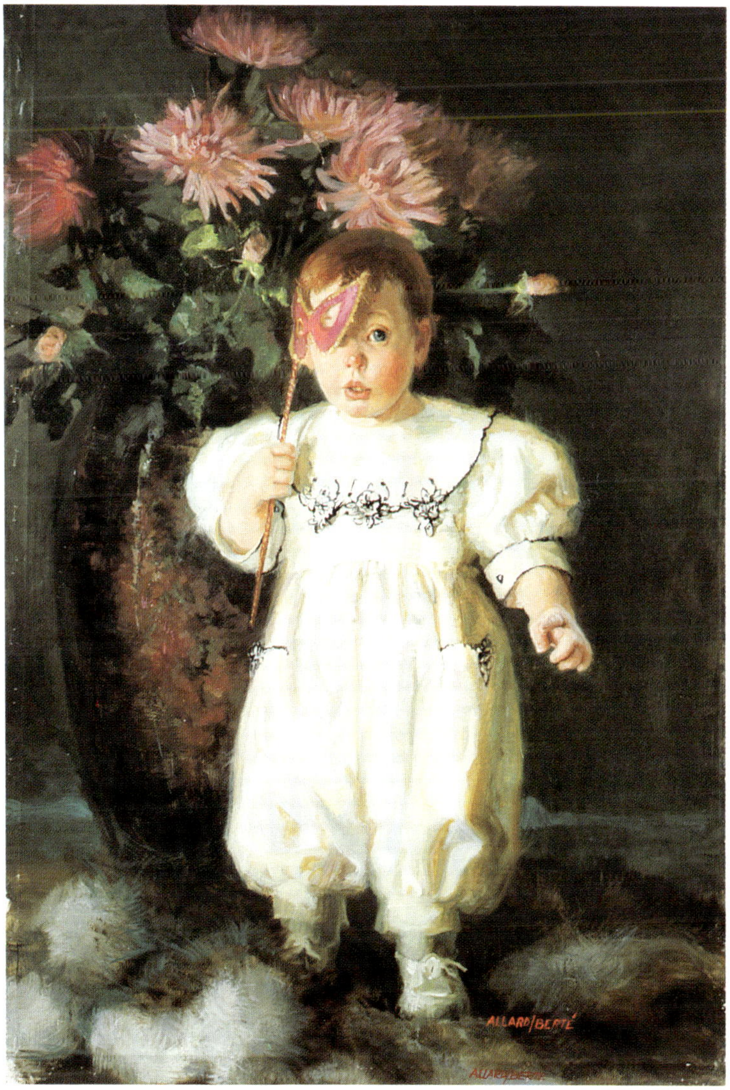

my personal epiphany.

How did you go about rechanneling your life?
I knew what I still had to contribute to maintain our lifestyle at home, but I was able to take some money and put it toward my fine art move. I began to cut back my fashion work. I gradually dropped my New York accounts, as I prepared to change direction. That summer, I signed up with Daniel Greene's workshop in North Salem, New York. I was there for *eight consecutive weeks*! Just painting. Soaking it up. I was a human sponge.

Had you done any painting, at all, before that?
I had not handled oils since art school. It was strictly watercolor, gouache, airbrush and colored pencil . . . and sometimes pastel.

I started that class at square one. Just like the most novice painter in the group. By the end of the eighth week, no one believed I had not painted beforehand. I was also totally exhausted, emotionally and physically. Thought I was going to die. But I stayed with it. There was no way I was going to quit.

How were you able to study all summer, and still hang on to your commercial work?
Ray came every weekend. He was teaching summer school, and he'd stay with me at the motel. He became the liaison with my account, and he'd bring my work with him. We'd play during the day. Then at night, he'd watch television while I pumped out my fashion work at a makeshift drawing board in the room.

For the first few weeks, I didn't tell any of my classmates about my commercial background. It seems strange now, but I was ashamed of it. Only later did I realize how much my fashion background added to my present skills, and how important that extra income was, too.

How necessary was it?
Ray's funds are totally channeled toward our home and his own expenses. Financially, it's just as if I were a single woman doing this. Every bit of my lifestyle – clothing, gas, art expenses – comes from what I produce with my art.

Are you saying that summer with Dan Greene made a painter out of you?
It was a start. Afterward, I painted all winter, and saved as much of my freelance money as I could. The second summer, I went back for four weeks. The third summer it was three, and the last two summers I went for two weeks. In between, it was paint, paint, paint, loving every moment of it. What joy!

Dan Greene, more than anyone, has been my role model. His teaching has been so sound. When all else fails me, and I'm at a loss, I can always fall back on his teachings. Later, I attended other workshops with wonderful artists like David Leffel and Harley Brown. Now, as I've become stronger and more aware of my own abilities, what they've taught fits me better.

You make it all sound very smooth. Was the transition to your new life really all that easy?
It certainly was not. That very year I had won

COUNTRY QUILT
1986
PASTEL
36″ × 49″
COLLECTION OF PELLINGTON GALLERIES, COLUMBUS, OH

This pastel, of a Swedish model who posed for me at our home, was painted in a realistic yet painterly manner. She posed for me in the sun, and the work was done à la prima, in part, on a wonderful kind of pastel board that used to be made for Dan Greene by Canson.

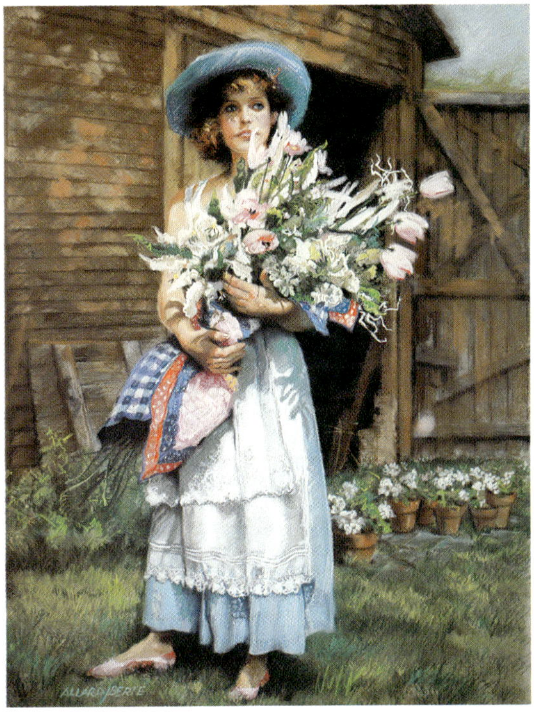

the Western Massachusetts Outstanding Artist award for my fashion work. So here I was at the pinnacle of my career, starting over again from level one.

Were you ever tempted to give up and go back to advertising?

There were times in the workshops, when I'd look at the artists around me, and I'd look at Dan Greene's work, and I'd think, "Just give it up and go home and do the dishes!" Yes, I did have my moments.

How long was it before you started selling your paintings?

That really began for me in 1983. There was this local tennis pro, whose sister I knew. I arranged to photograph him, and I did a portrait, totally on speculation. He never bought it, and it still hangs in my studio. But I used that portrait as a sample, and it was seen by a corporate president, who saw that I had captured a strong likeness, and that resulted in my first commission.

In '84, I rented a small studio in a nearby mini-mall. It had a glass front, where I could display a few paintings, and people could watch me work. I sold some genre paintings, and got several portrait commissions. I kept that space until 1988, when I bought my current studio.

Earlier, in 1986, I took some more of my commercial art money and invested again. I did an expensive portrait brochure. Full color. Die-cut. I sent that brochure off to dozens of galleries. The response was very disappointing. Subsequently, I found that this is how it works. If one in a hundred responds, that's a lot!

How many responses did you receive?

Exactly one! The Pellington Gallery in Columbus, Ohio, called me. The owner told me he ran a modern gallery, but had room for a realist in his space. When I was convinced he was sincere, I decided to fly out to Columbus to meet him.

When I saw the gallery, I realized that the work I had was really not pertinent to the local market, so I decided to make a further investment. I offered to do a portrait of his children, at no cost, which he could hang behind his desk as a sample of my work. I rented a small studio right there in Columbus, and began to paint.

That certainly increased your "investment in self." Did it work out?

Almost immediately. One of my large works sold to the president of a big retail concern. I was very pleased with that. I also received a number of portrait commissions from people who had seen that sample. That gallery still has some of my work, and sends me an occasional portrait commission.

My Columbus affiliation also produced two commissions for Cornell University, which I'm especially proud of. Some representatives from the law school had come to Ohio to visit one of the nation's first female lawyers. I believe she was 96 at the time. They saw my work in the gallery, and I was given the commission to paint her. The dean of the law school called me again in 1990 and sent me to San Francisco to do a portrait of Rudolph Schlesinger, a retired professor. It was unveiled at the law school's hundredth anniversary. Professor Schlesinger and his entire family were there. Ray and I were invited guests, and it was quite an event.

Are galleries your principal sales outlets today?

Yes, though a lot of my portraiture today is what I call "first generation." That is, direct with the client. My goal is to be represented in six really sound, good galleries. That should free me up to paint, while they do what they do best.

There's another advantage to having multiple galleries. When things are quiet with one, I can ship more paintings to the others, because each will have different peak seasons.

With all these galleries pushing your work, plus your portrait commissions, you must keep pretty busy. How do you handle the pressure of turning out all that work?

In 1988, I made another major investment in self. I bought a condominium unit in a renovated commercial building in downtown Springfield to use as a studio. I have to take it seriously. On the left side of my brain, mortgage payments, condo fees, utilities and so forth come due every month.

But once I'm here in my studio, and my music is playing and I begin painting, the creative side takes hold. That, plus I have a husband who helps me "play."

How does Ray deal with the demands your work puts on you?

He loves it. If Ray has a morning class, and he's finished close to lunchtime, he'll call me and say, "Let's skip away for lunch." We'll get away from downtown and take an hour or more. I can't explain it . . . it's beyond a husband-and-wife meeting. We feel very urban. It lends a lot of romance to an ordinary lunch. We don't fall into the typical husband-and-wife conversations. With all the life-threatening experiences we've gone through with Ray's cancer, we have placed a high priority on the time we have together.

When did that all begin with Ray?

You know, apart from his teaching, Ray was a singer. He took voice for twenty years, and

BARBARA AND JOHN
1988
OIL ON CANVAS
60″ × 60″
COLLECTION OF
MR. AND MRS.
THOMAS HAVENS

The Havens wanted more of a genre painting than a portrait. They're painted in only one-quarter of the canvas, for strong dramatic emphasis. Green tapestry behind Barbara's red hair strengthened my color composition. I directed John's gaze toward the viewer, from which the eye travels downward toward the joined hands.

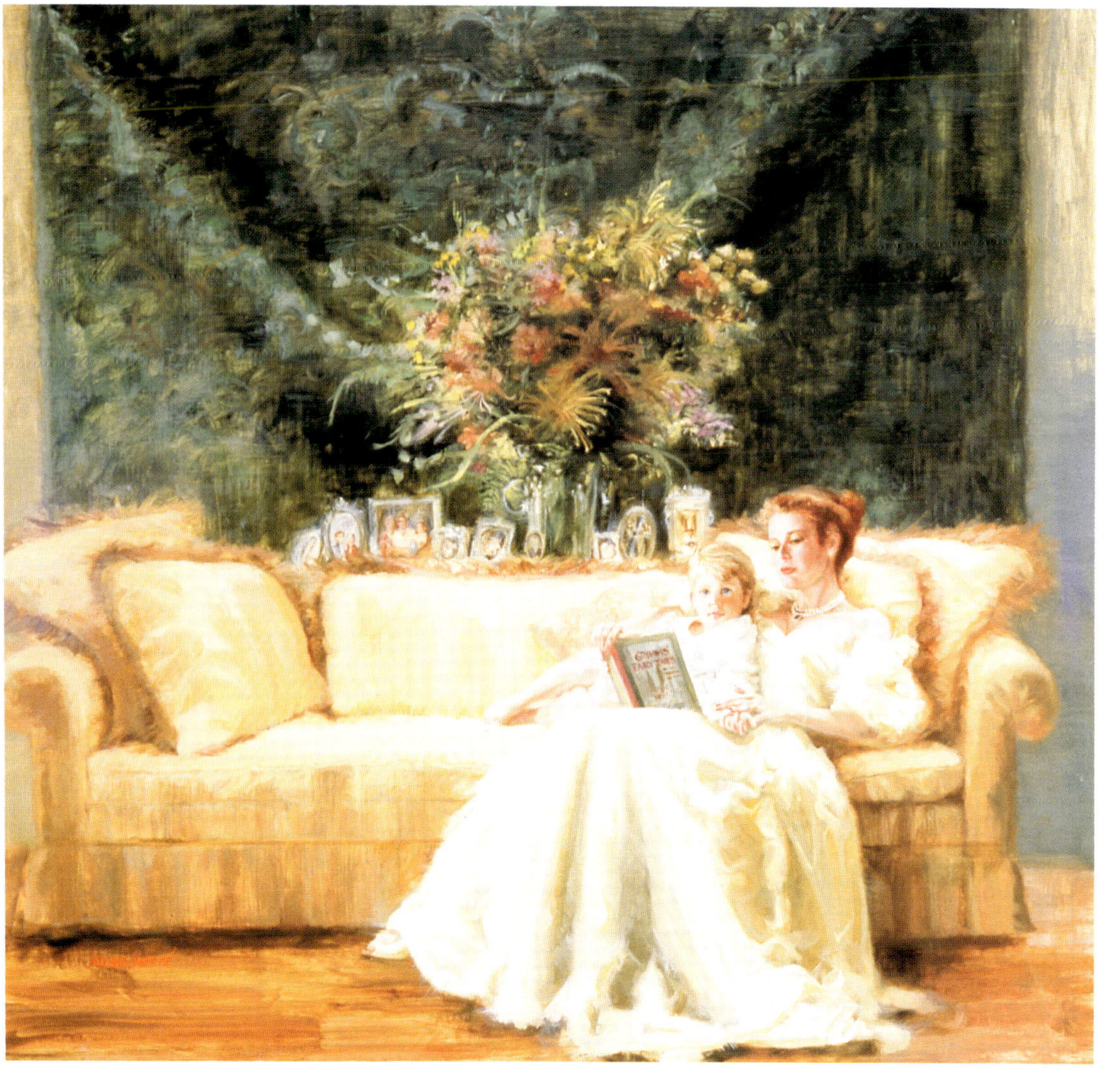

played in theater companies all over Connecticut. A lot of the John Raitt roles, like *Pajama Game*, *Man Of La Mancha*. They found his cancer in 1973, and he had his laryngectomy.

How was he able to continue his teaching?

He didn't teach for about three months, while he learned to use that device you hold up to your neck to speak. But that was only a steppingstone. He found a therapist who had never taught a laryngectomee, and convinced her that she could help him. He didn't want to learn from someone who taught traditional esophageal speech, because he didn't want to sound that way. He felt that with the abdominal muscle control he'd developed over all his years of singing, he could do better.

When school started in the fall, he was still using that awful device. He tells me that at his first class, he turned away from his students, and when he turned back again, they were giving him a standing ovation. That was when he knew he was doing okay. So he got through the first year. He was teaching psychology. Today he teaches "Psychology of the Handicapped." And he sees private clients here in Springfield. His voice, as you know, is nearly normal-sounding.

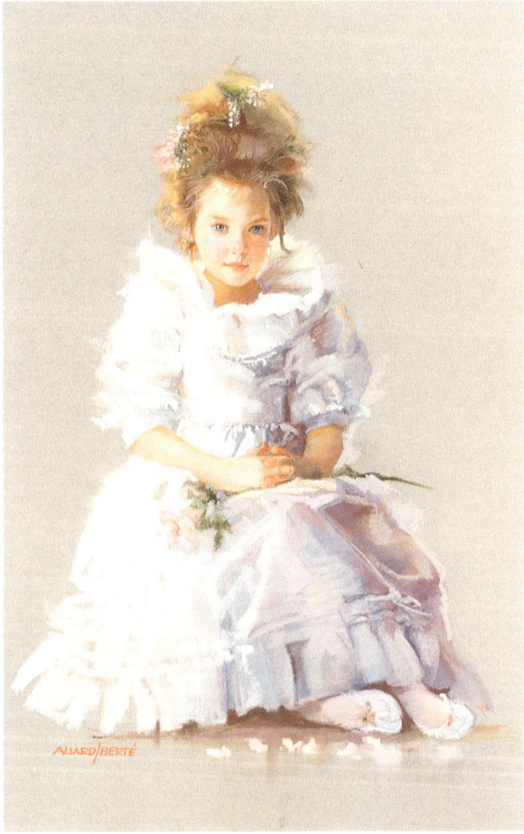

BRIANA
1990
PASTEL
32″×29″
COLLECTION OF THE ARTIST

This was created as a pastel portrait sample for Portraits South. I felt my subject was at a wonderful age, and it was an opportunity to paint in pastels—another example of investing in self, risking the work without having an actual buyer for the piece.

I'd like to go back, for a minute, to your beginnings as an artist. Where did it all start for you?

I always had this great desire to draw. I remember, I was in the sixth grade. My parents had just divorced, and I stuttered a great deal. I was taken to a wonderful speech therapist in the Springfield school system, and he stayed with me throughout my school years. He got my teachers not to call on me orally, but to have me write or draw my answers on the board.

I was ten years old that year, and my older brother and I were asked to do a mural for the hallway. We worked on it for a good part of that year, and it stayed on the wall for twenty years.

When I gave my acceptance speech as vice-president of my high school graduating class, my wonderful speech therapist was waiting in the wings for me.

Upon graduation in '51, I entered Pratt Institute, but didn't stay. After just a few weeks, I discovered Traphagen School of Design in Manhattan, and transferred over.

I was seventeen, fresh out of high school and living in Manhattan, a young woman in a hurry. I had already met Ray. I didn't have four years to go to school, and Traphagen had instructors who were actually out there in the industry. I didn't want to be taught fashion illustration by someone who had learned it twenty-five years earlier. I wanted someone who was doing it *now*.

Fashion design and illustration were your majors?

Yes. After being there for a year and a half, I got a part-time job as a dress designer. I stayed there for eight months, earning $125 a week . . . big money for a young woman in '52.

But I left to come home and marry. Of course, I could not find any job to equal it, so I took a job with a department store in Springfield, then a year later, with another in Hartford, Connecticut, where I stayed for eight years. Then another retail fashion illustration job for four years.

We were married eight years before Keith came in 1960, and then Jennifer in '63. Both our wonderful children are so special to us because

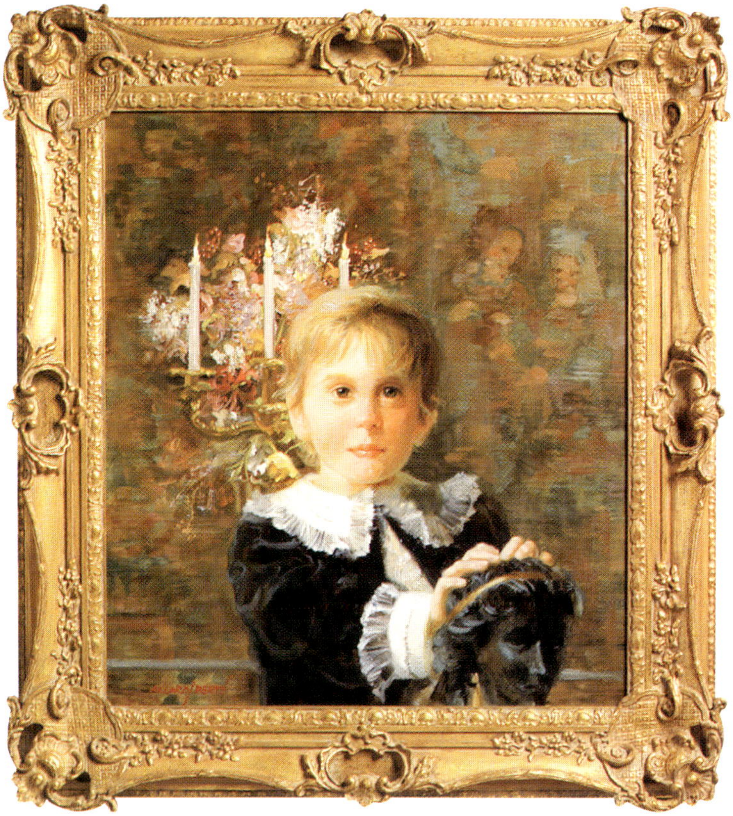

THE HEIR
1990
OIL ON CANVAS
32″ × 32″
PRIVATE COLLECTION

A blend of portraiture and genre, this painting conveys the mood of the portrait, with the tapestry and flowers of the background. I worked with a fine gallery/framer in Naples, Florida to achieve elegant framing.

they are adopted.

We eventually moved back to Springfield. That's when I signed up with an art rep from New York. I was with him for the next six years, doing work for Bloomingdale's, Saks Fifth Avenue, *McCalls*, Good Housekeeping, *Seventeen*, and others. I did book jackets for romantic gothic novels, too.

I'd meet him, my rep, on the corner outside of a Nedick's in midtown Manhattan. He'd buy me an orange drink and we'd discuss the day's assignments. I'd have to go meet the clients. One might be uptown, another on the east side, and a third in New Jersey. I'd get home, maybe by ten o'clock, put on a robe and get behind my drawing board. It was an incredible pace, but I kept it up for seven years.

You know, people look at me today and say, "How lucky you are!" And I have this inner reaction, that luck has had so little at all to do with it. It's all that has happened. It's all the time, all the planning, all the risks I've taken. But I guess I have been lucky, too.

If you had it to do over again, would you do anything differently?

I can zoom right in on that. I would have been painting twenty years ago. I don't even have to think about that one. And yet, because we learn, and because we are the sum total of everything that has gone before . . . perhaps what I have lived through is what is revealed on my canvas at this point.

If you were to talk to a group of artists who wanted to be professionals, what advice would you give them?

Focus yourself. Decide exactly where you want to go. Once you reach your first goal, push out a little further. Just continue to do that as you grow. Paint, and draw, and send yourself off to workshops. Find some of the artists who are out in the world this day. They're real. They're alive, they're painting, and they are successful. Avail yourself of their teaching.

You have to ask yourself, "What is really important to me? What am I willing to give up? What am I *unwilling* to give up? And where does my art fit in?"

There are things I could not personally give up. Like my precious time with Ray. Not at this point, at this age. Perhaps if I had done this when I was twenty or thirty, I could have devoted seven days a week, nine to nine, to painting. Eating, sleeping on a floor. I could not do that, and so I had to find a place for art within my life that would still leave me enough time to expand and grow. In that time of expanding and growing, you really have to focus in. You have to persevere.

Any final thoughts you'd like to leave with the aspiring professional artist?

I'm often asked to speak to students at nearby art schools. They ask me why some artists make it and others do not. Perseverance is the answer I give. I run into people I've gone to school with, and remember that they were outstanding. Why didn't they make it? They had ability. They had talent—often more than many of the other students. But they didn't have the drive, and they didn't persevere. So they didn't make it. That's the way I see it.

CHARLES SOVEK

Learn to Accept Yourself

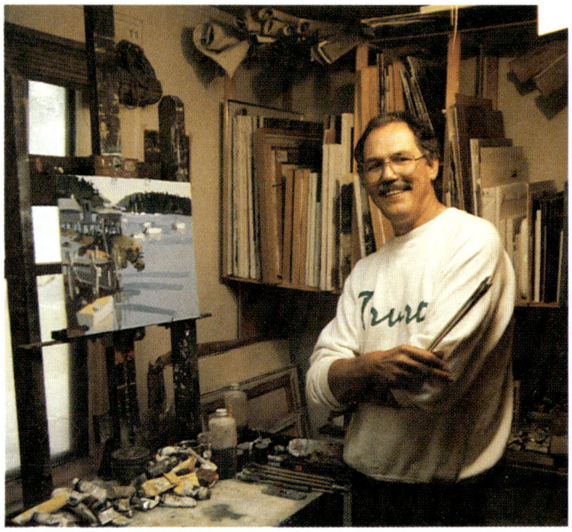

Charles Sovek, at his Norwalk, Connecticut studio. Photo by Lew Lehrman.

CHARLIE SOVEK'S HOME AND STUDIO OCCUPY THE UPPER FLOOR OF A two-story house down a quiet residential street in Norwalk, Connecticut. I have received a rare invitation there for this interview, and I mount the stairs under the suspicious gaze of the three cats who share his space.

On my right, at the head of the stairs, is Charlie's office. The walls are stacked high with heavily laden bookshelves; they dwarf a cluttered desk dominated by the word processor on which he drafts his books and articles. On the right, down the hall and across from the kitchen, is his studio. Dozens of canvases, completed and in process, early and recent, fill one wall.

Brightly sunlit, the apartment has a feeling of purposeful clutter. And the aroma of oil paint hangs faintly in the air.

How many books do you have in print now?

Three. First came *Painting Indoors*, in 1976. Seven years later, I wrote *Catching Light in Your Paintings*, which is the one that really put me on the map. My newest book, *Oil Painting: Develop Your Natural Ability*, is, I think, the best one yet. It's like a painter's version of Nicolaides' *The Natural Way to Draw*.

How did you get on the "literary track"?

The whole idea of writing a book had intrigued me for years. Al Michini, a painting buddy, approached me one day and said, "Charlie, I like the way you make pictures. How would you like to do a couple of paintings for a book I'm working on and write some text to go along with them?" I did. Something clicked. And I was hooked.

Walt Reed was the editor of North Light Books at the time, so I approached him and said, "I have an idea. Everyone's doing landscape techniques. How about a book on painting indoor motifs, like Wyeth or Vermeer?" He liked the idea, and I was off and running.

Painting Indoors took five years to complete. But even though it was a letdown because of the poor reproduction, the book sold twelve thousand copies. A couple of years went by before I decided to take another shot at it.

I was experimenting a lot with light around that time and scooping up every bit of information I could find. I had delved into the teachings of Frank Dumond and Frank Reilly and boiled down their theories into a simplified system of my own. And it really gave me a handle on painting light: edge light, back light, top light, front light, moonlight, match light, you name it! The system was fun, easy to understand, and gave my paintings a snappy, light-filled quality. I thought, "Gee, I should do a book on light." The result was *Catching Light in Your Paintings*.

What effect did the books have on your career?

I took off! They gave me a national reputation, a zillion students, and the luxury to turn down commissions.

You mean portraits?

Yes. Also paintings of estates. I do architecture

pretty well, and people would commission me to do their mansions—for big bucks, too. But it was more like illustration . . . satisfying somebody else's needs.

Catching Light got me out of that. It also got me into teaching and workshops. Then the teaching started to put such a big drain on my painting energy that I cut back. I do about twelve workshops a year now. One a month. That gives me forty weeks to do what I want.

It sounds like you've never wanted to do anything but paint.

Hah! Hardly. Let me go back. I grew up in a blue-collar Pittsburgh family. I had never painted a thing in my life. Music was more my interest. I played the piano. Was good at it, too. The summer I graduated from high school I wanted a car and took a job as a roofer. Then I had an accident. A bad one. I fell two stories and broke both wrists. The fingers on my left hand still don't function properly.

During the year it took me to recuperate I kept asking myself, "What am I going to do with my life now?" I had some insurance money coming and had just received a small inheritance from my grandmother. Somehow, I saw a catalog for the Art Institute of Pittsburgh and decided to check the place out. When I walked through the door and smelled the turpentine, I remember thinking, "This is it! I'm home!"

That's quite a leap. How do you account for it?

I really can't. But when I was fifteen or so, we had an encyclopedia. In it were some paintings by Thomas Eakins, Edward Hopper and a few others. I remember studying Hopper's painting of a lighthouse and saying, "Mmm. . . . that's really something." Never could I have imagined that thirty-five years later I'd set up my easel in the very same spot Hopper did and paint my own version of that lighthouse. At the same time, however, I knew absolutely nothing about painting—nothing! But I was itching to learn. At art school, I fell in love with the whole curriculum, especially the drawing of life classes. At night, I went to Carnegie Tech and took more life drawing and painting courses.

Still having some money left after graduation, I decided to really polish my skills and enrolled at the Art Center College of Design in Los Angeles. It was my first time out of Pennsylvania, and when I got there and saw the superb facilities, all I could say was, "Wow." I then proceeded to work my buns off.

I started out a fair-to-mediocre student. My major was advertising. But about midpoint in my second semester I saw an exhibit of paintings by a senior that left such an impression that I changed my major to illustration. I can clearly remember an inner transformation taking place and thinking, "That's what I want to do!"

I eventually earned a scholarship for my last two years. I took all the painting courses I could but skipped the academics. I studied with some excellent teachers, painted from life nearly every day, and made enormous progress.

Thinking I was hot stuff, I went to New York after graduation expecting fame and fortune. What I got instead was a chorus of, "Nice stuff, kid, but we're kinda slow now." Eventually I took a job as a sketch artist with an ad agency. I went to the Art Students League at

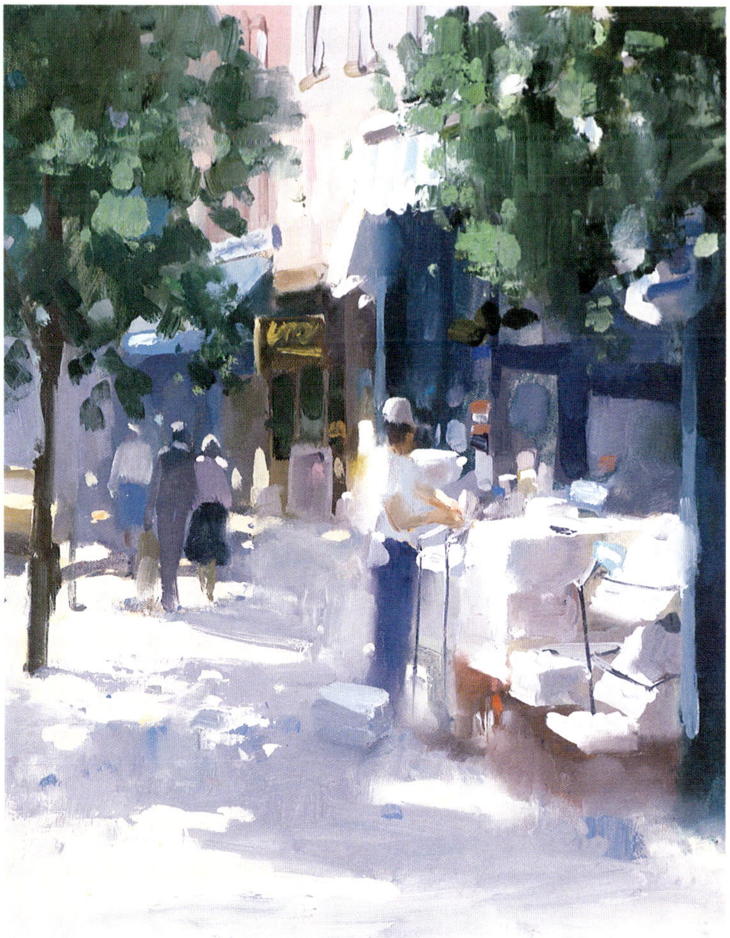

BLEECKER STREET
1991
OIL ON CANVAS
19" × 23"
COLLECTION OF THE ARTIST

This studio painting was done from sketches, photographs and thirty years' worth of recollections of wandering around the streets of New York. When doing this kind of studio piece, I imagine I'm painting on location, oftentimes to the point of imposing a three- or four-hour time limit.

The Tin Roof
1991
Oil on canvas
11″ × 14″
Collection of the artist

Light on interesting textures has always intrigued me. Here, the entire picture is built around the dramatic light hitting the tin roof of the building. I got so wrapped up in trying to capture its shiny surface that the rest of the composition clicked right into shape.

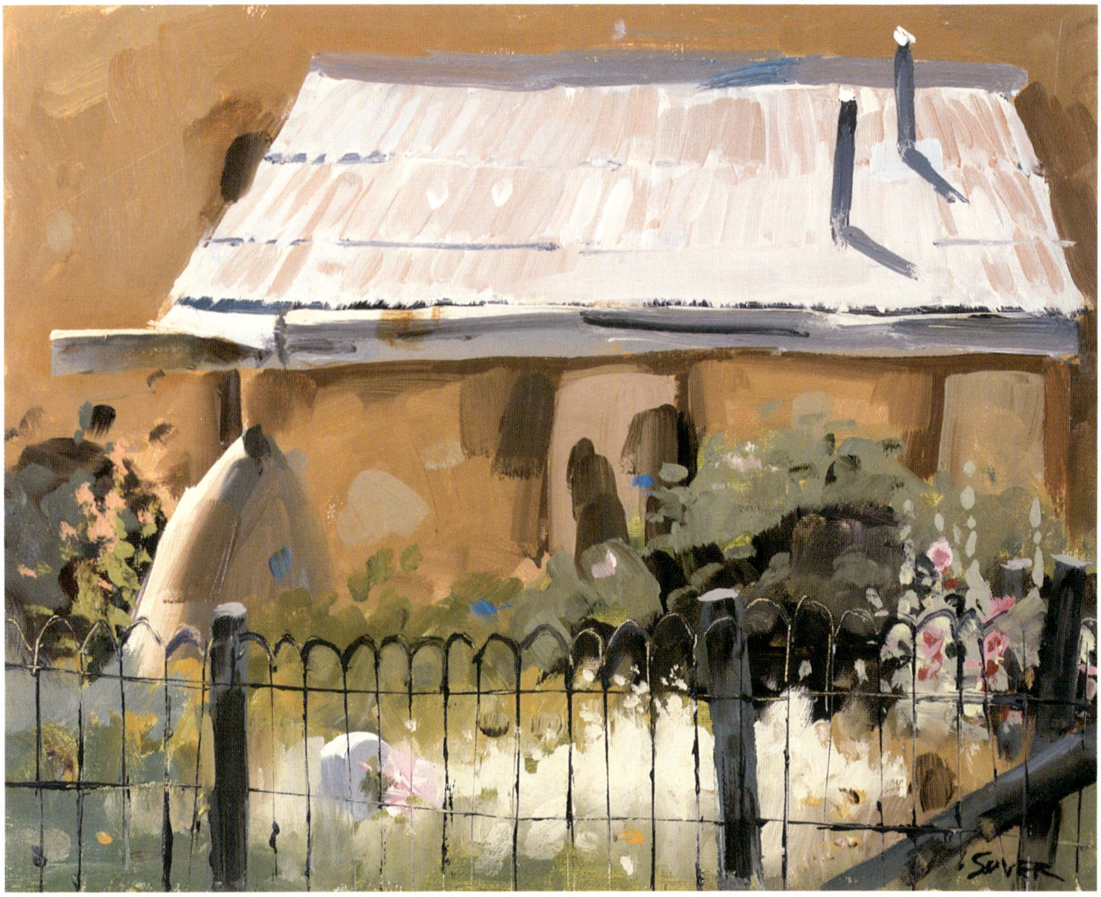

night and painted outdoors a lot on weekends. Still growing.

After two hectic years, I started freelancing. Mostly western and romance themes for paperback book covers . . . always painting. It was the revolutionary sixties, and illustrators were trying a lot of innovative techniques. More than a few knockout pieces came off my easel. But then the politics and lifestyles got more conservative and so did illustration. I realized if I didn't get out soon, I would find myself swimming in the wrong pool.

Anticipating the shift, I took a teaching job at Famous Artists School in Westport, Connecticut. I was assigned to the painting course and got to know people like Charlie Reid, Jack Pellew and Claude Croney, who also taught there. I began to see that you could really paint for a living. Met my first wife there, too. I left two years later and started phasing out illustration and focusing on becoming a full-time painter.

You were living in Westport and painting as well as freelancing?

More painting than illustration. Mostly portraits. I had been studying with S. Edmund Oppenheim at the League, and it seemed the natural way to go. I started hustling up commissions and was just about able to hold my own. Then, art groups started asking me to do demonstrations. I began exhibiting, entering shows and even winning some prizes. But it was still tough going for a while. The late sixties and early seventies were definitely transitional years.

How did you market your work when you were struggling to get established as a painter?

I started modestly, showing at libraries, banks and local shows to get exposure. It was then that I realized there are two types of painters: those who enjoy people and those who don't.

Now, I'm a pretty private person because I need my alone time to be productive. But when I'm with people I can be very gregarious. I'm comfortable, and I can talk with them easily. That was a big part of my success, because if a person thought about a portrait commission I would say, "Look, why don't I just paint your portrait? You keep it for awhile, and if you like it, we've got a deal. If not, I'll take it back and we'll call it a day." Easy-breezy. People like that. It relaxes them. I was very flexible, and that's what got me going.

If someone really loved a painting but couldn't afford it, I would let them pay it off in installments or even drop the price. On the other hand, if money was no object, I had no qualms about charging a respectable figure. But I've always stayed within a reasonable bracket. I've seen artists overprice themselves right out of business. Even today, I try to keep my prices affordable to everyone.

Did you start showing in galleries in the beginning?

Not until about 1975. I was doing pretty well on my own, and the commission was a nuisance. Later I realized the galleries had access to a lot more clients than I ever would.

Did you produce much income?

Enough to get along on. Mostly from portraits. I was starting to do scenes of New York City, which I eventually developed into a specialty. But I lived a pretty Spartan life at the time.

How did you price your work in the beginning?

I would charge about three to four hundred dollars for a sixteen-by-twenty-inch head-and-shoulders portrait. To price other subjects, I'd snoop around various galleries to see what the competition was charging. Then I'd set my prices somewhere in the middle to upper-middle bracket.

In 1970 my first wife and I bought a house, and we just squeaked by. That was nearly twenty years ago. Now I have the exposure and when people see my work in a gallery, they associate it with quality. I've gotten some professional recognition, too. I don't need a Mercedes or closet full of clothes. But it does feel good to have the respect of my peers.

Is your current path the one you'll stick to for the foreseeable future?

Painting-wise, yes. But I might make a move at some point. Cape Cod has always attracted me, but so has New Mexico. I have gotten involved with the Cape School of Art in Provincetown. Being affiliated with the same school that

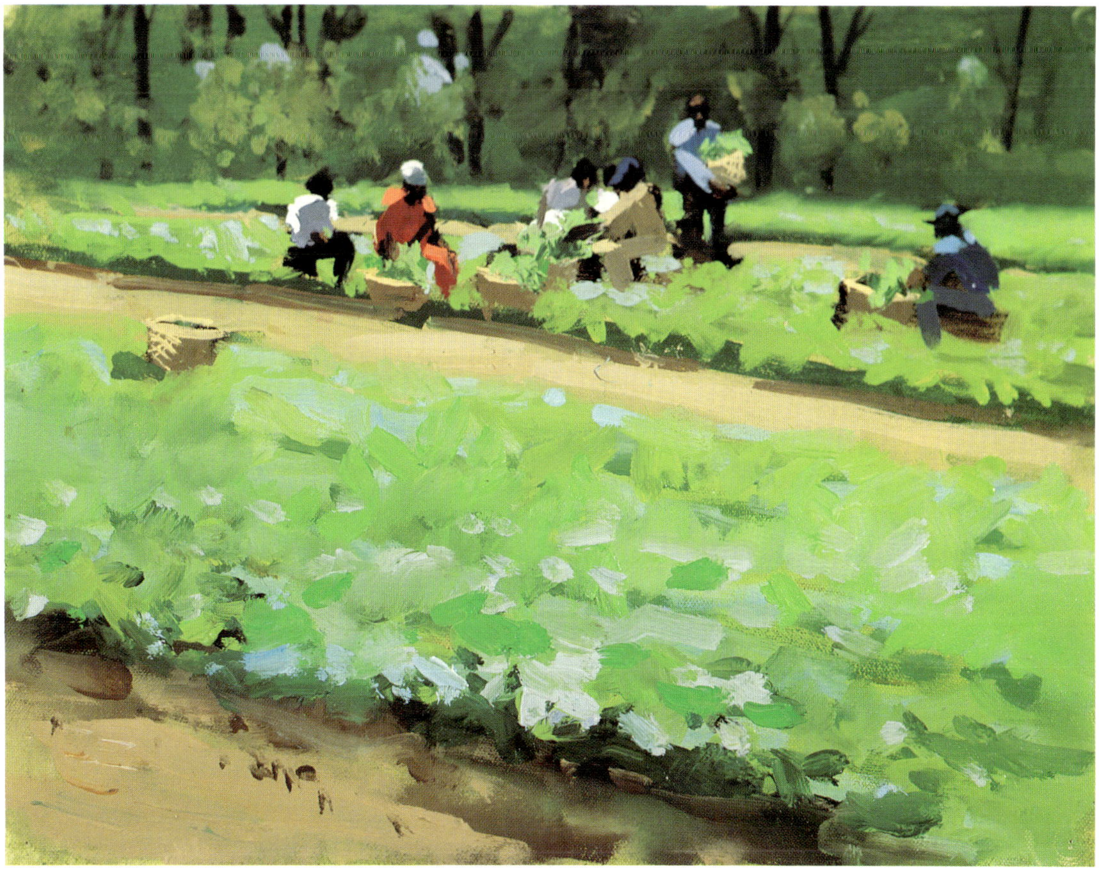

TOBACCO FIELD, KINSTON, NORTH CAROLINA
1991
OIL ON CANVAS
12″ × 16″
COLLECTION OF THE ARTIST

Batting small talk back and forth with the workers picking tobacco as we both toiled in the hot sun gave me an intimate feeling for the subject. I find it nearly impossible to contrive this kind of immediacy in the predictable environment of a studio.

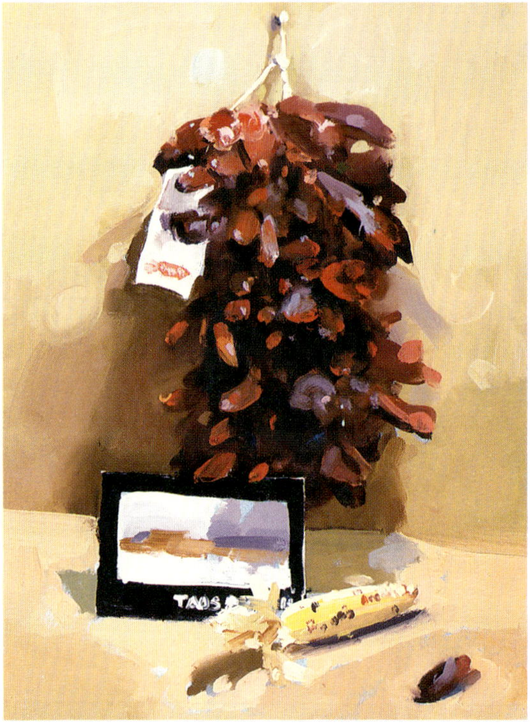

STILL LIFE WITH PEPPERS, CORN AND POSTCARD
1991
OIL ON BOARD
12″ × 17″
COLLECTION OF THE ARTIST

I painted this Southwestern motif in Connecticut. Having brought back the objects from a painting trip, I set them up and painted them under a strong lamp to simulate the effect of sunlight. More carefully executed than most of my work, the painting took nine hours to complete.

Charles Hawthorne started is a very attractive proposition. I've also painted and taught in Taos, New Mexico, enough to know the town pretty well and love the colorful motifs I see everywhere. Ideally, I'd like to spend half my time in the East and the other half out West.

Were you married a second time?

In 1980. My second wife was a neat lady. There was quite an age difference, but we had a good thing going. Unfortunately, we never resolved having kids. She wanted them. I already had two and didn't want to start over. We're still friends. I have the nicest ex-wives a guy could wish for.

Making the break . . . cutting the ties. Were you ever discouraged? Did you ever question the whole move?

Sure. Both times the break was painful, especially when it came to my kids. But it was the only option I had.

Are you ever discouraged about painting?

No more than a dozen times a week now! Years ago I was in a constant fret because I was trying to compete with every good painting I saw. Learning to accept myself for what I was got me out of that. But I still sweat out most pictures I do and can get very down when things don't go well. I can get mad, too. I literally have thrown paintings away. Once while on location I threw my whole easel into the Saugatuck River . . . the whole thing, painting and all!

Did you dive in for it?

Nah. A couple of days later I went out and bought a new one. I bounce back.

Do you ever get artist's block?

Not often. When I do I switch to a different medium like watercolor or gouache. Changing subjects also helps. So does teaching. I do occasionally hit a block trying to juggle too many different projects.

Can you point to a high point in your career thus far?

Right now feels pretty good. I'm able to do things with paint that I always wished I could. I have a fine following of students. A good reputation around the country. At the same time, I can see that I'm just starting to scratch the surface.

Tell me how you approach the discipline of work today.

I try to paint every day, seven days a week. It could be just a study of a walnut done with three strokes of color, or a full-blown cityscape. But like sourdough, I like to add to my skill every day.

I'm a night person. The later the day gets, the better I get.

Mornings are another story. I'll wake up and say, "Can I really paint?" Or I'll look at a picture I did the day before and think, "How did I do that? I know I can't do it again!" I just can't seem to muster up much self-confidence before noon. So I do all my chores. Clean house. Shop. Go for a run.

By 11:00 A.M. I'll head out on location. I have to discipline myself to do this because there's not a lot of enthusiasm. But once I get there, and see an effect, boom! The machinery starts to work. As I get to painting, all my doubts are forgotten.

On an ideal day, I'll go out to do a landscape. It'll turn out pretty well. I'll be riding high. All systems are go. My mind is sharp, and my facility's there, and the enthusiasm, too.

That's when the golden stuff comes out. I'll head home for lunch, then go out and start a second painting. I'll work until six or seven and have dinner after that. I am always amazed at how much better the second picture usually turns out.

Do you do much work in the studio?

Oh, sure. Still lifes and such. And this is where the night owl part of me surfaces. I do most of my still lifes under artificial light so I can keep working until the painting is finished. Or I'll paint from sketches. I don't work from photos much but when I do, I pretend I'm right out there on location. I even play tapes of forest sounds or waves to keep me in the mood. But I never work from any photographs except my own, and preferably a subject I've painted before. My studio pieces tend to be larger. But whatever size, I work on it until it's finished. I can go on for fourteen hours sometimes, often right through the night.

If I have to stop, go to bed, then get up and face a confidence crunch, it's hard to pick up my thread of thought again. I've tried for over thirty years to work on the same painting for more than a day but it's just not me. It's like jazz. I do a riff and that's it.

How do you market your work today?

I have a gallery in Darien, Connecticut, that fetches pretty good prices for me. And I do pretty well when I teach. I'll usually bring a batch of small paintings along and the students often take a few home with them. I've also made some gallery contacts in Cape Cod, New Mexico and California. I'm not pushing this yet because I want to wait until I have a substantial volume

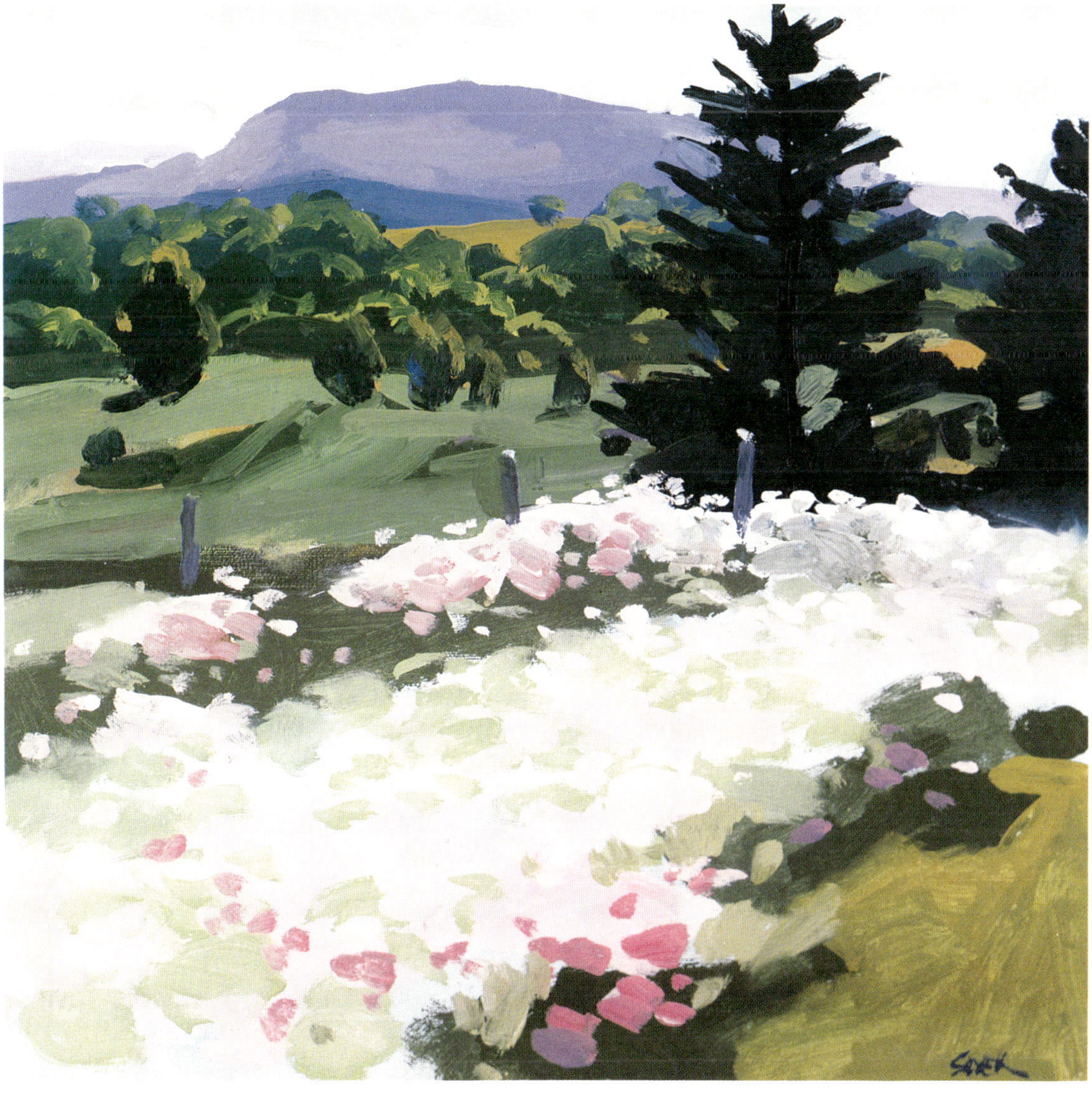

VISTA, WESTERN VIRGINIA
1991
OIL ON CANVAS
16″ × 16″
COLLECTION OF THE ARTIST

A busy, four-lane highway ran smack through the center of this seemingly quiet landscape. To preserve the pastoral quality of the subject, I eliminated the road and replaced it with a meadow.

Still Life With Pepper and Dish
1991
Oil on canvas
12″ × 14″
Collection of the artist

Getting risky with a still life is a challenge I can't refuse. What could have been a traditional vegetable-on-plate motif (had the drapery been unpatterned) became a pulsating riot of color. I did no preliminary sketches but jumped directly into the finished painting.

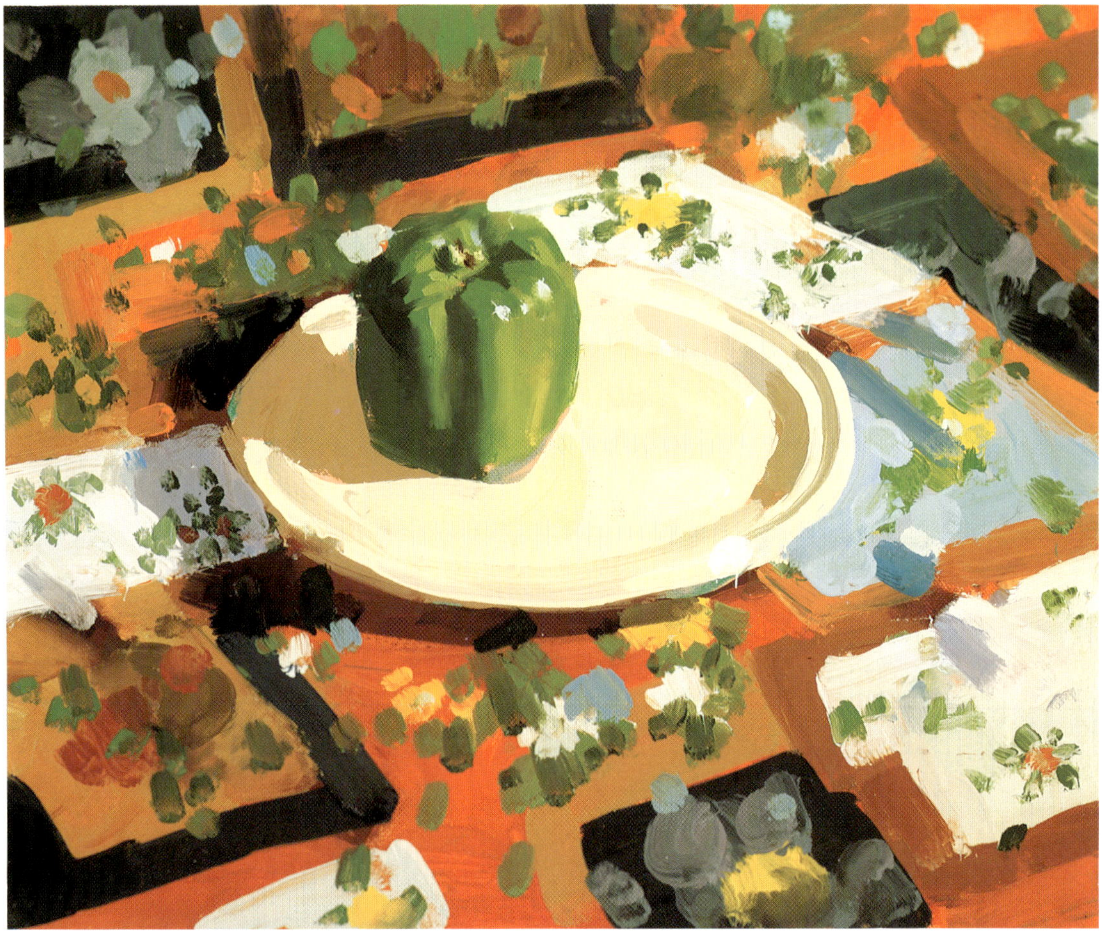

of work to choose from. It's not that I couldn't market what I have now, but I wouldn't have anything left to make a big splash with.

You must have a lot of canvases stacked up somewhere.

They're building up but not as many as I'd like. And there are a certain couple of little works—very small location paintings—that are hinting at new directions. I want to see where that goes, and if I start selling those, I won't have any touch points left.

As regards marketing, what are your plans for the future?

I want to put in another few years of intensive painting before I start getting serious with the galleries. By then, I should be able to command some respectable prices and begin beefing up my nest egg.

I'm fifty-four now and in pretty good shape. But it's getting to be time to start thinking about things like mutual funds and all those other goodies everybody else has. It's a little risky, but I've been a risky person all my life.

Why do you think some artists make it, and others never quite do?

There's no simple answer. You have to define your terms, because "making it as a painter" is one thing, "using your painting skill to make money" is another.

It's not that hard for an artist to make money. Wherever you live, there's always a demand for paintings of local landmarks and so forth. But then you have to ask yourself, "Is this really what I'm all about as an artist?" It gets risky.

But why do some artists end up going back to roofing?

Not working hard enough is probably the biggest reason. It's a long, hard pull learning how to paint. Then, there are the pressures from spouses and relatives to make money. That can be a real downer.

There are also people like students I've had who are all set to toss it in because they were discouraged about what they did. They keep comparing their work to the paintings in books they buy. Or they go to a Sorolla exhibit and want to throw their brushes away. Believe me, I can relate to that.

When you think over your career, is there anything you would have done differently?

I foolishly turned down a two-year teaching stint in Amsterdam that Famous Artists School offered me. Can't remember why. What a jerk! But to go back now and say if only I had taken that job . . . or not had that accident . . . or if I had majored in painting and not gotten into illustration. . . . But I like to think everything I've experienced, both good and bad, has contributed to the person I am today.

What advice would you offer to people who want to chuck their jobs and paint full time?

I tell my students, it's better to stay with your job for a while and ease into this slowly, than to jump off the deep end. I'd almost rather see a person paint weekends and be themselves than commercialize—and possibly lose—the very thing they cherish. There's that dichotomy again. Art versus money. . . .

They can't be separated. If you can't eat, you can't buy paints.

You really need to be flexible. If you have a knack for doing house portraits, sure. Do them. But never deceive yourself into thinking that this is all there is to you. Through all your money-making phases, try to keep defining your *real* artistic self. And eventually, you'll grow into that self.

My whole aim has been to discover who I am as an artist. Money is just a by-product. What did Joseph Campbell say?—"Follow your bliss, and helping hands will appear." I really believe in that.

I also believe you pay the price for being an artist because it can be a lonely, frustrating existence sometimes. Once you've accepted that, you can then reap the other, more considerable rewards: a wonderful peace of mind, the ability to live comfortably with yourself, and the satisfaction of knowing you're doing what you most like to do.

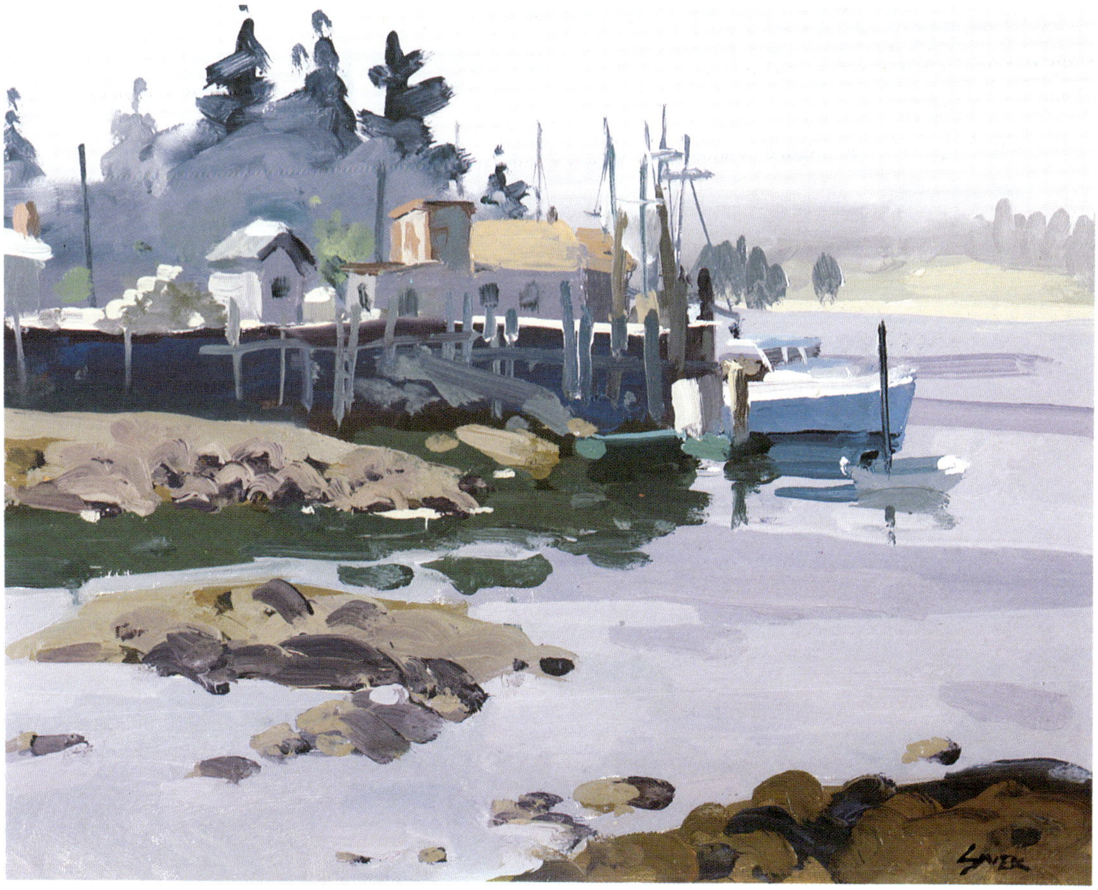

PORT CLYDE, MAINE
1990
OIL ON CANVAS
12″ × 16″
COLLECTION OF THE ARTIST

I came across this picturesque harbor as the fog was just lifting. I had to paint quickly to get the atmospheric effect in the background. It contrasted so nicely with the sun-filled foreground, an ambience unique to the Maine coast.

GERRY METZ
Your Work Has to Have Heart

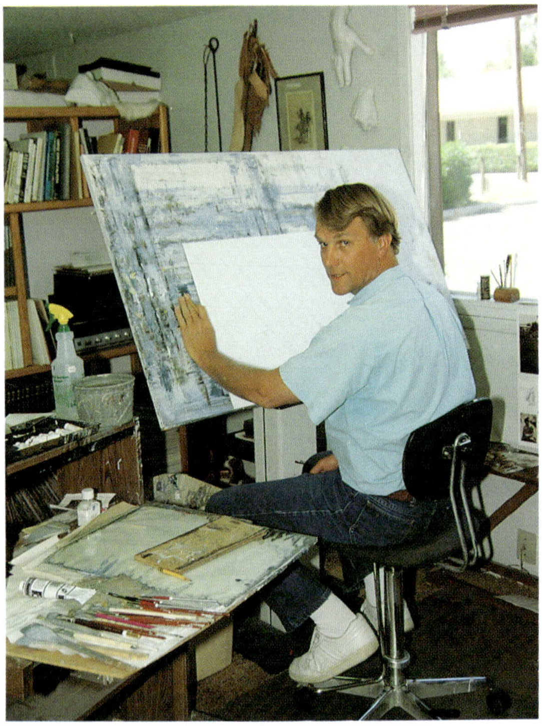

I can usually find Gerry Metz hard at work in the studio across the hall from mine. Photo by Lew Lehrman.

GERRY METZ'S STUDIO OCCUPIES SOME FOUR HUNDRED SQUARE FEET IN a trim one-story Scottsdale, Arizona office building. North light from a large, plate glass window floods his work area. Before him is a large, paint-stained pedestal drafting table turned nearly vertical; behind him a well-used oil painting easel; to his left, his taboret, covered with the large sheet of glass he uses as his palette.

Though he occasionally works in oil and is a proficient sculptor, his customary medium is watercolor on heavy board surfaces. His Winsor & Newton transparent pigments, however, are blended with Shiva's casein white. Gerry's paintings are a fascinating melding of transparent watercolor and the kind of opaque technique more commonly associated with acrylics. Finished paintings awaiting delivery are beautifully framed, but, surprisingly, unglazed. He fixes each painting with Krylon Crystal Clear, then applies a coat of acrylic matte varnish. It's a technique he developed years ago, and one that his many collectors seem to demand.

As I arrive for this interview, he is putting the finishing touches on one of his popular "mountain men" paintings. I settle into his well-worn lounge chair. He continues to work as we talk.

What chain of events led you to your art career? Please start at the very beginning.

Growing up in Chicago, I was always interested in art, but I just couldn't get into a high school art class. After graduation, I enrolled in an art program at Wright Junior College in Chicago. It wasn't long before I realized they were teaching me nothing, so I transferred into marketing, and stayed with that for two years.

In 1963, I had an opportunity to get into commercial art, and jumped at it. The opening was at one of Chicago's better art studios. Jobs there were rare, and people like myself would have been willing to pay just to get the experience. I started at thirty dollars a week. A year later, it went to fifty dollars. But I learned a lot.

We apprentices would draw on our lunch hours, we'd draw all evening and we'd draw all night. Next day, the illustrators would critique our work. After I was there a while, I enrolled in the School of Professional Art. For two years I attended three-hour classes three nights a week. My teachers were professional illustrators, and my classmates were professionals, too.

That studio, though, was my primary training, and I worked there for four years, learning everything I could. When the pressures of the job finally became too great, I left, and with a former studio colleague, went into an art school venture.

By that time, I was married, helping run the school, and painting in my spare time. A vacation trip to Arizona convinced me that Scottsdale was the place I wanted to live, and three months later we made the move. I opened a little art school in Scottsdale, where part-time teaching would leave me some time to paint. I never expected to make a living painting.

Then, one day in '72, a fellow named Roy Hampton walked into my school, and asked me if he could use some of the space as a studio. We became good friends. He was exhibiting in mall shows, and he asked me if I'd like to go into one with him. That's really how it started. I'd just been painting for myself. And then my works began to sell.

Was there anyone who acted as a mentor for you, who helped you a great deal in the beginning?

The person who probably helped me the most was Austin Deuel. When I arrived in '71, Austin was a top name in art here. We became good friends. I was really struggling in '72. The school wasn't producing enough income. My wife and I had just split up and I had a one-year-old son on my hip all the time. I had arrived here with enough money to last a year, and it was running out. I wanted to paint, but I had more damn problems. Austin helped me out quite a bit. He began to teach me painting and composition. He taught me that strong composition was often what made a painting sell. He showed me why you can walk into a gallery and immediately be drawn to a painting that's sixty feet away. It's not the detail . . . usually not the color. It's the composition.

Austin showed me how to do it. He helped me with every aspect of it. Even the marketing. He even gave me money when I was broke. That's the way he is. He's not primarily a teacher. He's just the kind of guy who'll help people out if he feels they sincerely want to succeed. And I have to include Roy, too. Without the help of each of them, I don't think I could have survived. Believe me, it was a very difficult time.

You certainly weren't making a living selling paintings in those days, were you?

Hardly! I was teaching one day a week at the Phoenix Art Museum, plus two days at my own school. We'd pack Roy's motor home full of work and head out. I was doing charcoal studies of Indians and mountain men in '72. The first show, I sold two hundred dollars worth of work, at about twenty-five dollars a picture. Fifty dollars was the highest price I had. That was a lot of money for me in those days. Later on, we got together with an organization that did mall

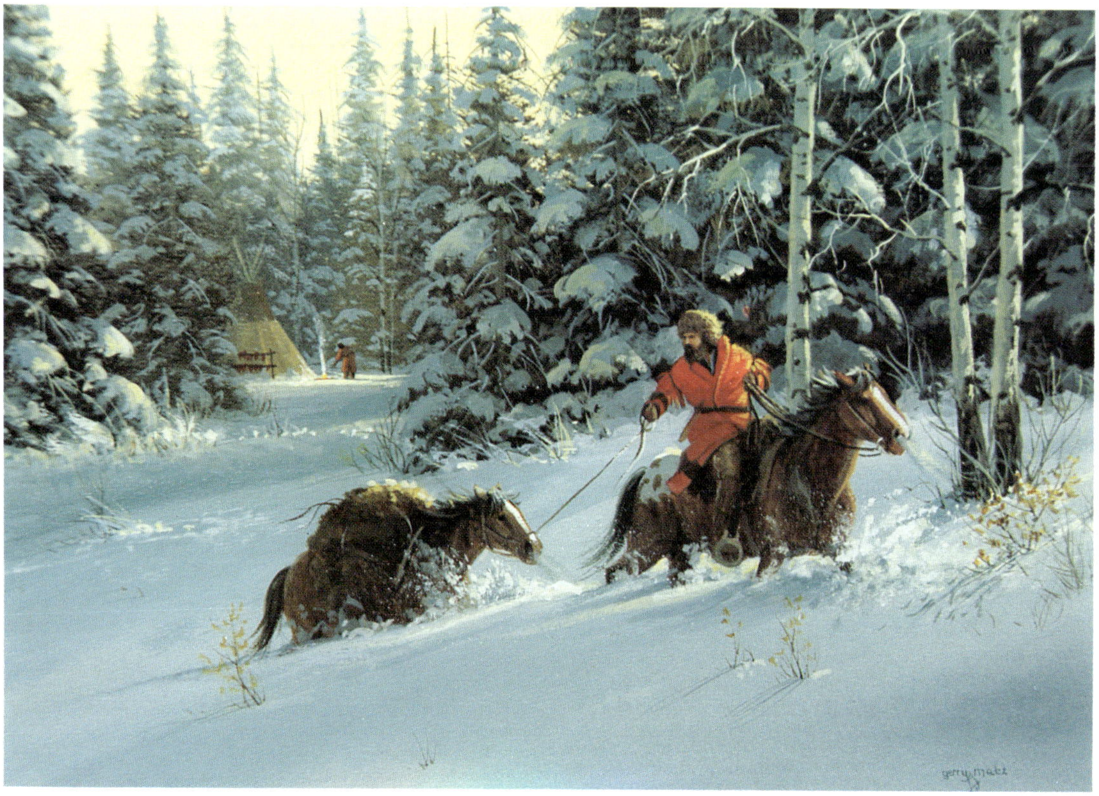

Deep Snow
1990
Opaque watercolor
15″ × 11″
Collection of Dale Teeters

A couple of years ago, I took a winter trip to Jackson, Wyoming with a model, to build up my file of reference material. We dragged our pack horses through the belly-deep snow, while I photographed from every angle. So you might say this painting was drawn from personal experience.

shows all across the country. Every week, we'd travel to a different show: California, Texas, Denver and such. Monday was a travel day. We'd arrive Tuesday, and set up Tuesday night. Wednesday through Sunday we'd work the show, 10:00 A.M. to 10:00 P.M. I'd sit there, selling my work, painting all the while, too. After closing, back at the motel, or in Roy's motor home, I'd sit up painting half the night. Constantly painting. Once in a while, when I was completely out of stock, I'd head for home, and start painting to build up inventory. I was cranking out a whole lot of work: mostly small stuff, charcoal drawings and paintings eleven by fourteen and smaller.

In those days, Scottsdale would close down in the summer. So in '72, Roy suggested we go up to Jackson, Wyoming for the summer. That's when my work really started selling. That first summer, I made six hundred to eight hundred dollars a week, grinding out twenty-five- and fifty-dollar paintings. I rented ten feet of wall space in a boot and saddle shop, set up my easel on the Western-style board sidewalk, wearing my cowboy hat and boots, and painted. The tourists would come by. "Hey, Mommy—look! A cowboy, a cowboy!" And they'd buy a painting to take home. Today, when I see what I was doing back then, I'd like to issue a recall notice. But I guess the price matched the art.

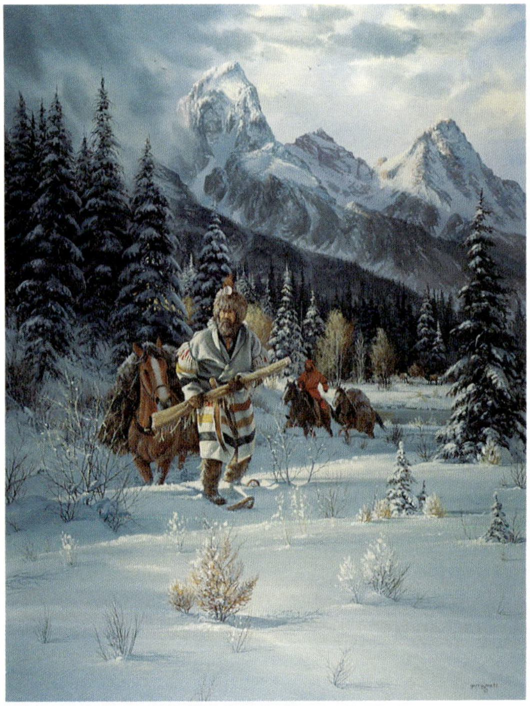

MOUNTAIN COLORS
1991
OPAQUE WATERCOLOR
40″ × 30″

The mountain man has always fascinated me. He lived and worked on his own, in a difficult, dangerous, yet romantic era. His coat, made from a Hudson's Bay Co. wool blanket, was a widely used garment, and indicative of the wealth of its owner.

It took incredible drive to stick with your chosen career at that point, didn't it?

Drive is a good word for it. I think it took more drive than talent. Many artists have talent, but can't make a living. So it's drive, and paying attention to the business end, that make the difference. I was interested only in painting in those days. I didn't think about making a living. I just wanted to get enough money so I could do another painting. It didn't matter whether the paintings sold or not. If they sold, I painted. If they didn't sell, I painted anyway. If I didn't make enough money selling paintings, I'd teach it. I did whatever I could to survive without having to get a regular job. But if I had had to get a job, I would have done that, too, and still painted.

I look back on those as my peanut-butter-and-jelly days, because that was all I ate. That, and cans of Dinty Moore Beef Stew, which I'd stretch out with dried bread. There were times I couldn't buy a frame until I sold a painting. The baby was with me all the time, too. We went everywhere together. Sometimes Roy's wife, Ann, would take care of my son while we'd work the shows. This went on for several years. I was involved in a bitter custody battle over my son at the time, too. It was very difficult.

In 1975, Austin, another artist, and I got together and shared studio space. We had a pact. A painting a day. It didn't matter what day it was. We each had to do at least one. So if I wanted the day off, I'd get down there at 6:00 A.M. and knock out a quarter-sheet painting as fast as I could. We painted all the time. Twelve to fifteen hours a day, seven days a week, when we weren't off doing the shows.

In 1975, I met and married a wonderful woman. Dayna and I have gone on to have three more sons, and to build a happy, full life together.

The show circuit, then, was really how you got established, wasn't it?

Yes. One thing would lead to another. Gallery people, and people running other shows, would walk through and invite you to exhibit. At my peak, I was doing fifteen to twenty shows a year. Practically none of my sales at that time were through established art galleries.

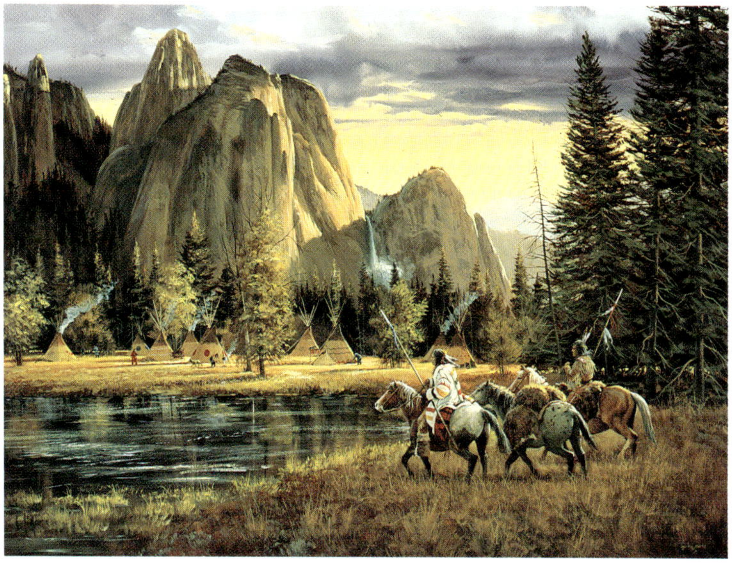

Morning Reflections
1985
Mixed media
40″ × 30″

Yosemite Valley is a spectacular place. I painted this camp scene in warm tones to show the intensity of the early morning light. We see Indians returning from a night of hunting. I go back in my imagination, to feel what it would have been like to be there during the early to mid-1800s.

How did you go about pricing and selling your work?

Roy helped me a lot with that. He'd taught creative sales. We'd travel down the road, and I'd be listening to Roy's real estate sales course tapes on my earphones. I just kept transposing "art" for "real estate" and trying to remember it all. I took the course, and Roy, seriously, and saw my sales increase by 70 percent in six months. I also learned the law of supply and demand. If the paintings were just sitting there, we'd keep the prices low. If they started selling, we'd raise them. In the beginning, fifty dollars was a good price for a sixteen by twenty. The faster they sold, the more we'd raise our prices. And if we had a really fine piece, we'd boost them a little more.

If your drive got you through the tough times, what keeps you at it today?

Fact is, I've never had a day when I didn't want to come to the studio. Those years in commercial art really helped, too. Commercial art taught me that you couldn't wait for inspiration to strike. You have to be inspired all the time. Deadlines are a fact of life. Even in my own business, the bills keep coming in, whether the paintings sell or not.

How did you start selling your work?

I was sharing space with Austin in '75, and dealers would visit our studio, interested mostly in Austin's work. One day, one of his dealers called me and said he'd be interested in handling some of my paintings. Austin was there, and he whispered to me, "Tell him that if he wants them, he'll have to buy them." With Austin coaching, I said, "Well, I'm really busy . . . backed up forever. The only way I can let you have work is if you buy it, because I have collectors waiting to pay me real money." To my surprise, he believed me, and began asking me for prices. That dealer came and bought several paintings, and that's how it began. It was great psychology, I discovered. After all, if the dealer had his own money in the painting, he'd be that much more intent on selling it than the painting next to it.

Is your income still growing? What's the trend these days?

My income is comparable to that of a top business executive, and it continues to increase . . . but so do my expenses. I guess that's always the way it is.

How are you planning for the future?

First of all, I don't feel like I'm ever going to retire, so I'm not really concerned about that part of it. Like most artists, I tend to spend whatever I have, so I developed the habit of buying land whenever I could, as investment. I've made contributions to a pension plan through my business corporation. I've tried to stretch myself with housing, too. I've owned about ten different residences in the past twenty years. And the last two we've designed and had custom built.

If you had it to do all over again, would you do anything differently?

Good question! [He ponders this one for a moment.] I probably would have remained a little more liquid . . . but, on the other hand, that contradicts what I said before, about tending to spend whatever I have. Maybe I wouldn't have partied as much . . . Naah! Come to think of it I'd probably have partied more!

What advice would you offer to artists who'd like to live by their art?

It's a difficult business. Working hard helps a lot, although being in the right place at the right time is important. Just remember that it's the "working hard" that puts you in enough places for the "right time" to come along. Above all, I'd advise artists to do it because they love it, not because they plan to get rich at it.

Why do you think some artists make it, while others never quite succeed?

It's that extra something that, for lack of a better word, I call "heart." I've tried to analyze that quality over the years. You see it in some paintings. It makes them stand a foot off the wall. It goes beyond what's on the canvas. Impossible to define, it's what can make a painting a fascinating, vital entity that will always hold interest for the viewer. And it's what makes that painting sell. Often, you, the artist, can't even tell whether it's there. I do believe, though, that if you're creating art only for the money, that elusive quality will never quite develop.

Whatever the art form, the artists who are most successful went into it because they love it. Those people will be creating for the rest of their lives. It may never make them rich, but money isn't the most important factor. Success can then become a matter of hitting that one lucky break.

Another thought: Most of the *really* successful artists I know are able to separate the art from the product. Too many artists fall in love with their own work. They let their egos carry them beyond their market. I'm not talking only about overpricing work, but believing that their work is better than it really is. I've met a lot of artists, especially in shows, who say, "I'm not selling because there isn't anyone here who knows anything about art." It's a convenient excuse that takes the pressure off. They aren't failing. They don't have to blame themselves.

Because they allow their egos to get in the way, they fail to ask the really hard (and important) questions: Am I painting subjects because they're popular and not because I love painting them? Is my work as good as I think it is? Should I be working on color . . . or composition? Should I rethink my pricing? Do I understand my market? Could I do a better job of selling?

Remember, it's important to get to know your galleries, but it's just as important that they get to know you. If you have a good, personal relationship with the people who are supposed to be selling your work, they'll be more comfortable and effective doing so.

Are sales skills really important? Shouldn't a good work of art practically sell itself?

You'd be surprised at how important the right approach to selling is. I've been studying it for years, and I'm still learning. Here are just a couple of thoughts: People who buy art are nice people. They're the kind of people you'll like. And you're the kind of person they'll be com-

BRINGIN' 'EM IN
1990
OPAQUE WATERCOLOR
30″ × 20″
COLLECTION OF BRADLEY VITE FINE ARTS

This is one of my favorite paintings. It's a purely made-up scene. I'm fascinated with old barns and houses. Here, I've used lots of nice, warm textures—rock, old wood, shingles, flowers in the foreground, trees in the middle ground. Just a quiet afternoon. Bringing the cattle in.

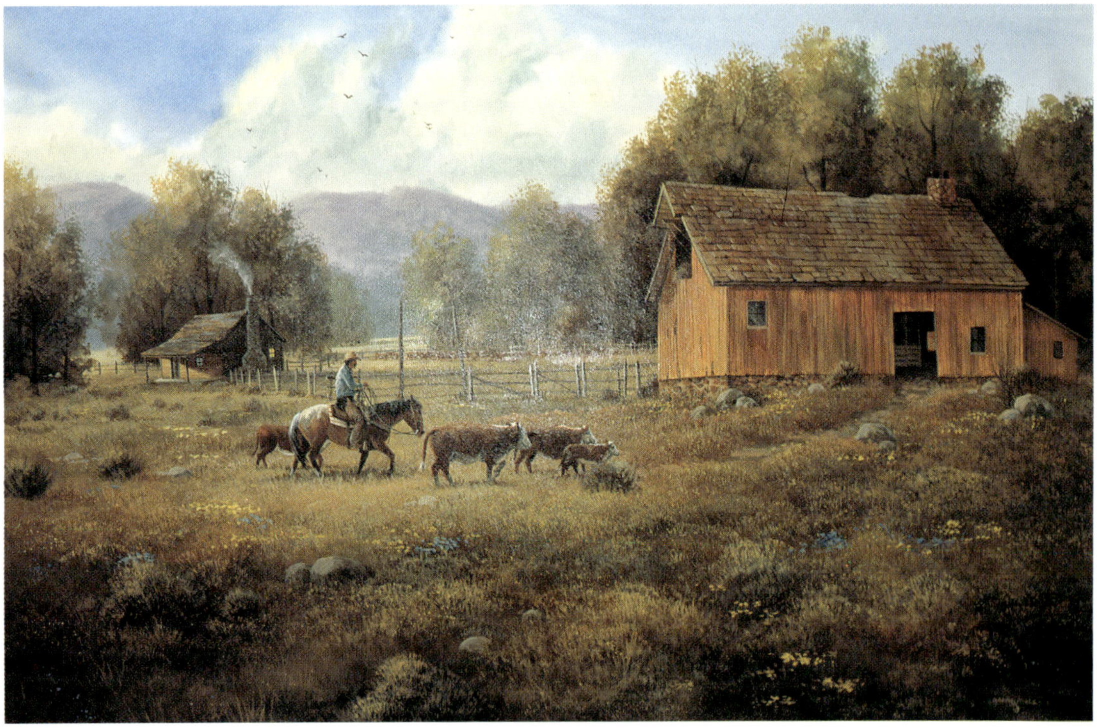

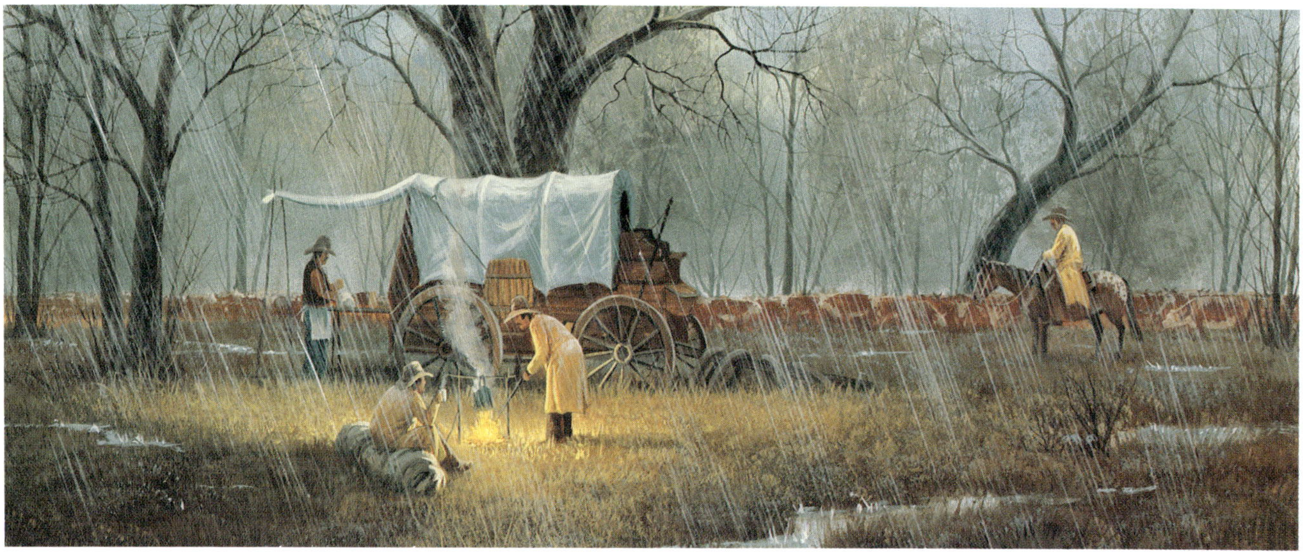

Hot Coffee on a Rainy Night
1991
Opaque water-color
24″ × 12″
Collection of Mr. and Mrs. Robert Harvey

The idea for this painting came to me during one of the trail rides I go on in southern Arizona. On the last couple of nights, it just poured like crazy. We'd end up around the fire, in our slickers, drinking coffee. I just painted what I remembered.

fortable with, too. Your art and you are very much alike, and folks who relate to your art will relate to you. So selling is never "hard selling." I find that most of my selling consists of establishing a friendly relationship with the prospect. Relationships with collectors of my work go back for years, and I count many of them as good personal friends.

When someone visits my exhibit at a show, I never pounce on them and say, "Can I help you?" That would warn them of an impending sales pitch and put them on guard. Their automatic response would be, "No, I'm just looking." Instead, I learned to let them begin looking, then to approach from the edge of their vision, in a nonaggressive way, and say, "If you have any questions, give a holler. I'll be right over there." They'd immediately feel at ease, and not be worried about having a big sales pitch laid on them.

I also learned to price every work, but to put the price around the side of the painting where it wouldn't be the first thing seen. That way, a person would have a chance to become turned on by the art before being turned off by the price. As you watch people studying your work, you can gauge interest by how they look at the art, the price, then back at the art. At that point you can try for the sell.

How important do you think matting, framing and display are in getting your work sold?

Presentation is a subject I can't stress too strongly. It's one part of taking your art, once it's ready, and turning it into a product. Right from the start, I spent a lot of time coming up with framing ideas so my work would be noticed on the wall. When I couldn't afford to buy frames, I made my own, cutting the moldings and staining them to harmonize with each painting. After a while, people wouldn't buy my paintings unless they had my "signature" frame on them. It consisted of a thin brown wood frame around the art, surrounded by a wide leather- or velour-covered liner, then another frame on the outside. At a time when everyone was using commonplace Mexican frames, they made my works stand out.

Do you have any final thoughts on fine arts as a way of life?

As an artist, you'll have to get used to the inconsistency of your income, and learn to handle it. It's not as if you have a check coming in every week. Sometimes you feel richer than hell . . . and sometimes you're scratching to pay the bills. I'm my own boss. But, of course, the boss ends up working harder than anyone else. Sometimes I may work right through the weekend. Another week I might take four or five days and get away with the family. I do enjoy the flexibility. As you can tell, I love it!

TOM HILL
Draw, Draw, Draw

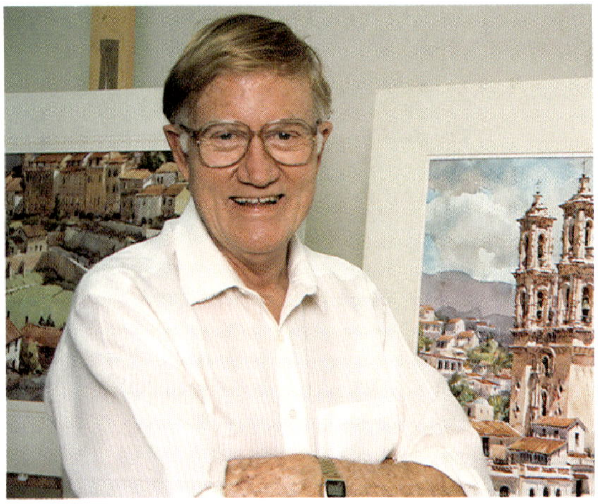

Tom Hill at his Scottsdale, Arizona studio.
Photo by Lew Lehrman.

I FIRST BECAME AWARE OF TOM HILL IN ABOUT 1986, WHEN I READ THE description of his watercolor course in the Scottsdale Artists' School bulletin. It was accompanied by a reproduction of a painting of Venice. I signed up.

Since first meeting Tom, I've spent four weeks in his workshops, and have enjoyed them immensely. His enthusiasm for art and the medium are more youthful than his 1922 birth date would suggest. His beautifully drawn paintings radiate an inner glow that would persist even in a darkened room.

Tom's dry sense of humor only serves to emphasize his careful, thoughtful approach to the medium. One knows that he has thought out every bit of his approach to color, composition, value and technique—a fact that is evident in his several books.

I interviewed Tom during the week he was conducting his class at Scottsdale. "Take it from the beginning," I said.

I grew up in southern California, and first became interested in art at around five or six. My mother would sit at her desk and throw papers in the wastebasket. I had a soft pencil, and I'd lie on the floor and draw on the envelopes she discarded.

In first grade I made a drawing of the Pilgrims' landing, with the Indians and Plymouth Rock, on a piece of laundry wrapping paper. Had my older sister fill in the sky and the water with crayon. I got a lot of recognition in school for that drawing, and of course it made me want to do more.

When I was about fifteen, I would go down to the farmers' market in L.A. and try to get some part-time work. There was a little restaurant there, with a hand-lettered menu board. I copied it on a piece of paper, and with poster paints my teacher had given me, did a fancy menu card. Illustrated and all. I took it to them, and they were delighted. They paid me, and began giving me more to do. Then the guy next door had me letter some price tags, and pretty soon, I was actually making a little money. In those years, I also did posters and invitations for the school dances. I'd letter and illustrate them, then take them to be printed.

The summer I was sixteen, I made some art samples and started visiting the biggest agencies and art studios in L.A. My stuff must have looked very amateurish, but they took the time to talk to me. And they kept sending me lower down on the scale.

I finally got a summer "art" job as a sign painter's helper, earning five dollars a week (including Saturdays), cleaning brushes and sweeping up. But I learned a lot about lettering, layout and all that.

By the time I got to eleventh grade, the sign painters had left town, and I was taking care of some of their old customers, making a few dollars. I had all these little art sources going. When I had saved up thirty-five dollars, my father gave me another thirty-five dollars, and I bought a Model A Ford to get around in and pursue business.

In California, we were hard hit by the depression, and I realized that if I was going to go to art school, I'd need a scholarship. The Art Center College of Design was my goal. I knew that they gave four four-year scholarships each year. (These scholarships were not endowed. Recipients had to do work at the school.) I had a one-man show at my high school, and my art teacher invited Mrs. Adams, one of the heads of Art Center school, to attend. She did.

After graduation, in 1941, waiting for art school, I worked for a neon sign company doing showcards and airbrush sketches of neon sign designs. By that time I was making about fifteen dollars a week.

I had other opportunities to show Mrs. Adams more of my best work. I entered the scholarship competition, and was awarded a full four-year scholarship.

Earlier, my folks had moved to Oregon, so I got a little room in an old rooming house: a couch that turned into a bed, my drawing board, and a gas plate. Refrigerator in the hall. Shared bath. Four dollars and fifty cents a week.

School was going to start in a week. I was down to my last three cents, and no job. I had been everywhere, and nobody needed anybody. I remember sitting in my room, thinking, "What am I going to do?" when there was a knock at the door. "Are you the kid that wanted the job at Ralph's Supermarket?" Yes! "Can you write showcards?" Yes! "Okay, fifty cents an hour. Start right away."

They put me to work selling fruits and vegetables. Another kid there showed me how to weigh things and run the register. And I painted those signs that read "Bananas, so much a pound." That's really why they wanted me.

How did things go for you at Art Center?

I loved it, but my schedule was a back-breaker. At Art Center, they really worked you. If you were playing at it, you didn't last long. They'd ask you to leave. That part of it was terrific.

I'd work at Ralph's every day from 4:30 to 8:30 P.M., and all day Saturday. Plus I got to keep overripe produce that wouldn't hold until the next day. I lived on overripe cantaloupe and graham crackers. Not much protein! I was skinny!

Then there was the hour I had to put in every morning at Art Center, for my scholarship. My job was to clean out fourteen sinks, take out

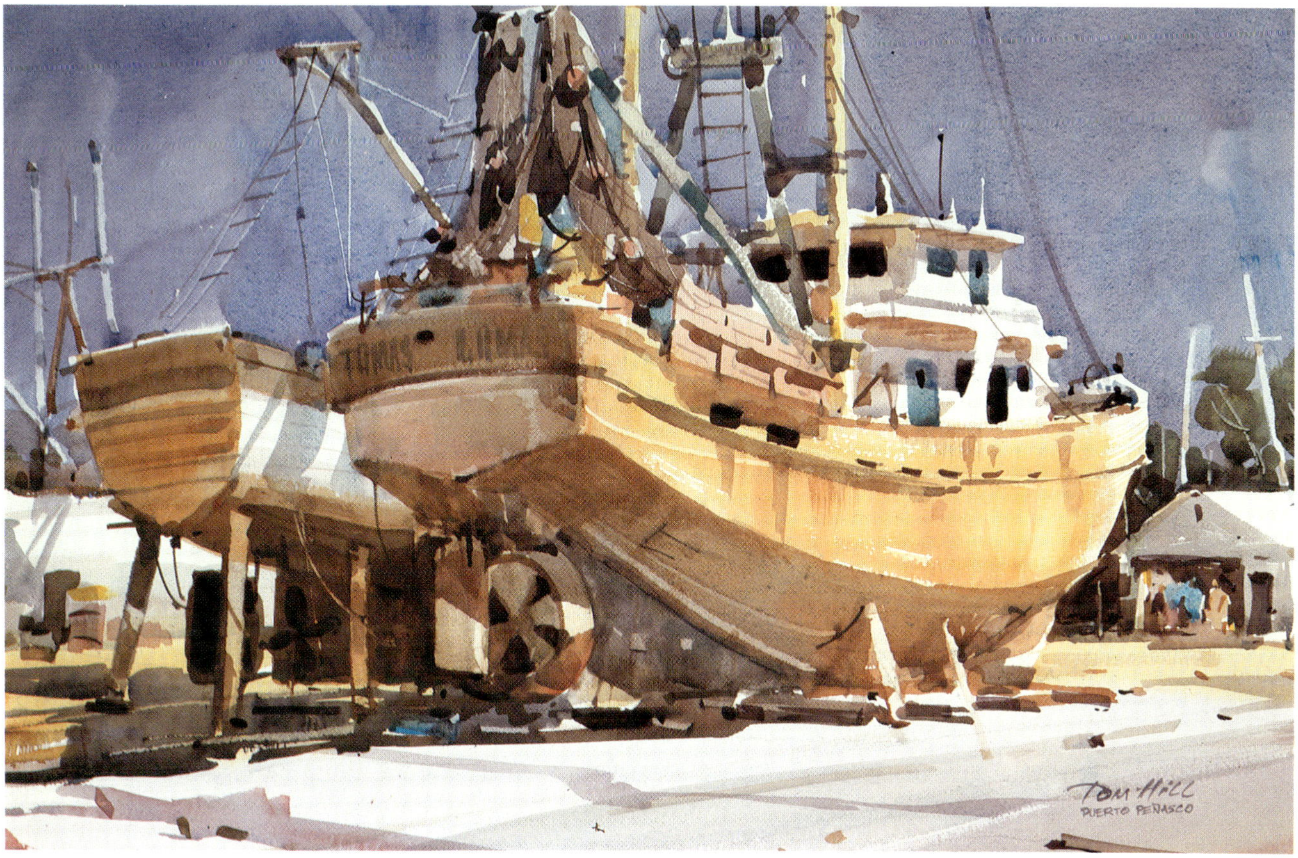

SHRIMP BOATS, PUERTO PEÑASCO
1987
WATERCOLOR
21″ × 14″
COLLECTION OF HARLEY BROWN

Capturing a feeling of brilliant sunshine was my special challenge here. Playing the boat's white cabin against a deep-valued cobalt sky while accentuating the crisp darkness of the shadows helped me achieve my goal.

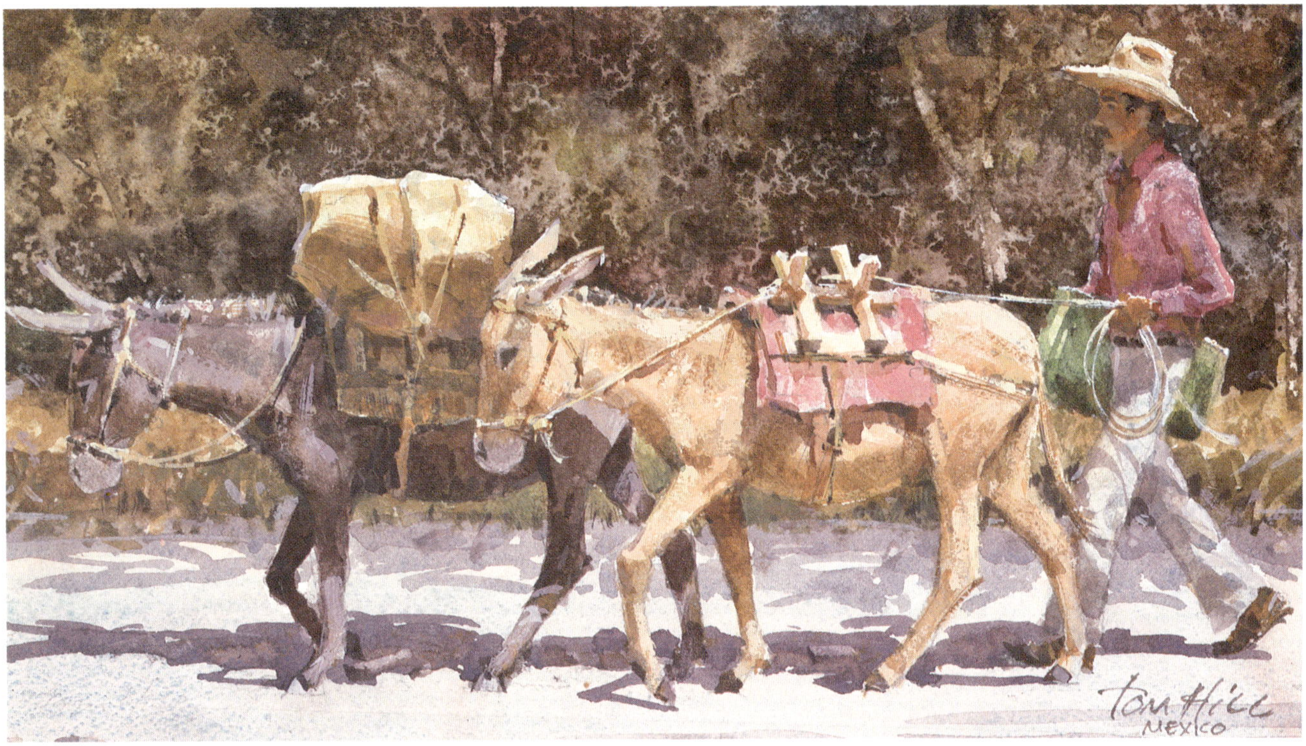

The Burro Man
1986
Watercolor
10″ × 5½″
Collection of
Walter Johnson

Even though Mexico is our next-door neighbor, there is still a lot of "foreign-ness" there. You can still witness scenes like this: burro power in an age of space travel. A lot of previous study and drawing of burros and figures helped me make the action convincing in this painting.

the trash, clean and mop eleven toilets. Not my favorite kind of activity!

Every night after work I'd do an hour and a half of homework, then go to sleep on that creaky couch.

In December, when the war hit, practically the whole male student body went down and volunteered. Mr. Adams tried to talk me out of going, but I went anyway, only to be turned down because of bad hearing in one ear, from a childhood infection. Mr. Adams had warned me (because I wasn't quite draft age, and the school needed my janitorial efforts) that if I went to volunteer I would lose my scholarship. And so I was out!

But right at that time, a group of people organized to develop production illustration for the aircraft industry. I signed up for a night school class that trained people to convert blueprints into three-dimensional drawings for production workers. Three weeks later I was hired by Douglas Aircraft Co., and I stayed with them until 1944, when I was able to get into the Navy as a visual aids artist under what they called "Limited Service/Special Assignment."

I was sent to a technical school near Pearl Harbor. There were three of us in the art department, and the school needed everything: diagrams, drawings, signs, cartoons.

On my days off, I'd go out watercoloring. I'd done a lot of watercolor in high school and while I was at Douglas. So when the Honolulu Academy of the Arts had their annual show, I entered a piece, and it took first prize. That prize led to the U.S.O. asking me to teach a watercolor class two nights a week.

Then the Academy of the Arts asked me if I'd like to have a one-man show. This was the top place in Honolulu. I knocked myself out, painted about thirty-five watercolors, and had the show.

When did you finally get out of the Navy?

April of '46. I went back to L.A. with the idea of going back to art school. But, as so often happens, I got sidetracked. I became engaged, and a job became a necessity.

Looking for a good art job, I answered a blind ad for a "continuity sketch artist." I didn't even know what that was. Ended up at Universal Studios, earning ten thousand dollars a year. Big money in 1946. They always had six or seven movies being made, and a whole room full of art directors and draftsmen planning sets. They needed artists to take set drawings and make them into pictures of how the sets would look, for directors and producers who couldn't make sense of architectural drawings.

Well, right about that time, I was introduced to a woman who was vice-president of an ad agency. She said, "Why don't you send your samples to a man I know in Chicago? He has a big art studio, and knows all the ins and outs of the business." I did, and he liked my work. He said, "I'm going to keep my eyes open for you." And one day he called: "How would you like to work for the *Chicago Tribune*? They need an artist who can do a little of everything."

That was all I needed to hear. I got married, left Universal, and went to Chicago to start work at the *Tribune*. The *Tribune* was very big in those days. Over two million on Sundays. Full color every day. They gave me a little studio on the twenty-seventh floor, and there I was, twenty-five years old, with a big job, doing covers for the magazine section, illustrating stories, going out on assignments. There was so much art to do! A great opportunity to learn and grow.

But I was always looking for new opportunities. Early in '52, when I heard the *Tribune's* aviation editor was going off to cover the Korean War, I asked him, "Don't you need to take along an artist?" I worked out a deal with Northwest Airlines and got my editor to let me go. We spent five weeks in Korea, and I'd airmail back drawings of what I saw. The *Tribune* ran them on the front page, "Our Artist In Korea. . . ."

When I got back, I wrote my own stories, along with my drawings and paintings, for the Sunday magazine section.

The Midwest representative for Scandinavian Airlines saw the articles and contacted me: "How would you like to go all over Europe and paint and write? S.A.S. will pay your way, if the *Tribune* will run your stuff."

Well, the *Tribune* went for it. So I took my wife, and toured ten western European countries. Got back and did stories on each. I'd lay out each article, write the story, and supply the paintings. They ran on the cover of the magazine section, and right across the centerfold, so I could have big, wide paintings reproduced.

That was some break for you!

It really came from seeing opportunities and taking them. Is it the same today? Probably. I believe there are always opportunities. But mostly you create your own. You see a possibility, and you develop it. Like asking that aviation editor if I could go along. Nobody had thought of hav-

TROPICAL LAUNDRY, MEXICO
1987
WATERCOLOR
29″ × 21″
PRIVATE COLLECTION

I had only a glimpse of this scene, while driving in tropical Mexico—not even a chance for a snapshot! However, I made notes and a memory sketch soon afterward. Two ladies chatting over outdoor laundry makes an appealing subject, but capturing the feeling of filtered sunlight was my main painting objective.

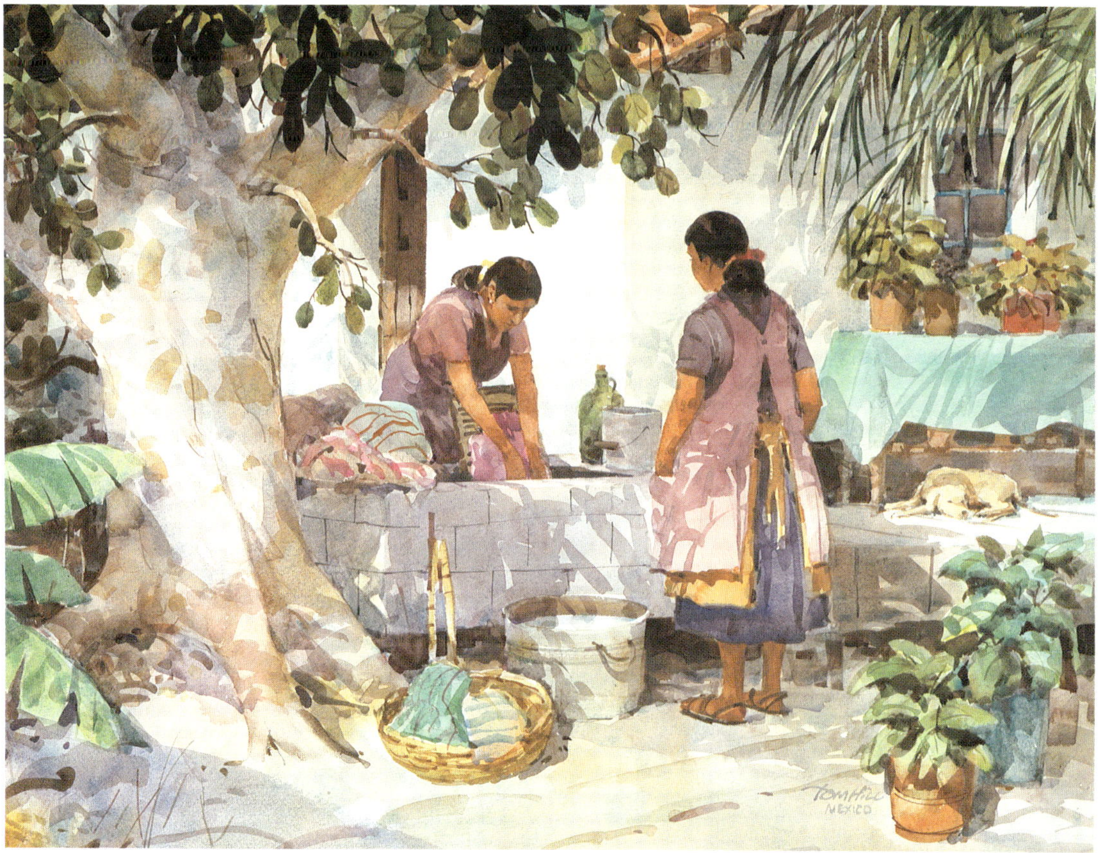

ing an artist there. And one thing leads to another.

Did all this success mean more money?

That was a problem. I asked for a raise, but my boss turned me down. "We're happy to keep you here, but we can't pay you more."

It was very seductive there at the *Tribune*, with all the benefits. But on my vacation, I went to New York and lined up an art agent. At the same time, S.A.S. had a big exhibit of my *Tribune* paintings and drawings in their window at Rockefeller Center in New York. Somebody from *Reader's Digest* saw them and contacted my agent. They wanted me to do some illustrations for them.

I had saved up some money, so I quit my job and we moved to New York. Rented a tiny house on Long Island and started commuting. I did a lot of freelance work for the *Digest*.

We had our second child and rented a house in Southport, Connecticut. That first year I doubled what I had made at the *Tribune*. My agent got me in with *Redbook Magazine*, and I started doing assignments for them, traveling to New England, Florida, etc. Then came work for *Argosy*, *Good Housekeeping*, the *New York Times* and the *Herald Tribune*.

After a couple of years, I decided to leave my agent, and opened a studio in Manhattan with another freelancer. Went down to the library, got the listing of ad agencies and their clients, and started with "A," calling on agencies that did travel work. I got so busy, I never did get to "B"!

I kept prospering, bought some land in Connecticut, and built a house. Then built a studio there and moved out of New York. By that time I was working at illustration all the time. Watercolor was a sometime thing. Oh, I would submit to the A.W.S. show every year (I was elected in 1954), but it was commercial art that took all my time.

What made you finally make the break?

Two things. The winter of 1963, I was forty-one. We had three kids, a big house, all those things. Nine years in New York and it didn't seem so great anymore. That January, I had a sinus infection and an injured hand. I was on penicillin, working every night and every weekend, grinding it out.

First, the artist I had shared studio space with in New York (he had moved to Arizona for his wife's asthma) came back to visit. At the same time, I got an assignment from a publisher in Boston to illustrate a book. Two hundred full-color illustrations—a whole year's work! My friend said, "Why don't you come out to Tucson and do your assignment there? I'll help you find a house to rent."

He did, and when we had the chance to sell our own house, we did. I figured that when we came back in a year we'd build another. Well, I was raised out West, and it was so nice to get back to fresh air and blue skies and warm winters, I never went back.

What did you do for income after that assignment?

I found another agent in New York, and he sent me work. By that time I was doing mostly book illustration, and the deadlines were longer.

When did you move to fine arts?

While I was in the Navy, I had met a guy who'd lived in Tucson. He'd told me, if I ever got to Tucson, to look up Gerry Peirce, who was a well-known watercolorist there. So I visited him. He looked at my watercolors and sent me to see his wife, Priscilla, who'd had a gallery in Tucson since 1938. I left three watercolors with her, and within a week she sold one.

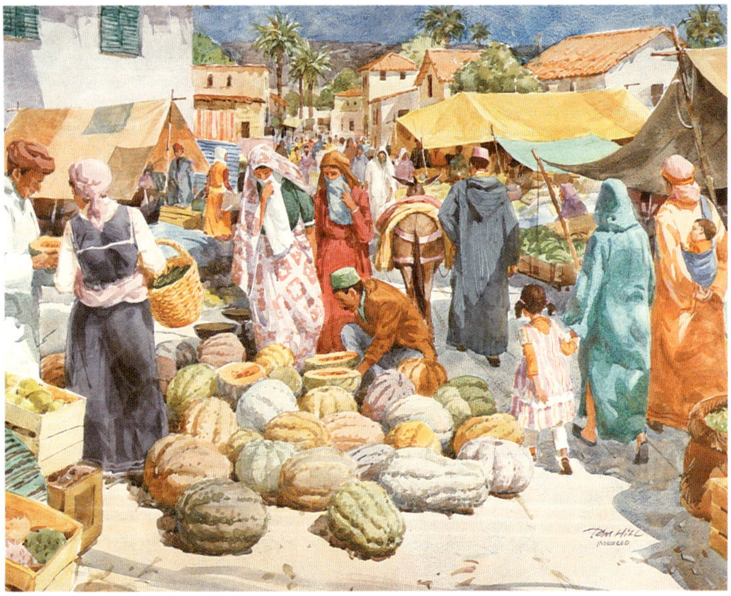

CALABASH MARKET, MOROCCO
1988
WATERCOLOR
29″×21″
PRIVATE COLLECTION

Morocco is a visual feast for any artist—especially in its busy soukhs and markets. Here, I strove to show the exotic busy-ness of an outdoor market, but at the same time I carefully planned my drawing and composition to avoid ending up with a confusing picture.

Old Gate at Fez, Morocco
1988
Watercolor
29″ × 21″
Collection of Mr. and Mrs. Ken Renard

All the mystery and intrigue of Morocco's past seemed embodied in this ancient, tile-covered city gate. And that's what I wanted my painting to convey. I added to the foreground market activity, while eliminating autos and power lines from the scene.

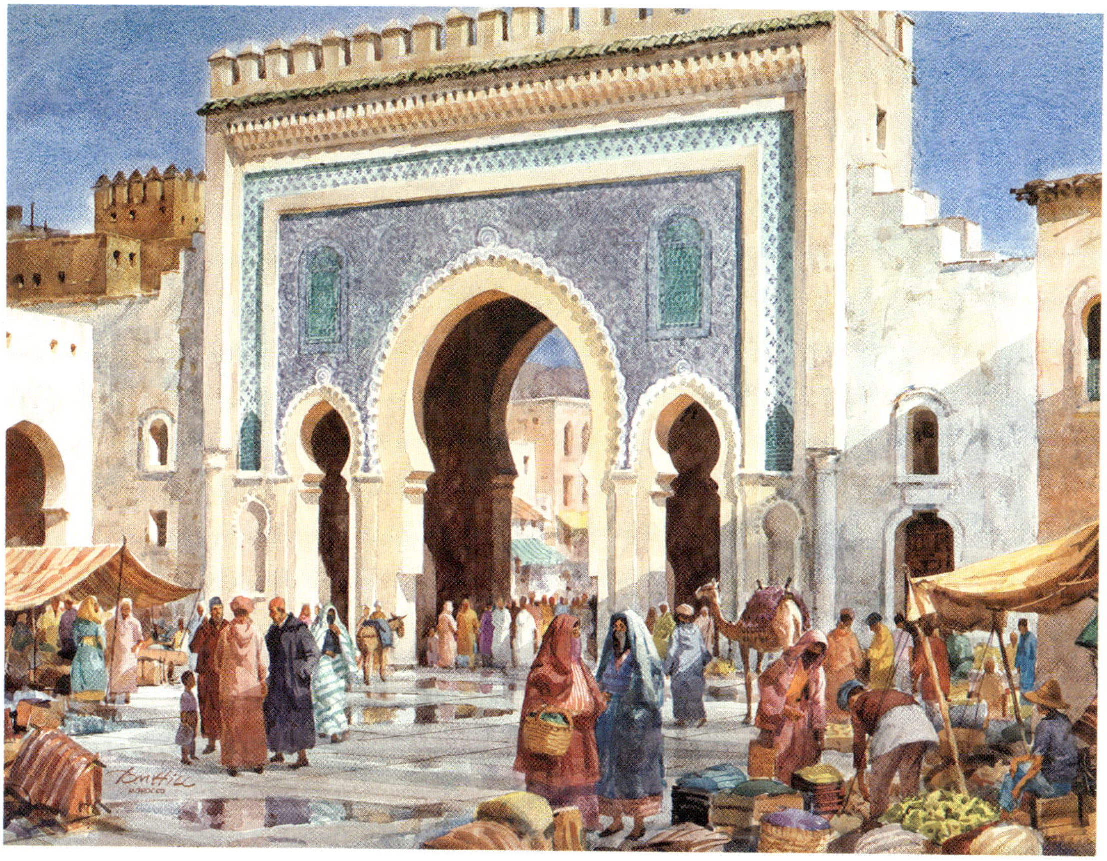

That was easy, and fun! I began painting more and more watercolors, still doing illustration, too. After a year or so, Mrs. Peirce offered me a one-man show. Well, all of Gerry Peirce's friends came to the opening, and all of the gallery clientele. But I didn't sell *one* painting!

That must have been a blow.

Well, she told me not to be discouraged, and she was right. Within a couple of years my shows were near sell-outs every time. I was with that gallery for ten years. By '73, I was totally out of commercial work.

Tell me about your first book.

In the early seventies, I won a prize in A.W.S., and when I went back to New York to receive it, I met Don Holden, who was editor at Watson-Guptill. I showed him some of my slides, and he asked me to write an article for the *American Artist Magazine* about painting in Mexico. (I had discovered Mexico in 1961, and had painted there a lot.)

After the article appeared, Don called me on the telephone and said, "I'm sure glad you're going to do a book for me!" A book? "Yes! Emphasizing color."

During that time, my wife decided she wanted a career of her own. She wanted to go this way, and I wanted to go that way. We split, amicably, in 1975, about the time *Color for the Watercolor Painter* came out (1975, Watson-Guptill, New York, NY).

In 1973, an operation called Painting Holidays asked me to join them, to teach watercolor in traveling workshops. A man named Tony Van Hasselt had started it. He'd go to interesting locales, check them out, arrange for hotels, get everything set up and organized, hire a workshop director, and all I'd have to do was teach. I did about sixteen workshops with Painting Holidays, and I have taken art trips to over forty countries.

Let's talk about the Tom Hill of today. Do you still paint every day?

I love to work. To me, it isn't really work, although some of it is plotting and planning. Not all of it is inspired hot brush strokes, by any means. Barbara, my present wife, and I built a house in Tucson. We each have studios, across the hall from each other. Barbara's interest is

View from the Alameda
1988
Watercolor
29″ × 21″
Collection of Dr. R. Valentine

Alameda means "shaded walk or park" in Spanish, and these really huge Indian laurel trees beautifully frame the cathedral on Oaxaca, Mexico's alameda. The figures help give scale to the trees and the massive stone church, all lit by afternoon sunshine.

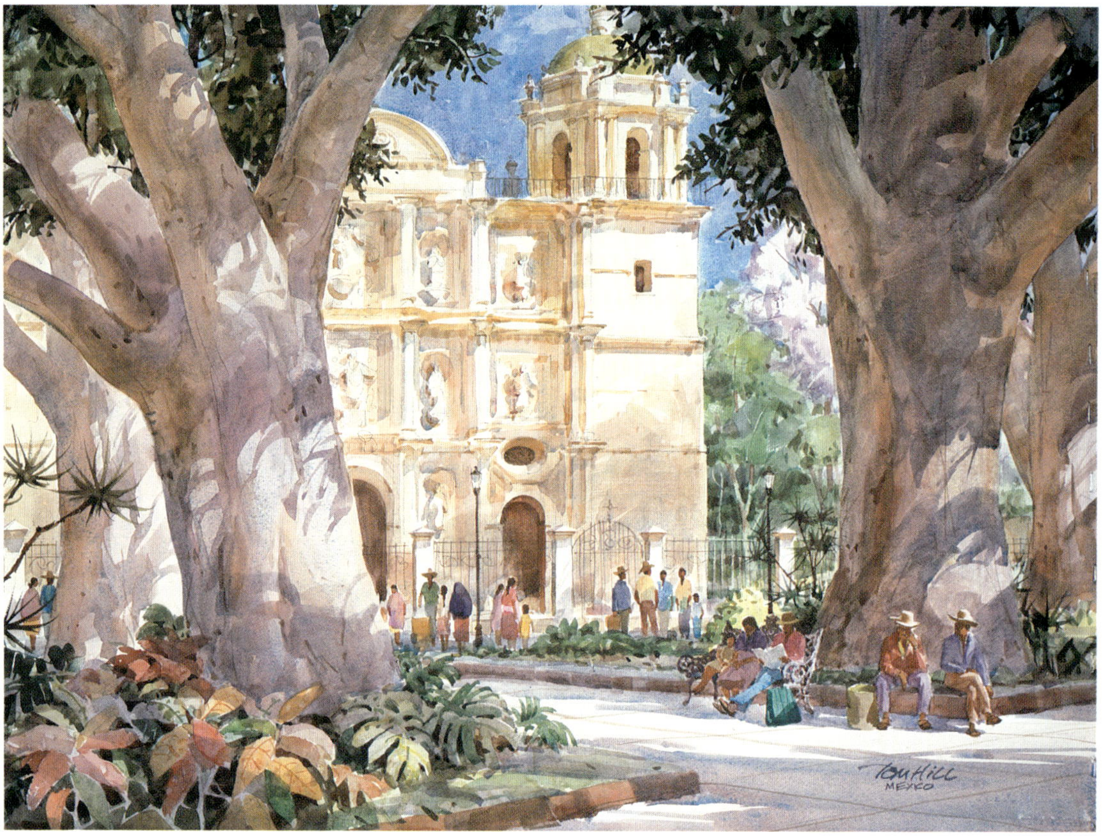

painting animals, in a painterly, aesthetic way. Her upcoming book is due in 1993.

I know you have another book on the way.

My third. It's titled *The Watercolorist's Complete Guide to Color* (1992, North Light Books, Cincinnati, OH). My second was *The Watercolor Painter's Problem Book* (1979, North Light Books).

Do you still give workshops?

A few. Scottsdale Artists' School, of course. And we've organized a few on our own. The last was in '89, at Taxco, Mexico. We might do some more. They're fun. With my books, and all the workshops I've done, I have a lot of people asking for more workshops. I could do one every week of the year, but now Barbara and I mostly just paint, and enjoy our lives.

Do you think ahead to a point when you might want to taper off and take life any easier?

Easier only in the sense of not trying to meet deadlines. I still enjoy painting, and I'll probably continue until I can't hold the brush anymore.

You know, you start on a painting: "Man, this is *the* one!" About a third of the way through, you're thinking, "*Maybe* I can save it." Once in a while you hit a peak. I just want to increase those peaks, and leave the rest out.

My view of art is that 99 percent of the people want to be able to understand a work of art, and not have to guess at it. So I try to speak in a language that everybody can understand. In order to speak that language, you have to be able to draw, understand composition and color, and have all your "smarts." *Then* you can interpret, convey an impression or a feeling.

Look at a Sargent watercolor, done a hundred years ago. Oh, man! The guy knew his subject. He felt it, and he portrayed it. The average person has no trouble understanding it. If my painting hangs on a wall, and people have the same feeling from looking at it that I tried to put into it, then I think the painting's successful.

How would you define success, Tom, in your own terms?

I don't think that just making a lot of money is necessarily being a success, though it's certainly nice to be comfortable. My idea of success is being able to continue to improve as an artist, and to enjoy the process.

What advice would you offer to artists who would like to live by their brush?

Start early. And persevere. Don't let your failures get you down.

Take advantage of any opportunity that comes along, or that you can create. Draw, draw, draw! Learn to *understand* your subject. Try to increase your appreciation, your knowledge, and your sensitivity toward good (versus poor) art. Ask yourself, "What do I really enjoy doing the most in this art business?" If you haven't been exposed to it, find out. Don't try to be everything to everybody. It won't work. Do what you want to do and become good at it, and you'll probably find your market.

But what can you say to the weekend painter who'd like to become a full-time painter?

It depends so much on the circumstances. There can be a terrible price, and a lot of people don't want to pay it. It's easier when you're young. It's harder to apply that extra pressure when you get to a certain age. Sooner or later it catches up with you. It's not like when we were thirty, and could work through the night.

But there's no reason a person can't get better. There is *some* free time. You can work to improve yourself as an artist. It took me about seven years to move from illustration to fine art. It was easier for me, though. I had my art training, and I had some breaks.

Do you see luck as a factor?

A minor factor. Mostly it's working hard. . . seeing an opportunity and grabbing it. I don't think there's any quick way to become a "famous artist," though there are always a few people who have a style or a gimmick that catches on for a while. I really don't know how important "talent" is.

Then what is most important?

That you just love it so much that it's the only thing you want to do. Like the first thing I mentioned: the feeling of that soft pencil on the back of my mother's envelopes, making a picture, and people responding to it. My way has been to do what I like to do best, and to get good at it. You can't do it all. You can't please everybody.

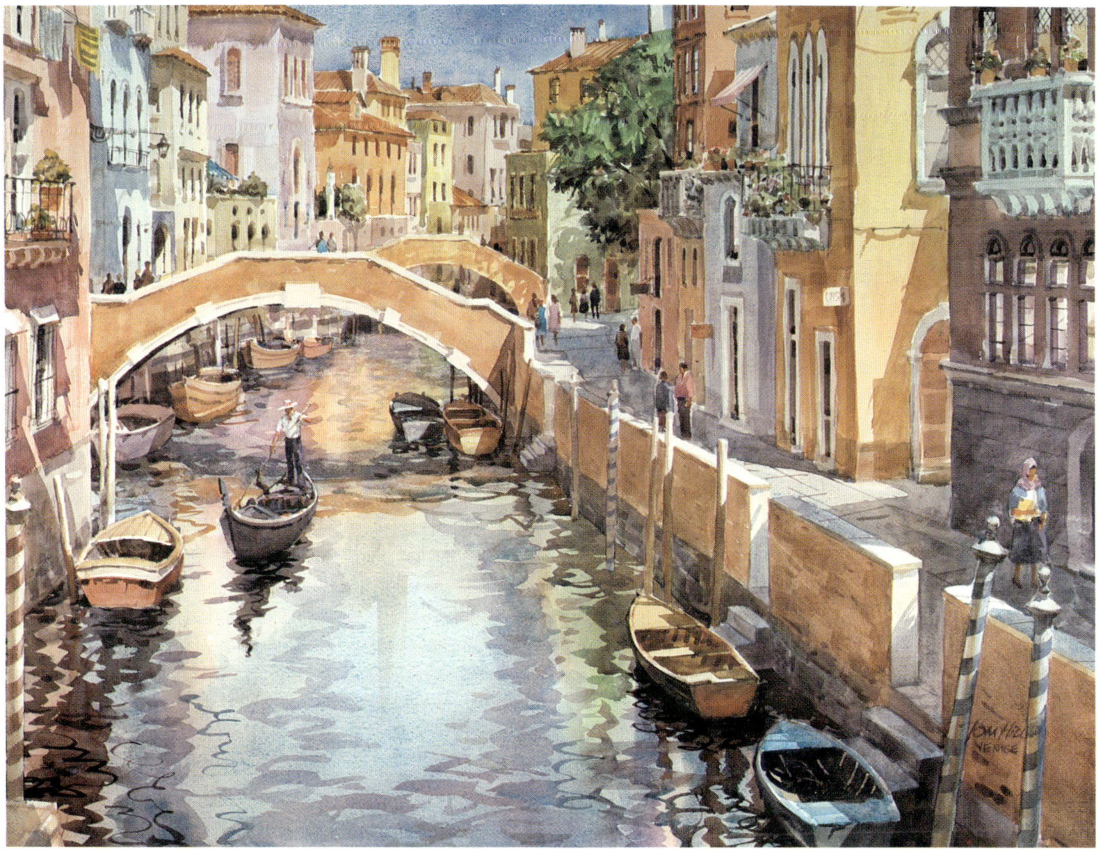

VENETIAN CANAL
1986
WATERCOLOR
29″ × 21″
COLLECTION OF
MR. AND MRS. BEN GOLDEN

On our first trip to Venice we had sunny, clear days and pleasant breezes. Intriguing to me were the old buildings, bridges and boats . . . and their myriad colorful reflections in the canals. I found, in painting this subject, that it was best to simplify detail in favor of impression.

ZOLTAN SZABO
It Has to Be an Inner Drive

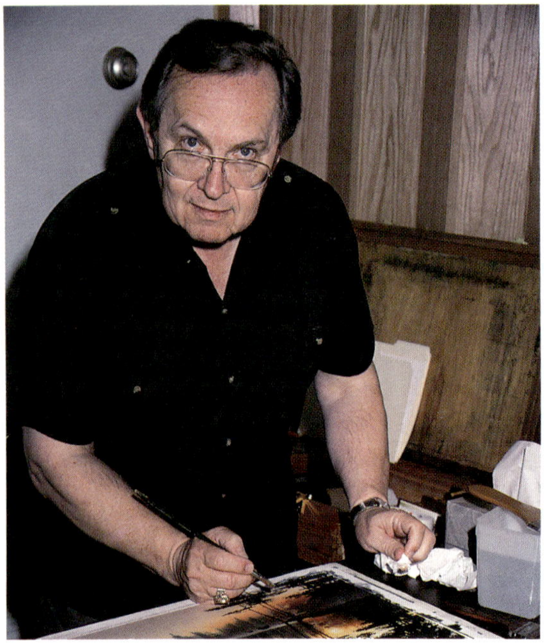

Zoltan Szabo completing a project for his upcoming workbooks in the studio at North Light Books. Photo by David Nutt.

I HAVE THE FEELING THAT ZOLTAN SZABO IS AS CLOSE TO BEING "the artist who needs no introduction" as I'll find anywhere.

Through his many watercolor seminars, demonstrations and lectures, he has (according to his own count) helped more than twelve thousand artists in the United States, Canada and Europe.

He is the author of six popular books on watercolor painting, and his videotaped demonstrations have achieved international popularity.

More than eight thousand of his watercolors, he tells me, are owned by private collectors all over the world, and are part of collections at the Smithsonian, the Hungarian National Art Gallery in Budapest, and other respected institutions and corporations.

I interviewed Zoltan at his Matthews, North Carolina home one Saturday morning, and began by asking him how he got started in art.

It started on the potty. My mother told me that the only way I would sit there long enough was if I had something to draw with.

I grew up near Eger, a small city north of Budapest, Hungary. By the time I was in high school, my interest in art was well established. The school system was very responsive to creativity in art, and I had a lot of help.

In 1946 and '47, I was in my first year at university, and we were very involved (as university students always are) in resistance to the communists. The problems concerning Cardinal Mindszenty (an outspoken churchman who resisted Soviet attempts to subjugate post-World-War-II Hungary), and everything, built up, and I had to leave the university and seek refuge in the West. I escaped to West Germany in 1948, and spent a semester in Munich as an unregistered student at an art school. In 1949, I emigrated to Canada, and started to work there.

My only other education was the Famous Artists' School course, when Norman Rockwell and the big boys were running it.

Did you complete the course?

Yes. It took me three years, but I enjoyed it. It gave me a lot of background. I still have their books, and they are my treasure.

What were you working at in Canada?

I got a commercial art job at a printing company in Ontario. After a while, I moved on to other jobs in art studios and engraving houses in Toronto. Eventually I began to freelance, and devote my spare time to painting.

Always watercolor?

I did some oils, too.

Finally I reached a point when, I thought, if my painting could create enough income to match that of my commercial art (never thinking it would happen), then I would quit and paint full time.

I was married, and we were raising two children. When I finally made the move, of course, it was a matter of giving up half our income. I was hoping that the extra five days each week would make up for it.

Was that a big decision? Or was it just something that had to happen?

It was wishful thinking. The people I knew at the time, the practical kind of people who worked at these places, said, "Oh, don't paint watercolor. You can't sell those things. Paint oils." So I started with oils, and gave away my watercolors, until somebody decided to have a little exhibition and sell the watercolors I had given him. I realized that if he could sell them, so could I, and I stopped doing oils after that.

How were you selling your work at that point?

I began doing things like going to Nova Scotia with a trailer, and spending my two-week holiday there, painting all week. Then on Sunday I'd put a sign on my trailer: "Watercolors for sale." I'd park on the side of the road, and people would come and buy them. The first Sunday I did that, I sold everything I had, and it gave me my first hint that there was something here that I wasn't aware of. A really good market.

How did you work out your pricing?

It's always a matter of supply and demand, and prices to match. I tried to be humble. This was the mid-sixties, and I felt that if I got fifty dollars for a quarter-sheet painting (about eleven by fifteen inches) I'd be doing well. And I did. It wasn't until 1972 that I sold my first five-hundred-dollar painting.

It was a gradual climb, checking every step of the way, watching how the public responded to my paintings. Before long I started getting into some galleries.

Which reminds me of an interesting experience. I was with a gallery in northern Toronto. They had three artists, including myself. One was a super-realist oil painter. The other was a totally abstract painter. And there I was, in between. They were attracting very high dollars—ten, fifteen thousand for a painting—and then there were mine at two or three hundred. I thought, "What am I doing here?" I even asked the gallery owner. She told me that she needed me more than I needed her. "I need somebody between these two opposites, and you're it. But I don't think you'll sell your work, because you paint like everybody else!"

That shook me. "What do you mean?" You know, the old ego gets started. She said, "Tell me, what's different about your painting?" I couldn't find anything. So I huffed and puffed, and pulled my work out and went home. "Obviously I'm in the wrong place!" I thought.

Not long afterward, I was going up north with a friend for a fall weekend. We had rented a cottage, and when we got there I discovered I had forgotten to take my watercolor case with me. I wasn't going to backtrack 120 miles to get it. My friend said, "We'll get along."

He gave me some mounted Whatman board, a few oil painting brushes, some watercolor paints and a palette knife. I painted sixteen quarter-sheets in three days, and that started a whole new trend in me. Mother of invention, I suppose.

Anyway, I brought the paintings home, and took them into that gallery. When she realized that I (and not someone else) had done them, she said, "Now you have something going!" Ever since then I have used bristle brushes for my watercolors, including a slanted style I designed myself. And I use a palette knife, too.

Aside from that gallery, how else were you marketing your work?

I did many of the outdoor and mall shows. Toronto is a big city, and the shows are the best way to get to know your customer. You meet

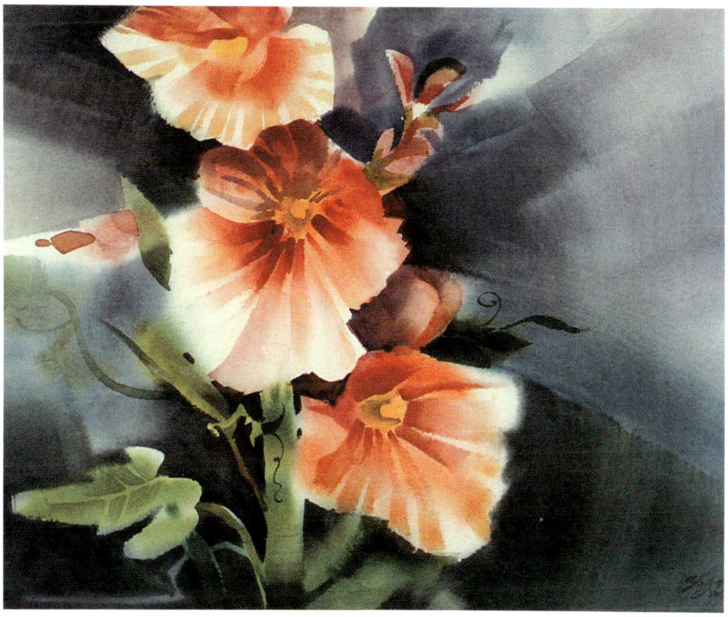

Hollyhocks
1990
Watercolor
20″ × 15″
Collection of the Artist

I chose a close-up section of an impressive stem of flowers in high contrast. The curvilinear design of the blossoms suggested a directional approach to the background. The composition depicts a lot of energy because of the healthy relationship between the subject and the background.

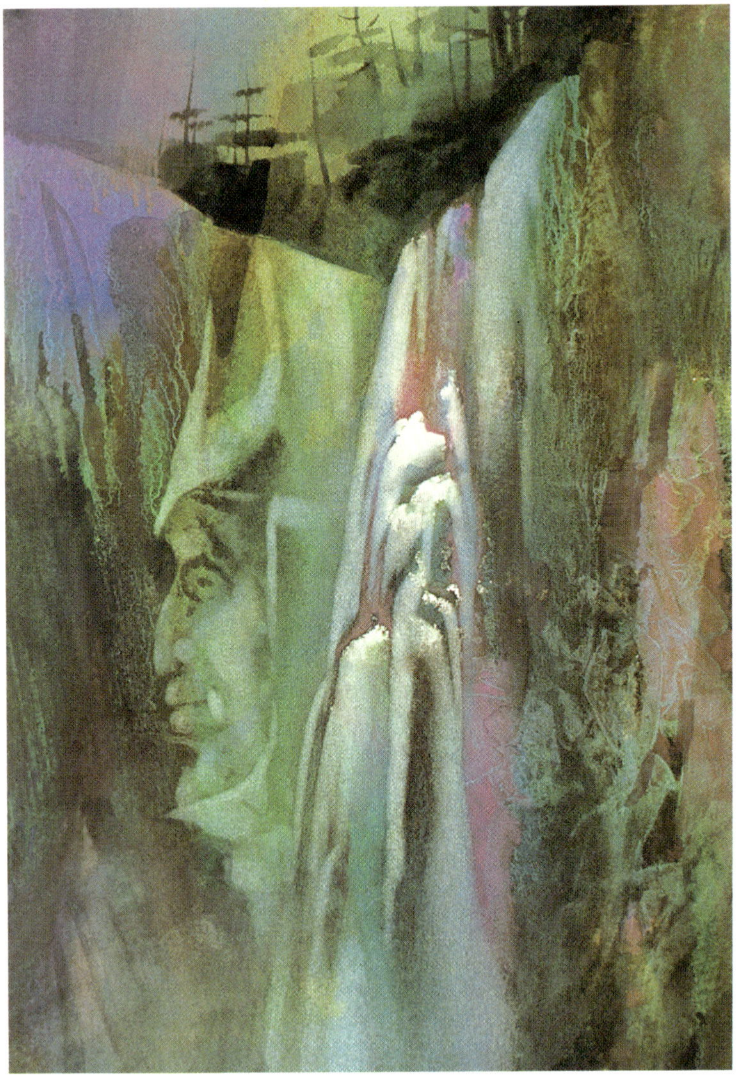

Warrior of the Mist
1990
Watercolor
11″ × 15″
Collection of the artist

I started this composition by pouring colors that created abstract images on the surface. As the washes mingled, shapes began to emerge. First I discovered the waterfall; second, the mystical impression of a face.

people face to face. They have no reason to compliment you, and they will tell you the honest truth about your work . . . sometimes without even being asked. You can read their response to what you have to say. The shows worked quite well for me. I did them for about ten years during the fifties and sixties, but not anymore.

It was also about that time that I started to do a little bit of teaching, on a beginner's level, first with oils, then with watercolor.

Then The Gallery Of Ontario, which was at that time a Toronto art gallery, hired me to teach a series of evening watercolor classes. I prepared a very structured plan for the course, and a friend of mine suggested that I submit it to a publisher. I went to Watson-Guptill. Of course, there was a lot of work involved in it, but that outline became *Landscape Painting in Watercolor*, my first book. *Creative Landscape Painting* was published later.

Soon, my books were doing so well in the United States that I began to think, "Well, if they give me such a large percentage of my income, is it fair for me not to pay my taxes there?" So I moved to the United States in 1976, to Tempe, Arizona first. I lived there until 1988.

How many workshops do you do a year?

Twelve to fifteen. Most of them run two weeks. I used to do more than that, but I have been slowing down a bit, trying to cut it to about four or five a year.

Do you ever think in terms of retiring, and taking life easy?

Never. As long as I have my faculties, which I hope will be for a long time, I intend to work. I can't just sit and do nothing. Pushing that little brush around does not take that much energy. Even the traveling is an enjoyable experience.

Tell me about your activities today. Do you try to paint every day?

I don't know if anyone can paint every day. I know I can't. I try to spend my mornings painting, and sometimes my afternoons. I try to keep three or four hours each day, when my mind is freshest, for creativity.

But after the mail comes, at two, I end up doing whatever else has to be done. Business details, answering letters, working on my videos.

I gather that teaching is a very important part of your life right now.

It is. I like the interaction between adult artists and myself, people who relate to what I'm doing, and vice versa. We're playing with a medium that's temperamental, and little surprises happen. Watching my students grow is really fun, and I enjoy it.

I find teaching is a big help in my own work, too. Because when you have to spell out something verbally before an audience of twenty to thirty people, and most are at least as intelligent as you are, you have to plan and think, and clarify what you are going to do. This results in more courageous, more unusual paintings. After all, many of my students come back, and I don't want to do the same thing over and over.

Teaching has really been a great benefit for

MAKEUP ARTISTS
1989
WATERCOLOR
20″ × 15″
COLLECTION OF THE ARTIST

Rhythm is a theme in this painting. The rhythm, that the leaves and blossom play in sharp and dark images on the orchid, is repeated in the soft technique in the background. These elements are enhanced by the strategically located white shapes.

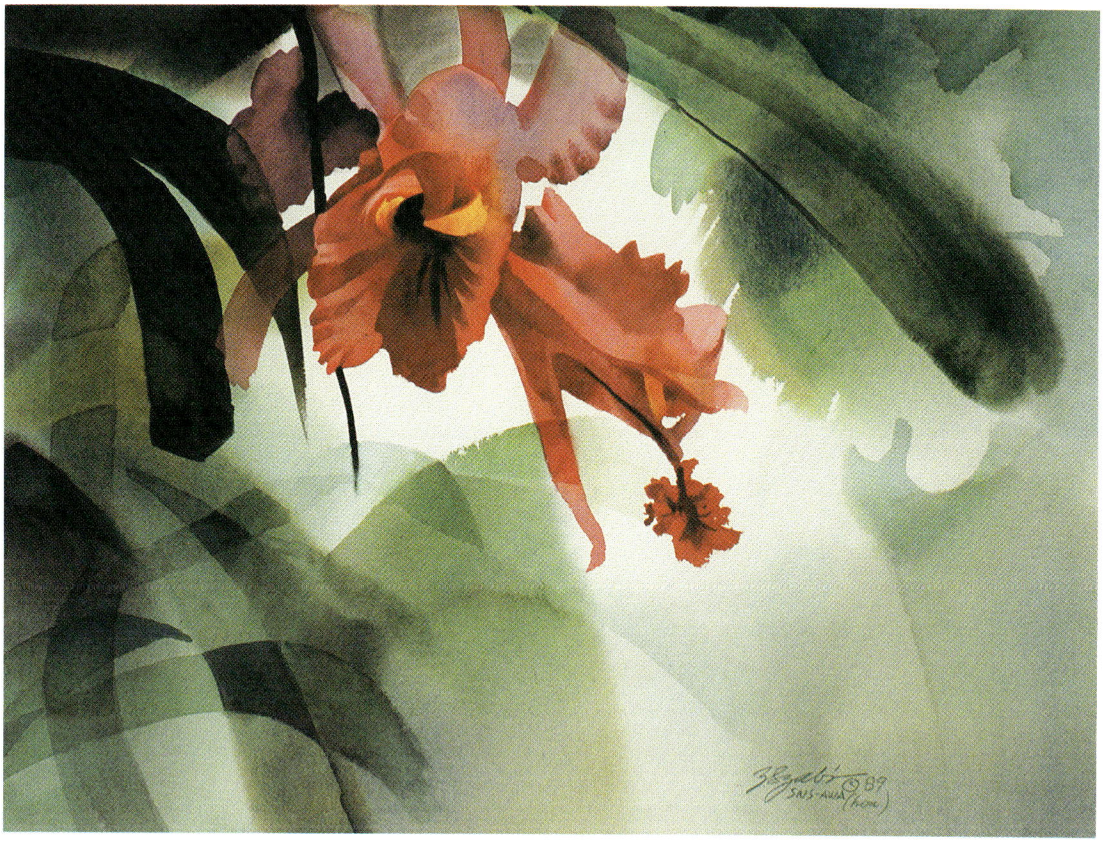

my creative growth.

Let's talk about the future. Where do you see your career headed?

Today, at sixty-two, I am seeing a very exciting change in my ability to express myself – from my more realistic style, to a more design-conscious, simplified, inventive, creative way of painting. I am in the process of expanding on that. You might call it "half abstract design-y realism."

Is this showing up in your teaching?

I don't think you can teach personal taste or creativity. What I do teach is technique, and I'm doing that as sincerely as I can. The beginning painter relates very well to reality most of the time. You know, if it is a house, it has to look like a house, and every curlicue will end up on their painting. I'm not teaching that, but I am showing my students how to paint, the technical aspects of watercolor: lost edges, wet-into-wet technique, and so on.

Let's talk about artists in general. What do you think it takes to make it as an artist today?

I don't know for sure, but I have many suspicions. I know that in this country, promotion (either by yourself or having somebody else doing it) has a lot to do with it. This country is very conscious of promotional impressions. Take Andy Warhol, for instance. I'm sure promotion had an awful lot to do with his success. And you can look around, and see similar patterns building up. But even in the case of Andy Warhol, the gutsy uniqueness of putting Campbell's Soup labels on paintings took courage. Most of us wouldn't get away with it, and I don't really know how he achieved his fame. The point is, he became very successful with his approach, plus the right kind of promotion.

In the long run, though, I don't think anything will take the place of originality. If you are unique in what you do, the public will notice that. Your work will be picked up, and it will support you. If you look at some of the present giants, you will see the truth of that. Andrew Wyeth is a good example. His unique approach, which came as a result of the steadfast demands he made upon himself, ultimately paid off.

That steadfastness is very important, isn't it?

You can't be a temperamental prima donna in

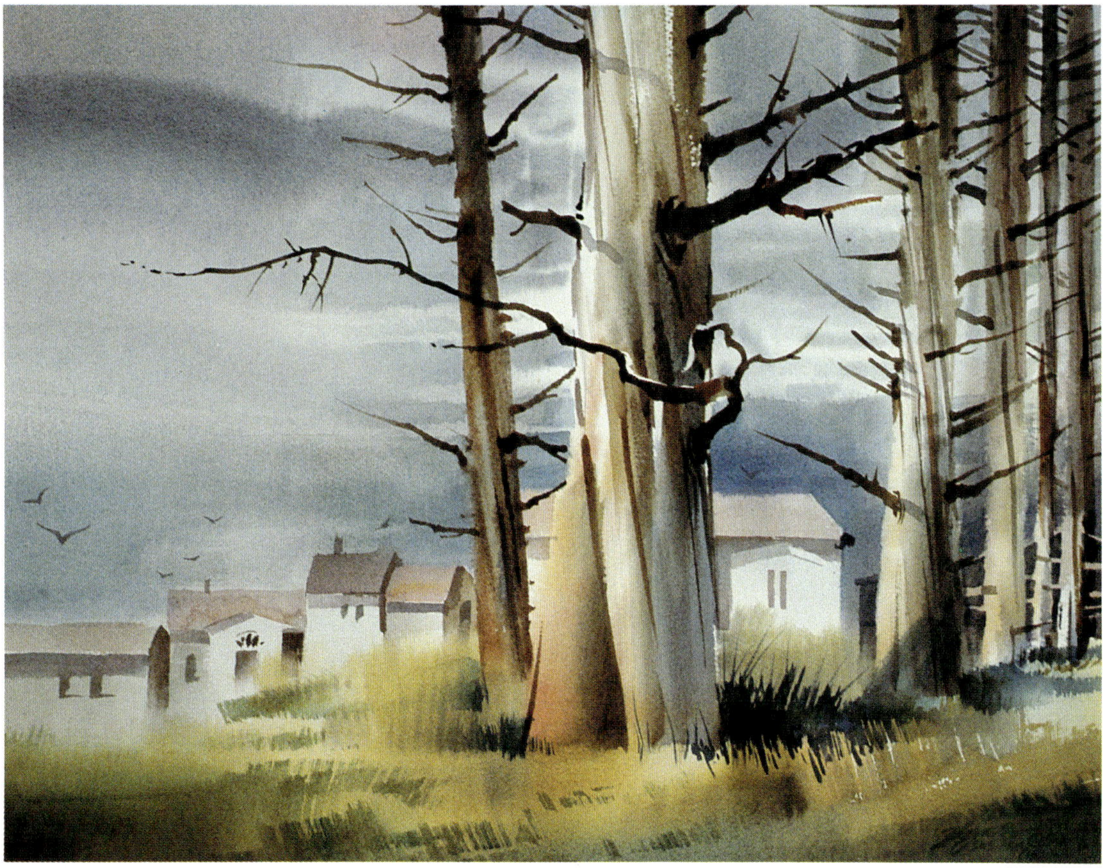

Coast Guards
1988
Watercolor
20″ × 15″
Collection of the artist

I interpreted a natural subject paying attention to negative and positive relationships. The soft, simplified background enhances the contrasting foreground trees. Colors are subdued in the middle and background and emphasized in the foreground.

this business. "I don't feel like painting, so I won't work for a month and just have fun." It has to be an inner drive. If it's not there, you probably should be doing something else.

What do you think makes some art so wonderful, while other art is essentially lifeless?

Leo Tolstoy said that a work of art has to have emotional content, or it is not a work of art. It is only craft. This emotional content is very difficult to give to a work. But if you, the artist, are excited about the subject, it transfers to the viewer, and the work becomes lasting.

What advice would you offer to artists who would like to live by their work?

Start humble. And watch like a hawk. When the demand for your work becomes higher than you can supply, that's the time to raise your prices a little. Don't start high. It's better to sell a work for fifteen dollars than to have a basement full of paintings. When they get to know you, the prices will raise themselves.

That's one bit of advice. Another is to never, never question your ability, and never quit. Stick with it and you'll make it. I particularly remember a statement I heard from the last living member of the Canadian "Group of Seven," A.J. Casson. He said, "You know, the real secret of this business is to outlive your competition!" He was doing very well when he said that. It was about ten years ago, and he was eighty-four.

Tell me how you would define success, in your own terms.

It's not monetary, though that's part of it. If you don't have a comfortable environment to live in, or if you have to worry about what you're going to eat next week, or if your family is in rags, that is a pressure.

To me, having my work accepted is success. When society says, "I read what you are saying. I think you are contributing to life with your presence and your work," that is success. Not everyone can be a Picasso or a Michelangelo, creating on a level that so far surpasses our own. But when you achieve something, and society recognizes it, that is a version of success I can relate to.

Any final thoughts on fine art as a way of life?

I look at art as the real joy of life, expressed in something that is a luxurious – not a practical – commodity. Beauty is something we all want to live with, though many people live without much of it. If the artist creates something in that category, as a result of a lifetime commitment, to whatever extent he is able, then that art will never, never die. Art will always be at the head of human achievement. We are the only species that has the privilege and the ability to be creative for creativity's sake alone. If we do not take advantage of that, it is our own loss.

In my case, fine art has become an obsession. It's something I can't do for just two hours a day. It's a twenty-four-hour, seven-day commitment, and I live it all the time. If you don't live it that way in your heart, I don't think you do justice to your art.

And one final thought: There is one area through which I feel artists have been ridiculed, blamed and criticized through the centuries. And those same forces – critics – seek to control art and artists today. Tolstoy had a wonderful way of describing the critics. He called them "Eunuchs. They know a little bit of the theory, but nothing about practice!"

You can ask, "How many artists do you remember from the last century?" and almost anyone can name a dozen or more. Now ask, "How many *critics* do you remember from the last century?" There will be a big silence, and this tells the story.

My God! If there is one freedom left untouched in this country, it is creativity. Don't let politicians mess it up. I grew up in a country where this actually happened. Believe me, the freedom we enjoy in the United States is better. I would rather allow all that porno junk to fly around freely than to turn off the tap for creativity. If there is to be freedom in one area, this is the one we must fight for. The critics will fade away and be forgotten, but art must live. We must stick to our guns. If we give up the freedom to create, we will have lost freedom.

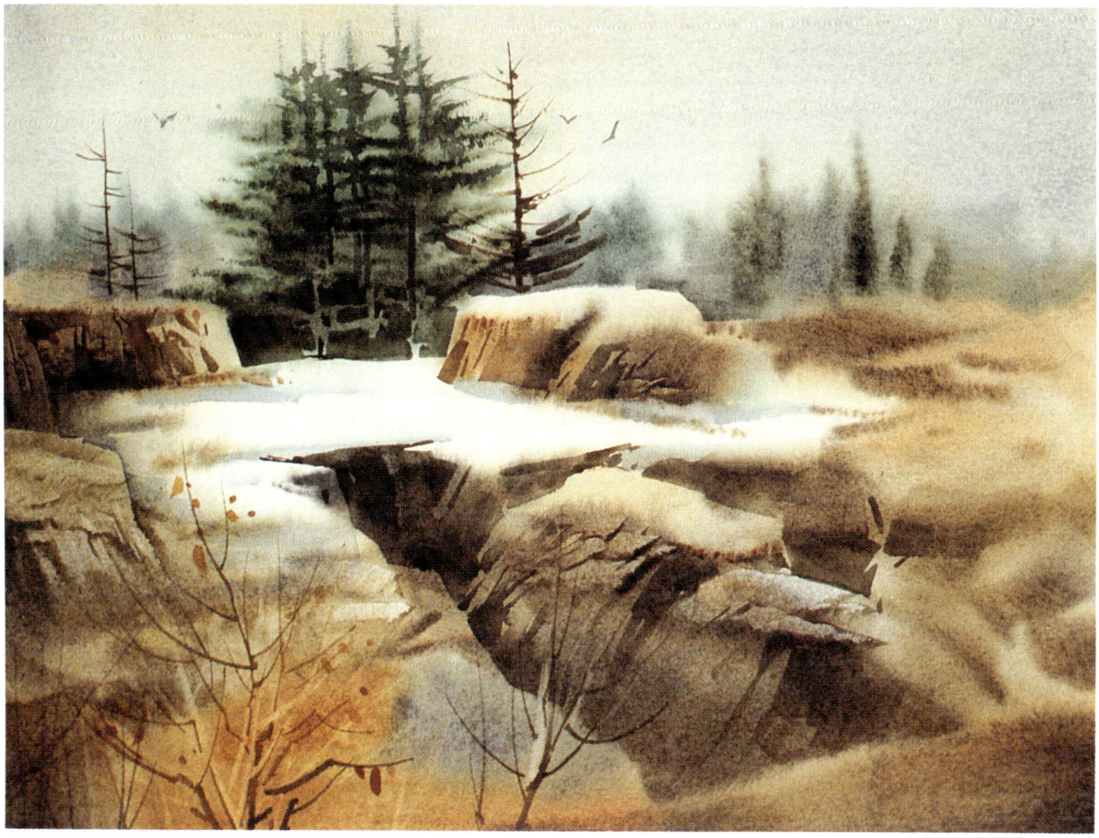

Soft Rock Music
1989
Watercolor
15″ × 11″
Collection of the Artist

My goal here was to keep high contrast between the snow, the dark evergreens, and the dark side of the rocks in order to focus instant attention on the snow.

LIESEL BOOSE
Everybody Needs Publicity

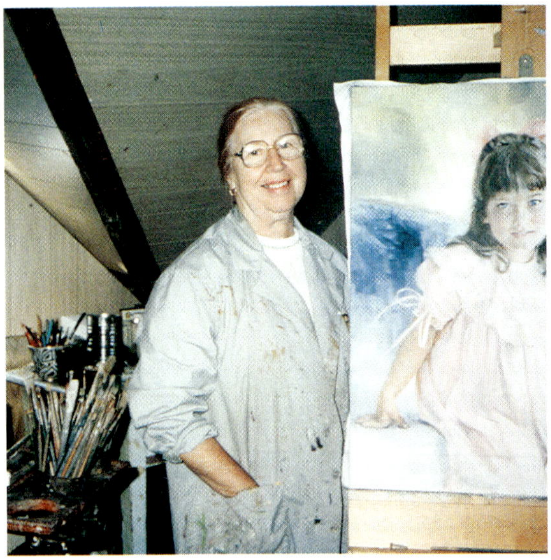

I photographed Liesel Boose in her "garage-penthouse" studio. Photo by Lew Lehrman.

LIESEL BOOSE, AND HER HUSBAND, DON, HAVE BEEN CLOSE FRIENDS OF mine for more than thirty years. I met Liesel in 1958 when she walked through the door of my little design studio, offering her services as a freelance fashion illustrator. At the time, the Booses lived in a tiny house in North Bellmore, Long Island. We became close friends. I was still single then, and spent many an evening at their home discussing art, life and philosophy over the wonderful dinners Liesel prepared, and countless glasses of wine.

Today, the Booses own a summer place in New Hampshire, and live in a big, old colonial home in Freeport. Liesel's studio is perched atop their garage, overflowing to a shed alongside.

Lola and I arrived on a warm, early-autumn morning, and after a tour of the studio we adjourned to the kitchen, where we lunched on delicious sausage-and-mushroom quiche, salad, and coffee. We reluctantly declined dessert: cake remaining from their fortieth anniversary party the previous weekend.

Finally, Liesel and I returned to the living room:

You've told me that on your first visit, you have to get to know your subjects and their personalities. But you paint largely from photographs. How does that work?

When I meet a subject, my first impression is, "What great eyes. . . . " Or, I recognize a quality like shyness, or whatever. I try to capture that in the pictures I take, and in my on-scene sketches. I do a whole lot of pastel studies. They're almost memory sketches, especially with little kids, because they're always in motion. But they're enough to familiarize me with the face and the color feeling. Then I take dozens of pictures in black and white.

With all the pictures I take, I find that people tend to repeat gestures. They're characteristic of the person. I incorporate them in the picture, and people will say, "Oh, he *always* does that."

You were telling me, before, about the portrait you recently finished, which your client was not satisfied with. How do you deal with that?

I don't get mad at them. I understand it. They're human. I try to make it right. What happens is, you really begin to like your clients. You've become friends, so it's not a relationship like any other business relationship. You want them to be happy. You're thrilled if they're pleased. But you also realize that you may encounter a mind that doesn't want to accept what yours does. That's what happened in this case.

Fortunately, I haven't had too many problems with that. I can think of only three over the years. But in some cases, no matter what you do, it will never be what they're looking for. I do my best. But if everything I try should fail, I'd cancel the commission and return their deposit.

What did you end up doing with that last portrait?

I did a second painting, and they loved it.

You seem to be very busy. Are you in the studio,

painting every day?

Yes. Every day. Even Saturdays and Sundays, except those dark, rainy ones when the light's not right. Sometimes I have to fight to do that. You know, the house is a wreck, and I have to do this or that. But painting is the strongest pull in my life now, and when I'm away from it for any length of time, I feel at loose ends. I feel very happy over in my messy studio, and if I just go through the studio door, I'm all right.

Do you ever think in terms of retiring?

I thought about retiring about ten years ago. But I've given up on the thought. As long as I'm well, and I do feel fine. . . .

Don has been a big help since his retirement. He's the reason I can still do all this out-of-town travel. He does the driving, handles the emergencies, and carries the heavy stuff. He handles all my finances, and he's a wonderful traveling companion. So why would I retire? I'm enjoying what I do, and I feel like I'm thirty-six!

From talking about retirement, let's head the other way. Tell me about your beginnings, and how you decided to become an artist.

I couldn't do anything else! My public school teachers in New York used to pick up on that. Even when I was little, back in Germany, my teacher noticed something.

My father was an artist, and I didn't pay any attention to my own ability. I thought everybody could do that. But gradually I noticed people making remarks about it, and I realized there was something I could do that was a little bit unusual.

When I was twelve or thirteen, my father began to show me how to use oil paints. He taught me the basics. We couldn't afford linen canvas, so we used oilcloth, on wooden stretchers he made. We'd take long walks together, and he'd talk to me about painting.

How old were you when you came to the United States?

I was eight. It was 1928.

When I was in the seventh or eighth grade, my teachers told my parents about Washington Irving High School, which was an arts school for girls. My mother would always back me in anything. My father, too. I had to go up there with my portfolio, and I was accepted, even though the school was outside my district.

The art classes consisted of figure drawing, more than anything. They didn't teach the use of oil paints, but we did use watercolor, Conté crayon, or anything we wanted to. We had four periods a day of art and art history, and two periods for all the other stuff, like English. I'm terrible at everything else.

In English, I was commissioned to do two portraits for the set of *School for Scandal*. I had to paint the girl, who was playing the male lead, as both a young man, and as an old man. I got a 95 in English that year, and I never even went to the class! I was so busy painting those portraits.

Did you do any other portraits in high school?

There was a teacher at Washington Irving whose grandfather was a Methodist minister from North Carolina. He was in his nineties, and she wanted a portrait of him, as a surprise, to be painted from newspaper clippings and photographs she had. It was almost like a contest. And everyone from the class had an opportunity to try for it.

I did the portrait in Conté crayon. They loved it, and they chose it. One teacher stopped me in the hall and asked me how I managed to capture his spirit. So there you are. I think it's the way I see people. But, of course, I was concentrating on becoming a fashion illustrator. I

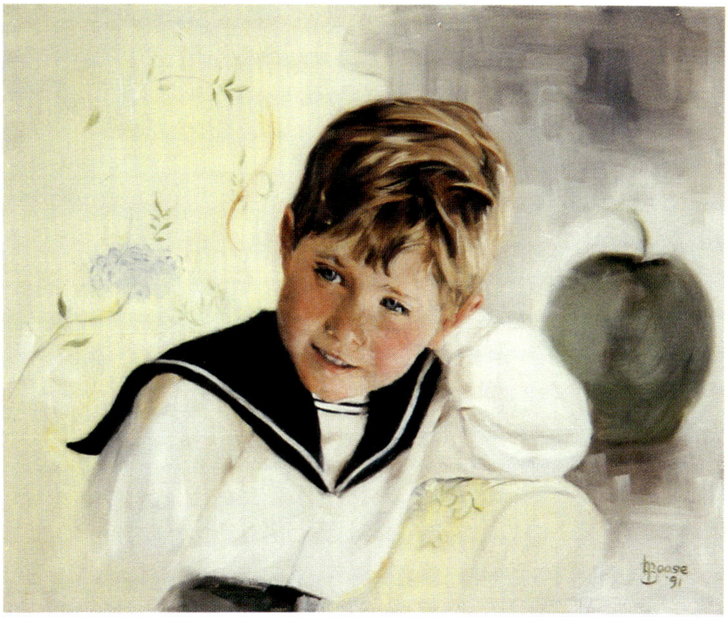

WILLIAM
1991
OIL ON CANVAS
16″ × 20″
COLLECTION OF
MRS. DOROTHY
HENRY

In this portrait, the shape of the collar delighted me, and I jumped at the chance to use a shape that pleased my eye. I contrasted the sturdy little boy with the suggestion of flowers in the background as a way of indicating the innocence of his age.

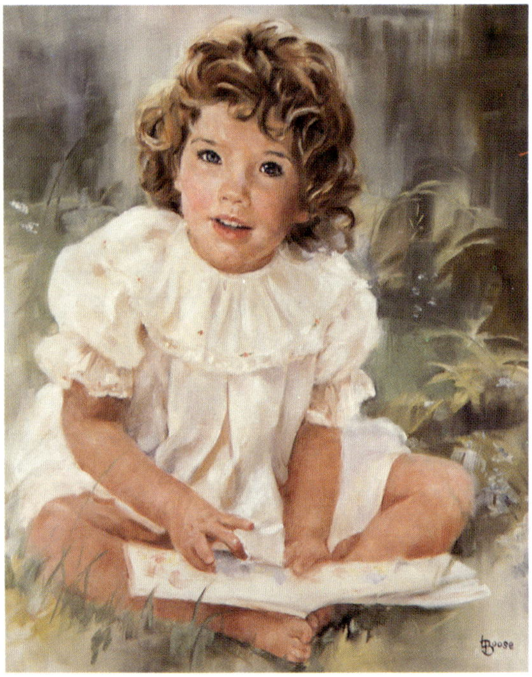

Favorite Story
1981
Oil on canvas
20″ × 24″
Collection of Mr. and Mrs. White

Though the finished portrait is in oils, I find pastels best for quickly sketching an active child. It's catch-as-catch-can, though. A quick smudge can correct an eye askew when the pose changes unexpectedly. Often the parents request my pastel preliminaries.

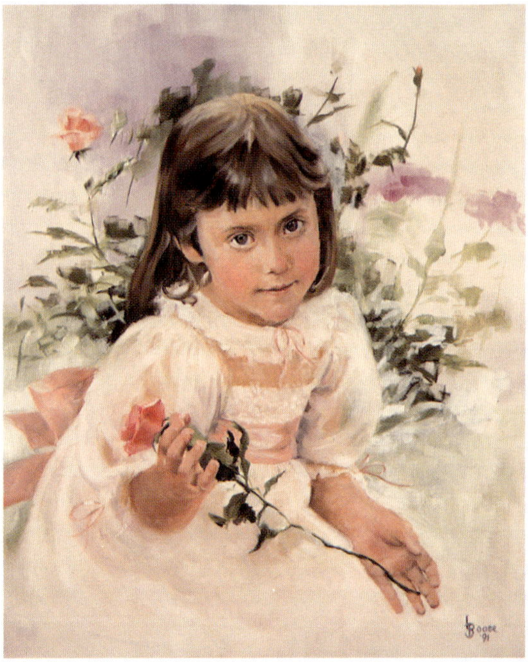

Courtney May
1991
Oil on canvas
20″ × 24″
Collection of Mr. and Mrs. Cabaniss

Courtney May's dress was actually constructed by me and redesigned from her mother's wedding dress, which I saw on a hanger, and in a small color photo. My experience in fashion illustration, not to mention childhood paper doll designing, came to the surface here.

never dreamed I would be a portrait painter.

I had taken a fashion illustration course my senior year. We worked with models, and we did plaster hands and skeletons, and copied drawings that Michelangelo had done before he painted the Sistine Chapel. And we were prodded into sketching what my teacher called "the beautiful bums" on the subways. And people everywhere.

We had no money in those days. I couldn't afford anything. But still, the school furnished wonderful supplies.

When I graduated, and my parents moved to Long Island, I stayed in New York and got a job. Not long after graduation, I went back to see my teacher at Washington Irving. She'd sold a painting I had done, to the assistant principal. I got five dollars for it. I had gotten five dollars for the minister's portrait, too!

Were they the first paintings you had ever sold?

Not really. I remember a postcard of wonderful splashy sunflowers in a wonderful splashy vase. Each petal was one stroke. I was twelve or thirteen. I fell in love with it, and I copied it in oils. My father framed it and my mother put it on the wall in the living room. One day I came home from school, and my mother said, "We sold the painting! Some people came in and saw it and wanted to buy it!" That was my first sale.

What happened after you graduated from high school?

That was a hard time. It was 1938. Washington Irving had what was called "professional class." There was a teacher there, who'd help you with job-hunting. You could use their phone to make appointments. I remember the horror of making appointments for a job interview. I'd have to call the art director, and go there with my portfolio. And they would say, "This is very good, but it isn't what we want."

I remember going to Altman's Department Store. To my surprise, the art director said I could do some display work for them. He asked me how much I charged, and I had no idea what to say. He read me like a book. "You've never done this before, have you? I think we'd better wait until you have more experience." And that was that.

Well, I needed money, so I went to New York State Employment and got a job for twelve dollars a week with Norcross Co. They made greeting cards. I got it because of my art background, but they had me checking labels on packages. It wasn't what I had been looking for, but it was a job.

I wanted to get into the art department, so I began to submit designs for greeting cards. They bought some of them, but did terrible things to them afterward.

It was a long time before they moved me

into the art department. And at that time, with the war on, being German was giving me trouble. The girls would all be talking, and I would mention the Germany I remembered as a child. It had been my home, and I had no pain there. A supervisor in my department called me a Nazi sympathizer! Can you imagine? Another time, there was an Asian-American artist, working in the same building, who asked me to lunch. I was called aside and told that since we were both enemy aliens, we shouldn't be seen together. And he was American-born! Anyway, I stayed at Norcross for five years.

DON
1979
OIL ON CANVAS
30″ × 36″
COLLECTION OF THE ARTIST

This portrait of my husband was painted to show that I was capable of painting portraits of men. It hung in a gallery for quite some time, but nothing much came of it. I am very pleased to still have it, however, as it is of Don.

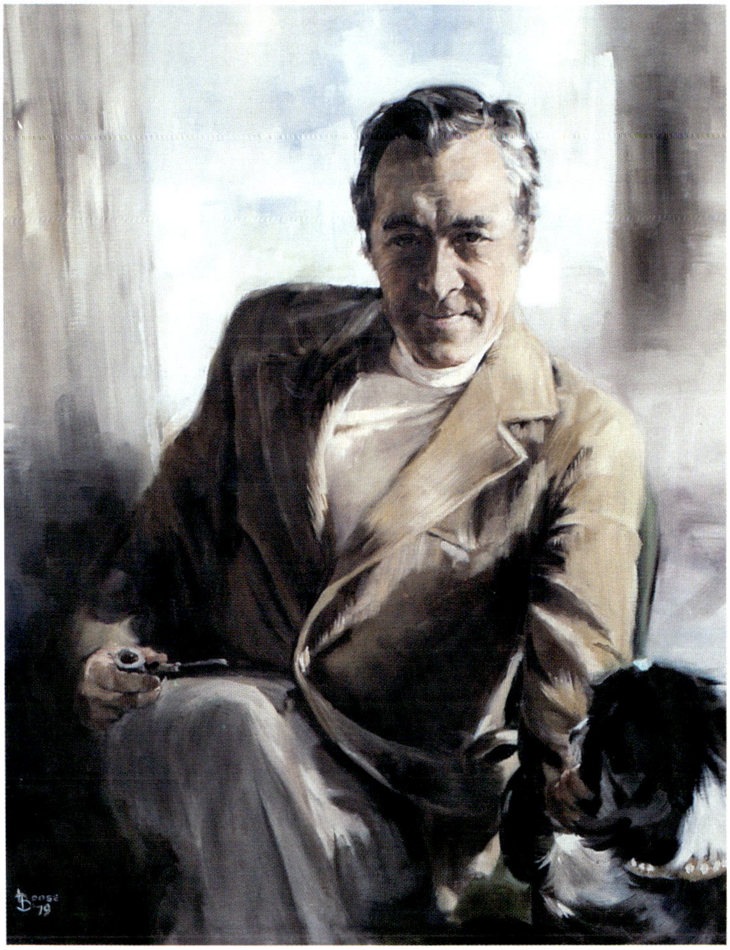

You weren't checking labels all that time, were you?

After what seemed like a very long time, I got promoted to the stenciling department for sixteen dollars a week. It was factory work. You'd have a stack of cards, a brush and a stencil, and have to lay down a swath of color through the stencil, on a thousand or two thousand cards. It was so monotonous. I'd have to work out the most economical brushstroke and do it over and over. I was terrible at it. I was always making a mess. It was piecework, and I couldn't make out.

My supervisor knew I had talent, though, and eventually she moved me into the airbrush department, and some time later, into the art department, but not the creative part.

When the war really got going, and jobs became available, I left Norcross and got a job with the Army Exchange Service, filing literature. My salary increased too—to twenty-two dollars a week.

While I was there, I learned that, if I wanted a job as an artist, I had to go to an employment agency that specialized in artists. I'd never known that! Right away, I got a job as a fashion illustrator with a buying house. I was drawing dresses and pocketbooks and basic stuff. I thought up a way to get shading in my sketches with grease pencil, and the buyers loved it.

One day a school friend, who was a successful fashion illustrator at Stern's, told me about an opening at *Women's Wear Daily*. "Go there, Liesel!" she said. It meant more money, so I took my samples, and ran into this nasty art director: "Do you call this drawing? Anybody could do this!" "Well, I don't especially want to work here anyway!" I replied, and that interested her. So she hired me, and despite her nasty temperament, I stuck it out for five years, until things got so bad that I would wind up crying half the time. I finally quit, and did some freelance work for *Vogue* and *Simplicity Patterns*.

About that time I met Don. We were married in 1950, and I moved into his apartment. During my first pregnancy, I had to stay in bed, and, through an agent, I got some work for *Bride's Magazine*. There I was, sitting in bed and sketching bridal gowns in our fourth-floor walk-up, with messengers bringing dresses, and an unemployed actress friend modeling them for me.

After my baby, Christina, died at five months, I got a call from *Women's Wear*. They had a new art director, and they said they needed me back. I think they did it to help me over my loss. I returned there until I was very pregnant with Christopher.

Did you continue your freelancing after that?

No. Christopher, Jonathan and Stephen came

Jonathan
1977
Oil on canvas
16″ × 20″
Collection of
Jonathan Boose

I waited a long time before doing this portrait, because I hoped Jonathan would have his hair cut. But I'm as pleased as he is to have caught him as he was then. "I'm ready now," he said, as he looked at the finished painting, "to look more respectable." The haircut followed a week later.

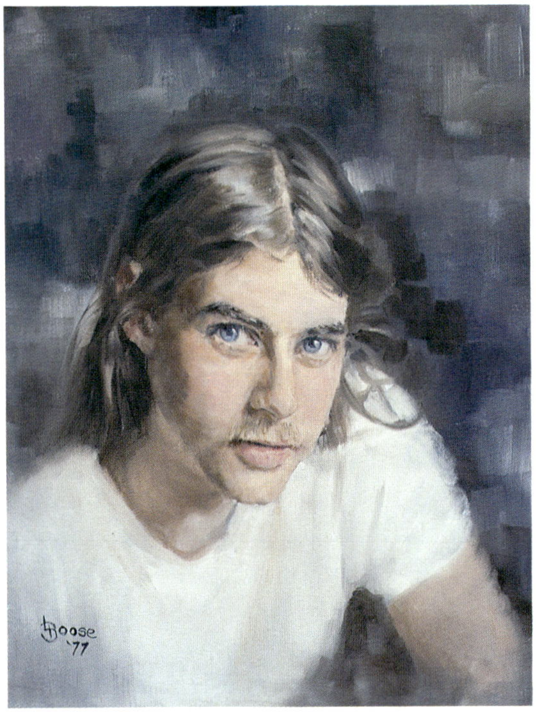

thirteen months apart. The next freelance work I did was in 1958, when I came to see you.

Some very good friends insisted that we get out of the city with the children. So we borrowed a car and went house hunting, and found the place in North Bellmore. They helped us with the down payment, and we moved in 1956. It was heaven for me.

Anyway, I had the babies. All of them were in diapers, and I started doing flowers and landscapes, mostly in watercolor. When Stephen, my youngest, went off to kindergarten, I went out painting with an old friend who lived nearby. She was a portrait painter, and I said to myself, "If she can do portraits, I can do portraits." That was what started it.

Then Don asked me to paint a portrait of our boys. He does such beautiful photos of them, I thought, "Why should I paint them?" But to please him, I did. In watercolor. Friends and neighbors saw the portrait, and asked me to watercolor them. One of our friends saw the painting and asked me to paint his wife and children, but in oils. We all went up to his country place and I did them. He paid me $150 each. It doesn't seem like much now, but I was also spending fifteen dollars a week on groceries then. Each portrait led to more portraits, and I began to get busy.

Then I saw an ad for Portraits, Inc. in *New Yorker* magazine. It showed a portrait I liked very much, and I decided I wouldn't mind being represented by a gallery like that. Don made some slides of my work, and I took them in, and met the director, Mrs. Appleton-Read. She looked at them and said, "Where have you been?"

And the rest is history?

It took a while, because people like to see that you've done a lot before they really trust you. So I didn't make much in the beginning. Though it was always a lot as far as I was concerned. It was nice to have that extra income.

It's really word-of-mouth, isn't it?

Word of eye. Portraits, Inc. really got things going, and one thing led to another. They showed my paintings around, and the more I did, the more they could show.

Do you have a big backlog of work?

I did have a big backlog for a while. It was very nerve-wracking. I couldn't do anything but paint portraits. Now I have what I'd call a "good" backlog. A few in the studio. One that's waiting to be started. And quite a few to be started next year. And I've begun work on my grandson's portrait.

How did you price your work?

I was really bashful at first. I was afraid to ask. Andrea Erickson Hogan, the director at Portraits, Inc., suggested a price, and we went with that. I was always afraid to raise it. Every time I did, I felt awful. Until the last time, when I said to myself, I've got too much work. If I raise my prices, I'll get less work, and I'll retire. So I almost doubled my prices. And, you want to know something? I still have enough work to keep me busy every day!

Do you mind my asking your rates now?

Not at all. A single portrait, twenty by twenty-four, is ten thousand dollars. A group of three young children might run thirty-one thousand or more. Each person in the picture counts as a separate portrait. I charge a thousand dollars extra for a recognizable horse or dog in the foreground.

Summer River in Texas
1986-87
Oil on canvas
60″ × 48″ (approx.)
Collection of Mr. and Mrs. Charles McCord

My commission read, "Mother, two teenagers, two shaggy dogs and a quarter-horse (on a greeny-bluey river)." When I stayed with the family and Mr. McCord saw photos of my paintings, he decided he wanted to be in the picture, too.

You seem to enjoy wonderful success with your work. Can you point to a key factor in that success that might help other artists?

For one thing, it isn't anything you can fool people with. You do a portrait, and either they like your work or they don't. You're selling in a very direct way. It really is a business, although I do get help from the people who represent me. I wouldn't be able to make this kind of living if I didn't have people out there showing my work.

There is a catch to that, though. I think that I'm being presented as a children's artist. Other artists prefer to paint judges, or politicians, or bank presidents. They don't get asked to paint children. I suppose it's because my representatives have more photos of my children's portraits than anything else.

What thoughts would you offer to artists who would like to make their living doing portraits?

You need representation. In portraiture, the people who sell do so through a gallery. Somebody has to be there to push the work, and expose the public to it. An artist can be in his studio painting, and nobody will ever know about him, unless there's somebody representing him. Especially in this day and age, everybody needs publicity, and to be talked about, and to get noticed.

Any last thoughts on fine art as a way of life?

It's great. I think it gives you an understanding of people. But I can't speak for every portraitist, because every one is different. Their attitudes are different, too.

When I paint, I really experience my subject. I don't paint velvet without feeling that buttery softness. And shiny hair, or hard metal, or textures. You really experience the physical world by looking and understanding.

For me, the greatest pleasure is what I see. I just love a line. I can sit at the table with Don, sometimes, and his hand will fall . . . just so. And I'll just love the line of his hand. Like some people love ice cream. I don't even have to paint. I just enjoy seeing. I think painting does that for you. It makes you see better.

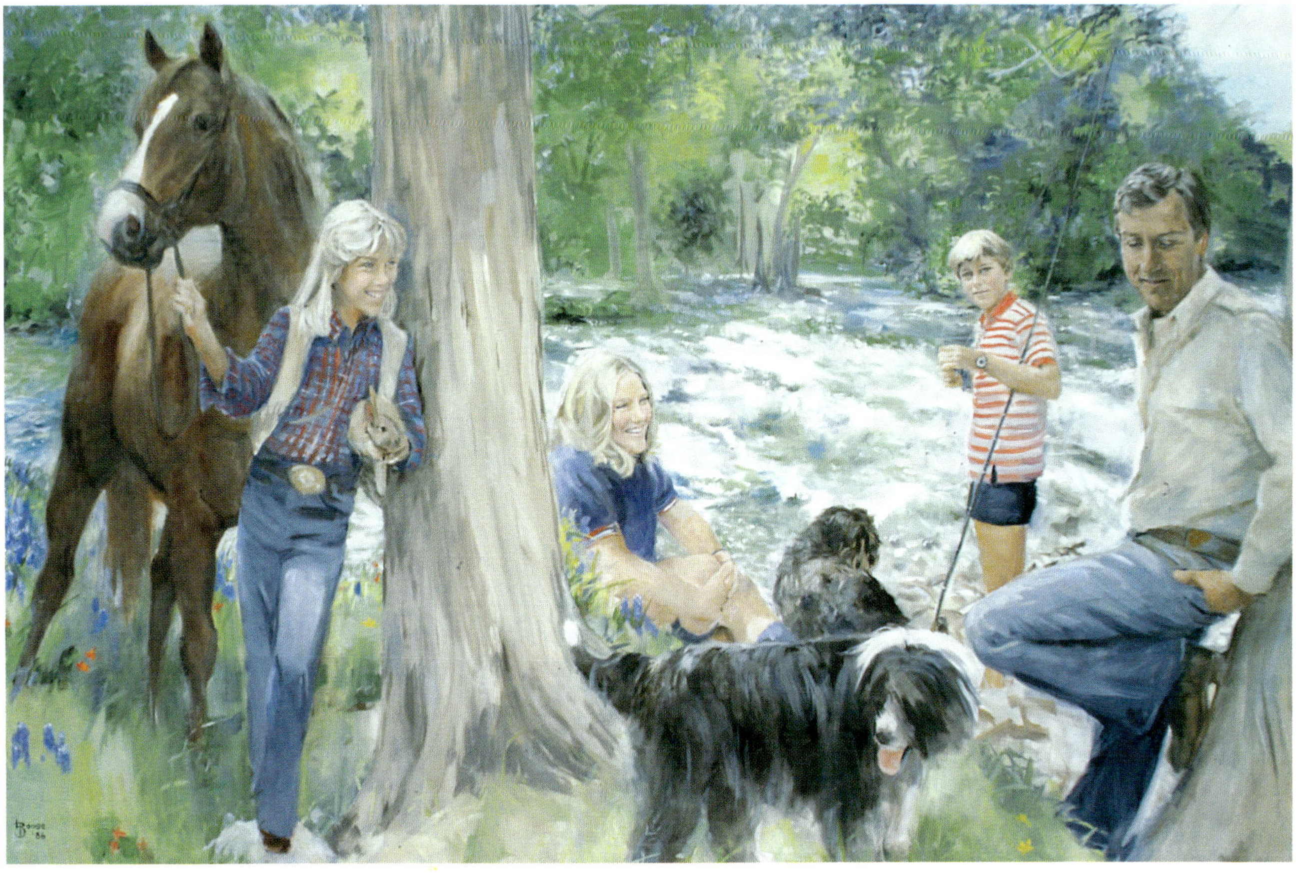

FRANK WEBB
When Ability and Opportunity Coincide

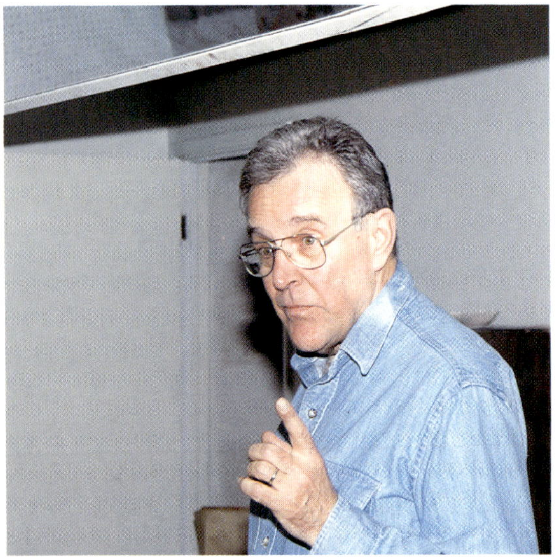

Frank Webb at his Arizona Watercolor Association demonstration. Photo by Lew Lehrman.

I WAS DELIGHTED TO LEARN THAT FRANK WEBB WOULD BE IN PHOENIX to conduct a watercolor workshop for the Arizona Watercolor Association. Part of his schedule included an open demonstration at the Arizona Artists' Guild one evening, and I was there in the crowd. The place was packed. Several hundred people filled the seats and lined the walls to watch and listen as the artist worked his skillful way through a dockside scene.

The movements of his brush were decisive as he attacked his subject, now hovering hawk-like above the paper, now swooping to pounce upon some detail. Through it all, his witty patter and commentary on matters both painterly and philosophical kept the audience thoroughly involved and entertained. I was equally impressed with his skill on both levels.

The following evening, as we sat in his motel room, I commented on his demo and on his busy workshop schedule.

I thoroughly enjoyed not only your dialogue with the paper, but also your monologue with your audience. How is it, being the Bob Hope of the brush?

It's fun to deal with the humor that grows out of such a serious occupation. Painting is very serious business, because you're dealing with some of life's deepest issues, while being confronted with your own limitations—not to mention the unexpected that happens while you're doing it. But I don't think the humor would surface unless I had the ease that results from long experience.

With a public demo, you have so many people attending (many of whom may be seriously studying painting) that with all the information you wish to impart, the humor helps to keep them engaged . . . and awake.

How many workshops do you do a year?

From twenty-two to twenty-five. And I begin each workshop day with a demo. That demo is an assignment I give to myself, and my students are witness to the various and differing approaches I use. Then most of them go on to try these approaches, using their own subject matter. I try not to suggest that this is *the* way to paint. There is no such thing.

I've watched many demos over the years, and yours, more than many, gives the sense that you've lifted the hood so we can watch the machinery at work.

I've never heard it expressed quite that way, but that's what it's meant to be. My idea is not so much to communicate how I do it, but to convey the principles, the thought processes behind it.

Beginners watching a demo may not see that. They will be pretty much absorbed in technical matters, and there's nothing wrong with that. They need that information until they are able to express themselves in paint. Later they will be concerned with developing their conceptual powers, because what ultimately separates one artist from another is the power to formulate concept . . . a unique aesthetic concept that will make this artist's work something that has never been seen or felt before.

Do you think it's possible for the artist to do that? Hasn't everything been said, to some extent, before? Is there yet anything new under the sun?

Every work of art ought to be new. All the books have not yet been written, nor all the plays. And all the pictures have not been painted. It seems to me the world is crying out more than ever now for the quality of uniqueness. We live in an age when our culture tends to routinize, almost brutalize our everyday lives. The sameness of mass communication (we all get the same messages every day), of products (we all eat foods processed by the few), have left it to art to lift us, give us a vision, a glimpse of what might be, more than mass communication and mass production can.

Why is it that some art communicates so personally with the viewer?

People respond to life. If a work of art gives them a glimpse of what life is like, they will respond to it. I think a good play, or a good book does the same thing.

I think this happens because art gives us a glimpse into the hearts and minds of those people we call artists. Works of fine art have no other reason to exist than to be perceived: to celebrate, to communicate, to be felt, pondered, savored. Not to impel us toward being in sympathy with any cause, though this is not to say that art cannot be enlisted for that purpose. That's called propaganda. Or advertising. And many of us, myself included, have been involved with that to make a living.

Tell me a bit about your life in art . . . and advertising.

I was born in Pittsburgh, Pennsylvania in 1927. Went to a very small school with two grades in each room. I had no art training, but I always drew. Neither my parents nor I had ever known a living artist, but they encouraged me, though it never occurred to any of us that one might make a living at it.

Then there was World War II. I went right into the Navy out of high school, and did quite a bit of drawing there, on my own. Afterward, on the G.I. Bill, I went to the Art Institute Of Pittsburgh. Had some fine instruction and enjoyed it very much. It was a happy time of life for me. That was when I met my wife, and began

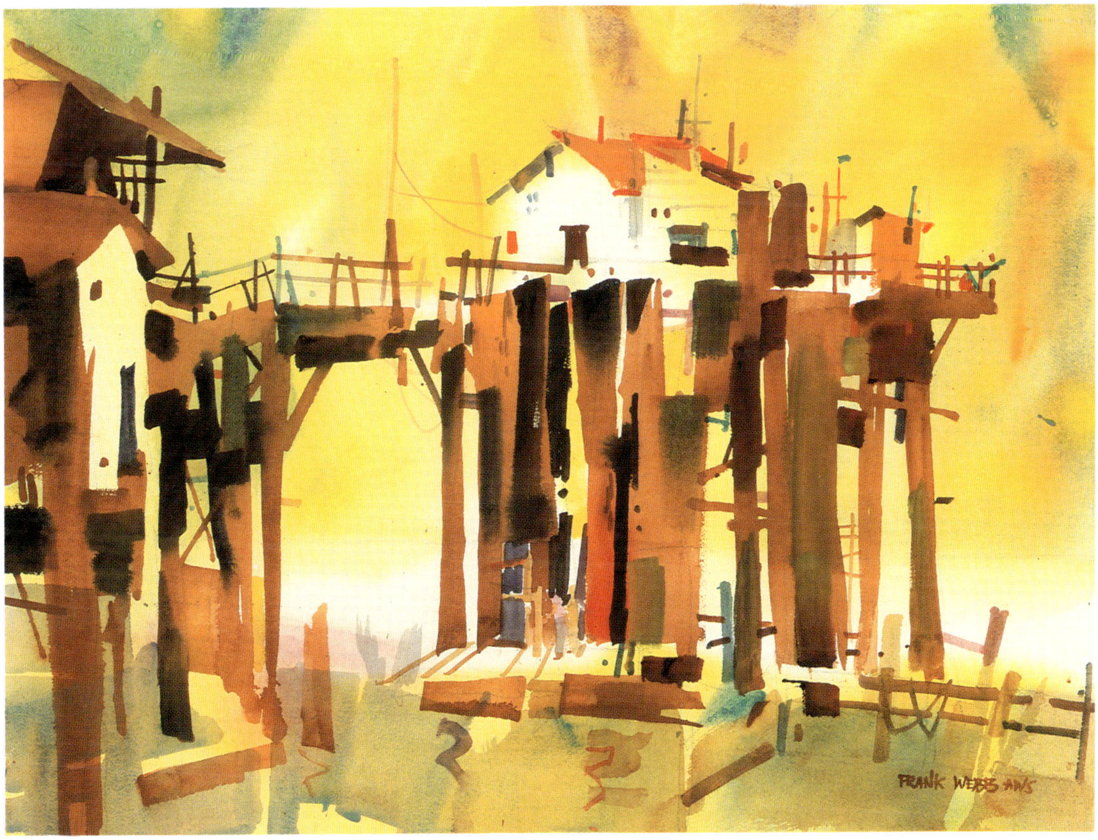

RANDY'S LANDING
WATERCOLOR
30″ × 22″

A yellow wet-in-wet. Whites were spared for the shacks and the horizontal ocean. As this dried, I applied a flat burnt sienna hard-edged wash; before that dried, I charged the sienna wash with pure colors and darks.

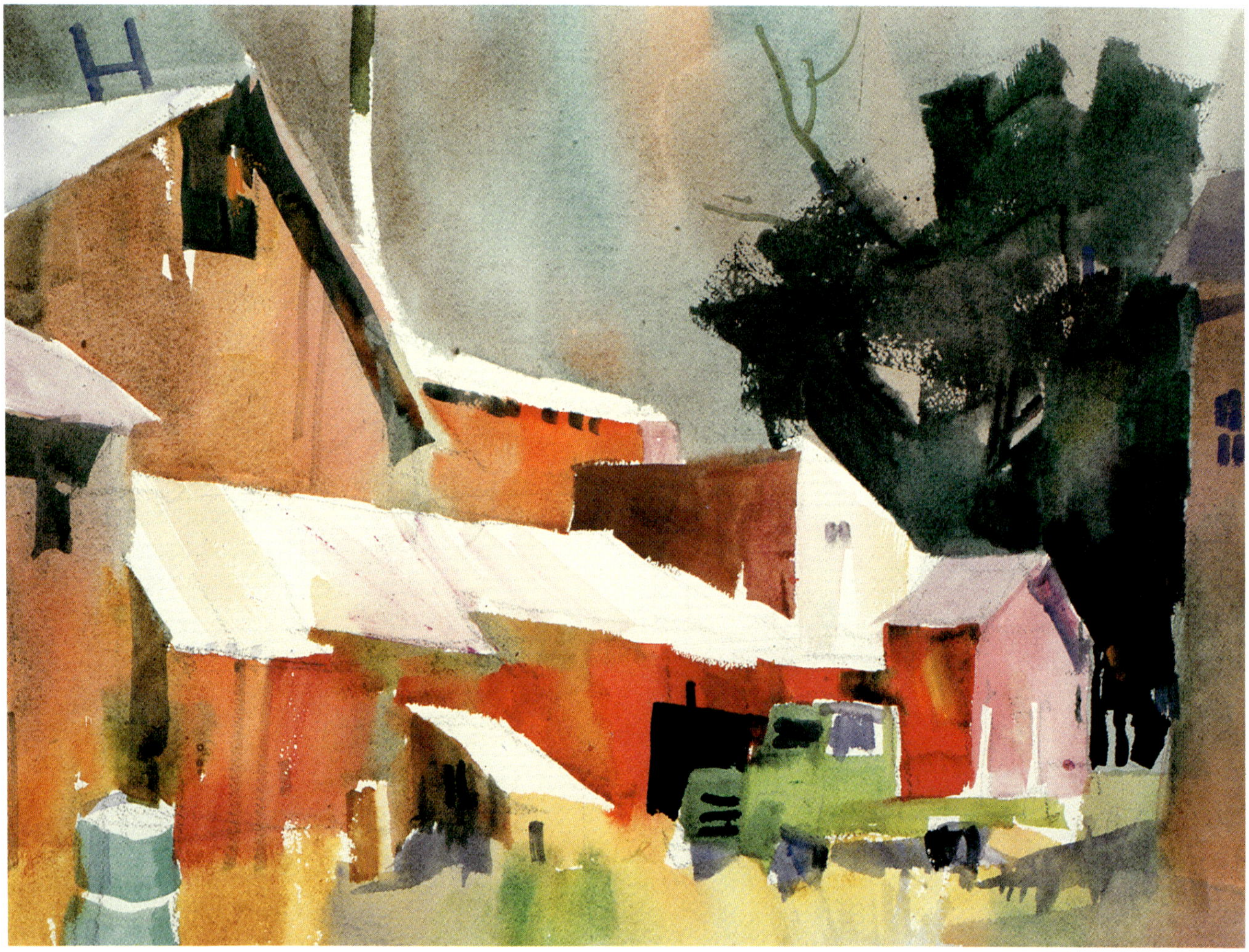

CATSKILL FARM
WATERCOLOR
15″ × 12″

Painted directly with greens and a wide variety of reds. As usual, white shapes were invented using the roofs to indicate sheet metal. Reds were charged into the sky to integrate sky and barn. When painting a red barn, I avoid having an equal amount of green and red in the composition.

my career in commercial art. I worked at it for about three years, until the Korean War started, and was then recalled to the Navy for another two years.

In '52, I returned to the studio where I had worked previously, and in 1957, the owner, who was elderly, decided to make two of us his partners. I eventually became the senior partner. I worked at that until 1980, when my partner announced that he had reached retirement age and would be leaving. That got me thinking. I began to visualize how it might be to escape the responsibilities and the deadlines, and decided that I would leave as well. We decided to give the studio to our employees. We handed them the lease, the equipment, and, as much as possible, the goodwill we had earned. I left to do more teaching and more painting.

How did you get involved in giving workshops?

Back in 1970, I took the family along and attended an Edgar A. Whitney watercolor workshop in Kennebunkport, Maine. I watched Ed working, teaching, painting, doing demos, giving critiques. I enjoyed that week, and it started me thinking.

The next two years, I organized my own five-day workshop in the Laurel Mountains, near Pittsburgh, based in a small town called Farmington, going out to different locations each day to paint.

How did you go about filling your class?

I had joined the local watercolor society in the mid-sixties, and had won some prizes. There is an artists' grapevine, and word gets around. I did a brochure to announce my workshops, and mailed it out. You develop a following.

By 1973, I was doing a little traveling for workshops and demos. I enjoyed that, but didn't think I'd ever want to make the break to do it full time. The children were still in college, still living with us. But by 1980, they had graduated and gotten married, and were off to good starts, and the timing was right. I felt that any risk I might be taking with this move would not involve them. In fact, there was no risk at all, but we don't know these things ahead of time.

That first year, I ran a simple ad in an art magazine, listing about twelve of my workshop locations. I received many inquiries, and that was the only ad I ever ran.

Today, your workshop schedule must keep you on the road fully six months each year.

I do twenty-four workshops a year, and most are five-day affairs. Allowing a day for travel out and another for return, that's twenty-four weeks out of fifty-two. But when one works at a job, as I did for many years, one has even less free time. My wife often joins me for these trips, always when I drive.

And your children?

Today, we have a musician daughter, a speech pathologist son, and a manager daughter. Four grandchildren (who are our abiding interest now), and all doing well. Nobody paints.

How were you selling most of your work during those first years of your career?

Then as now, during workshops a large number of my paintings were sold to the workshop participants. I bring a number of paintings with me to each workshop, and of course there are the demonstration paintings. I usually pin them on the wall and make one modest announcement that the paintings are for sale.

When you were becoming established, did you market through galleries, as well?

Yes, but more importantly, I was showing in juried shows. That began back in 1970. For many years I entered as many as fifteen shows a year. Juried shows aren't necessarily selling opportunities, but a strategy for long-range goals. They're a forum where you can get a notion of your status, compared to your peers. To be accepted is good for your morale. To receive an award or to sell a painting is certainly a boost. No one ever gets enough of that. And to get into the traveling shows puts you in touch with the grapevine I mentioned earlier.

Then the workshops are your principal sales outlets today.

That's right. And there are no gallery commissions, and no framing costs. I always feel that the paintings I sell at workshops are bought for the right reasons (not that there are wrong reasons

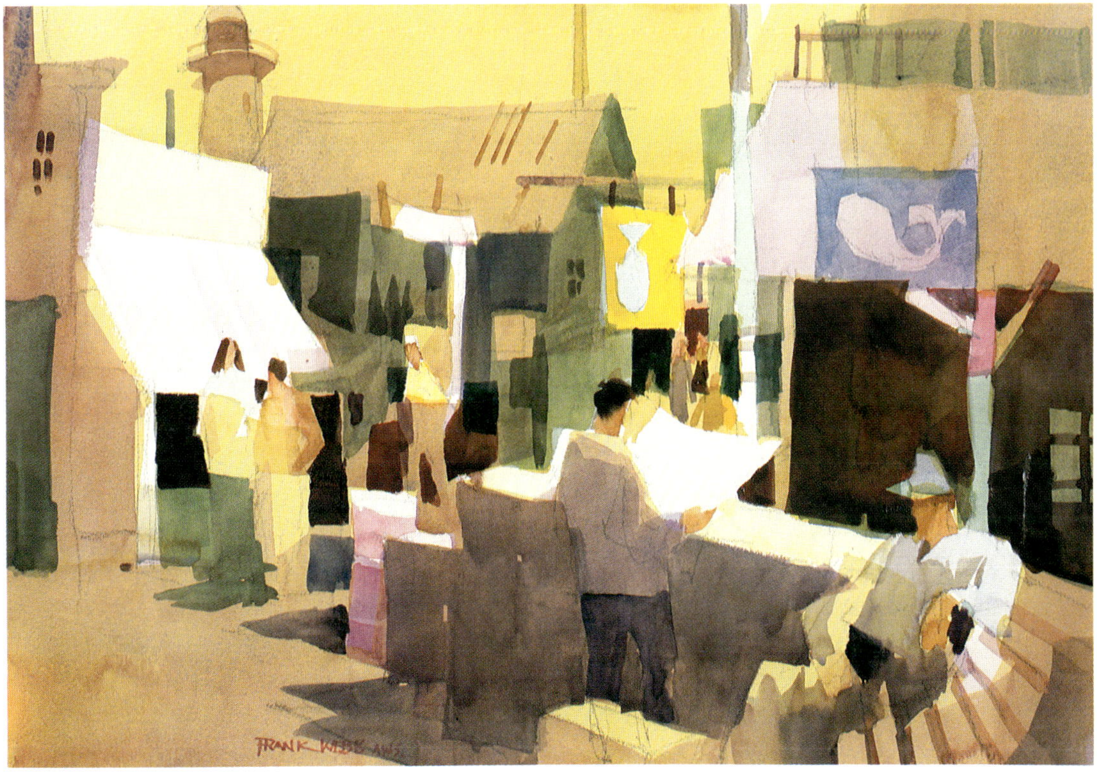

FISHERMAN'S WHARF NO. 1
WATERCOLOR
22" × 15"

To make the reference drawing for this painting, I stood on a park bench like the one on the right. I was less of a spectacle than the nearby organ grinder with his monkey. The painting was built from a succession of flat, overlapping, warm washes, keeping all edges hard.

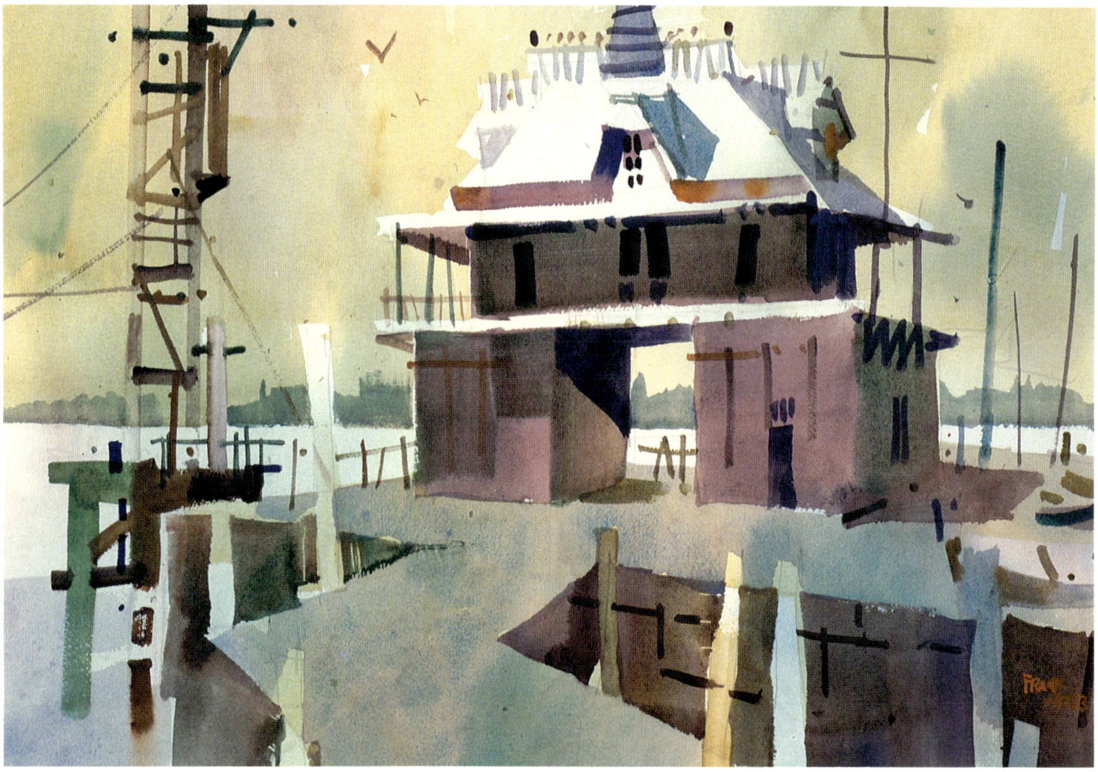

YACHT CLUB
WATERCOLOR
22″ × 15″

This Delaware River subject intrigued me because it was a "see through," surrounded by a rich lacework of rails, towers and masts. Abstract underpainting was first applied, followed by flat washes, and the brushwork calligraphy was added to complete it.

for buying a painting), because these are people who study painting.

When did you do your first book?

Watercolor Energies appeared in 1983 (North Light Books). I had never written before, so when I got started, I picked up a copy of Will Strunk's and E.B. White's book, *The Elements of Style*, and learned a little about writing. That book helped me to clarify and focus on principles I felt I could teach wholeheartedly. *Webb on Watercolor* was published in 1990 (North Light Books).

How should the artist of today make him- or herself ready to be a professional?

The answer is very simple. You learn to draw by drawing. You learn to draw and paint by drawing and painting. In *The Shape of Content* (Vintage Books, New York, 1960), Ben Shahn, the artist, wrote on the education of a painter (and I'm paraphrasing): "To become an artist, you get a job on a farm and draw and paint and draw and paint. You get a job in a factory and draw and paint and draw and paint. You go to a university and draw and paint. . . ." I think he was quite right. It's not a matter of going through some system. Art is not so much "knowledge about." It's hands-on knowledge.

The focus in most careers is outward: getting the promotion, getting the client, getting the power. On the other hand, when you work at your art, you are developing *inward* power. It's in-dwelling knowledge, and the only way you get that is by drawing and painting . . . the way of trial and error. To prepare yourself professionally for art, no matter what your job is, you draw and paint, the way a dog chews a bone. It's what you want to do.

But at what point do you make the break, quit the job, and try your wings as a professional?

I can only speak for myself. Would I have run out on my family like Gaugin to follow my dream? No. That's not me. I felt there were other claims on me that were more important. I was parent, spouse, employer, and I didn't take any of those roles lightly. But patiently I worked away at it, and eventually the opportunity presented itself. There's certainly nothing wrong in life with learning to work for long-range goals. I think the need for instant gratification is a sign of adolescence.

In the final analysis, I would tell the aspiring artist, "Work, do the thing you love to do. That's the only way you can become unique. If you drift off in some direction for the sake of selling something today, you'll lose direction. I can't overemphasize the importance of trying patiently to run the long course, even though you might have to do something else temporarily to make a living. Don't be trapped into thinking that if you really want to be an artist, that becoming a businessman is somehow beneath you." If you suddenly decide, "Yes, I like running a business and making money!" then obviously you found your real call.

Do you believe that there is an element of luck involved?

The best definition of luck I ever heard was, "when ability and opportunity coincide." You've got to believe that the two will come together at some point. And when the opportunity presents itself, you want to be ready, with all your skills honed. You'll have imagined, studied, sacrificed, been knocked down and gotten up, you'll have entered shows and been rejected and kept on entering, and practiced and improved, and learned to live with the world's indifference.

Looking ahead a bit, where do you see things going for you?

Just more of the same. I notice that when the world decides to write about an artist, they focus on his odd behavior, his irresponsibilities, his neuroses. I think an artist's life is not particularly measured by the events in it. An artist is a person, working, for the most part, in solitude. Like a broadcaster, he sends out work and is not immediately witness to the applause. Unknown people buy his works, and the artist may never know their names.

So when I say "more of the same," I mean drawing and painting and teaching. Cogitating on matters of art. You know, when you write a book, and teach a great deal, you get a lot of feedback and mail. I have a drawer full of letters thanking me for "helping me become this . . . " or "showing me how to do that." There's a great deal of satisfaction in that. I've already been rewarded, so I can't imagine being greedy enough to think this is a stepping-stone to something even greater.

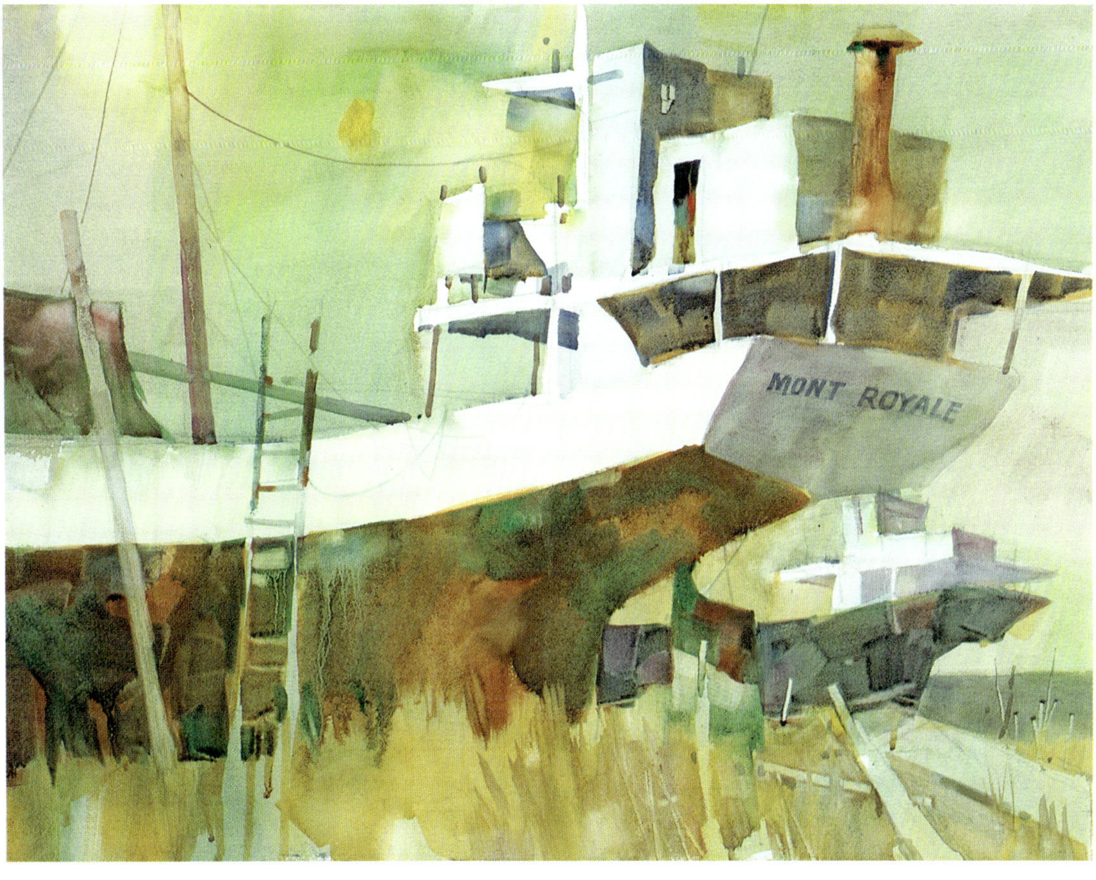

MONT ROYALE
WATERCOLOR
30″ × 22″

These two wooden derelicts languish on the shores of the St. Lawrence in Quebec. Since the shapes have such a definite movement to the left, I used vertical masts and the ladder to slow down the leftward thrust. The large, dark hull was alternately painted with viridian and burnt sienna.

DEAN L. MITCHELL
You Can Make a Difference

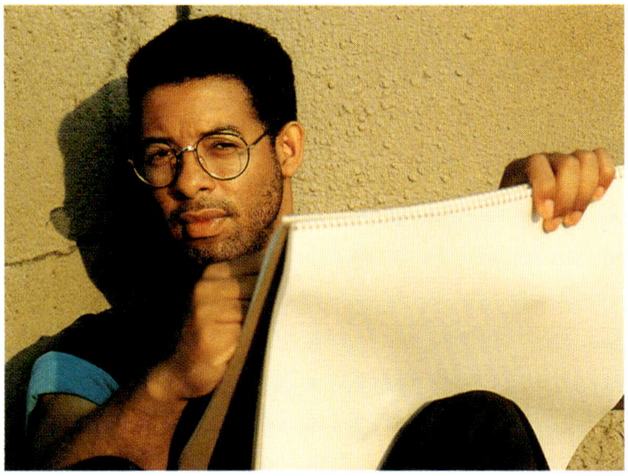

Dean Mitchell. Photo by Julie Robertson.

AS I WAS SEARCHING FOR ARTISTS TO INTERVIEW FOR THIS BOOK, ALL AT once, several people mentioned Dean Mitchell to me. I reached him at his Kansas City home, and he sent me several magazine articles about himself and his work, plus one of the most voluminous résumés I've ever seen.

I came away from our interview impressed with the talent of this young man (he's just 34), his determination and his accomplishments. Dean is a totally committed professional, serious about his work, and cognizant of his importance as a role model for emerging black American artists. At the same time, plainly audible in his voice is bemusement and boyish wonder at his own remarkable success. But it was Dean Mitchell, role model, that interested me first.

Why do you think there are so few professionally successful black artists?

Recently, I became familiar with the works of Henry Tanner, who is probably the most famous black American painter. Of course, he's been dead now for fifty-some years, but his painting, *The Thankful Poor*, brought the highest price ever paid for the work of a black American painter. It was recently purchased by Bill Cosby for a quarter of a million dollars.

Reading Tanner's life story, one thing he did say was that when he looked back on history, he had no role models to pull from. I found myself dealing with some of the same issues, the same problems when I was coming up. There were no books to read, no magazine articles to tell me that what I wanted to do was possible here in America.

My Mom kept harping on me, all those years. "If you're going to go anywhere with your art, you'll have to go to Paris. You just can't make it in America!"

Because of the race issue?

Yes. That's exactly what Henry Tanner had to do. But I felt, well, that was fifty years ago. Today should be different.

Was it?

In some ways. One conclusion I've reached is that black people are just not interested in art.

Why not?

I think it's because America has not embraced the black American painter and escalated him to the realm of an Andrew Wyeth, or a Jasper Johns, or a Warhol. But when you see somebody like a Michael Jordan, or a Bill Cosby, or a Michael Jackson . . . that's high visibility. There has yet to be a black American painter with that kind of visibility, or on that economic level. Until we have at least one or two, most black kids are not going to be interested in art, because they see no future in it.

And the black people who buy art, the few who can afford to, buy Matisse, Picasso—the things they see as investments. They don't see the works of black Americans as a sound investment. "Well, history says black painters' work just doesn't go up."

Are there many black artists striving for the success you speak of?

There are, but they're not breaking into the mainstream. There has not yet been a traditional painter, like myself, or like Hughie Lee-Smith, a social realist, to do so.

Unfortunately, it's money that brings visibility. When you're not making any money, the press is not interested. People are not interested. Museums are not interested.

It's the American way.

Sure. Museums are interested in making money too. When they host an exhibition, they want to know it's going to draw people, sell books, get press coverage. I don't see any major exhibits, any books, any coverage for a black American artist of any age.

Do you think the situation is changing for the better?

I think so. Once people see museums and collectors buying, I think it will change even faster. I notice now that as I get a lot of press, I'm able to verbalize things that at one time were controversial. Now I run into artists who say, "I read that article, and I'm glad somebody had enough nerve to say that!"

You faced discouragement as a child, yet you persisted. What kept you going?

There certainly were times when I felt like giving up. But every time I'd think, "I'll forget this and just illustrate," something would push me to keep on.

What was that something?

I guess it was a little bit of faith, and wanting to make a difference. I see so few portraits of black people. And I think, "There's really a void here. A big void in American art. You can make a difference if you stick with it!"

Tell me about your own background.

I was born in Pittsburgh, Pennsylvania in 1957, and raised by my maternal grandmother in Quincy, Florida. My mom was the first of my grandmother's four children to go to college.

I started drawing very young. I was fascinated by animation, and drew lots of cartoons. By the time I got to fifth grade, I had discovered the *Saturday Evening Post* cover art of Norman Rockwell, whom I greatly admired. I bought my first set of oils when I was in the sixth grade, but my mom had met a guy who was a commercial artist. He said, "You can't make a living doing this stuff." So she wasn't real encouraging.

My grandmother was my biggest source of encouragement. She'd gone to school, but she wasn't college-educated like my mom was, so she didn't understand the complications of making a living. But she was very excited about my

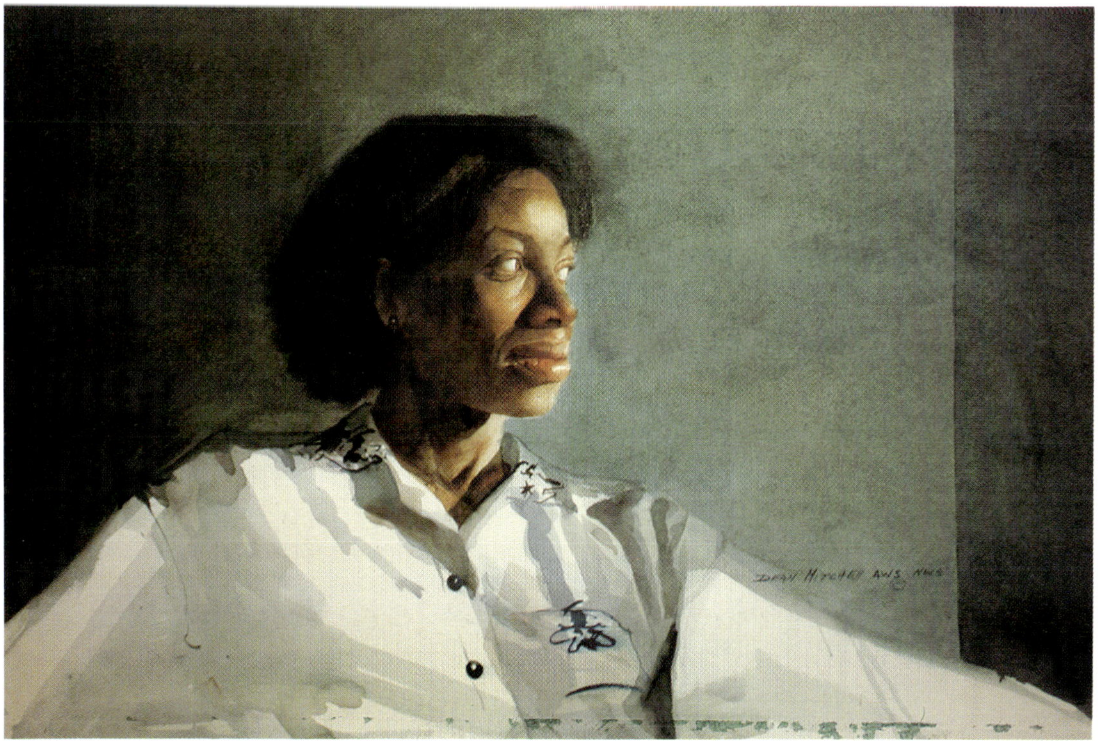

CAROLYN
1988
WATERCOLOR
20″ × 15″
COLLECTION OF THE MISSISSIPPI MUSEUM OF ART

Carolyn is the daughter of Elouise Mitchell Favors, my maternal grandmother's oldest daughter. We were both raised by our grandmother. The bond we share is like a brother-sister relationship.

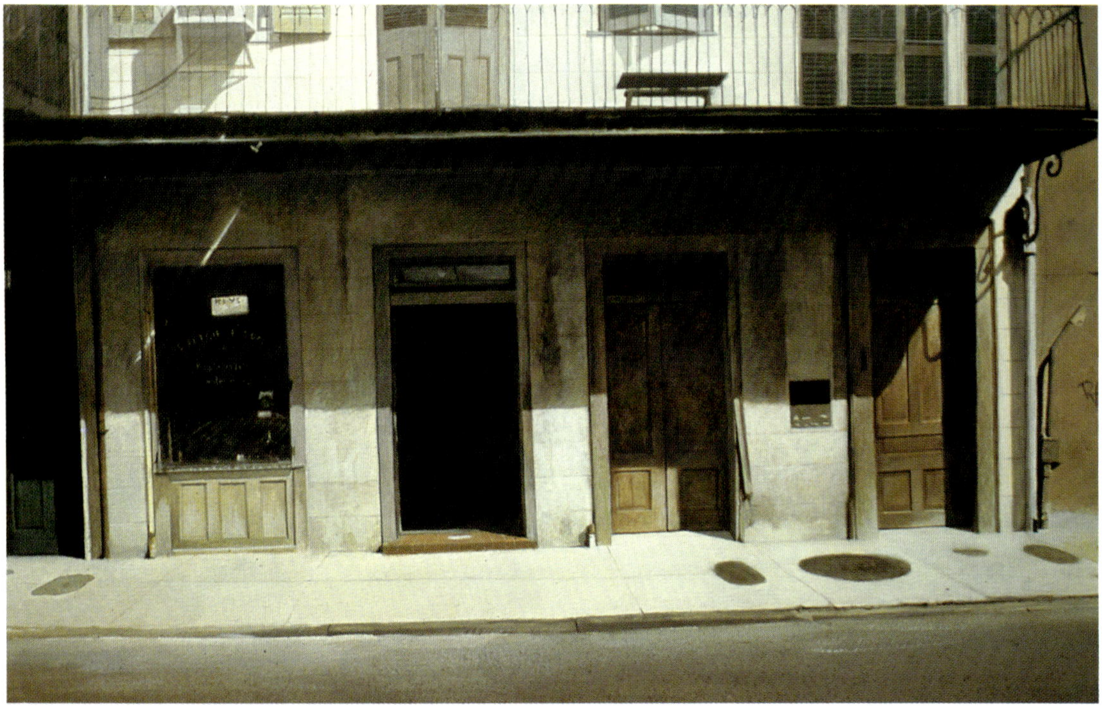

New Orleans French Quarter
1985
Acrylic
15¾″ × 10″
Collection of the artist

This painting gives us a sense of sunlight, bright yet somber. There is a spiritual emptiness—its haunting use of color and space makes the viewer question what has taken place there.

work, and I think that gave me the sense of security to go on with it.

At the high school I attended, there was an art teacher who would take his "special" students to a lot of the art fairs. So I got a chance to see what professionals were doing. They had competitions at these art fairs, and I entered, won a few prizes. I did some things for the local school teachers. They'd pay me maybe fifteen or twenty dollars, which was encouraging for a child. But I realized that I'd have to think realistically about what I was going to do with my life.

I decided I wanted to pursue art, so I got some college catalogs, met with the counselors at school, and submitted applications to four or five colleges. I was accepted at the Columbus College of Art and Design, in Ohio, and I went up there, by myself, to begin. I worked hard and got some grants to see me through.

How did you handle that college transition?

Right away, I realized how far behind I was. A lot of my classmates had had private instruction, and I found myself wondering if I could even stay there.

I was in a state of shock! There was a lot more to it than just knowing how to draw.

That first semester I lost about thirty pounds. When I got home at midyear, my grandmother looked at me and said, "You can't go back to that school!" My mother said, "You've got to go back!" So I did. And it worked out fine, as I started getting used to the workload.

After my freshman year, I came home and got a job at the cannery. But I realized that I'd have to work hard to build my drawing and painting skills. So I quit, and began painting, and tried to sell my work.

Then my mom saw an ad in the paper for some kind of competition being held in Panama City, Florida. She said, "Why don't you enter this?" I looked at it and said, "This includes all of north Florida. There's no way I'm going to get into this." She said, "Oh, take a chance on it." So I entered, and I got in, and I won a prize! I went down there and the people were really excited about me. They said, "You're the first black person ever to enter our show!"

That led to a call from a boys' club in Panama City, and I ended up teaching a children's drawing class there for ten dollars an hour. It was there that I met a lady, Joanne Dickerson. She thought I was so gifted. (I had no self-confidence.) She took me around to some of the galleries, and in Fort Walton Beach, we just happened to luck into a gallery that loved my work. He leaped at everything. In fact, he bought a few pieces for himself, on the spot! And he began selling my things.

I also got another gallery in Panama City.

In fact, he still handles my work. I had my first gallery show there. People came, and they bought. Of course, I was getting around twenty-five dollars a painting, but for a kid it was great. In fact, when I got back to school, I'd send my watercolor assignments to him after they were graded. He'd sell them, and that paid for my supplies and paper.

My junior year, I entered a piece in the A.W.S. show, and it was accepted. What a high!

What were your career prospects after graduation?

Every year, Hallmark would come around to the school and recruit graduates. In fact, my junior year, they tried to get me to come to Kansas City. Said they'd pay for the rest of my education, but I refused. I liked Columbus.

My senior year, I sent my portfolio to Hallmark, and was offered a spot. My mom was excited. Hallmark Cards! Everyone knows Hallmark! But I wasn't sure. I had about ten other job offers. Finally I flew out to Kansas City, and saw the facility. A lot of talent there. The art department was huge. Like a factory.

An important consideration for me was that I be able to continue painting. I asked the Hallmark people about that, and they said yes, that was fine. So I took the job. After a few months there, I began to feel that they were really not in favor of having their artists do things outside the structure.

How did you become aware of that?

There was this ad in *American Artist*, for a show in London with a two-thousand-dollar first prize. I thought, "Boy, it would be neat even to *hang* in London!" So I entered. Two or three months later I got a card saying I was accepted in the show. I was ecstatic! All my co-workers were excited. But my supervisor got jealous, and that's when the stuff really started happening.

Anyway, I only had three hundred dollars in the bank. I found it would cost me one hundred dollars to frame the picture, and another one hundred dollars to ship it. But I took the chance and sent it. And I won first prize!

Wow!

Two thousand dollars! That's when the jealousy really started snowballing. I entered a lot of shows that year. I won a thousand-dollar first prize at a show in New York. I won a thousand-dollar award in the National Watercolor Society competition. I was in A.W.S., and Rocky Mountain Watermedia, and a lot of others. But at Hallmark, after that, man, my career just went down. All of a sudden I couldn't do anything right. It

GRANDMOTHER
1987
ACRYLIC
14½" × 9½"
COLLECTION OF THE ARTIST

I was raised by my maternal grandmother. Her moral and spiritual influence gave me a sense of self-worth, pride and inner strength to pursue my dreams. In this small, frail body was a deep commitment to the well-being of family, always giving unconditionally, reinforcing love above all else.

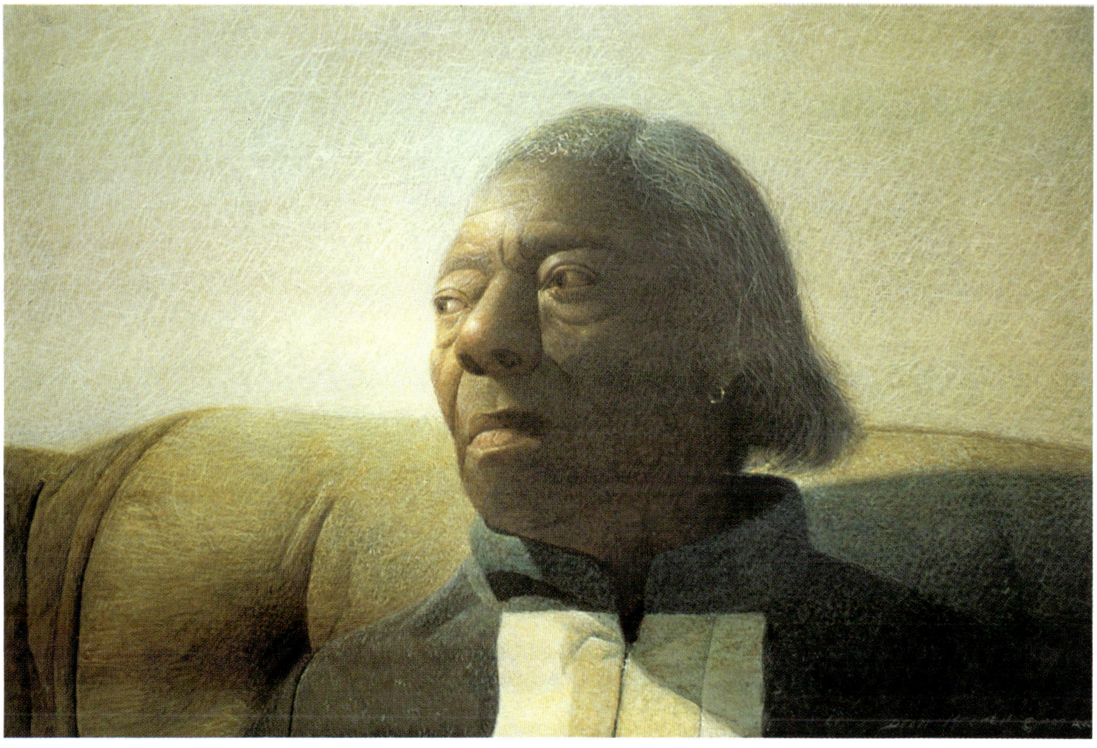

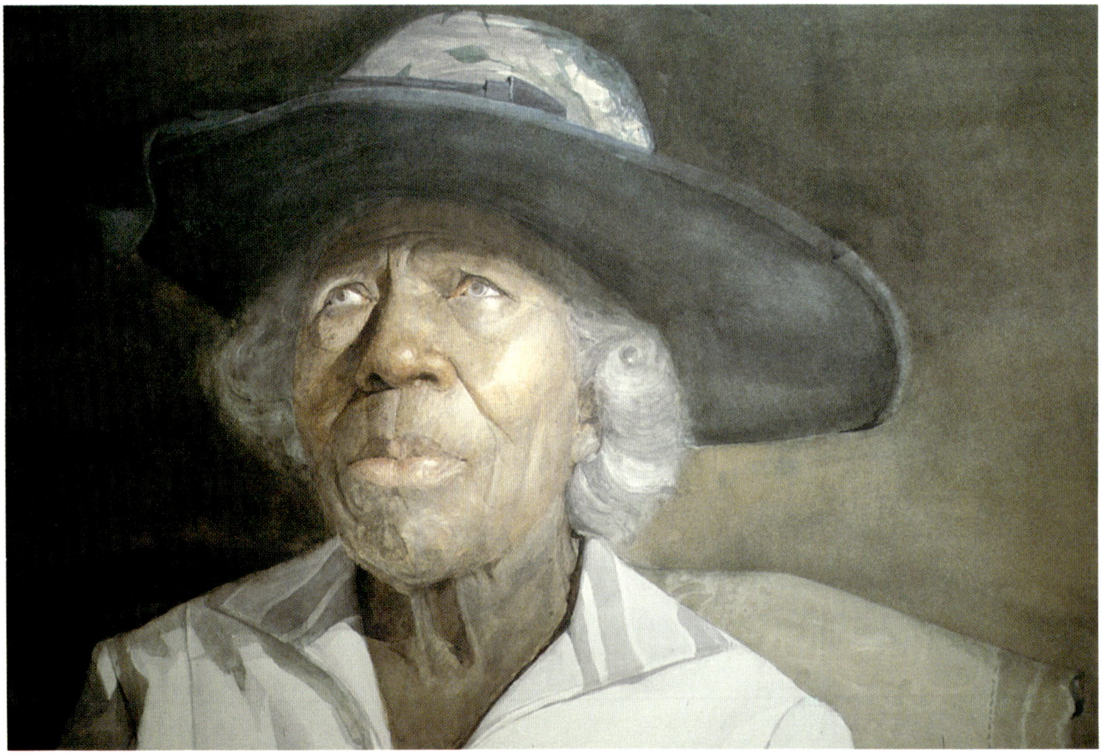

Keep Your Eyes on Jesus
1990
Watercolor
30″ × 22″
Collection of Mr. and Mrs. Jan Adams

Through these warm eyes the world has seen God. What a wonderful human being God has created in this, my Rowena.

was unbelievable!

I don't really understand that.

I think I was motivating the artists to start doing things outside the structure, and they didn't like that. Finally they said, "No more painting outside!" I just kept doing it, and they ended up firing me in November of 1983. I've been on my own ever since.

Let's focus on that breaking point in your life.

The firing was totally unexpected, and it devastated me. I had just gotten married, and had bought a new car. It was a rough time, and my marriage just fell apart.

Every artist who dreams of making the break from a paying job worries about this transitional time. You didn't even have time to plan for it. Describe how you handled it.

I went around to all the agencies and studios, but nobody wanted to hire me because I had been doing greeting cards for three years, not commercial art. And I didn't have any printed samples. Finally one agency guy said to me, "You've got to make up your mind if you want to be a fine artist or an illustrator." I thought about that and decided I wouldn't interview anybody else. I'd go forward on my own. So I went out and bought a copy of *Artist's Market* (North Light Books, Cincinnati, OH).

I contacted all the card companies, and hooked up with some of them. I began doing cards again, but this time for royalties. I did some freelance work to stay afloat.

Then I remembered a project some friends of mine had worked on for Anheuser-Busch. It was an ongoing series called "The Great Kings and Queens of Africa." I knew that if I could get that assignment, it would tide me over for three months. So I submitted slides, and I got the job.

Meantime, I began showing with a gallery in town called American Legacy. They insisted I keep my prices down. I worked about three months to put together my first show there. My work sold well, but I cleared all of nine hundred dollars, after commissions and framing.

After that, I raised my prices, but at the next show, things sold sporadically, which was really frustrating. What was I to do? I decided that I would start entering my best paintings—portraits mostly—in shows. I entered *every* show I could possibly enter. And I began winning!

Just going through* The Artist's Magazine *and* American Artist *every month?

Yes. It was amazing! Sometimes in the course of a month, I would win $5,000. I suddenly realized that I had a better chance of making a living competing for prizes than showing in all those galleries. I entered more and more shows. I kept winning.

People started seeing my name over and over. Someone from *The Artist's Magazine* saw my piece in the Rocky Mountain Watermedia show, and liked it, and I was featured in the magazine (February 1984, pages 46-51).

About that time, too, I got a call from American Legacy. They said, "We've got this mural job. It's 4 feet high, and 140 feet wide. It pays twenty-five thousand dollars. Are you interested?"

"When do they want it finished?"

"Seven weeks."

You're kidding!

That's what I said. But they told me I could give it a shot, or it would go to some guy in New Orleans. So I took the job. I don't know how I completed it on time, but I did. The subject was jazz. A lot of research.

You must have worked on it twenty-four hours a day!

During those seven weeks, I don't think I got more than three or four hours' sleep a night. I did it on fourteen four-by-eight-foot Masonite panels. When they delivered the masonite to the room they rented for me, I took one look and thought, "Were you out of your mind when you took this job, or what?" Anyway, they loved it, and it tided me over pretty well.

So between the mural and the competitions you were supporting yourself?

I was still with American Legacy Gallery, too.

At the N.W.S. show in Tucson, a woman saw my painting, thought it was stunning, and invited me to be in her gallery's "American Watercolor Invitational." I sent her two paintings, at two thousand dollars apiece, and she sold both of them! I thought, "Wow! I'm in!" And then she just up and decided she was going to get married, and closed the gallery! So I ended up going with Wolfe Galleries there. I'm still with them.

Tell me about "Art for the Parks."

A friend told me about this back in '86, when it started. I sent for the literature, and noticed that the Truman house was on the list. I thought, "Well, shoot! That's only about a half hour from me." So I did a painting of the Truman house, and won a bronze medal. I was ecstatic. And to top it off, a curator from the National Gallery saw it in the show, and suggested that the National Parks Academy purchase it for their permanent collection. Which they did.

The following year I entered four paintings again, and they accepted three. My painting of a soldier was a real favorite with the audience, but it didn't win.

Even before this, I was invited to the Hubbard Art Award for Excellence competition.

What exactly is that?

I had read about it in *American Artist*. You

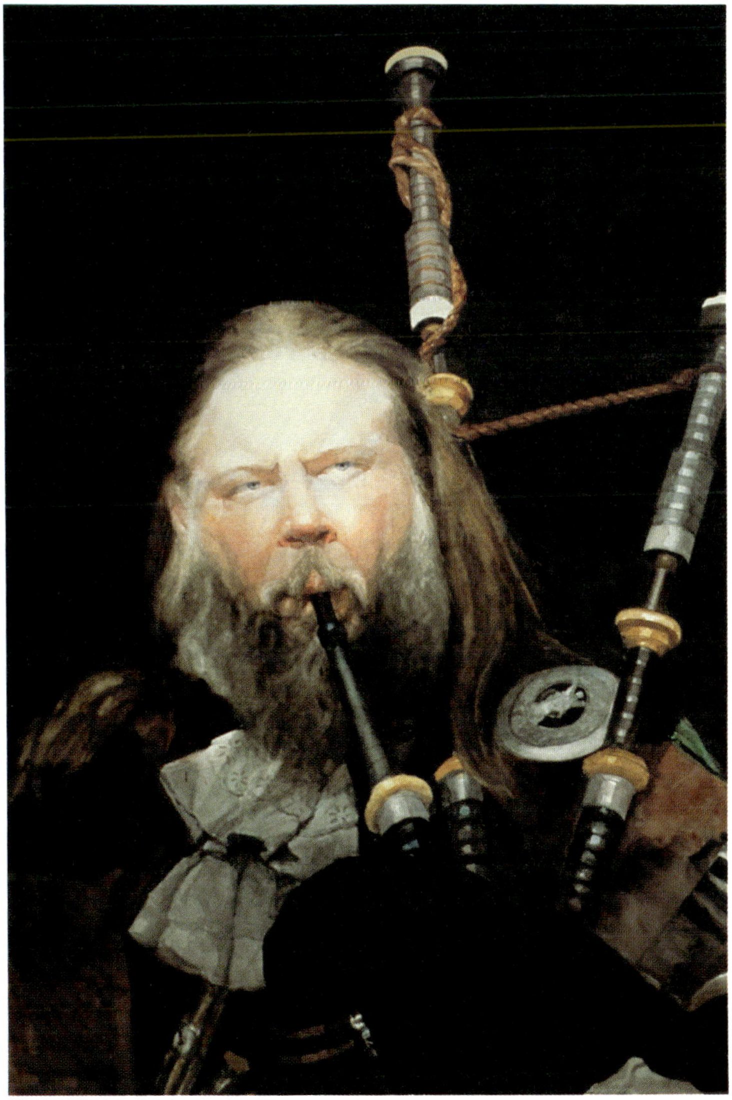

MIGHTY IS THE PIPER
1990
WATERCOLOR
20″ × 30″
COLLECTION OF MS. SHIRLEY BAKER

This painting gives us a sense of the old masters' use of light. It is a powerful display of energy, while keeping the focus on the piper and his pipes.

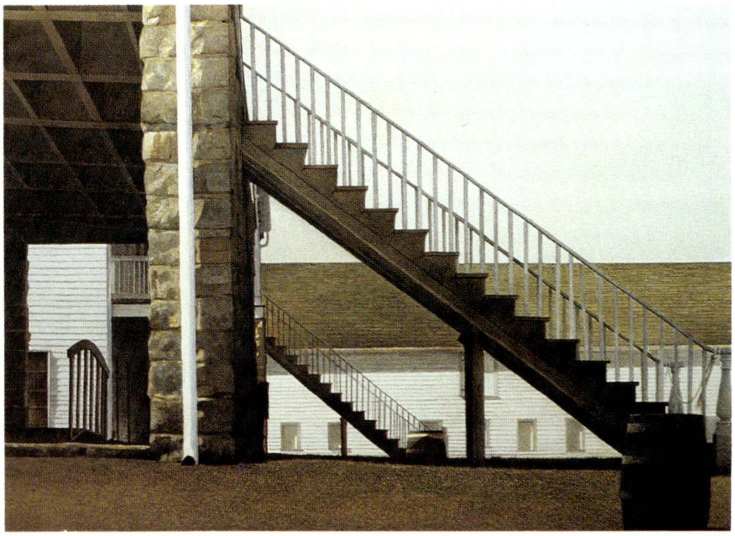

Fort Scott
1989
Watercolor
24″ × 18″
Collection of
Dave Usher,
Greenwich
Workshop

The fight for freedom and equality for all . . . this is the spirit I felt deeply present on the grounds of Civil-War-era Fort Scott, in Kansas. My wish is that it be a reminder to us all of the heavy cost that racism has exacted upon some of America's greatest lives.

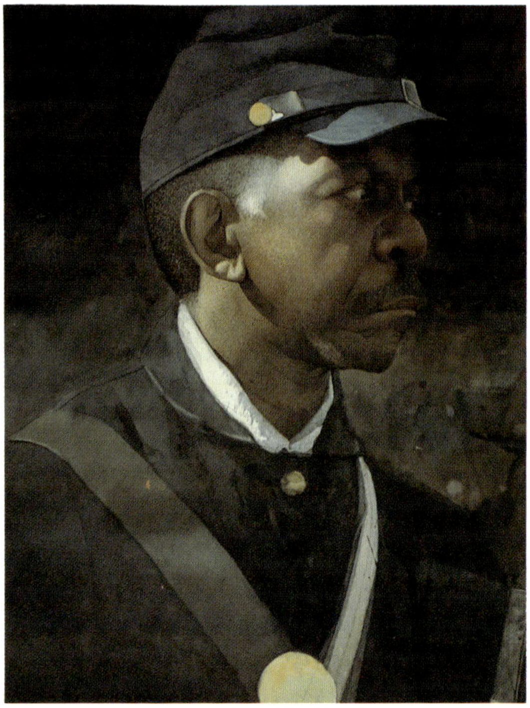

Fort Scott Soldier
1990
Watercolor
18″ × 24″
Collection of
Mr. Philip
Schneider

Kansas was the first of the free states to enroll Negro soldiers, and the first during the Civil War in which American Negroes were permitted to fight.

couldn't submit for it, but one day I got a call telling me I had been nominated. It seems they give a quarter-million-dollar top prize, based on that artist's contribution to the genre of American realism. Howard Terpning got the award last year. Artists like Jamie Wyeth, Henriette Wyeth, Gordon Snyder and Richard Schmid were nominated too.

Some pretty heady company!

Not only was I nominated, but I ended up in the top six! The painting I exhibited was of an elderly black woman. It was titled *Rowena.* The night of the opening, people bid on paintings they wanted. I didn't get a single bid. I wasn't surprised, because I've found that when I do a painting of a black figure, it doesn't usually sell.

The Hubbard family ended up buying my painting the next day. That evening, when the six finalists were announced, my painting received the biggest applause from the audience. People said, "Where were these people last night when the bidding was going on?"

The Hubbards came over afterward and said, "You got bigger applause than the person who won. Won't that make news!" And it did. That's my career up till now, in a nutshell.

While your focus has understandably been on the problems of the emerging black artist, I'm sure you'll agree that most aspiring professionals face many problems in common. Let's talk about how you approach them.

I've never let my career be in any one person's hands. Gallery, museum, whatever. Most artists sit around, thinking someone is going to come along and discover them. That's naive. I have always taken control. If nothing is going on, I make something happen.

How do you make things happen?

I send press releases to the local papers. I make sure that my name is in print as often as possible. When I win anything, I try to get extra catalogs, and I mail them to people who have bought my paintings. When the award list appears, I highlight my name on photocopies and send them to people who have bought my work. This is how to get known. People talk. Through word of mouth, your name gets around.

Do you maintain a mailing list?

That's a big part of my marketing. You can be gifted and have a wonderful product, but if you don't get the product out there and get people to look at it and be interested in it, they're going to bypass you.

Whenever I can, I talk about my work. Artists ask me, "How do you know what to say about your work?" It's easy. I'm emotionally involved with it. So when I talk about it, people feel the honesty there. What you say about your work can also intrigue viewers, because they feel they're getting a part of your life. And that's one

Dance With Me
1990
Watercolor
20″ × 30″
Collection of
Julie and George
Strecker

This painting of a festival dancer has a wonderful attitude of power and control. The way she grips her dress reminds me of the same attitude displayed in John Singer Sargent's El Jaleo *– adding to the power and performance of the dance.*

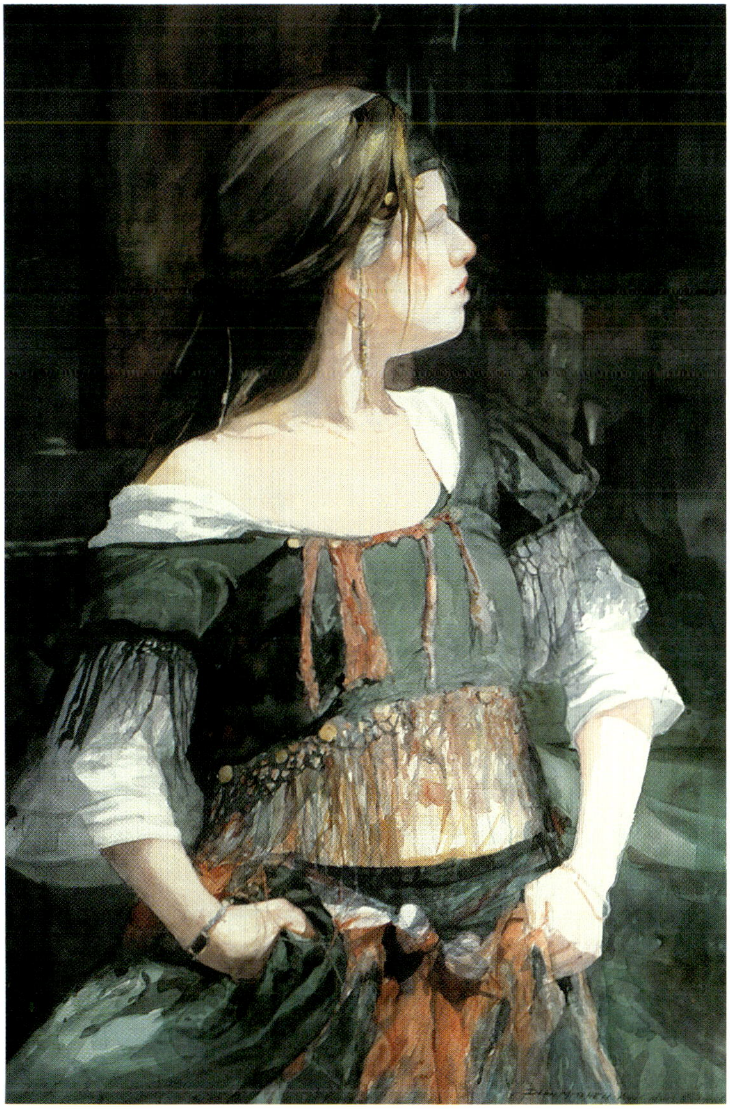

thing collectors like. They're not just buying an object; they're getting a part of you.

Another important point: Some artists paint something because it's going to sell. No no no! Terrible mistake. Don't do that. You'll end up painting something that you don't even want yourself. I figure if something doesn't sell, I'll hang it up and enjoy it myself.

What advice would you give artists embarking on their careers?

When I talk to young people, I always try to paint a realistic picture of the field. I don't try to discourage them. I only tell them my experiences. And experience varies for each person. I never try to tell them what they should do, because they'll come back and tell me, "You told me. . . . " No no no! You have to make your own decisions.

I tell them, "Don't compare yourself to me, or to anybody. It's not healthy. Everyone's career is going to take different turns, and the breaks will come at different times."

Don't say, "I'm going to do this or that by such-and-such date." Don't give yourself deadlines that will only frustrate you. The money may not come exactly when you want it to.

I lived in one room for a long time, with my drawing table, everything. Everybody else had big studios and spent every dime they earned. I pinched pennies so I could afford to enter more shows. I kept my overhead low. When I started building a financial base, I moved to a little larger place. A career is the sum total of many things, not just one thing that's going to make it take off like a rocket.

Don't lose patience. No matter how insignificant you think it is, each step is another stepping-stone. Some artists say, "I don't want to be fifty by the time I make it!" Let me tell you, there are people well in their fifties, who've been at it for years, still trying to get established.

You also have to have a sense of faith. You know, there are some people who can walk down a tunnel without a light. They can walk on their faith, and pretty soon they'll see a light. But there are others who will stand at the end of that tunnel and say, "Boy, it sure is dark in there. I don't know. . . . " Your whole life can go by while you're standing there saying, "I don't know." I've ventured down that tunnel in the dark. There are no magic answers. I've just felt my way as I've gone.

Any final thoughts on fine art as a way of life?

One thing that's kind of nice is that I have managed to do a lot of paintings of the people who have been very dear to me. They're not stars. They're just people. Like my grandmother. She works for wealthy people in this small Florida town. She's just a simple person, but she's been a very important force in my life. Through this gift the Lord has given me, and His blessings, people will know her. That's the nicest thing. To me, that's the ultimate success, when I can put these people on paper or canvas, and know that they will be remembered.

AUSTIN DEUEL

Paint 'Em, Pack 'Em and Peddle 'Em

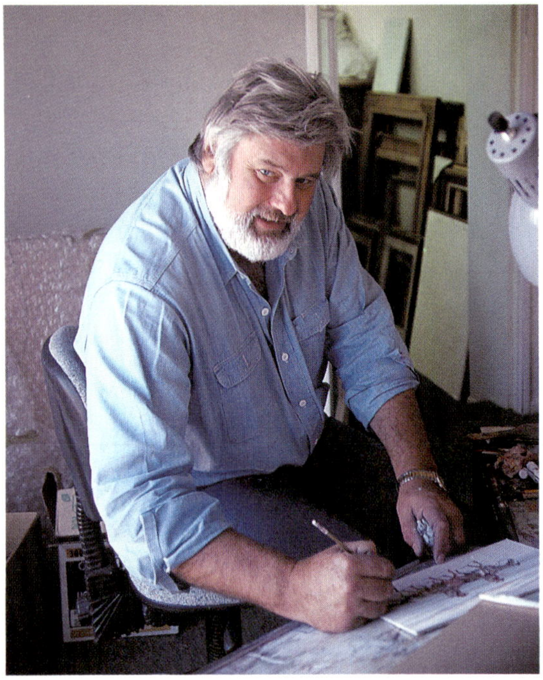

Austin Deuel, in his Scottsdale, Arizona, studio. Photo by Lew Lehrman.

A BIG MAN, AUSTIN DEUEL SEEMS TO FILL THE TINY STUDIO IN SCOTTSdale where he paints, as well as the cluttered office down the hall that is the base of his company, Desert Winds Press.

At times he works far into the night, preparing for some show or exhibition, completing work commissioned by a collector, or finishing art for a publisher of prints or cards. At other times, he'll pace the hallway of the small building, seemingly unable to settle in one place, being driven by his enormous, undisciplined energy.

Austin readily admits that he has a penchant for doing things the hard way. It often appears that, given the choice, he will opt for the more difficult (or more controversial) way every time.

I've known Austin for several years now, and have been fascinated by his unique views on life, and art, and the pursuit of both. Our interview lasted several hours one evening, and as I expected, he rambled widely—and wildly—from subject to subject.

When we were done, I knew I would have lots of editing work ahead of me. But I also knew that I had on my tape some ideas, and a viewpoint, that were unique to this one man.

I was born in '39 and grew up in Pittsburgh and Philadelphia, Pennsylvania; and Gary, Indiana. My dad was turn foreman on a rolling mill . . . a "mill hunkie." My environment, I would say, was not too attuned to art.

How did you get interested?

Mothers always showed you the other side of the coin. They wanted you to have culture, feelings, sensitivities. The male end of it was, "You've gotta be mean to live!" Those were the two worlds I grew up with.

I'd never heard of "art." But I could draw. The guys used to have me paint on their trucks, flame their valve covers, paint their jackets.

I took art in high school, but flunked it. I was a troublemaker. I was working as a butcher, had no use for the educational system, barely got through my junior year before they kicked me out.

Some time later, I decided I'd try to be an artist, and started night school for commercial art. Daytime, I worked for a department store, decorating windows. I was nineteen. It seemed the whole department was gay, and I became very confused and nervous about it. I lasted about ninety days. Finally I said, "If this is art, I'm never going to be an artist!" and left to join the Marine Corps.

Actually, the Corps is responsible for my being an artist today. I was in boot camp on Parris Island, and up on the bulkheads were all these posters and drawings, signed "Sgt. Tom Lovell." I admired the stuff and thought, "He's a Marine. He's all right!" Six months later, I finished my active duty, and went home to Pennsylvania. When I told Dad I planned to work in the mills, he put three hundred dollars on the kitchen table and said, "You have a choice. You can go to California with this three hundred dollars, or I'll take you out in the backyard and beat you up."

So I went to California, met Charrie, got married, had a couple of kids, and worked my way through the factories. Wound up as a bill collector with a finance company for three and a half years.

I was twenty-five, and restless, and didn't know why. My parents had moved to San Diego by then, and Dad was selling real estate. I mentioned to him that I had started drawing again, and he told me about some artist who had a gallery in Lake San Marcos, just starting off. He was looking for a partner to run the place.

I had nine hundred dollars in a savings account. I quit my job, moved down there, bought a house, and went into his business. Ramone's Gallery. Only his work. Cement floor, unpainted Sheetrock walls. I put my money in, and he split! Left me with fourteen paintings. I had two hundred dollars, a family and a house. I couldn't paint. I didn't even know an artist!

Sounds like a sure formula for disaster!

Well, I remembered a story my dad had told me, about a man he'd met who claimed to be the nation's top can-vending-machine expert. Dad asked him how long he'd been doing it. He said, "Four weeks!"

Dad laughed. "How could that be?"

"I've been across the country three times in the past four weeks. I've put coins into every machine in every airport, every bus station. I know their problems, their bad points and their good points. No president of any of these vending companies has done that." That story stuck with me.

I got in my truck and started driving: Scottsdale, Santa Fe, Pasadena, Hollywood, Beverly Hills. And the first place I'd go to in each town was the art supply store. They'd always tell me who the most successful galleries were. I'd go to each, pick out their stars, and ask where I could find them. Naturally they wouldn't tell me, but I was an old bill collector, so I knew how to find people. I went after the artists I enjoyed most. And I got them.

After a while, I got a feel for what I was doing. I had seen all the best galleries, so I built a new 3,500-square-foot gallery that was just gorgeous! I ran big shows. Had an annual invitational that drew more than thirty thousand people. Showed all those artists that now sell at $150,000 and up.

But what does this have to do with your own painting?

Well, I'm getting to that. It seemed the artists I went to never had any paintings. They were always very busy. So the only way I could get work out of them was to go sit in their studios all night

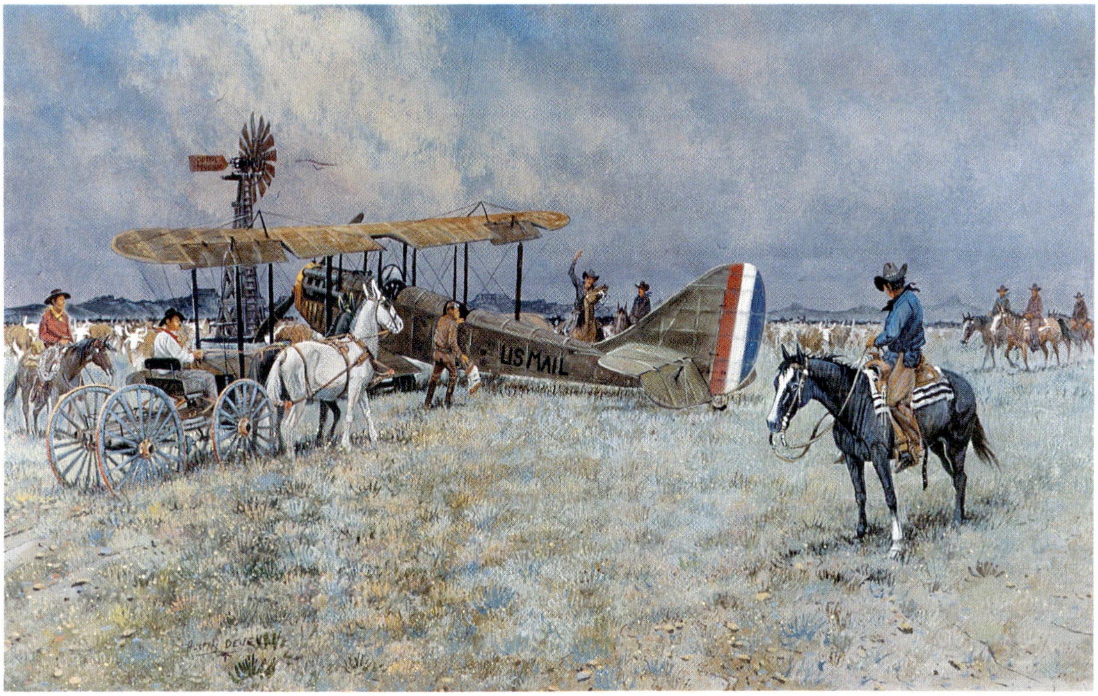

Mail Call, West Texas
1990
Dry-brush watercolor
40″ × 24″
Collection of the artist

I've driven a lot through west Texas, doing the shows, and this painting is an idea that occurred to me during one of those trips. The time is the twenties, in the Fort Stockton area, when the mail was delivered by air to the big ranches in the area.

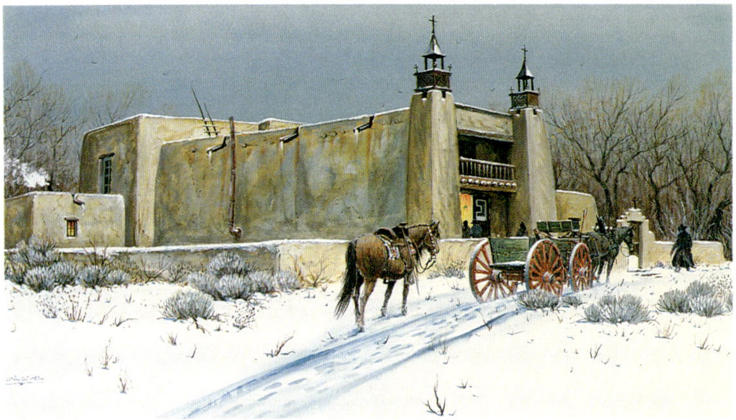

Las Trampas
1990
Dry-brush watercolor
36″ × 22″
Collection of The Gold Coast Casino, Las Vegas, NV

Las Trampas is a very famous mission along the back road to Taos, New Mexico. I've painted it frequently. A classic Santa Fe scene.

and watch them while they painted.

Frank Hamilton was king at that time. He sold as fast as he painted. He was a night painter, working from two in the afternoon to four in the morning. My way of getting paintings was to close my gallery, go to Frank's and stay up all night with him.

After a while, I said, "If I'm going to stand here and wait for paintings, I might as well grab a brush and learn." I spent seven years studying with him, and he was the best teacher I ever had. Taught me everything about painting. He was the only artist I ever met who knew why a painting sells. And he was absolutely right! I've passed that along to all my students.

What does make a painting sell?

Three things have to be in every painting.

One: Tell a story. Like that Andrew Wyeth painting. A water pump, a board, and an old bucket. That bucket is the story. Because that puts the human touch to it. They'd been there, left something. Smoke out of a chimney, light in a window. That kind of thing.

Two: Create a dramatic mood. Fog. Snow. Rain. Sunset. Even the heat of day with all the shadows burned out.

Three: Dramatic composition. Every painting has to have a strong vertical in it. Now everyone will argue with me on this, but you can go back in history, and every artist from Michelangelo to Tiepolo . . . they all used strong verticals. It's what draws you across the room, and it has nothing to do with style or subject. I've spent more than twenty years in the game, and every time I've gone outside the bounds of Frank's formula, I find he's right.

Let's get back to your gallery.

So I have the gallery, and I'm learning to paint with Frank, and I have the greatest learning material hanging right on my walls. Absorbing it all.

When I finally felt ready to show my own paintings, I went into the Death Valley '49ers show. I sold out that first year. But at that show, some gal came up to me and asked me how I'd like to be a combat artist for the Navy. Without saying anything at home, I followed up the lead she gave me. Very quickly I found out that the Navy saw me as a civilian, and wouldn't send me anywhere near where the action was.

But I was an ex-Marine. I stopped in at Camp Pendleton and said, "You guys need a combat artist?" They sent my stuff through to Washington, and I got approved. So I went down to San Diego and rejoined the Marines. I still hadn't told my wife. When I got my orders, I finally announced it to Charrie and the kids. At first she didn't believe me, and then we had a couple of days of this and that . . . but that's the way it was. I lined up a friend, Steve Scott, to run the gallery. Charrie, of course, would help. Off I went to Vietnam.

That was the first time the Marines had ever sent an artist into combat. It was '67, and nobody had any real opinion on the war yet. But we had just started taking heavy casualties, coming up to the Tet offensive. I was in two of the first major battles, and I became totally bizarre on the war. I just couldn't believe they were allowing this to happen. I went over as a hawk, and came back three and a half months later an avid dove.

As a combat artist, and, incidentally, a body guard for the press corps, I had a high media profile. When I came home I unloaded in the *L.A. Times* and *San Diego Union*. There was even a TV special on me.

But why had you taken this route in the first place?

Outside of my normal curiosity, I was going over there to become nationally known. I was going to put my gallery on the world map. This is what I thought was going to happen. It just shows how far I was willing to go.

You placed a pretty high value on promotion,

didn't you?

That's another lesson I had to learn the hard way. Every artist says, "I've got to be promoted!" So when he goes into a gallery, he doesn't ask what they sell. He asks, "How are you going to promote me?" He wants an ad. He wants to be in the art magazines. And that's nonsense!

What should he be asking?

He should be asking how many paintings the gallery sells. If they're paying you for twelve paintings they sell for you every month, that means a lot more than having a big ad, while they only sell three.

I had tons of publicity. I hired one of the best media artists in the business. I staged a showing of the Marine Corps Combat Art Collection at my gallery about that time. Had major "Walter Cronkite" coverage. Tens of thousands of people came to see it. Had hours of TV coverage. All the major shows. And there were absolutely no results!

What supported the gallery was my painting, surprisingly enough. That's how I lasted as long as I did. In 1971, the gallery hit the mountain, and I ended up coming to Scottsdale.

I thought you were doing well. What happened?

California is still an enigma. It's a place to go to buy art, not to sell it. I just couldn't sell enough to survive. Finally, I couldn't go on. Everything collapsed. My gallery, my marriage. I stayed around for about six weeks, then left for Scottsdale with my son, Sam, who was eight.

Why Scottsdale?

All I had was twenty dollars. I couldn't get any farther. Sam and I lived in an old army ambulance. I'd go to bars and hustle paintings for twenty dollars. Gradually one thing led to another, I got into a gallery, and things started to happen.

The art system in Scottsdale was as incredibly great as the system in California was bad. I went from army ambulance to substantial income, and a new life.

Tell me about your Vietnam memorial.

In '86, I did a Vietnam war memorial for San Antonio, Texas. It's the largest since the Iwo Jima monument.

You can't believe the publicity I got. Every sculptor thinks if he gets one commission like

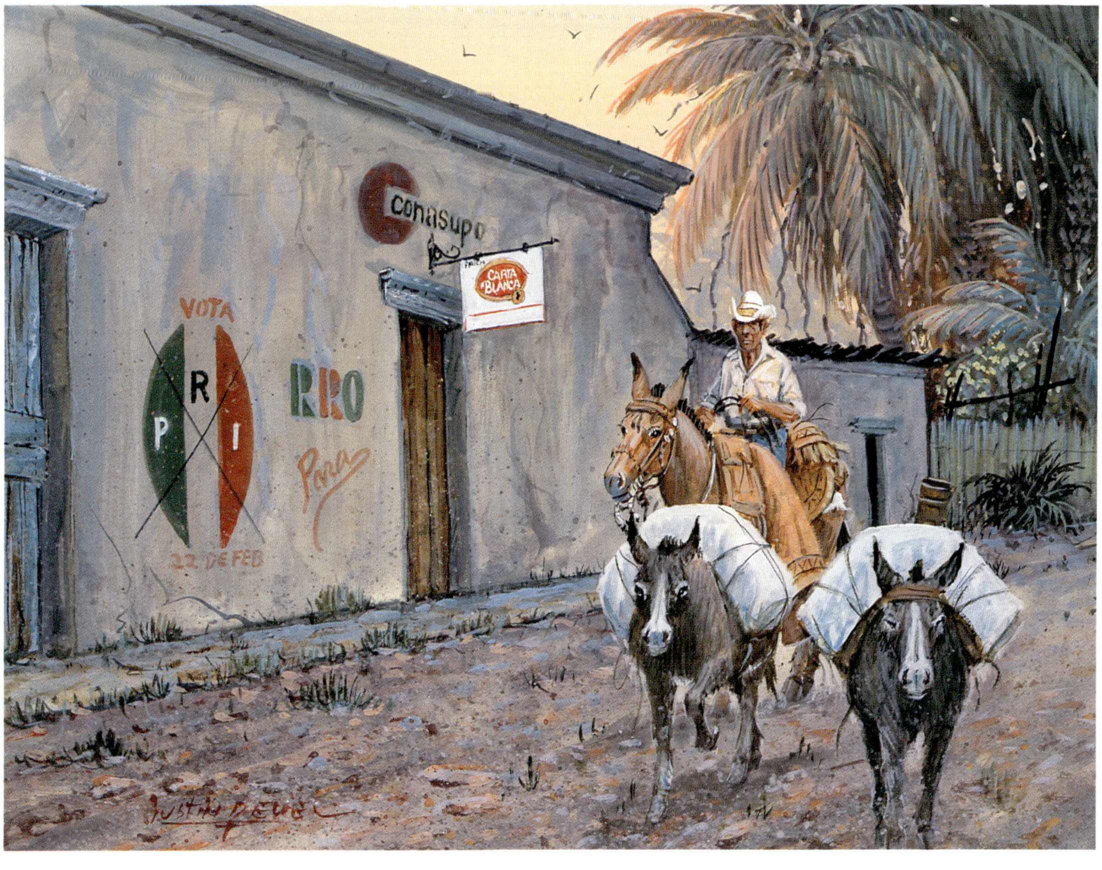

SAN IGNACIO
1990
DRY-BRUSH WATERCOLOR
15″ × 11″
COLLECTION OF THE GOLD COAST CASINO, LAS VEGAS, NV

A quaint mission town of about 2,500, this village in the center of the Baja is one of my favorite places.

Moving Out
1982
Oil on canvas
30″ × 40″
Collection of Trinity University, San Antonio, TX

This painting appears in my book, Cañon de los Artistas, *in which I detail my exploration of this remote area of Baja, California. Deep in this special land, I became one of the few Westerners to see the incredible cave paintings, painted some eight to nine centuries ago.*

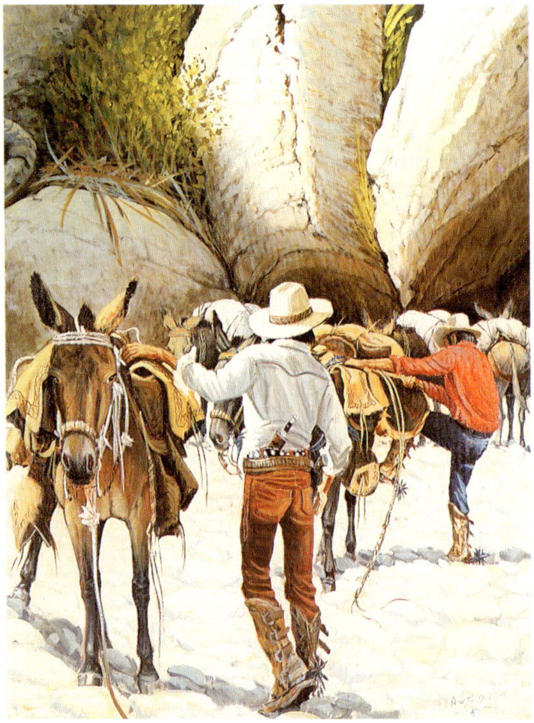

that, he'll be busy the rest of his life. Nonsense! A painting on a wall in somebody's house does you more sales good than a ton of promotion or an ad in *Southwest Art*. That's your best advertisement. Word of mouth.

What do you see as the role of the artist today?

We're a service. Like a mechanic. We have a job to do. We're here to communicate: Causes. Reasons. Whatever. And we can't disregard that.

I'm talking about those artists today who totally poo-pooh the public. "If you can't understand my work, you're just not educated!"

Not true! We need the public not only for our own personal growth, our own egotism, but to communicate with. If we totally turn them off, they're not going to listen.

Tell me about your books.

Writing is another medium. Another outlet. My first book was *Cañon De Los Artistas* (1987, Desert Winds Press, Scottsdale, AZ). It is about my travels in the Baja, to a place so remote that when I first went, not six hundred Anglos had ever been there. I was very protective of it. But *National Geographic* exposed it, so I wrote the book. *Even God Is Against Us* (1989, Desert Winds Press) is about my experiences in Vietnam. The paintings are real events. It's not only to share my experiences, but to prevent their ever happening again. Now I'm finishing *The 20th Century Art Warrior*. In a humorous way, it's about being an artist at this time in history. My Alaska book should be finished soon.

Let's get back to living as an artist. It looks like you've seen it all, from bottom to top, and back again. What can you tell artists who'd like to make a living at it?

The most important thing is to have guts. Guys with talent but no guts never make it.

Define "guts."

Desire. A fanatical desire. But that's true of any trade. Real estate, or whatever.

Another important thing: You have to show up! Keep that energy going. If you sit, you're dead. You just keep moving, and doing.

Tell me about your way of selling art.

Marketing in art is a fact of life. It's exposure. And you have to get off your butt and drive. I drive thousands of miles, do auctions, sales, try to be everywhere I can. I call it "the three P's": Paint 'em, pack 'em and peddle 'em. Even the big boys work that way.

You've obviously done many of these shows over the years.

I did the malls, came up through the system. An artist, just beginning, should do the malls. It's the greatest training ground in the world for artists. In fact, the shopping center is the most important thing that's happened for the artist in the past five hundred years, other than the camera. It allows the artist freedom in spite of the system. Artists have only been free for about three hundred years. The gallery system is only a couple of hundred years old. Before that, art was controlled by the kings, the royalty.

Today, the artist is the mountain man of the twentieth century. He has to live by his wits.

Did you have a school? Or teach in one?

Nah. I'm not a teacher. I've never charged for my art lessons. The guy who taught me never charged me. But he said, "Pass this along." And I do. I never taught what to paint. What I taught was how to think. That's very important. And the discipline. Artists don't take days off.

I used to tell my students that you have to do a thousand paintings before you're an artist. Think about it. When you've done a thousand paintings, who can say you're not an artist? Beating your brains out for days on one painting isn't going to do it. It's going on to the next one, and putting in that mileage.

Another thing: Don't paint at home. You've got to have a professional place to go. I don't care how messy, or where it is. Because that's part of what makes you a pro.

The other is to learn to paint under pressure. House payments are behind, the kids are sick—most guys fall apart. Performance under pressure. That's the difference between a professional and an amateur.

You have to learn to paint under social pressures: "Why don't you get a job?" "Why don't you wait until your art starts selling?"

Well, how are you going to sell until you've put in the mileage? This is not a game you can walk out great at. You have to begin selling things for thirty-five or forty dollars, bringing in some income. Then it's just that you're not making enough.

What would you say is most important for a beginning professional?

Express your own experience. Take Poe and Hemingway. Poe was a sickly person, and wrote of the experiences in his mind. Hemingway lived his art.

N.C. Wyeth went out West, was in bar fights, brothels. The excitement in his paintings is from life experience.

Andrew Wyeth's consciousness was bounded by Chadd's Ford and Maine, the only two places he had ever been. That's what makes his work so magnificent. He saw corners of life in a way that people who are living life haven't got time to see. That's what an artist has to do. Express his own personal experience, whatever it may be.

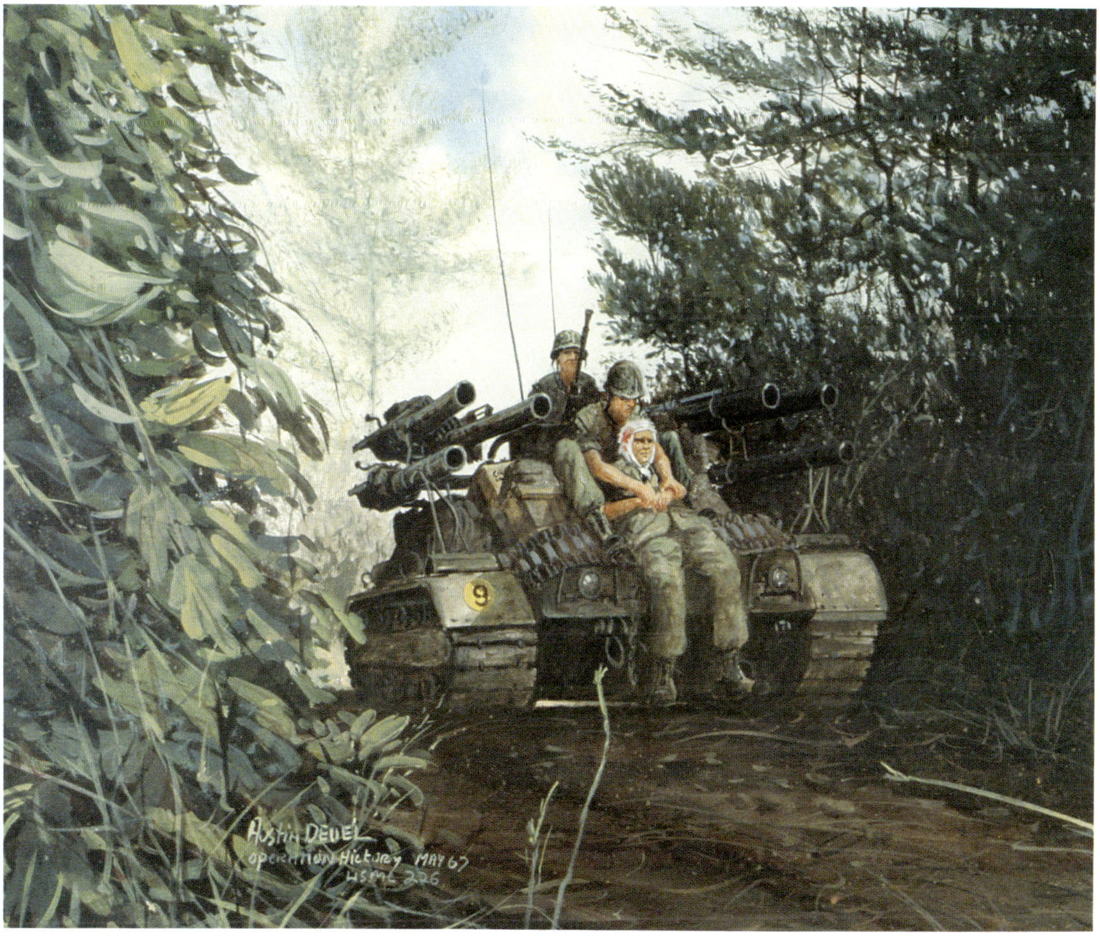

OPERATION CROCKETT
1982
DRY-BRUSH WATERCOLOR
22″ × 18″
COLLECTION OF THE ARTIST

I did this painting for a Vietnam show that was held at the Lyndon Baines Johnson Library, in Johnson City, Texas. Operation Crockett was a Marine Corps operation, the first invasion of the D.M.Z., by the 226th Marine Batallion. It took place in May of 1967. The memories of that era are still clear in my mind.

BETTY LOU SCHLEMM
Never Give Up on Yourself

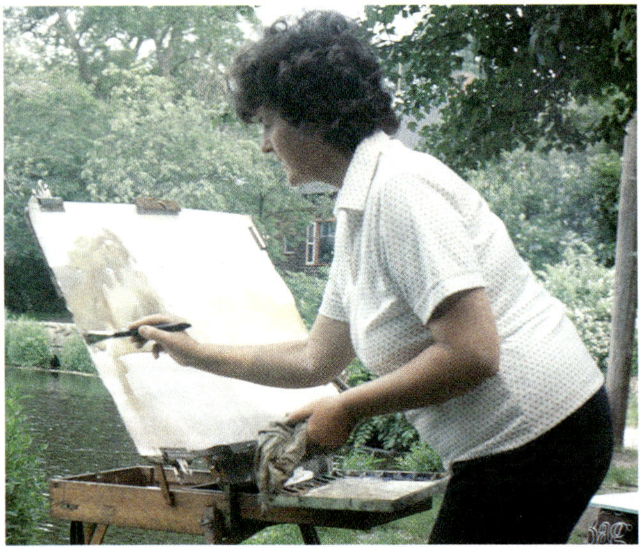

Betty Lou Schlemm at work. Photo by Lew Lehrman.

ROCKPORT, MASSACHUSETTS IS A PLEASANT OLD SEAFARING VILlage located somewhat north of Boston on historic Cape Ann. Its attraction for artists, plus a steady flow of tourists to keep their work moving, make it a sort of art capital for this part of New England.

I arrived at the home and studio of Betty Lou Schlemm on a warm, sun-sparkled morning in late summer, to be welcomed by the artist and her three dogs. After introductions all around, and a brief tour of her painting- and book-filled home, we settled in her kitchen, where, over glasses of orange juice, we began our conversation.

Art? It was always there . . . since I was a little kid in New Jersey. When I was eight years old, I'd paint pictures, get on my bike, and peddle them to the neighbors for twenty-five or fifty cents. By the time I was in high school, I was very serious about art, and just wanted to get out into the field. But I had to wake up to reality, so I went to New York Phoenix School of Design (it's part of Pratt Institute now), and studied commercial art. It was the early fifties, and, at the time, I didn't think they were very good at commercial art, because they constantly kept me working with the figure.

I was broke most of the time at Phoenix. I remember we'd go for the five-cent coffee at the White Tower every morning and afternoon. When it went to ten cents, we'd only have coffee in the morning, because none of us had the extra ten cents. I was living at home in New Jersey, working weekends to make a little money, and commuting to New York all week. I got very sick, so I decided I had to live in Manhattan. I moved into a girls' residence club, and had my cereal with water in it, and walked thirty blocks to school. I don't like to talk about those days, because nobody would believe them.

After three years, a whole bunch of us quit school. We thought we knew everything. It was a bad mistake, because in that last year I would have studied portraiture. I'm still trying to make up for it.

Anyway, I moved back home to New Jersey, and got the first in a series of jobs in advertising. I got fired from just about every one.

Finally, I quit a job that paid me one hundred dollars a week, which was good money in those days, to take a job at Norcross in Manhattan at thirty-five dollars. I really wanted to be around artists. Everyone there was a painter. We did greeting cards. I couldn't wait to get to work in the morning. I'd come in early, and look forward to lunch hours when we'd go running around looking at gallery shows. We'd put up our own shows in the hallways. That was the art world for me. That's how it started. I was twenty-four, and painting all the time.

Well, one day, the whole group was talking about summer vacations, and going painting with Ed Whitney. I really couldn't imagine spending my summer vacation painting all the time, but everyone was going, so I went, too. I never could do watercolor. I flunked it in school. I couldn't do it at all. But I followed Ed Whitney's demonstrations exactly as he did them, and

Mother and Child
1980
Watercolor
22" × 30"
Collection of the artist

I tried to show the great love between mother and child by their position. The child is holding the mother with his hands and his feet in center stage. The mother's head, placed less importantly, gives strength to the child. A great diagonal, from upper left to lower right, ties this painting together.

I was on my way. I saw how, and then I could paint. At the end of the week, Ed said, "You know, you could become an artist." That week changed my life.

I stayed with Ed for six years, going from New Jersey to Douglaston, Long Island every week. Lots of people from Norcross would go. I wasn't earning much, so Ed gave me the job of picking people up, and then I didn't have to pay. To buy supplies, I'd do little jobs, like cutting mats for the other artists.

About that time I started to exhibit in the Greenwich Village art shows, and won some scholarships. It was an exciting time. I was doing well with the shows. The art bug had bit, and I was determined to make it on my own, so I left Norcross. That was a very rough period for me. I couldn't make enough money to live on. I just wasn't ready, so I ended up going back to Norcross for another year.

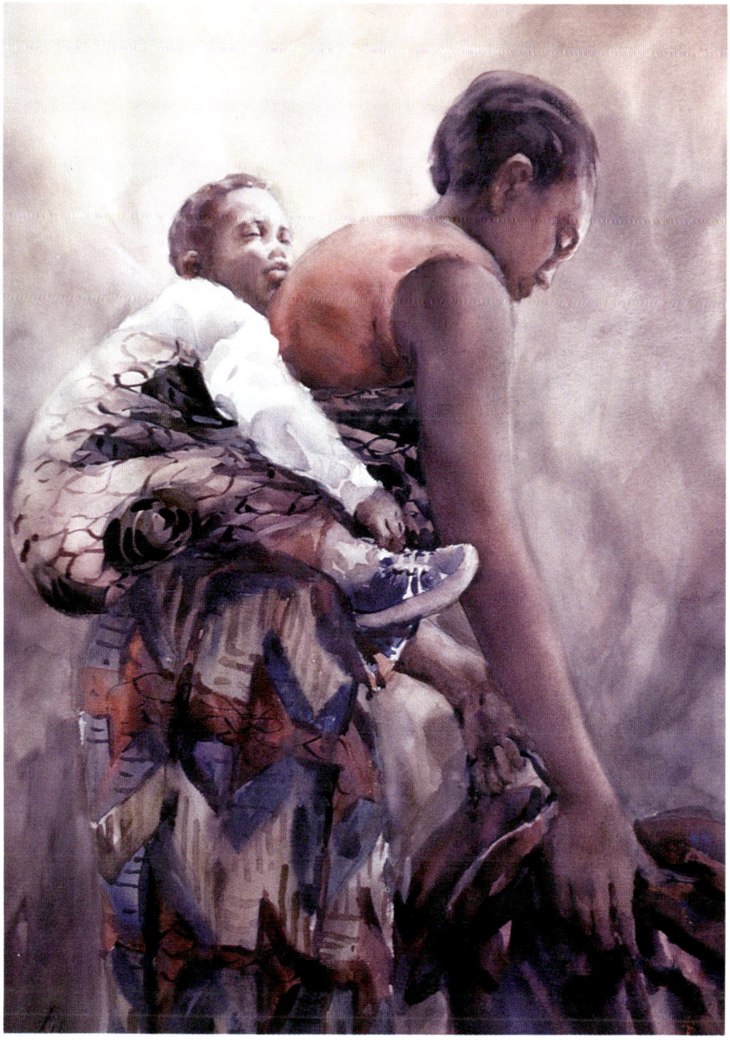

Tell me about that final break from Norcross.

In 1961 I was twenty-seven, and I had taken a trip across country. I stopped at Rockport. I think everybody eventually finds where they belong, and this was it. I just kept coming back. I'd go home to New Jersey, and then the next week I'd be right back.

Finally I rented an apartment here. It wasn't even finished, and the bathroom was downstairs. To take a shower, I had to go to a friend's house. For almost a year, I had no furniture. Slept on a mattress on the floor, and traded paintings for furniture. . . . Food, too. I had two dogs. My landlord, who owned the market, used to give me ribs for them. He'd leave a lot of meat on the bones, so I'd cook them, keeping the meat for myself and loading the pot with vegetables, mostly celery. I called it celery soup, and for about a year I lived on that.

What did you do for income during that time?

When I got here, I did everything I could to make a little money. I cut mats for the local frame shop. I did all the outdoor shows. The Greenwich Village show ran five weeks every summer. There were only about four hundred artists, all painters. It was a wonderful show. You had to be juried in. Artists would come from all over the world to show there.

Did you travel around to do shows too?

For two winters I went down to New Orleans and sold my paintings in Pirate's Alley. The New Rochelle show was big. Atlantic City was big, too. They were my only real travel. I stayed mostly in the Northeast. That's where the big shows were. But when I was here a while, I developed an eye problem. I found I could no longer drive the car or do the shows. So I decided to start teaching to supplement my income.

How did you make the transition into teaching?

Paul Strisik was one of the first to help me when I decided to teach. He gave me about forty chairs, so I could do demonstrations. Don Stone told all his students to come study with me. Everybody in this town just backed me all the way.

I started by setting up still lifes. They're a basic. You have to be organized and learn to

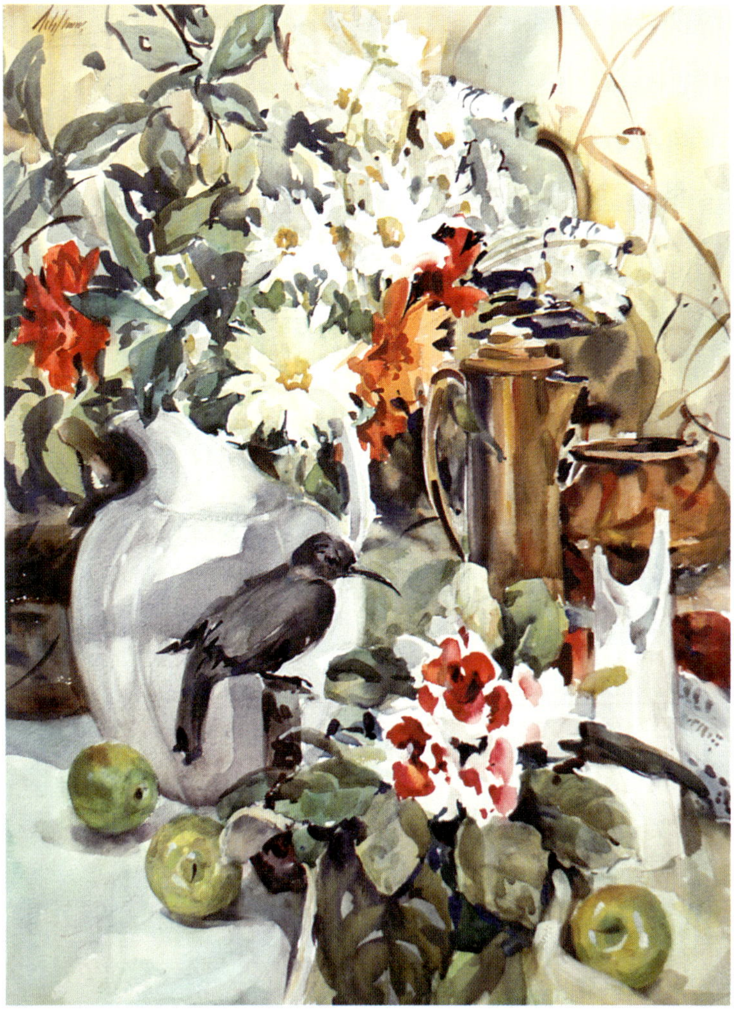

STILL LIFE WITH BIRD
1991
WATERCOLOR
22″ × 30″
COLLECTION OF THE ARTIST

This old bird had been in a fire somewhere. I placed it on the left golden section, both horizontally and vertically, to give it importance. I quickly declared center with the large leaf at the bottom, creating an anchor for the painting.

draw. I wanted to *stress* drawing. Anyway, I'd set up this still life, and nobody'd come. It must have gone on for a year, before I signed up one student. I got all my friends to come to class, to make it look like I had a group. Little by little, people started to come, and I began one-week workshops. Eventually I was busy all summer.

After I was teaching for a few years, Don Holden, who was editor for Watson-Guptill, saw my work and wanted me to write a book. At first, he wanted it to be a flower-painting book, but my ideas didn't fit into that. Eventually, Don wrote to tell me he'd been thinking about everything I had to say, and it all seemed to deal with light. He came up with the title *Painting With Light* (1978, Watson-Guptill, New York).

I couldn't begin to write a book myself, so Don asked me to do it together with Charles Movalli. I didn't know Charlie, but met him on the beach while walking my dogs. It took us a year, just sitting here like this, talking and demonstrating. I had an inexpensive camera, and he bought a book on how to take pictures. It was great fun, and we've been wonderful friends ever since. The book's still in print, and it's used in colleges as a text. It's even been published in Japanese.

Was the book a help with getting students?

By the time the book came out, all my classes were filled. But suddenly it expanded things. I was asked to teach in other places. Robert Wade, an Australian artist, found my book in a Singapore bookshop, and called to invite me to Australia. I was the first American they had invited. The book also resulted in other invitations from around the United States.

It took you a long time, didn't it, to establish yourself as a professional?

It was a very slow process, and it's still going on. At first, nobody knows who you are. So you have to be there, and visible, and selling your work. Slowly, it starts to come together. You sell a painting. It hangs in someone's home, and then someone else sees it there and wants to meet you. That's how it begins.

Let's go back to your earlier days in art. How did that progress?

I knew I had a lot lacking. I was a hit-and-miss painter. I didn't like experimenting. I loved the world as it was. But then I got hold of a book on John Singer Sargent and his watercolors. And that was the second big change in my life. Someone had asked me why I didn't "paint the day," and I couldn't. I didn't know how. I didn't have a clue. The Sargent book showed me what I should be doing. And once I got that truth into my painting I could extend it, or change it, or subdue it, or do anything. Sargent was my hero, and he still is.

Then there was this big Cezanne show in New York. I used to brag that I didn't like Cezanne. But I was going to the show, so I decided to read up on him. That show was another breakthrough for me. Suddenly I knew how to handle surface. I learned color composition looking at Cezanne's works. Now I love Cezanne!

Garden Statue
1985
Watercolor
22"×30"
Collection of the artist

I did this painting a long time ago, when I first became aware of the space arrangements in a painting. I divided the paper into two vertical golden sections—one with the statue on the line of the left section. The green leaves fill the other section, right up to the line, but not using it.

One day Charles Movalli and I went to have breakfast with George Faddis, a Rockport artist who has since passed away. He was a great teacher, and had been a museum director. When we left him, we were excited at all the knowledge he had that we didn't have. Here I was, a professional painter, and I didn't even know what he was talking about! I was chairman of education for Rockport Art Association, so I begged George to do some lectures. He talked on art history, and how paintings were knit together. But even with his slides, I couldn't see how. One day I asked him to show me. He took out the great masterpieces and put tracing paper over them, and in one evening he showed me all about dynamic symmetry. All of a sudden I could begin to express my emotions in paint.

Then I had the biggest breakthrough of all. A giant step. I went to Frank Stella's lectures on "Working Space" at Harvard. It was 1983. It was like heaven opened up. I just learned everything. I learned how to move color back and forth. I remember when he showed the Kandinsky slides, I said out loud in the hall, "I see it!" And when he was showing Titian's *The Flaying of Marsyas*, I had to bury my head. It was so powerful, because all of the artist's emotions were right there. I've been teaching Frank Stella's lessons ever since.

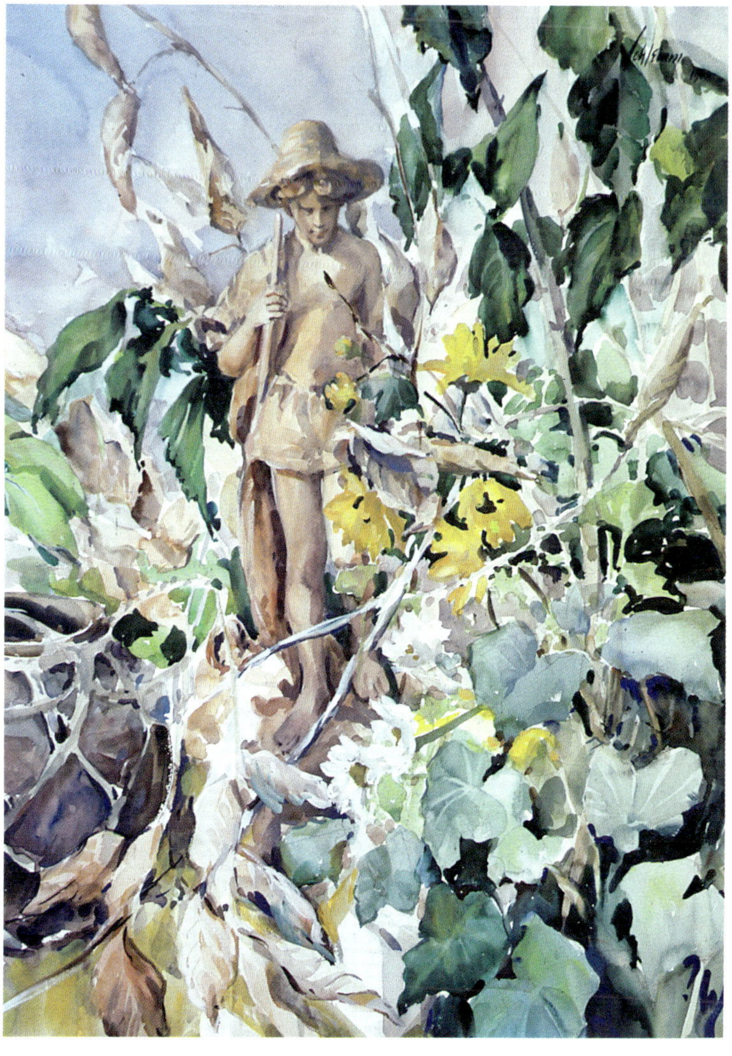

Do you try to paint every day?

Yes, but I don't. I seem to work in spurts. Once I get going, though, nothing else matters. I'll paint like crazy for a couple of weeks and let things go to pot. Then I have to pick up my life again. That's when the thinking goes on. I have to get charged up, and then let go. There's never a day when I'm not thinking about painting.

How did you price your work, as you were becoming established?

Pricing was never a problem. I would look at my painting and decide whether I'd rather have this much money or the painting. As soon as it was balanced, I had my price. I still sell my paintings for very little. I decided at one point that I didn't want to be the biggest collector of my own work. But if I turn out a really good painting, I won't sell it for anything—that is, until I can do a couple more that I like as much. I go through very dry periods, and I need them to look at and carry me through. I always feel the good paintings are yet to come.

Was there a person in your life who was particularly helpful in your career?

Really, there were two. One was my father. I don't know what I would have done without him. The other was Ed Whitney. I always say I've had two fathers: Ed Whitney and my father. I owe so much to them both.

My parents used to live in New Jersey and they'd come here in the summer. After my mother died, Dad moved up. I had my own gallery on Bearskin Neck (a popular Rockport tourist shopping area) from 1964 to 1985. He took it over, and made something out of it. Even way before that, Dad would show up on the weekends, and put everything up, and sell for me at the outdoor art shows in Greenwich Village. I couldn't sell my own paintings. I just wasn't

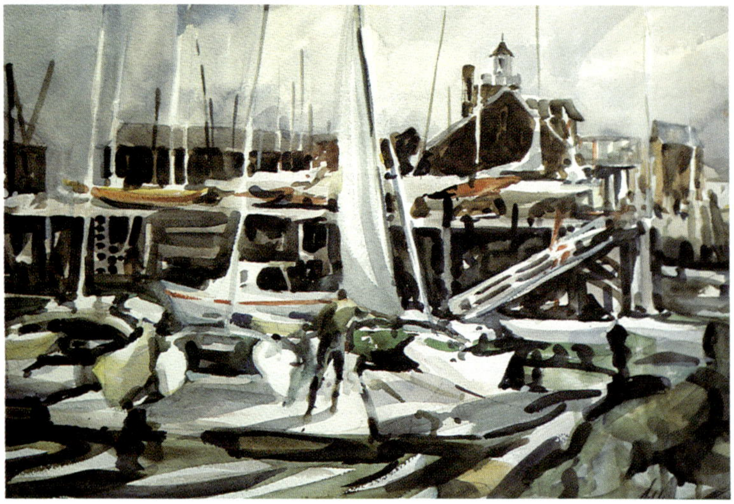

SANDY BAY YACHT CLUB
1986
WATERCOLOR
15″ × 22″

I started this painting by putting the figures lower on the paper, so the sails would appear high. The figures lead downward to the boat, as do the light patterns on the left. At the boat, the directions change and rise upward with the sails in two diagonals, which give a sense of movement.

interested, I guess.

Your father set you on the track, didn't he?

I remember, even when I was twelve, trying to sell those little paintings, he would tell me, "It doesn't matter how much money you get. Give a little to your mother, put a little in the bank, and then do what you want with the rest." I do that to this day. Even if I have to scrimp, I'll always put something in the bank. That's for my future. I don't want to lose my house someday!

What happened to your gallery?

I had it for seventeen years. When my Dad died, I just wanted to get away, so I closed it.

Do you spend a lot of time marketing your work?

I'm terrible at marketing my own work, but others sometimes do it for me. They've done some prints of my paintings, and those sell. I don't like marketing anything. It's a personal thing. I like to paint. I like to teach. In teaching, my market is there waiting for me.

You do market your workshops and classes, don't you?

I think the best marketing I can do is to teach and give it everything I've got. I really don't have to advertise anymore. It's all word of mouth.

How many workshops do you give each year?

This year, I'm only giving ten. The most I've done is seventeen. I start my schedule in the spring, and run through to the fall. But I may not be able to continue it this way much longer.

Your eye problem?

My schedule has been pretty intense. I've wiped out my eyes. I may be going in for corneal transplants, and I know I won't be able to abuse my eyes like before. I'll probably have to work out new ways of doing things, and I'll enjoy that, too. Who knows? It may all be just fine.

What will you do if you can no longer teach?

If I stop teaching, and it looks like I may have to, then next year I'll really have to promote my work. I've already begun. My portfolio is ready. I'm saving paintings now, because I realize that I may have to start going to the galleries.

What advice would you give to artists who want to work with a gallery?

You may have to try many, in different areas of the country, before you find one that's right for you. Rockport is very different from, say, Provincetown. It's purely trial and error. Suddenly you fit right in somewhere, and you've found where you belong. Never give up on yourself. If they don't like your work . . . pity! Go somewhere else.

When you do get accepted into a gallery, be sure to keep your work moving. Give the gallery six months. If nothing happens, don't leave, but bring them other work. Keep changing and switching your work, because art buyers keep coming back. Each gallery will have a certain type of clientele. If you haven't done anything in about a year, you're not right for the gallery. That doesn't mean you're a bad artist, but you haven't found where you belong.

Why do you think some art lives, while other art just sits there?

Construction. Inner construction. Color, composition, value. As I said before, its how you compose the painting that makes it come alive. A painting has to be constantly moving. It's a living thing. A whole world in itself, and that world has got to be created.

If you were given the opportunity to start over, what would you do differently?

I wouldn't have quit school before the fourth

year. And I wouldn't have waited until I was in my fifties to do some serious figure painting in oils. My advice to anyone who wants to drop out of school: Bear with it. Don't quit! You'll pay for it the rest of your life. Of course, you can try to catch up, but you miss that intense student life with nothing to do but work, day after day, scraping the paint off and doing it again. I'd also have taken a lot more art history courses, and not have had to find it on my own. I'm still trying. It's so hard to study on your own, with no one to guide you.

What advice would you offer to artists who'd like to live by their art?

Quit your job, and get another job part time, so you have a little money and don't have to panic. Get a job where you don't have to think. Wash dishes or dig ditches. Anything physical, because then you can constantly think about your art. Give art everything, but save 10 percent of yourself to make a living.

It takes a long time to begin making a living at art, especially if you're going to do it right and not take any shortcuts. If you take shortcuts, they'll haunt you for the rest of your life. You'll only go so far.

Another thought: Don't make the mistake of thinking that your work is too precious. The best way to make a living at art is to get your work into people's homes. My advice would be to price your work as low as you can. Just keep it moving. Maybe you'll have to work twice as hard, do twice as many paintings.

Any other last thoughts you'd like to offer, regarding fine art as a way of life?

I think everyone should do a little teaching, because it's giving something back. It's also another way of earning a living. If you're going to teach, it's also important that you enter shows. You've got to be seen.

For the beginning artist, shows are a way of evaluating your art. You think you're good, or maybe not so good, but when you see your work on the wall with other artists you can look at it impersonally and judge it more clearly.

And a final thought: Paint with good painters. Go find yourself some good painting friends. They're the best friends you can have. You back each other up.

CHILDHOOD MEMORIES
1985
WATERCOLOR AND OIL COMBINED
30″ × 22″
COLLECTION OF THE ARTIST

This painting was started as a watercolor, but I soon lost the feeling I was trying to convey. A quick whiff of damar varnish was applied to seal the paper. I used only turpentine as a medium because the oil would "eat up" the paper.

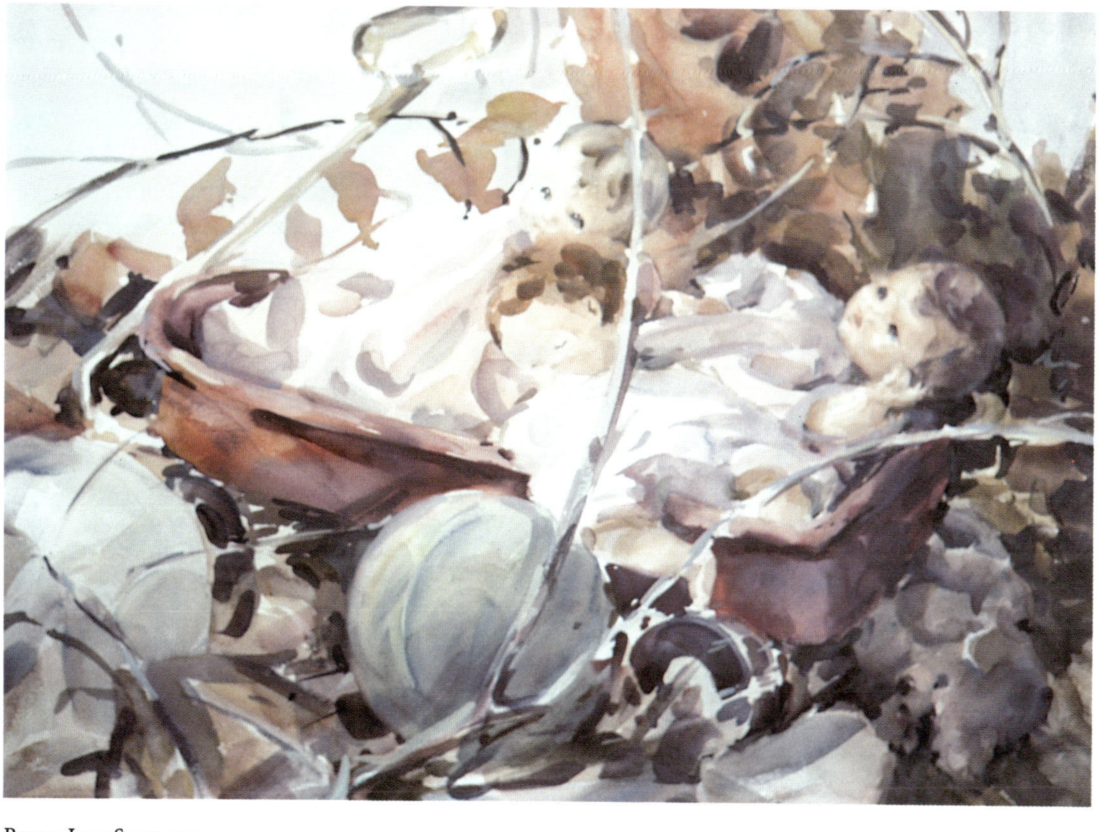

GARY AKERS
Treat Art As a Business, Not a Hobby

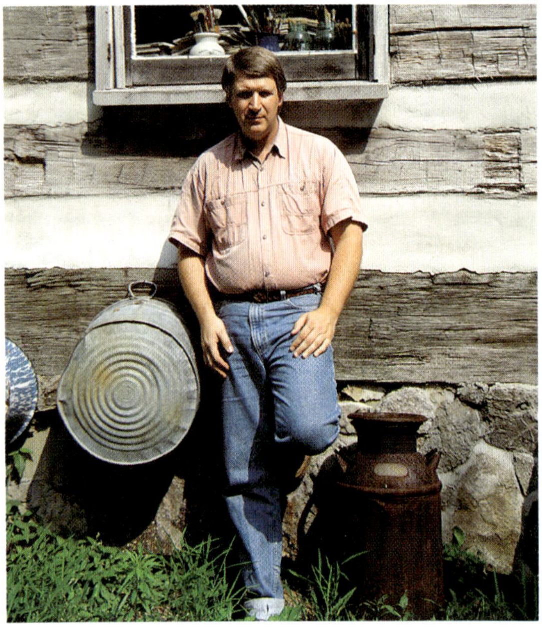

Gary Akers posed outside of his log cabin studio. Photo by Lew Lehrman.

EVEN BEFORE I HAD THE PLEASURE OF MEETING GARY AKERS IN PERSON, I felt as if I knew him. My first real contact with Gary came when I sat down and watched his video, *A Quiet Way of Life* (Gary-Lynn Galleries, Inc., P.O. Box 100, Union, KY 41091. VHS, 60 min.). I came away feeling as if I had spent an afternoon with him, and had achieved some insight into his personality and approach to art.

Then, on our spring trip back to New England, we finally visited the Akers at home. We were welcomed into their beautiful home, aglow with the light that comes through huge, segmented-circle windows. The house, which the Akers designed themselves, is hung with many of Gary's paintings. The crisp, modern lines of the weathered board structure are in sharp contrast to the rustic, chinked-log architecture of his comfortable studio, situated about a hundred yards away.

Later, as we drove home, I reflected upon how well Gary's video had captured the sense of history that is so readily evident about the region, and upon his reverence for that feeling.

Tell me about your video. How did that come about?

I had painted frequently since 1980 at the farm of the Borders brothers. William, Elmer and Woodrow were three bachelor farmers who shared a way of life that is rapidly disappearing from America. My only real purpose in doing the tape was to capture the way these men lived. They were getting up in age in 1988, and I knew their way of living was not going to last. Their old farm had no electricity, no running water. I thought, "If I don't record it now, it's never going to be this way again."

Doing it was one of the best experiences I ever had. My wife, Lynn, wrote the story line, and we got a very good local video company to do the shooting. We published it ourselves. The video works on several levels. Though there is a demo on it, it's not just a demonstration video. It's really about a way of life, and the way an artist goes out and sees subjects.

A lot of nonartists have told me how much they enjoy watching it. It's not boring to them. And I'm glad I did it when I did, because the two older brothers are gone now, and the farm is empty and up for sale.

Your work seems to revolve strongly around Kentucky themes. And yet rural Kentucky seems an unlikely locale for an artistic career as active and successful as yours. How did your career—and your success—come about?

I was raised in a little place called Grethel, in eastern Kentucky. It had no galleries, no museums, no arts community at all. But I guess I had a knack for drawing. Instead of playing with toys, I'd doodle and draw, creating my own little world. Of course, I did have encouragement from my mother, who was a school teacher. But there was never an artist in my family.

I attended two-room rural schools, in various communities. One room was for the first four grades, the other for the upper grades, with a pot-belly stove in each. My first art class was in high school, and I took art all four years. I really enjoyed having an instructor who was educated for that purpose. She was the one who recommended the fine arts program at Morehead State University, which is in eastern Kentucky about two and a half hours from home. It was a fine program, because the first two years were all drawing. No painting until you had completed all the drawing classes. I worked hard at anatomy, structure, perspective. A lot of students complained that they wanted to paint. I just wanted to get a good foundation. Then I started painting.

I graduated in '72 with an A.B., and before starting to work on my master's I spent a year teaching art in the neighboring county. I taught all grades, one through twelve. What an experience! I had to do it, though, because I needed the money for my studies. I also received a graduate assistantship at the university, which really helped. That graduate year was exciting, because most of my classes were independent studies. I had developed an interest in egg tempera. I'd go to my own studio, paint for several weeks, then show my instructor what I was doing.

Why egg tempera?

I had seen egg temperas by artists like Robert Vickery, Andrew Wyeth, and even Botticelli and Giotto. I loved its linear quality, almost like an extension of drawing, and I felt comfortable with it. I began experimenting. It's a difficult medium, and though my instructors could help me with color, composition and so forth, I was pretty well on my own with the actual technique. A lot of trial and error.

I received my master's in 1974. That was when Lynn and I got married. We had met in high school. I played basketball, and she was a cheerleader. We moved to northern Kentucky, and took art teaching positions at different schools in the same system.

It sounds like you had the beginnings of a comfortable life. What got you moving toward your present art career?

While I was still at Morehead State, I spent a lot of time in the library. They had a wonderful librarian, and an excellent arts section. I would go through all the art magazines, and that's where I discovered a listing of artists' grants. One of them was through the Elizabeth T. Greenshields Foundation of Montreal, Canada.

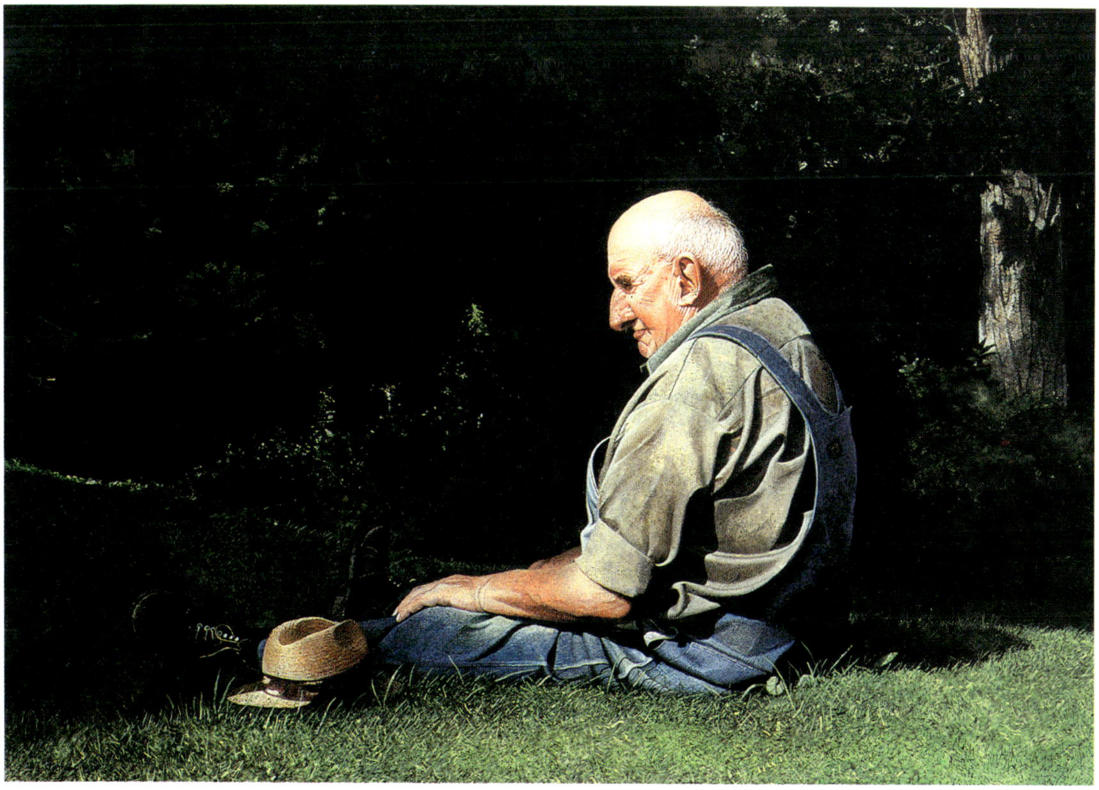

SUMMER AFTERNOON
1985
DRY-BRUSH WATERCOLOR
30″ × 20″
PRIVATE COLLECTION

This painting was exhibited in the Kentucky Watercolor Society's "Aqueous '85," and was awarded the Kentucky Artist Award. The juror stated that the award was not because of the details of the figure, but because of the "masterful handling of the background."

SEA ROSES
1989
DRY-BRUSH WATERCOLOR
29″ × 19″
PRIVATE COLLECTION

What attracted me to this subject was the simplicity of the white clapboard house, the pink roses in full bloom, the play of light on the porch, and the contrast of the deep dark greens in the background.

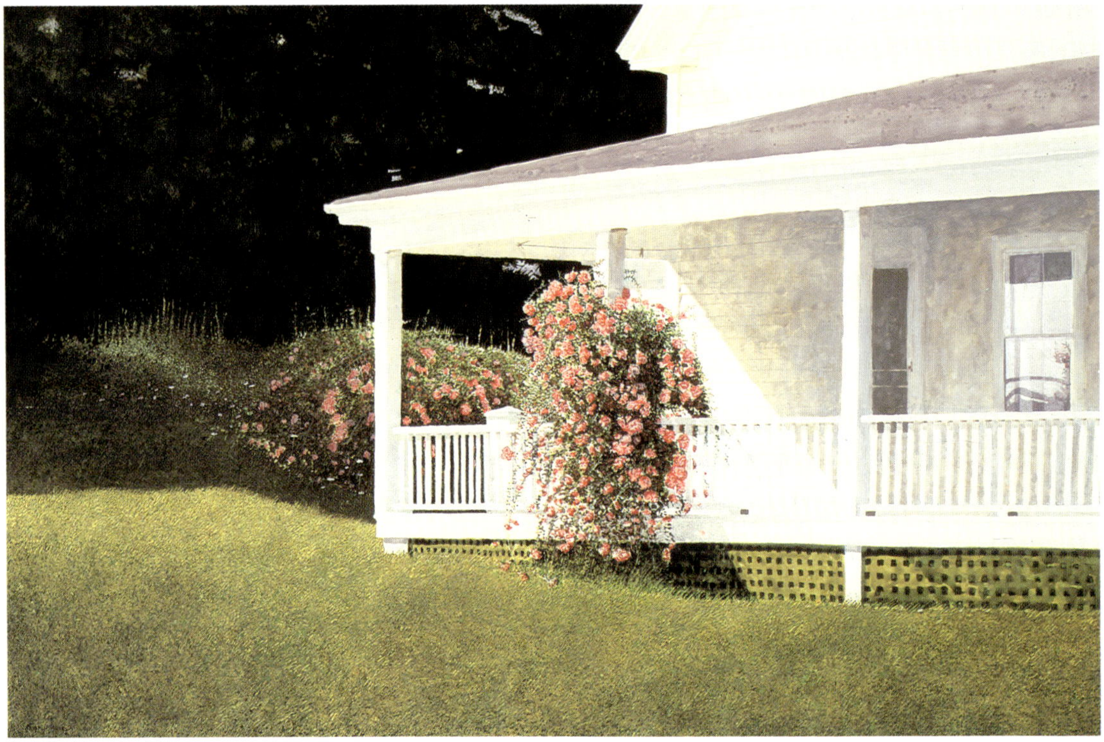

It was targeted toward serious young artists working in a realistic style, and I certainly felt I fit the profile.

I applied for the grant, sent ten or twelve slides of my work, plus one of my early egg temperas, and was accepted. That grant took the financial pressures off me for the year so I could paint and learn more about my craft. I took a leave of absence from teaching (so I'd have something to fall back on if things did not work out), and began with a trip to New York's Metropolitan Museum, where I got permission to go into their library and research egg tempera. They even brought out temperas from their vaults so I could actually see how artists from the thirteenth and fourteenth centuries had painted. It was a wonderful experience. I had been doing egg tempera without even knowing what it really looked like.

Then we went on to Maine, where we stopped at the Portland Museum—which had some Andrew Wyeth works in egg tempera—and the Farnsworth Museum in Rockland. That really opened my eyes to what other artists were doing!

The rest of the year, of course, I painted. I logged all my paintings, and sent in reports of my activities to the foundation.

That grant was really what started my career as a full-time artist. Though even when I was teaching, I was painting, publishing some prints, making appearances, and marketing my work.

Your work was already selling?

Even when I was in college. I'd put my work up anywhere I could. The college library . . . any place at all. Some of my pieces were selling for ten or twenty dollars. Not all of the shows were successful, but I always exhibited as much as I could. Producing, and getting some money for it. That was always important to me.

Was the grant all you needed to start your career rolling?

I did have another big break, when I was elected as a member of the Kentucky Heritage Group. The group was established by one of Kentucky's senators as a nonprofit association limited to twelve artist members. It is quite prestigious to belong. I am not one of the original members, but one had died, and another had moved out West, so there were two openings. I was nominated and elected. I'm still the youngest member of the group.

It was a big break for me, exposurewise. Every weekend, the group would travel to one of the state parks in Kentucky and set up an ex-

BORDERS BLUE
1990
EGG TEMPERA ON PANEL
19″ × 28″
COLLECTION OF DONALD S. TYLER

For many years, I was fascinated with how the light struck this beautiful blue wall in the Borders' farmhouse. I had a feeling the house would not remain standing for long once it was empty. So I did this, in egg tempera, my last at the Borders farm. On May 17, 1991, the house was destroyed by fire.

hibit. Each park has a nice lodge and restaurant, and great recreational facilities. We'd pay only for our room and meals. The paintings and prints we sold were our income.

Another thing I liked about the group is that we exhibited and demonstrated for hundreds and hundreds of school children. Most of them, especially where I was raised in eastern Kentucky, had never seen an artist before, and I think it really opened their eyes.

I know egg tempera takes a lot of time. Were these all you were doing?

I was also doing watercolors, and selling those with some success. The egg temperas, though, were not really moving. They'd sit around a year or two with no interest in them at all.

So what did you do?

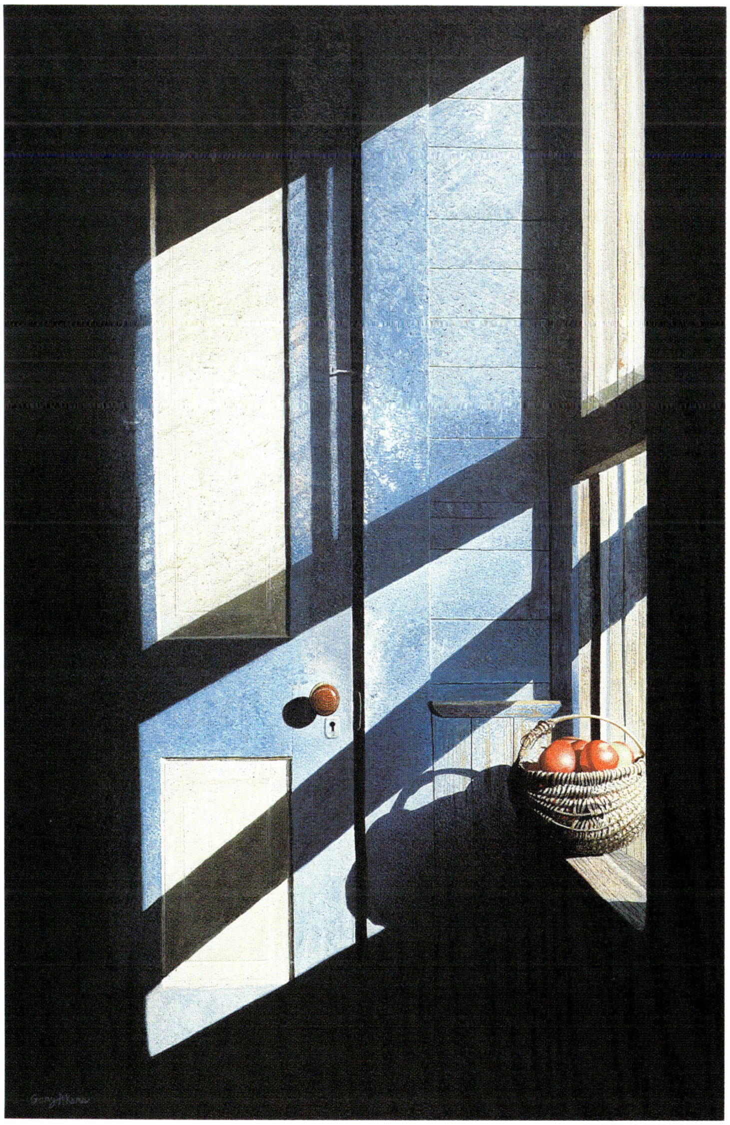

I had started by pricing my tempera paintings at $350 to $400. I decided to get some attention for them by doubling my prices.

A bold move! Did that do the trick?

Well, I was at a show in Lexington and left my exhibit to get some lunch. When I came back, the director told me that a doctor had come by in my absence and wanted to buy one of my temperas. I had priced it at nine hundred dollars, and in '77 that was a lot of money to me. I was really excited. The doctor bought that work, and then the next time I did a tempera, he bought it, too. That was how I began selling them. It wasn't long before I started to have a following.

Did galleries play a part in your marketing?

No. I've dealt with a few, but I've done almost all of my marketing myself. I started by publishing prints of my egg temperas. They retailed for about twenty dollars.

You'd take a painting to a printer and have it done?

Yes, to a color process lithographer, and I'd pay for the proofing and the printing. Then I'd sign and number them.

Then what did you do with them?

I spent many hours and many days, wearing a suit, calling on every print and frame shop (not the high-end galleries, but the places that sold the low-end products) and gift store . . . as many as I could. I'd introduce myself as one of the Kentucky Heritage artists, which really helped me, and if I was lucky and persistent, maybe I'd sell them one ten-dollar print.

You had to do a lot of pavement-pounding to make a day's pay, didn't you?

A shop might take one print, or none at all. I knocked on a lot of doors, and some never opened at all. But what I had in mind was to at least get established. If they bought one print, I was in the door. Then I could follow up by phone and ship them work. I'd give them three weeks, then call and follow up. That's very important. I'd ask, "Have you got it framed?" or make some conversation.

End of an Era
1989
Dry-brush watercolor
16″×24″
Private Collection

This is the last painting I did of William Borders. I was working on it when he died, which is the reason the painting is left unfinished. William is standing in the doorway of his barn, to which he would sometimes go in the afternoon to take a nap.

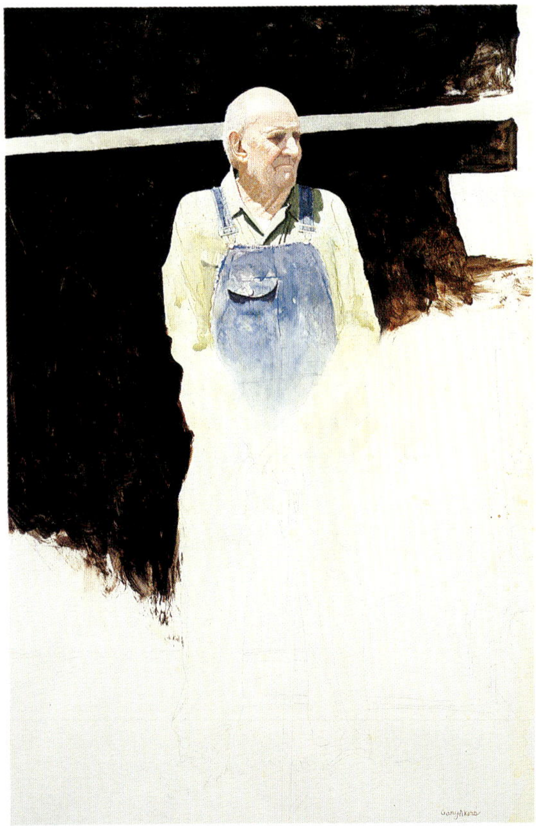

Did they, in fact, sell and reorder?

Yes. We were quite successful. Originally, my editions were too large—950. So I decided to print five hundred or less. Then they started to sell out completely, and that generated more demand. It got so we'd sell out an edition of five hundred in about six months to a year. Finally I increased the price of some of the prints to thirty-five and forty dollars. I didn't see any slackening of sales, but I'm cautious about getting too high.

You must have been quite busy, doing all that sales work and follow-up.

We were in the print business. We had between seventy-five and one hundred shops that we supplied frequently. I was doing four or five egg temperas a year, making prints and marketing them. I didn't have a lot of originals to sell.

Were you still doing watercolor in between?

A lot of watercolors were preliminary studies for the temperas. They were selling well because they were much lower priced. Sometimes people who'd buy a print would want an original study to go with it. So I had no problem selling the studies, and I really pushed them.

Was Lynn still teaching during this time?

Yes. She taught for eight years, and that gave us a steady income to cover the necessities.

Did you have children?

Not at that time. Ashley was born in 1984. But back then, trying to get my career off the ground, we decided to hold off.

Were you working out of your home?

Back in 1976, we lived in an apartment in Florence, Kentucky. I rented a store front about a half mile away, as a studio and gallery. Approximately twelve hundred square feet, with a studio in a back room and two front rooms for the gallery. People would drop by, and I started to build a local clientele. I also offered picture framing. Anything to keep me in business. Not ashamed of it whatsoever. I'd paint all day, then come home and frame pictures for my customers late into the night.

In 1983, we moved to a larger space in a strip mall in a nice business district and opened a larger gallery. That's when Lynn gave up teaching to take part in the business. She's run the gallery ever since, typing the letters, and answering the phone, and doing the publicity work.

Was your studio still in the back room?

No, in 1980, we moved from our apartment to a house in Union. And I restored a 150-year-old log cabin as my dream studio. It's about 150 feet from our house, nestled back in the woods, and very private. We're surrounded by about five hundred acres of open field, with cattle and horses and such. A lovely setting. I spent my days there, and not at the gallery.

After Ashley was born in 1984, we decided to bring our gallery and sales functions back to our home and studio here, and that has worked out very well. We have private collectors out to our home, where we have the gallery area set up. We don't have steady traffic or anything like that. It's all by appointment or invitation.

And we have been going to Maine every summer. That has played an important part in my career.

How so?

It started with my grant. Every summer since '76, we'd try to get away to Maine for a week or two, just to be there, and be inspired. We'd stay in different spots around the Rockland area each year. After Ashley was born, we'd stay for six or eight weeks. In 1990, we bought oceanfront property in Spruce Head, Maine, and began building a home. We conduct shows in Maine the way we do here in Kentucky.

Please tell me about your shows.

Right now we put on three a year, and that's where most of our income comes from. Since 1980, we have held a show in April, usually at my studio. We try to make it an event, either by releasing a new print or a new series of paintings. Something that no one has seen before. In the summer we hold a similar show in Maine. We rent space at the grange hall for the first weekend in August. People there know, now, when the exhibition will be.

We send out press releases to as many publications and radio stations as we can, and we do a nice show poster, which we plaster up in as many places as possible in a 75- to 100-mile surrounding area. We send out a mailing to about a thousand of our friends and collectors. That's all on our computer these days, and we can do our mailings a lot more efficiently than when we started. We'll get as many as five hundred people coming through in those two days, and most of my works will be sold, usually in the first two to three hours! Plus lots of prints. The show poster is especially popular. We try to have a poster that's unique each year, and people like to collect them.

But our main goal is to sell the originals. My subject matter is done from the area, so people can relate to it. Lots of people vacation there, and they like to take my work back to Kansas City, or wherever, to remind them of their good times in Maine.

We return to Kentucky in September, and have the third show at my studio in late October. I'll show paintings I've done while I was in

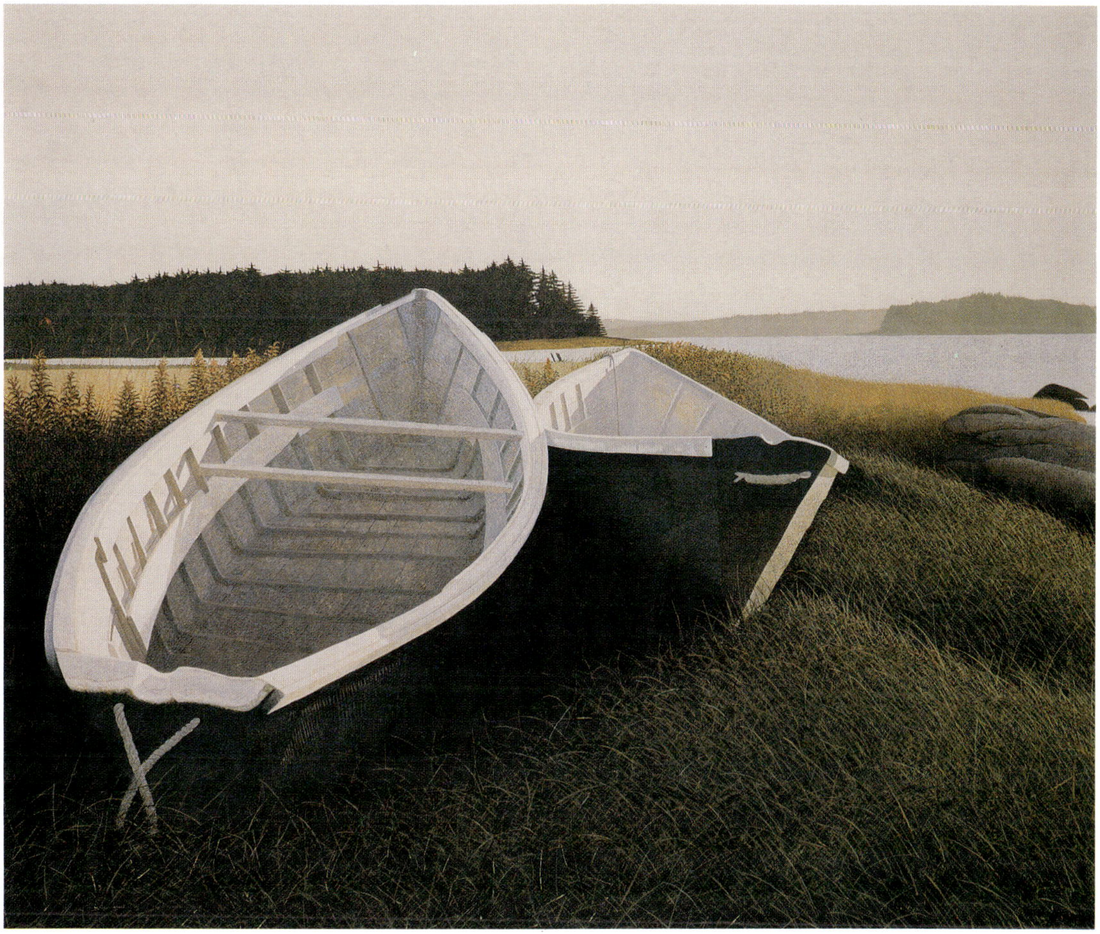

SEAWARD
1990
EGG TEMPERA ON PANEL
33″ × 27″
PRIVATE COLLECTION

This subject was painted on the coast of Maine. I chose an unusual vantage point, to show the skeletal structure of the boats. I spent a lot of time building up the grasses, as I want the viewer to feel the breeze coming off the water.

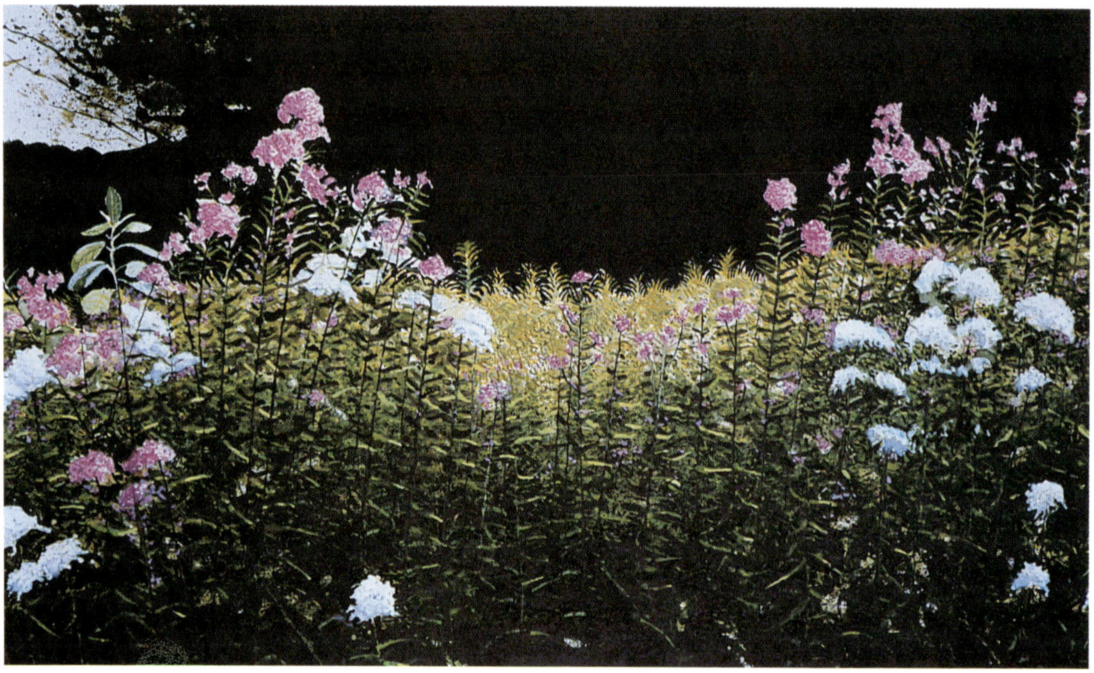

Maine Wildflowers
Watercolor
20¼″ × 13″

When I saw these wildflowers, I knew they would become a painting. I like the contrast of the pink and white flowers to the rich dark greens in the background.

Maine, plus possibly a new print release.

Of course, I sell privately between those shows, to collectors and people who come by. Sometimes I'll have a piece that I think a particular person will be interested in, so I'll contact him or her. Or someone will call and ask, "What do you have?"

How many prints have you published?

We've done about 25 to date, and at least 15 are sold out. We come out with two or three a year now. Always one in the spring and one in the fall. We don't want to just crank them out. We produce only what we can efficiently market. There's no use having them out if you're not selling them.

How much time do you spend doing one egg tempera?

I usually work a full ten- or twelve-hour day on just one small section of one piece, building it up. Sure, it's intense, but once I get into it, I don't want to do anything else. I spend at least two to three months on a piece. I can't work on two or three pieces at once, but in between temperas I'll work on some watercolors—and I think it helps my watercolors because they are the opposite of how I was working for those intense months.

I know you're an active instructor on the workshop circuit. Please tell me about that.

For the last several years, I have been teaching five-day watercolor workshops from Maine to California. Originally, I offered egg tempera as an alternative, but not anymore. It's too time consuming, and five days are just not enough to get into it. I've cut down on the number of workshops I do, now, too.

Have you set up a pension or retirement plan?

Not exactly. I'm investing in properties, though.

Another thing: I've always felt that my work will be more valuable some years down the road, and so I keep a certain number of my most successful paintings as a kind of investment. I completely believe in my work, and I have watched it increase tremendously in value over the years.

I recommend that artists keep some of their best work during their careers. Not the ones they can't sell, but the ones they know they could sell just like that!

What other advice would you give to artists who would like to live by their art?

You have to believe in yourself first and foremost. And then you've got to treat art as a business, not a hobby. The business part enters in, no matter what.

But what does that mean, exactly?

You have to be business-minded, set up your venture as a business, be able to relate to people, talk to them, and show them your craft. Be proud of what you're doing. Get excited about your work, and they will too.

You can't *just* create in your studio and be discovered. They won't come and bang your doors down. You have to get out there.

Start out locally. That's a must. Get your work shown at the bank or in a store. Getting started, I did appearances anywhere I could—hardware store openings, anything. Join the local art league or club, and enter the members' shows and the juried shows. Start your marketing efforts locally, then branch out regionally, and save your national efforts for later.

And be prepared to make some sacrifices. That's what I had to do those years when I was teaching. I painted long hours into the night, to build up a body of work before anyone would want to see it. In a sense, you've got to work two jobs: one to feed your family, and one to develop your craft. You have to really be serious about your work, and put in the hours.

You know, there is still this misconception about artists, that we really do not work. I'm usually at my studio by eight in the morning, and I'll work until five-thirty. Then I'll put in a couple of more hours after dinner. Yet even today, I'll have people call the house at 10:00 A.M. and ask, "Is Gary up yet?"

Do you set goals for yourself?

Yes, and I always have. Back in college, in the library, going through *American Artist Magazine*, I decided one of my big goals was to have an article about me in that publication. I thought that if I did, I'd feel like somewhat of a success. I set that goal, and it finally came about. Another goal was to become a member of A.W.S. I reached that, too. I think you've got to set goals in order to reach them. You can't just go along from day to day, with nothing to reach for.

One goal was to sell a piece for a certain amount of money, at a certain age. I reached that goal. I still set myself realistic goals, and try to reach them in a realistic time.

I remember the summer of 1983, when Lynn was away in Europe. I spent practically all summer with the Borders brothers, painting them. I said at the outset, "By the end of this summer, I want to be able to paint the figure." I did dozens of paintings. Some were awful and I threw them away, but by the end of that summer, I had added that new dimension to my work. That was a high! It's interesting to note that, having set goals, attaining them became the high points in my career.

MONHEGAN LIGHT
1991
EGG TEMPERA
60″ × 30″
PRIVATE COLLECTION

This was a fifty-thousand-dollar commission for a private collector, whose only requirements were the size, and that the subject be from Maine. The work took more than four months to complete, and is the largest egg tempera that I have painted.

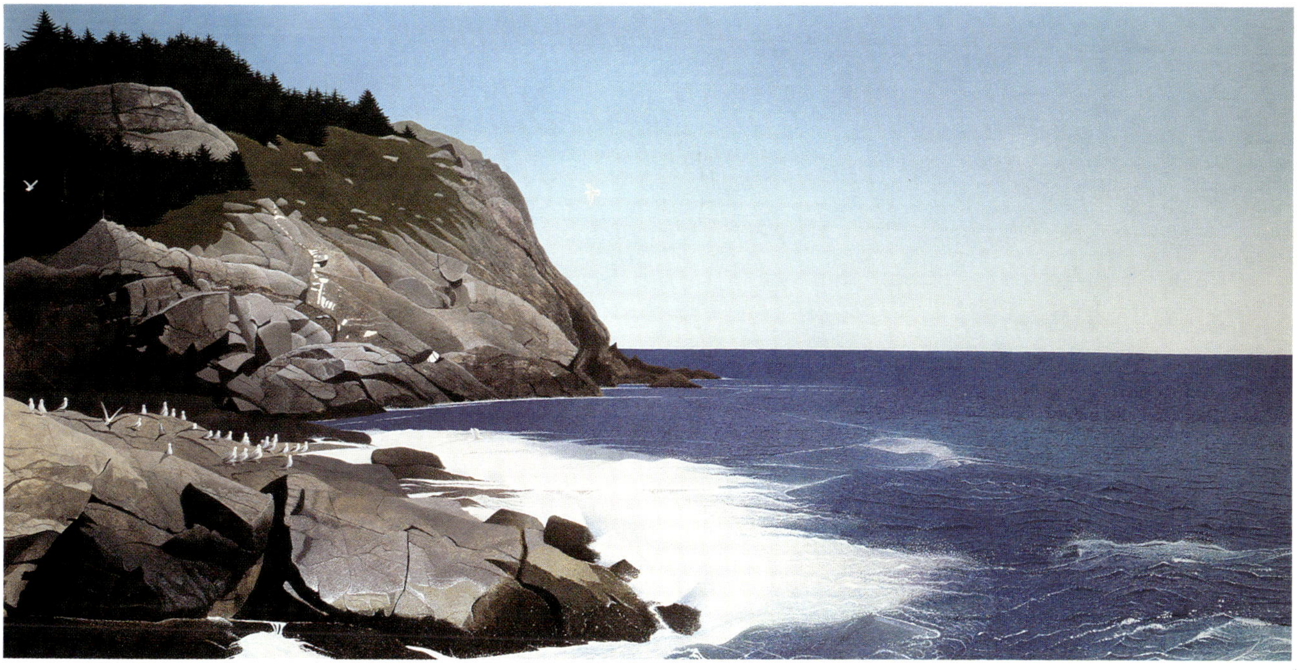

LIN and PAT SESLAR
Sell Your Work As Early As You Can

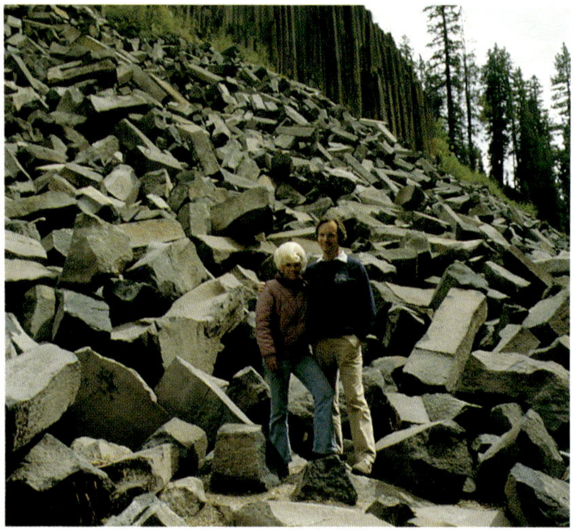

Lin and Pat Seslar at Devil's Postpile National Monument, California.

WHEN I HEARD ABOUT THE SESLARS, AND THEIR LIFESTYLE, I WAS ESPEcially eager to interview them. After all, they had achieved not one, but two of the kinds of dreams that many of us harbor.

Not only are they living from their artistic efforts, but they seem to have successfully cut the ties that bind the rest of us to one place on the map.

For the past seven years, Lin and Pat have made their home in a travel trailer, which tags along behind their van as they travel the highways of America, stopping where they please, painting wherever they go, and enjoying the best of what our wonderful country has to offer.

I caught them at their winter stopping place in Florida. Their story is all the more intriguing for its inauspicious beginnings: a go-cart!

Lin: It was 1972, and Pat was just getting out of the Navy. He had always wanted to build a go-cart, and that Christmas I bought him a hobby welding torch. Trying to figure out how to use it, we started making little sculptures. Nuts and bolts and pieces of scrap became sailboats and turtles, and who knows what.

By the time we learned how to use the torch, Pat was working for the county of San Diego, and he began to take some of his pieces there. I was working at the University of California as a staff research associate, and I took some there, too.

At first we gave them away, but pretty soon we had used up all the scrap that had been given to us. So we told our friends, "If you really like these, we'll charge you, at least, for the materials."

Pat: That torch took control of our lives!

Lin: I really related to the torch . . . to building things with my hands. And once he showed me how to light it, I never gave it back!

Anyway, one thing led to another, and someone suggested that we might like to try selling our sculptures at one of the local outdoor art exhibits. That first weekend we made seven dollars. We were so jazzed! Well, one outdoor exhibit led to another, and . . .

Pat: Within a year, we decided to put together a plan.

Lin: We would pay off all our bills, and see if we could earn one person's income from our art. We'd still keep our full-time jobs, do the shows on weekends, and make sculptures in the evenings.

We started doing the mall shows, too, and some of the professional art shows, testing designs, learning what people liked. We did our first mall show in May of '74, and earned more than I did in a month at my job. The next month I quit.

Pat: Everyone thought she was crazy.

Lin: That June I signed us up for a four-day mall show. We were the top-selling artists on our end of the mall! Pat had been planning to work at his job until January before giving notice. But I had done so well that he quit his job in July. Everybody thought we were *really* nuts then. But we never looked back.

Eventually, we sold enough sculptures to

graduate to a full-fledged welding outfit. Then it really opened up for us. We could create all kinds of interesting things.

And where did this all lead to?

Lin: Eventually, another artist asked us if we would go into partnership with him and open a gallery on Coronado Island—a high-quality area. We did, and we ran it for about a year and a half, but the partnership didn't work out. However, the experience gave us the confidence to pick out a location and try it on our own.

Pat: It was about that time we decided to try our hand at painting. It seemed like a natural progression.

Had either of you had any formal art training?

Pat: Neither of us, when we met, had any predilection toward art. We had gone to school together, and begun our careers together. But art blossomed like a shoot of grass coming up out of the ground. One day it was just there. I have this theory that there are people who are born to do certain things. It's something innate that drives you, almost beyond control, to that destiny. You start out in life becoming what other people want you to become. You hope, in the course of your life, you'll find out what *you* want to become.

My father was a Methodist minister. We moved all over the place, so I only had the basic kinds of educational opportunities. Some of the schools I went to had art classes, and I remember peeking in the doors and wondering what they were doing in there. My only intimation came in my last semester of summer school at Purdue, when I took an art appreciation course. I just loved everything about it. But that was all. Then the Navy came along, and Vietnam, and all that other stuff.

How about you, Lin?

Lin: Nope. Nothing. I had no drawing classes. No art classes. Nothing.

Pat: When we decided to try painting, we did take a course. One of those "Anyone Can Paint" courses you always see advertised. After three weeks we discovered that painting wasn't nearly as technical as we'd thought, and that we could move ahead faster on our own, so we dropped out.

What about composition, color, drawing? How did you pick all that up?

Pat: A tremendous amount of reading. Going to the museums in San Diego. Looking at what

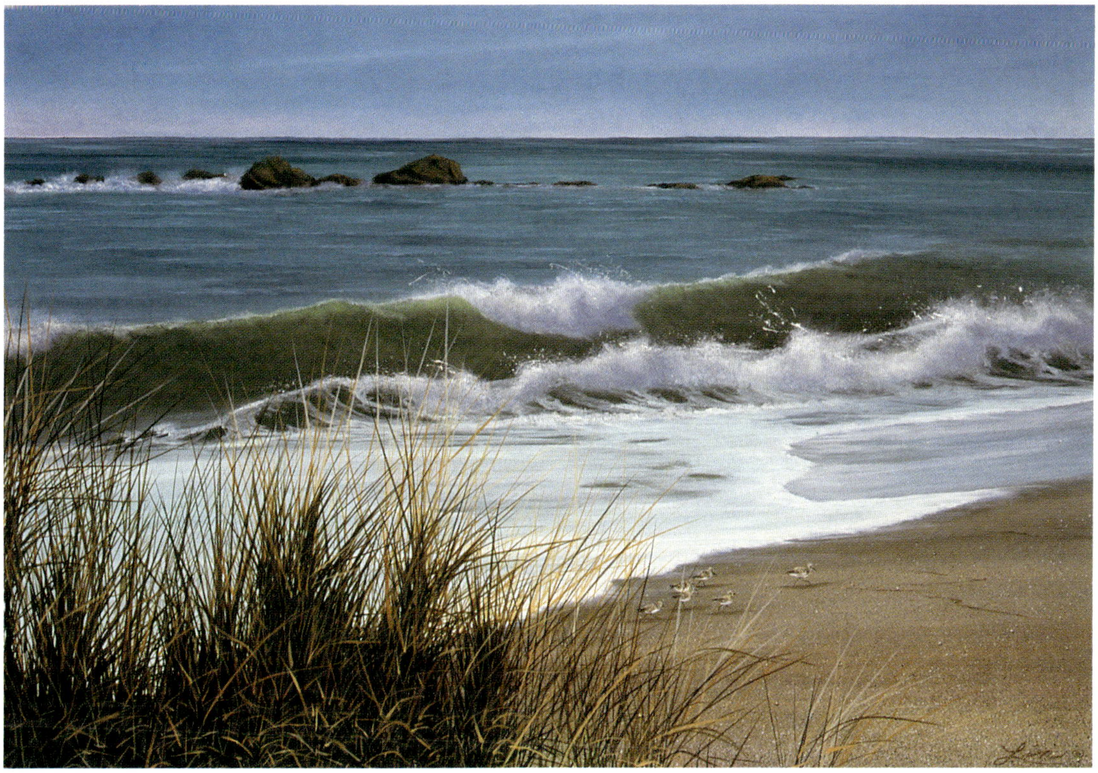

LIN SESLAR
SPARKLING SURF
1990
OIL ON PANEL
20″ × 14″
COLLECTION OF MR. AND MRS. TOM AKERS

After many years and many, many seascapes, I still see each new painting as an opportunity to capture some new nuance of color or motion. Here, I was intrigued with the soft light in the wave and with the frothy veil of foam spilling forward onto the beach.

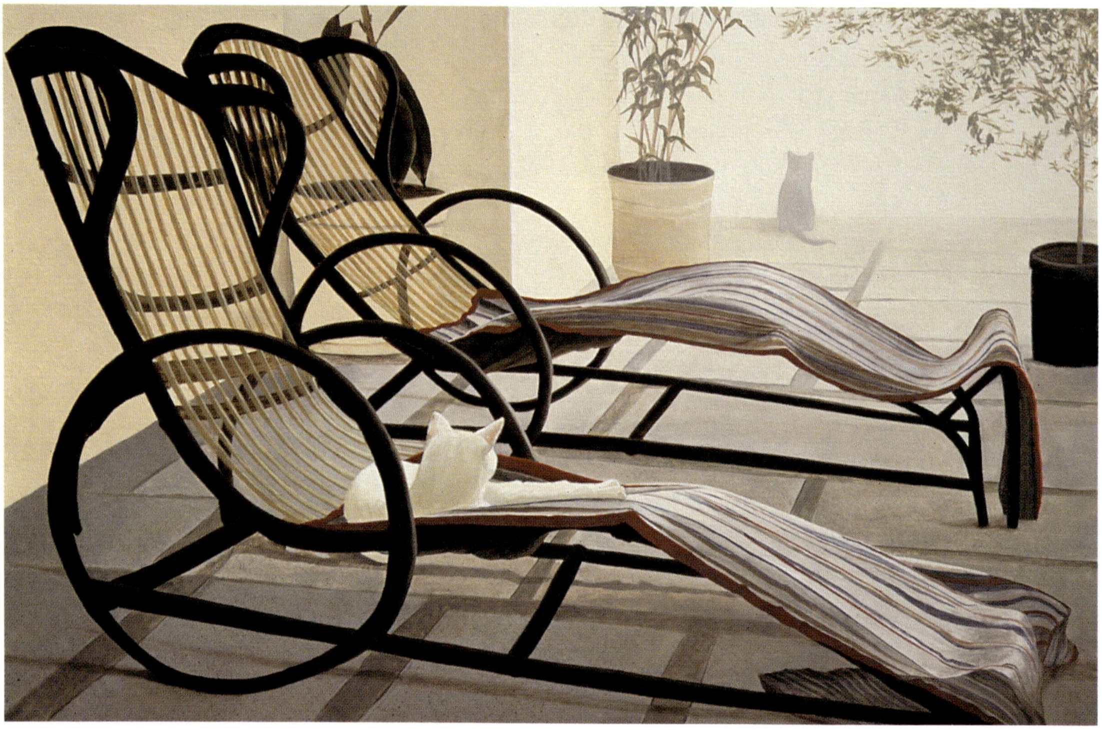

PATRICK SESLAR
TAKING IT EASY
1991
OIL ON CANVAS
30″×20″
COLLECTION OF
STEPHANIE
VANDERVENTER

On a tour of the Hemingway house in Key West, Florida, I couldn't help but notice the nonchalance of the home's only current residents—about thirty cats, all descended from Ernest's own pets. I made several quick sketches, fearing my model would move before I finished. I needn't have worried. The cat still hadn't moved several hours later when I'd finished my tour.

other artists had done. . . .

Lin: And practice, practice, practice!

Pat: There's so much to learn. You get a lot of it by reading, but mostly you get it by painting.

How long did it take between starting to paint, and selling your very first painting?

Lin: I must have painted a full two years. Just painting and tossing, and trying to find out what worked and what didn't.

Pat: During that time, she must have painted a couple of hundred oils.

Lin: Most of which were failures. I kept them to remind me of where I had come from.

And Pat, what were you doing?

Pat: We were between galleries at that time. Our first partnership had dissolved, and the new gallery was not yet open. I started doing some pencil drawings, and toying with watercolor and gouache. It took me about a year before I started to sell. We had this two-year interval when we were still doing shows with our sculpture, beginning to show a few paintings, trying to build our skills and become reasonably proficient.

Where was your studio?

Pat: We had our house in San Diego. About twenty-two hundred square feet with a two-car garage and a basement, pretty much all of which was devoted to one aspect or another of what we were doing. Our painting studio was an upstairs bedroom. The silkscreen shop was downstairs (We had taken an adult ed course in serigraphy, and were doing that, too.) Welding was in the garage. And storage everywhere.

Long before, we had decided against raising a family.

Back to the gallery . . .

Pat: We opened in Marina Village, not far from Sea World, in 1980, with about twelve hundred square feet. Lots of wall space. We had decided that we wanted to show only our own work, because that's where the best mark-up was.

Opening day, we sold seven thousand dollars worth of work. They just about cleaned us out! We were a little concerned at that point whether we'd be able to do enough work to put on the walls and the sculpture displays.

Lin: We also realized that possibly our pricing was a little low.

Pat: The gallery was wildly successful. By the middle of the second year we had a nice little Porsche, money in the bank, and all the dreams any artist could have.

Where was all this traffic coming from?

Pat: San Diego is a big tourist area. We were in a specialty shopping center that drew the right kind of people. There was a huge marina associated with it, and the Islandia hotel was just a half block away. We did plenty of advertising: *San Diego Magazine*, *Guest Informant* (which goes into the hotels) . . .

Lin: We did radio.

Pat: We made some television appearances. Hired a public relations firm for a while, to get some visibility. But we found that we were scheduling our time so completely that there never was any time for us to grow. No time, even, to be aware of our lives. We found ourselves back on a different kind of treadmill, not too different from a lot of other people.

Though we were doing great, the shopping center was having its problems and we could see the handwriting on the wall. Our three-year lease was coming to an end. Between what was happening with the center, and our personal thoughts about what we wanted to do, we didn't renew.

We decided to take time for ourselves, work on our art, see what artists around the country were doing, and travel . . . enjoy ourselves while we were still young enough to do everything that occurred to us.

It was December of 1983 when we closed the gallery. I was thirty-four.

Just like that? You closed the gallery and off you went?

Pat: It really happened over the course of a year. We had begun thinking about it in early '83. We already owned a travel trailer, which we were using for short getaways. "Full-timing" became part of our master plan. A few longer trips convinced us we'd need something larger, and we upgraded to a twenty-seven-footer. We spent that year getting our house sold and outfitting our trailer and van. In January of 1984, we were on the road.

Lin: The van was set up as a sort of mobile studio. We carried all our art materials and framing in it, where it would stay out of our way. That way we could keep our living quarters separate until we wanted to paint.

So you were on your way . . .

Lin: Traveling and painting!

Pat: The first two years we went everywhere. A lot of national parks.

Every part of the country. We'd drive for a day or two, then set up somewhere and split our time between sightseeing and painting. We also visited the art enclaves and the great muse-

LIN SESLAR
BREAKERS ASHORE
1990
OIL ON CANVAS
18″ × 12″
COLLECTION OF
MRS. DOROTHY
BLAIR

There is a rhythm and movement to the ocean almost like music. Breakers are the grand crescendos that carry but do not overpower the subtle harmonies of light reflected in shadowy foam or translucent water.

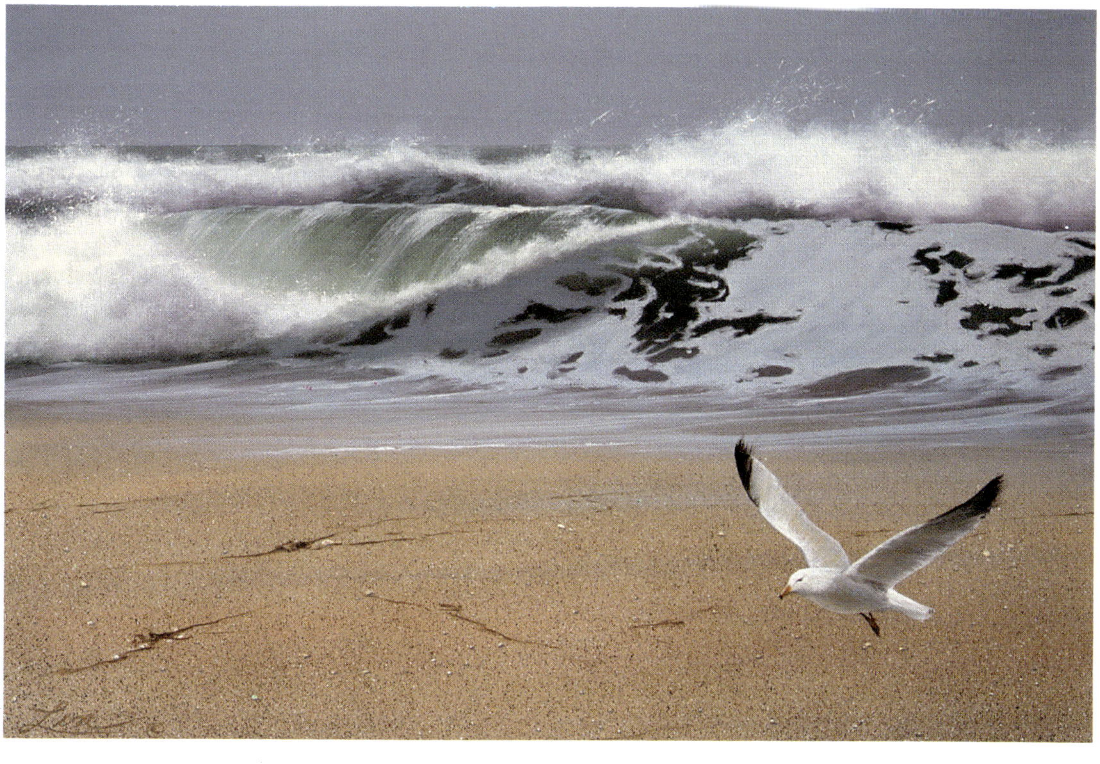

PATRICK SESLAR
BY THE POOL
1989
OIL ON PANEL
14″ × 11″
COLLECTION OF
HELEN D. CARTER

During my visit to the Hemingway house, I discovered another cat lounging by the pool in an ornate cast-iron chair. I wanted to capture the play of light and shadow, and the contrast of natural color against the bright aqua pool. Once again, my feline model remained blissfully unaware of my presence.

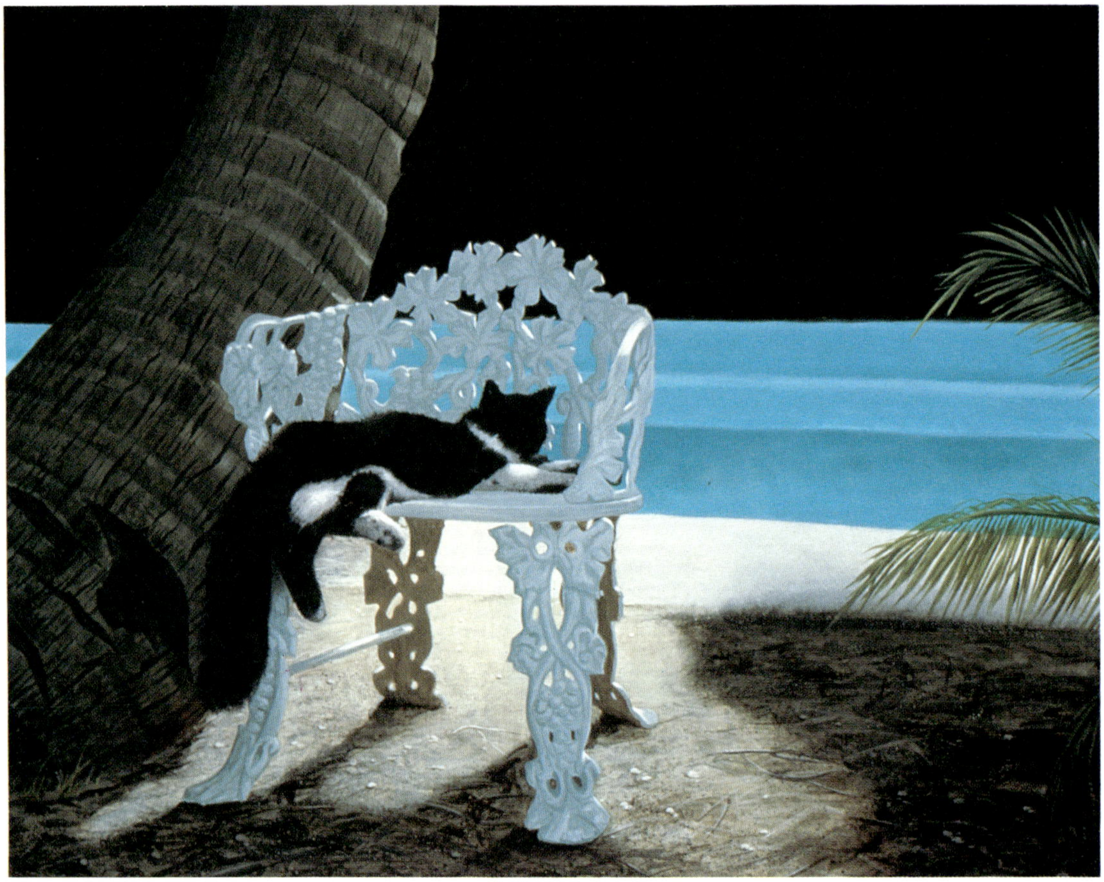

ums, where we could see the real thing, not tiny reproductions.

How long did this nomadic life continue?

Pat: Really, it still continues. We winter in Florida, living in our R.V. We rent studio space to make life a little easier, travel and paint the rest of the year. We spend a lot of time in the Sierras.

Pat, you also do a lot of writing, don't you?

Pat: When I was young, I didn't know I wanted to be an artist. But I did want to write. I wrote for the school paper, that kind of thing. But my serious writing came much later.

Back while we still had the gallery, I wrote for the computer magazines. Once we were out of the gallery and traveling, I had more time to spend on it, so I began to submit more . . . and be rejected more . . . and eventually made some connections. *The Artist's Magazine* was just coming on the market about that time, and I must have had what they were looking for. I've done quite a bit of writing for them over the years. Basically on marketing and art techniques.

Lin: After the first article, North Light Books asked us to do a book, *Painting Seascapes in Sharp Focus*.

Are you still doing the sculptures?

Pat: No. They're not practical on the road. We're concentrating on painting, because it's fairly portable.

Lin: We sold all our welding equipment, so we wouldn't have to pay for storage.

Pat: We want the time to put everything we can into our art. To experiment. To be everything we can be. Not to be driven by money to the point that we'd hack off paintings to earn income. What we wanted was to paint, first, for us. Then for money. And to relate much more to life in the world than most people seem able to, when they work at regular jobs and conduct their lives afterward and on weekends.

Do you foresee the day when you might want to settle in somewhere?

Pat: One day we might open a seasonal gallery somewhere. Of all the ways to market your work, provided your choice of location is right, having your own gallery is probably best.

Lin: We'd still travel the rest of the year.

Pat: We want to continue traveling, to develop different markets, to continue exploring our art. To us, that's the most vibrant and successful way to live our lives.

How would you define success, in your own terms?

Pat: I'm a great fan of Thoreau. *Walden* is just about my bible on successful living. Success is having enough, not being ruled by your possessions, nor the pursuit thereof, and coming in contact with your world. For us it's spending our summers up in the mountains with the pines, listening to the crunch of gravel, all that romantic stuff.

What advice would you offer to artists who'd like to live by their work?

Pat: My most important advice would be: (1) Paint a lot. It's only a wish until you pick up the brush. It's the only way you progress, and the only way you have anything to sell. (2) Create a body of work. (3) You're never going to be completely satisfied with what you do at any point in your career, but there's generally someone out there who's prepared to buy what you're producing at that point, because that's where *they're* at. (4) Get to selling your work as early as you can, because that will give you confidence.

Another important point for people who are starting: In the beginning, you think every break that comes up is going to be the one that makes your career. As you go on, though, you find that this is very seldom the case. Though you may lose a bit of your enthusiasm, your naiveté, you do gain a more realistic attitude. Lin nearly had a *Reader's Digest* cover, early on, and an almost-article in *American Artist*. Everyone has those kinds of disappointments. They can be painful, particularly in the beginning.

What thoughts would you have for the aspiring artist, Lin?

Lin: I think it's much more difficult for a woman. We've both known several women artists whose husbands were not artists, and that seems to be especially hard. If your marriage partner is not supportive and understanding, it becomes difficult to have the time to grow, to show, sell, promote, and do those other things that are so important. That support is absolutely crucial.

In a marriage situation, where the husband works all week, and the only time the wife can show is on weekends, they never see each other, and that can put a big strain on things. But if you want it badly enough. . . .

Any final thoughts for the reader?

Pat: I'd say, read *Walden*. Because Thoreau's life philosophy is perfect for the artist. For anyone, really.

That's been a touchstone for you both, hasn't it?

Lin: Absolutely. We read it all the time.

Pat: There's so much in it. Particularly today. I think that in the years since we began, the pace of society has accelerated. The pursuit of income, and material possessions, has gotten totally out of hand. People think they can buy happiness. They tend to forget what life is really about. Thoreau puts your head on straight.

PATRICK SESLAR
THE BACK PORCH
1989
OIL ON CANVAS
16″ × 12″
COLLECTION OF
KATHRYN MORRIS

In a world all too swiftly being overtaken by cheap plastic siding, it's nice to savor a bit of real clapboard and peeling paint, or a weathered half-barrel straining to contain its sprawling cargo of geraniums.

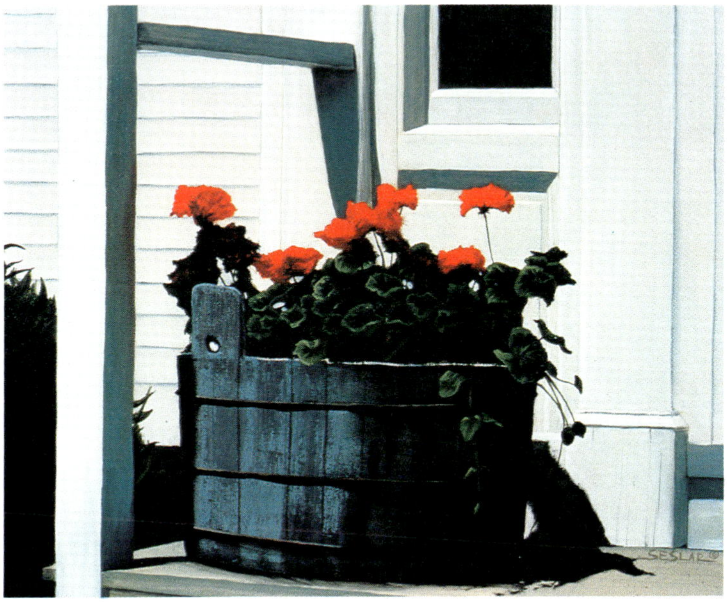

ARNE WESTERMAN

Don't Worry About Making Mistakes

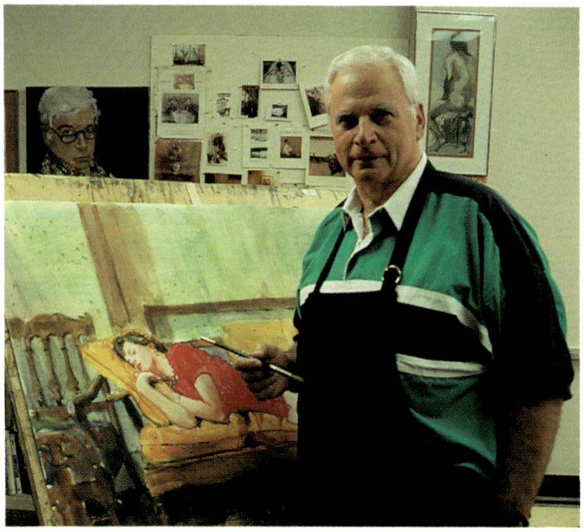

Arne Westerman in his Portland, Oregon, studio.

*I*T IS READILY APPARENT TO ME THAT PORTLAND, OREGON WATERCOLORist Arne Westerman is, first and foremost, a "people person." Not only is this clearly reflected in his work, which invariably deals with people, but it's reflected in that of all the artists interviewed for this book, Arne was the only one who started by asking me to send him slides of some of *my* work. Perhaps he felt that it gave him insight into the person who would be asking him all those intimate questions.

When we had finally gotten through the preliminaries, Arne and I spent a productive hour or two talking about art and its pathways, our conversation mingled with bad jokes and common experience. But throughout the course of our conversation, his affection and reverence for people came strongly through.

How long have you been at this full time?

Since about 1981.

And is it supporting you at this point?

Oh, yes.

From the sale of your work, or the workshops you teach?

Mostly from the sale of work. It's a thrill.

I set up my studio downtown because I wanted to be where people are. I also wanted to paint street people—still do (I've gotten to know many of them)—and to do that, you've got to be downtown. Anyway, for furniture I found junk—things from drop-boxes and stores going out of business. Because I never thought I could make much of a living at it. Thought it would be a hand-to-mouth kind of life. But things have gone quite well, and I've finally bought some furniture.

Do you paint every day?

Sure. No matter what, unless I'm sick or dying. I love doing what I do. Any time I look at paintings or a book with some paintings in it, I get all excited and I've got to start working again. Even though I'm my own boss, I feel guilty if I'm not painting. I look at a book on Whistler, or any great artist, and say to myself, "Damn! I'm an artist! I can *do* this!"

It's not like saying, "I can do this on the weekend and then I've got to go back to work."

People told me, "Wait until you get to be an artist full time. It'll be just like anything else. Work is work." That isn't true at all!

How did you get started in art?

I always liked to draw, and I always loved to cartoon. Ever since I was a little kid growing up in Portland, Oregon. Strangely enough, I never did well in art classes. I never could follow orders. I wasn't listening. When everyone else was getting praised for cutting out little squares and circles, I was trying to do my own thing, and I generally got lousy grades in art.

But that didn't matter, because my parents wanted me to be a doctor anyway. I thought I didn't have the brains to be an attorney (I know better now), but I did like the idea of being a doctor.

So I started taking premed at Reed College, in Portland, though I ended up in the Army in 1944. I was seventeen, just at college having a good time with the girls, and stuff like that. I never opened a book. The war was on. I knew I was going to go into the Army. I spent my time drawing cartoons on the blackboard, being an all-purpose kind of clown, and earning a 0.65 grade point average.

And then I got drafted. After a stint with the medics, I gave up medicine and took the advice of a cousin who had been with the *New York Times*. When I told him I wanted to be a writer, he said, "Don't! Any fool will write for nothing just to see his stuff in print. You need to do something they pay money for. Try advertising. At least it keeps the amateurs out."

So I got a degree in journalism anyway, and wound up in the ad business. It incorporated writing, and art, which I loved, and all kinds of creative things. There aren't many professions around in which you can have fun, exercise your creativity, and still make a good living.

I worked for a couple of agencies first before I opened my own. Eventually I had a staff of artists and writers to handle the creative work. I handled the clients. At one time, I had a staff of ten—fairly big for Portland. I was in that for thirty years.

When did painting begin to motivate you?

The last five or ten years in the business, I was becoming kind of bothered by my life. Advertising is so transient. The ad you prepare that's so good today is nothing in a few days or a week. There's no stability. No longevity. I started searching for something that had a little more meaning.

I had gotten to that age in life when I was starting to worry about death. That's one of the reasons I chose to be an artist. Because I didn't want to die. My wife told me, "Your children will go on after you, and that's how you live on." She wasn't wrong, but I was looking for a different kind of longevity. I felt that, as an artist, my things would hang on the wall, and be there long after me.

That's a kind of immortality, I guess. The thought has occurred to me.

I think we all want to cheat death somehow or other. We all know it's going to happen. But,

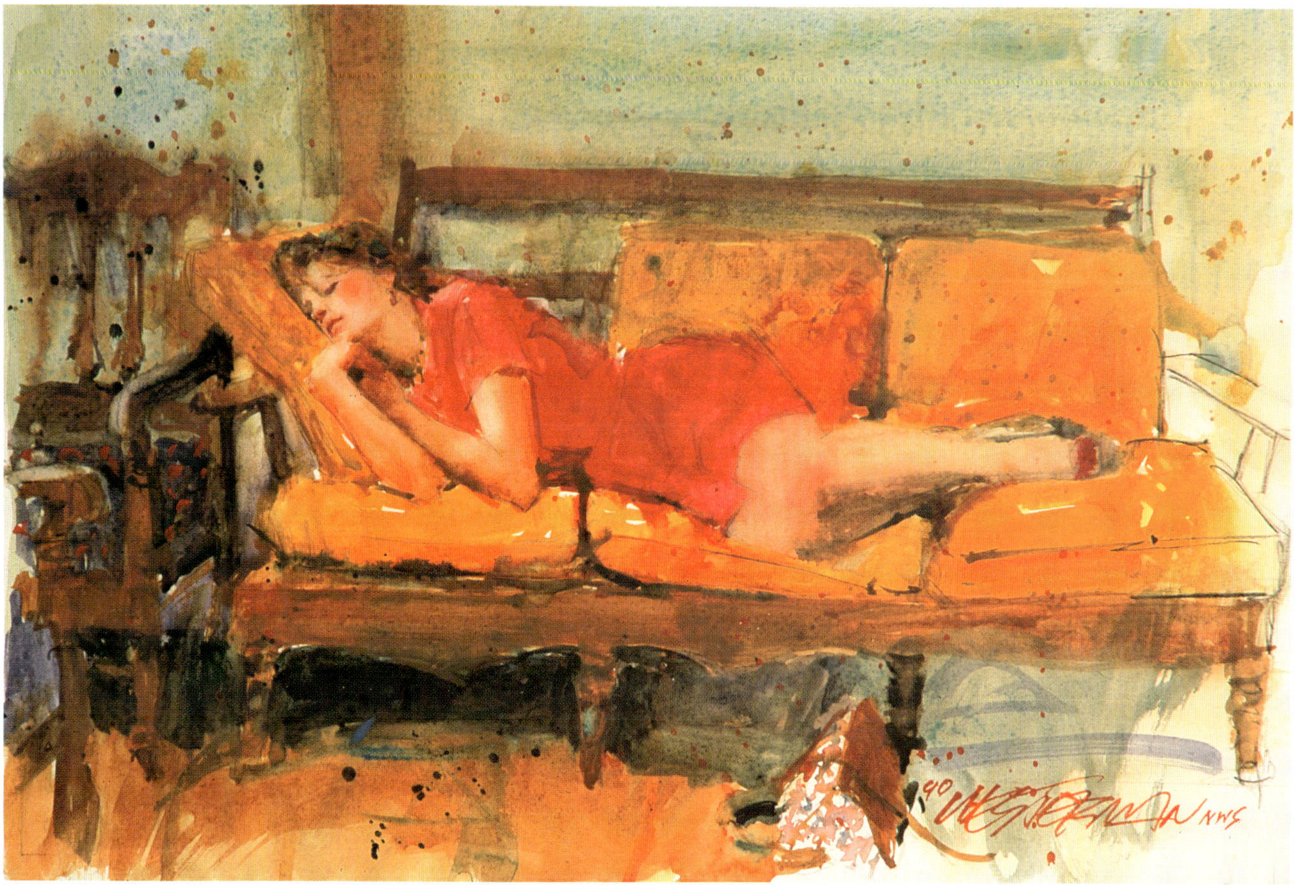

DeAnna's Lunch Break
1990
Watercolor
42″×31″
Courtesy Attic Gallery, Portland, OR

This is a study for a larger version. A young woman from an office down the hall was to be found, almost every noon, fast asleep on the world's most uncomfortable sofa in the women's lounge. (What, you may ask, was I doing there?) Anyway, it was so serene, I thought it would make a pleasant painting.

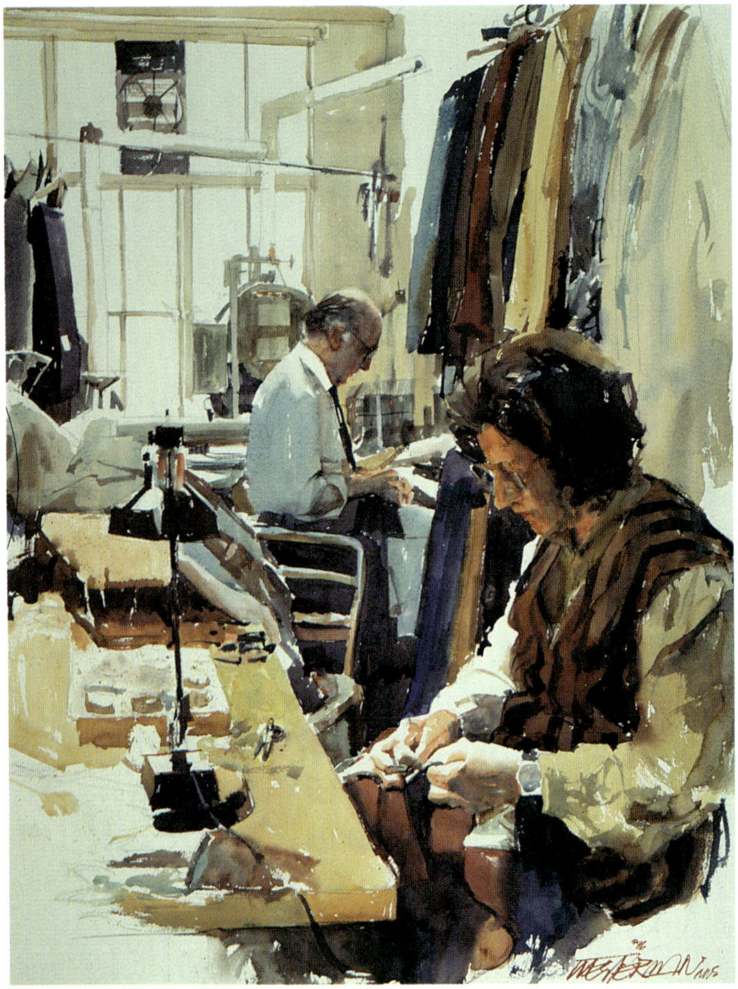

George the Tailor
1986
Watercolor
20½" × 25½"
Private Collection

George Nichol's tailor shop is next door to my studio. He and Vasso chatter in Greek while their fingers fly over the garments they alter. I wanted the viewer to focus on their fingers and the piles of scattered clothes. The frantic pace of the shop is suggested by the loose brushstrokes and spatter.

through children, or painting . . . some way of creating . . . giving life . . . we mean to go on.

Had you painted at all at this point?

Occasionally. But just for my own amusement. I had probably done three or four paintings in my life. If I wanted to fill a wall with something, I'd cover a piece of hardboard with stuff. That was the extent of it.

Then I heard about an artist here in Portland who did a certain kind of watercolors. I took his class. He did barns . . . and the brook running through the trees . . . and the two fishermen. George Hamilton. I thought he was fantastic. God, he was good! Still is, though his style had changed considerably since those days.

Anyway, at that time he was doing the typical kind of watercolor. A zillion people went through his classes, hoping to paint like he did, and I was one of them. He'd have people taking his classes so long that he'd finally have to tell them to leave. The wonderful thing about George was that he could fail. And that helped me believe I could become a painter.

Can you explain that?

I'll give you an example. I also took a class with Sergei Bougardt. Sergei was A.W.S., but he was best known as an oil painter. A tremendous painter. Russian. Bougardt never made a mistake. When he painted a demo, every stroke was right on the button. Just perfect. He never wiped anything out. You looked at his stuff and said, "I could never do that." Intimidating!

On the other hand, Hamilton could make mistakes. Sometimes his demo painting would get progressively darker and darker, and he'd start using opaque paints, and you'd realize that even the best of them can blow it. That helped convince me that I could do it. I could work at it. I might not be perfect, but I'd be able to paint.

You still had your ad business at this time?

Yes. It was to last for three more years. I was painting snow scenes, barns, little fences, that kind of stuff, until I realized that landscape painting just didn't hold lasting interest for me. I was more interested in people, so I started trying to paint them.

About 1978, I came across Charles Reid's work, and tracked him down to find out he was teaching at the Silvermine School in Connecticut. I flew there, and spent a week trying to learn how to do what he does. Of course I was terrible for the next two months. I couldn't paint worth beans, I was so intimidated. Everyone in his class was so good! Real pros who came from all over the country. And I was *"pfffft!"*

I know the feeling.

Reid was fantastic. A great teacher. A great guy. It was a wonderful experience for me, because two or three months later, all of a sudden, little bits and pieces started showing up in my pictures as I realized what I had learned. I could start to feel what he had done, and I didn't have to imitate him. (Though if I could have, I would have.)

I wound up painting the kind of things that appealed to me. From that point, it just progressed to the point where I figured I could sell the agency and get started. I appreciated that I wouldn't make much of a living, but I decided that was what I wanted—to be an artist.

Did you have a wife and family at that point?

Yes. A daughter, two sons, and my wife. We got divorced about that time.

As a result of this decision?

No. . . . I don't think so. The kids had left home, and I wanted to start a whole new life, and be a whole new person. So I went that route.

I remarried some years later, to a woman who is artistic, and shares a lot of my interests. We each have our own children, and their spouses, and grandchildren. . . .

Anyway, I sold the business to another agency. That was my stake, and I went from there. Ever since then, I've been managing to make a living painting, and doing some teaching, which I love.

In becoming established, who was your main role model?

I guess that would have been George Hamilton to start with. And Charles Reid. Add Burt Silverman and David Levine. And Milt Kobiyashi. Fine painters. I like the feeling that each artist imparts to his work. I've got a library here that I love to just soak into. An awful lot of great old and modern painters. Some of the Russians: Serov, Berthe Morisot and the impressionists, Richard Diebenkorn and Sorolla. What a great mix for inspiration! There's so much to be gained by looking at their work. When I get really depressed, or things really go wrong . . .

Do things go wrong much?

Not as much as they used to. Back in the old days, I dumped nine out of ten things I did. Now I have a much better track record. I think in part that this has to do with time, training, workshops, learning what to do and how to handle the medium.

Are you doing anything like prints or videos yet?

No. I haven't gotten into them. At this point, I guess I'm not sure the kind of thing I do makes a great poster. All I know is that I sell almost everything I do . . . around fifty paintings a year. About six hundred since I started.

I'll tell you something really interesting that happened: I had to contact people who owned my paintings that were to appear in *Splash* (1990, *Splash! America's Best Contemporary Watercolors*, North Light Books), to see whether they wanted to be named in the captions, or to remain anonymous. I mentioned to

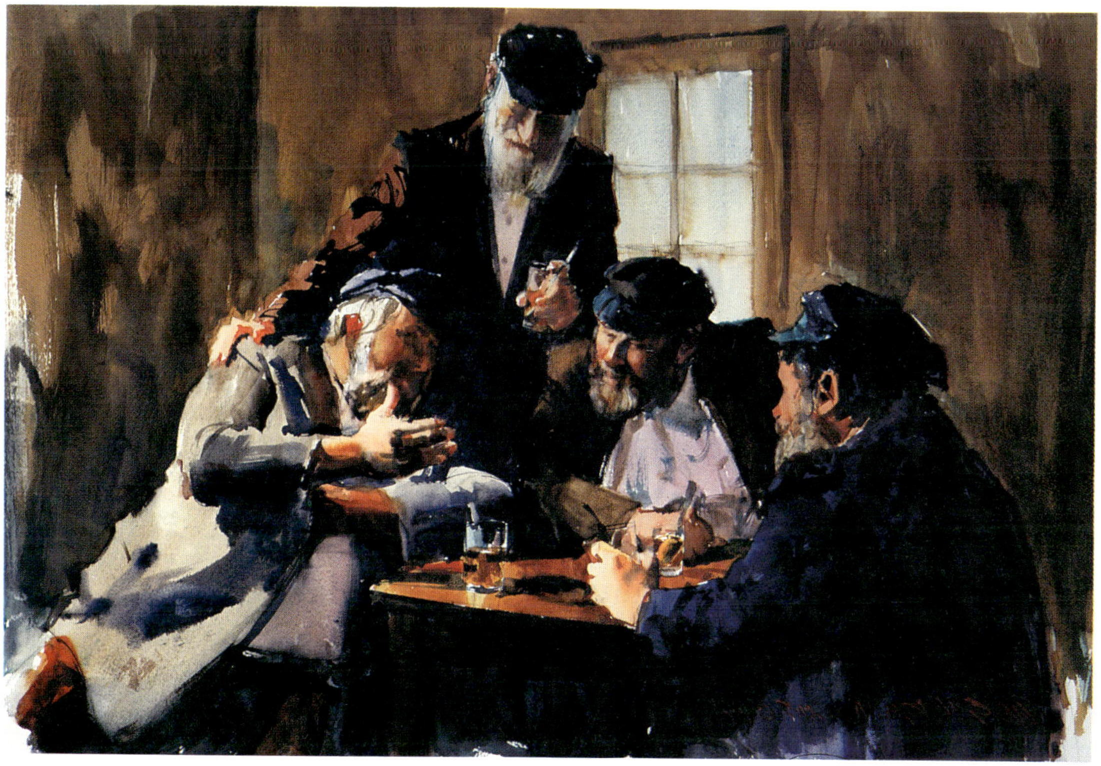

A Little Business
1990
Watercolor
25″ × 17½″
Private collection

My series of "shtetl" paintings has always been popular. Here I have some of my friends posing in eastern European costume, drinking glasses of tea (colored water, actually). I exaggerated the gestures and used strong, warm colors, trying for dramatic lighting.

one woman, who owned a particular painting, that I was thinking of sending out a mailing regarding some of my paintings that were not in galleries.

I asked her, "Would you like to be on that mailing list?"

She said, "Of course! I have twelve of your paintings!"

You didn't know she had them?

I don't know who's got what. I have a number of collectors who contact me, but most of my sales are through the galleries.

How would you define "success" in your own terms, as an artist?

I think success means being satisfied with your work, satisfied with yourself. I know you can never be totally satisfied. I know as an artist I'll never paint as well as I can see in my mind's eye. But I can be satisfied that I'm making some kind of progress, testing my skills, tackling things of greater difficulty and succeeding . . . daring to take chances and face failures.

Also, in order to continue practicing your craft, you have to be successful at selling your work. People have to say, in effect, with their pocketbooks, that they like what you do. Ultimately, success has to be measured in terms of sales. Luckily, this is probably the best time, historically, for an artist to be selling his work, what with the number of collectors in this country buying original art.

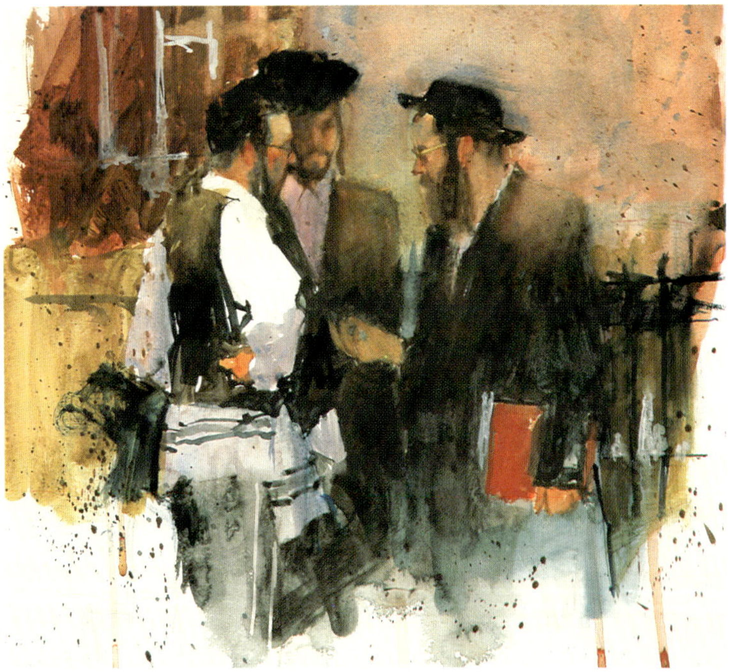

Three Hasidim
1990
Watercolor
13″ × 11½″
Private collection

This scene is from the Williamsburg section of Brooklyn. Three Hasidim are talking to each other in the street. The problem with scenes like this is, what do you do with the background to keep it from intruding? In this case, I chose to use abstract shapes, suggesting something, yet nothing.

Why do you think so many artists fail to achieve success?

I've never found out. I know too many artists who are fantastic, and don't sell worth a hill of beans. And I know other artists who are incredibly "thin." Sometimes clever. Sometimes not even that. And they still sell. And sell well.

Why?

I credit it to several things. First, your paintings have to be saleable. Second is luck. The third is chutzpah—a lot of good artists don't know how to sell themselves. You can't be bashful talking to a gallery owner. Talk his language: business. You've got to get out there and find a gallery that covers your audience and will be aggressive about making a market for your work, then personally get out there and sell them on it.

The main benefit of being in a gallery where the owner and staff like your stuff—really like it—is that they'll move it. You can have fine work, but if the gallery isn't doing anything to sell it, it's just going to sit there on the wall until they put it into the stacks, and you'll die there.

How did you go about finding the right gallery?

From my years in business, I felt I knew what the galleries wanted. They're just in business—looking for something they can sell. They're not so much interested in promoting art for art's sake, as they are in promoting art to keep their doors open and make a profit.

When I was still in the ad business, I went down to L.A., around Rodeo Drive, because I figured my work wasn't that bad, and I was showing promise. I was kind of hoping somebody would say, "I like what you're doing. Why don't you come back and see me in another month or so, or a year or two?"

I hit thirty-three or thirty-four galleries, and each one of them said no in a different way. "We don't talk to artists on Thursdays." "The boss is the only one who chooses." Etc., etc. And I thought, after I left each one, "Drop dead! I'm still making a living, and it's your loss!" But I also thought how bad I would feel if I were in it

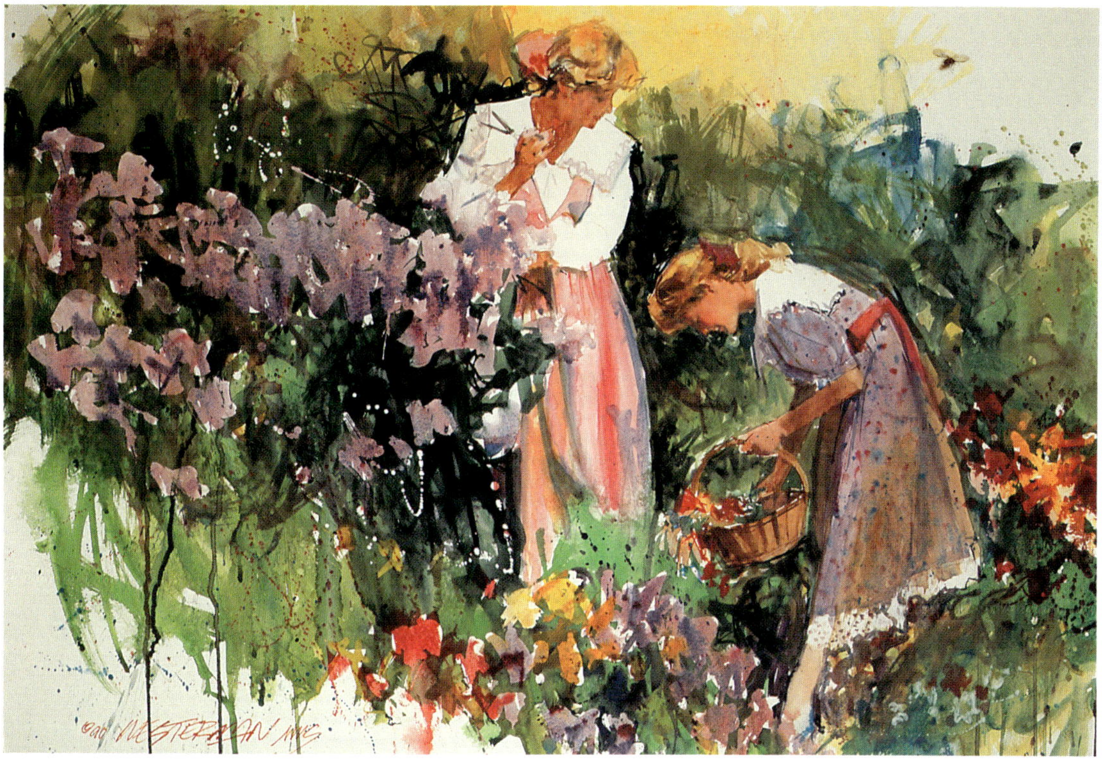

Shoemaker Garden
1990
Watercolor
39″ × 27″
Private collection

What could be sweeter than a pretty mother and daughter in a flower garden? The flowers are only shapes and colors. I'm afraid that if they were too representative, you wouldn't see my models. The background is formed of abstract shapes designed only to complement the verticals of my figures.

for my next buck, and they were saying, "No, no, no!" Anyway, I went to the ad business, and I kept painting.

The next time I went south, I stopped in Carmel and started with this one gallery, Bob Kaller's Galerie duTour. He was on the phone, and he put his hand over it and said, "If you can be back here in ten minutes, I'll take a look, but I have a lot to do and I'll be leaving here in about ten minutes." Well, I went outside, and I couldn't remember where I parked the car with my paintings. Carmel is full of cute little shops, not to mention eighty-two art galleries, and all the streets look the same to me. I finally managed to get back about fifteen minutes later. He looked at my paintings, and he said, "I'll take this . . . and this . . . and this . . . " I was three feet off the ground! And I was thinking, "Here's heaven! This is *it*!"

And what's funny is, we went out and had drinks and dinner, and we talked all night long, because he used to be in the ad business, and he used to be a journalist, and we could talk about a zillion things. We had a ball, and he *didn't* have any place to go! He was just using his "I'm-the-gallery-owner-and-I'm-too-busy-to-talk-to-you-with-my-busy-schedule" routine. This was his system. I loved this guy.

He's not still selling for you?

He died a couple of years ago, of cancer. All his galleries closed, one by one. That's how I was selling, and I said, "He died, and I'm dying too." I got real depressed, and I thought, "My life is ending. Nobody else wants my stuff. He did, but who else?" It was a real depressing period, and I thought, "I can always live on my Social Security, and I'll still paint a little."

What finally pulled you out of it?

The Attic Gallery in Portland. All of a sudden they went from selling a few, to selling most of what I could produce. Bang! Just like that! God knows why. I think people just decided they liked my work.

Then Zantman's in Carmel. They started slowly, and they went bang, too. Southwest Gallery in Dallas also sells some work. And I've got another gallery scheduled for Washington, D.C.

Today my problem is being able to paint enough to satisfy the galleries as well as my private sales. And now teaching is coming into the picture. . . .

Tell me a little about your teaching. Do you do many workshops?

My painting schedule doesn't permit many. I

West 72nd Street, Spring Rain
1990
Watercolor
42″ × 32″
Private collection

In all my New York street scenes, I try to focus on one or two individuals—in this case the young woman at center. The dark figures at the edges emphasized the light around her, and helped create the dramatic effect I was looking for. What could be dreary turns into a warm spring scene.

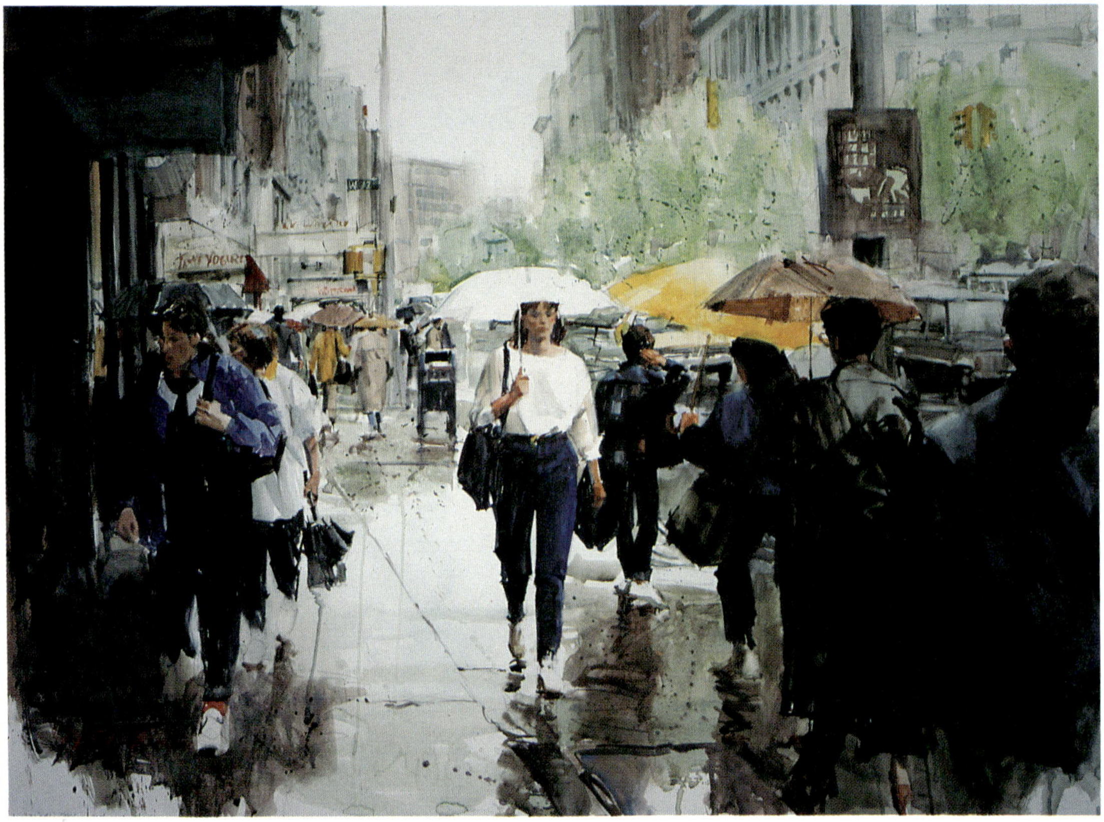

give some workshops in the Northwest, and have a fall class at the Scottsdale Artists' School. I'll be teaching in Fort Lauderdale, too.

I love doing it. I mean, I really have a ball. Teaching is just plain fun for me. I love people. My job, as far as I'm concerned, is not to have them paint like I do, but to get them so excited that they can hardly stand *not* doing it. That's what happens in my class. They just get excited! I've had people tell me, "Maude, well, she never did anything in any other class, but she can't stop painting now!" I like to hear that.

Suppose that someone in one of your workshops says to you, "I want to become a professional artist." What advice can you offer?

One way is to enter competitions. It gets your work seen, sometimes opens gallery doors, builds your reputation, looks good on your résumé. Donate paintings to appropriate causes—it opens up an audience to you.

What's your feeling about the mall shows, and such?

They're one way of doing it. I didn't want to do that. George Hamilton sells through the mall shows. But somehow I think that, in order to "arrive," you have to sell through a gallery. On the other hand, people make wonderful livings selling at malls. George does very well.

You were talking, before, about achieving a sort of immortality through your work. That "life" that we talk about in a successful painting . . . can you define it?

I think paintings that have some kind of emotional content, even if they're crude, last. The paintings that are cute, and clever, and technically just right . . . I think people look at them and say, "Isn't that neat?" and pass them by. They don't seem to have much staying power.

I don't know how long purely abstract art will last. Some of it may have staying power, but I'm not really sure. . . . The things that seem to go on and on are people, landscapes, things people can put themselves into, and take feelings out of. That's a clue. The emotional content somehow keeps registering, sending out feelers. And those feelers are caught up by people, and people respond to them.

What other thoughts might you offer to the aspiring professional?

If I were talking to somebody who wanted to be

an artist, I think I would probably say, first off, that you shouldn't worry about making mistakes, because you are going to make them. And that's how you're going to learn. And that you want to take what's inside you, and use that for your work. That you want to be emotionally involved in whatever you do. When you are, then it will show in your work. When you don't care what you're doing, then it's not going to have the same kind of meaning, either to you or to the people who look at it.

Another piece of advice for getting into galleries: Try to separate yourself from your work. Learn to talk about your paintings objectively, as if you were the agent rather than the creator. That may help reduce your sensitivity to rejection.

My ad background seemed to help me with that. I could recognize that gallery owners were just like most business people I had dealt with. They're nothing without artists. They have no inventory without us. The ones who peddle art for art's sake don't last long. That insight, I think, helped me talk their language. I believed strongly enough that my work was saleable that I was able to sell myself and my work to a gallery. I had a slow start, but I was sure there was an audience for figurative work. Time has proven the market for my "people paintings."

So many artists, it seems, want to paint what they want to paint, and only think about selling it after it's done.

I paint what I like to paint. I paint people. People like to buy paintings of people. Mind you, that doesn't go well for institutions, which seem to prefer the more abstract themes. But people who have homes seem to like looking at paintings of people, and reading things into them. It's like listening to a symphony, and hearing new things in it every time you do. I think when you pass by a good painting, there's always something new to see.

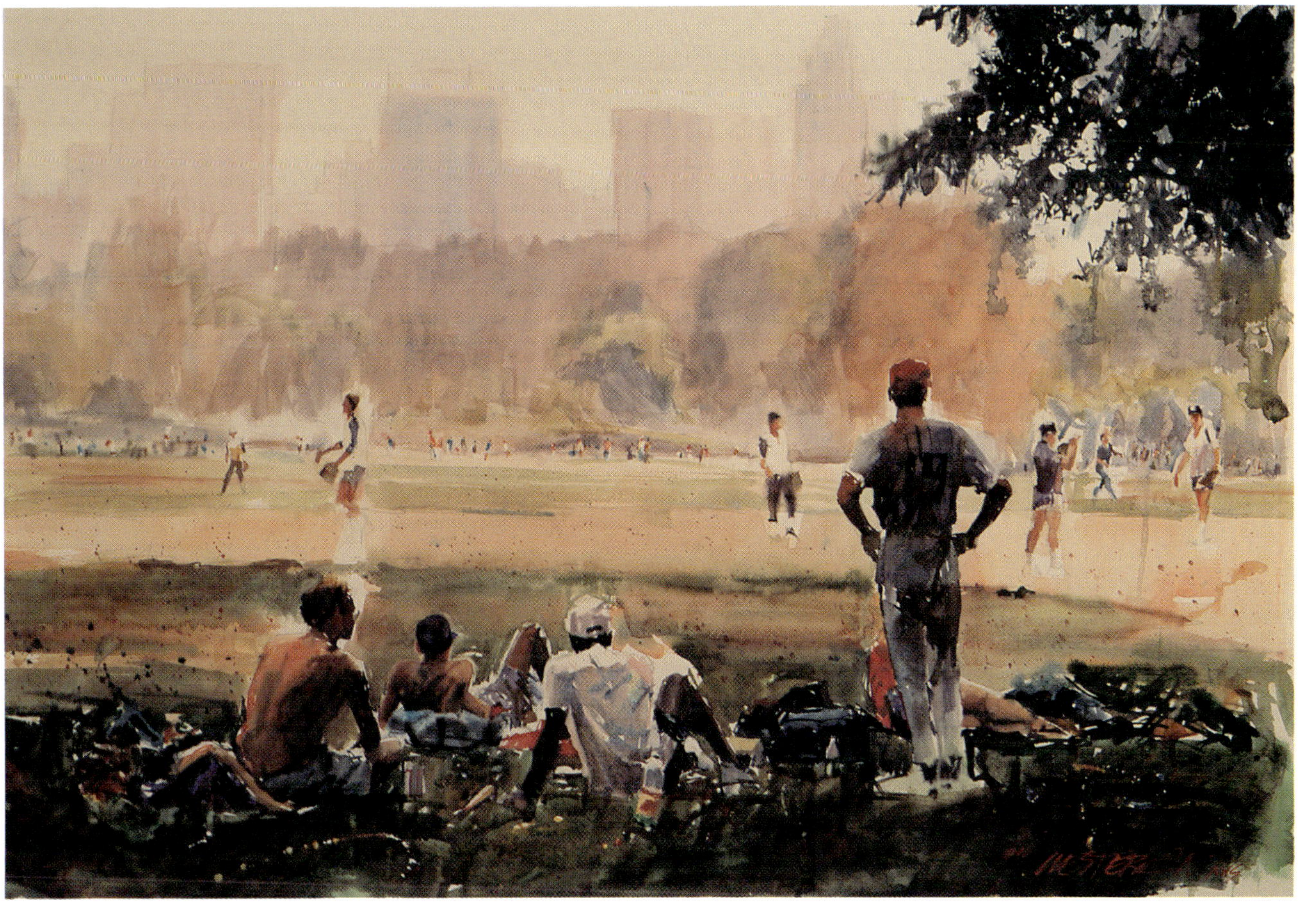

Ball Field, Central Park
1990
Watercolor
40″ × 27″
Courtesy Zantman Galleries, Carmel, CA

New York is a great place for a painter. Look in virtually any direction and you've got a painting. Here is a scene of contrasts: dark figures in the foreground, a light background. Loose handling of the ball players and plenty of white paper showing through, all add to the movement and sparkle.

DONALD PUTMAN
Know Your Subject and Paint Truth

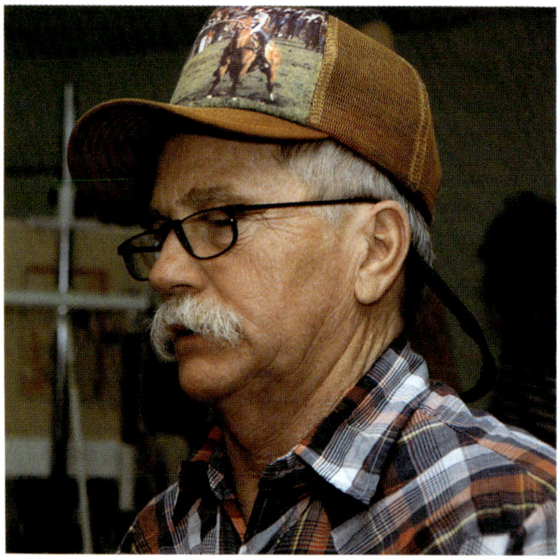

Donald "Putt" Putman demonstrates during his Scottdale Artists' School workshop. Photo by Lew Lehrman.

THE FIRST TIME I SAW ONE OF DONALD PUTMAN'S PAINTINGS—A WONderfully expressive, sure study of a straw-hatted man, legs crossed, reclining atop the dribbles of paint that ran down from his loosely painted blue suit—I was floored.

Enrolled in his Scottsdale Artists' School workshop the following year, I watched his demos with delight. Putt brings to mind a middle-aged Mickey Rooney, with whom he shares boundless energy and enthusiasm. When he wasn't painting, he continually made the rounds of his students, suggesting, helping, getting things back on course, and occasionally commenting to the whole class on matters such as color, edges, composition and contrast. Ideas and insights flew, and I wished for my tape recorder to capture all of them.

So impressed was I with Putt's ability to communicate his concepts that I returned the following year to repeat his workshop. I'll probably do so again.

Though Putt does not talk much about himself, clues about his background emerge during the workshop week. His portfolio of slides holds several circus paintings. And I'd heard that he had spent time under the big top. I didn't know the half of it:

When I left the Art Center School in Los Angeles in 1955, I had decided to go to Europe to bum around awhile and paint. Well, there had been this girl at Art Center, and driving through Massachusetts, I decided to visit her. While staying there, I got into a basketball game and sprained my ankle. My plan had been to work my way to Europe on a steamer. With this big cast on my foot, I couldn't. So I got into my old '36 Chevy coupe, and started heading down the coast, visiting museums along the way—Boston, New York, Washington—painting and studying, on my own, a free soul.

One day I found myself in Sarasota, Florida. I remembered that this was Ringling Bros. & Barnum & Bailey Circus' winter quarters, and decided to go out there to paint. I had always loved the circus. In school, my brother and I had put on shows at halftimes, hand-balancing and such. I did comedy diving routines in college, too. That was during the Esther Williams era, and there were lots of water shows. I was always a funny person, doing all these comedy routines; and I dive well, do all the tricks.

Anyway, as I was setting up my easel there, I realized they were tearing down all the tents. A worker told me, "We open at Madison Square Garden next week." Well, right then and there I decided to go with them. I had nothing holding me back except my cast, so I cut the damn thing off! I couldn't wait for it to get well. I went to the circus employment office and asked, "Hey, could you use a clown? I used to be a comedy diver and I'm very funny."

"No, we're all booked," they replied. "But there's an opening on the train for a porter." Without even knowing what was involved, I took the job. I found that I was to take care of two cars: the clowns' and the ring stock's. It was quite an experience.

I had to feed and fix drinks for all these people when they'd come back after each show. I'd fix meals for the snake lady, and the giant (who was close to seven feet tall, although he looked taller because he wore a ten-gallon hat and boots), and the Doll Family, who were all midgets. And the clowns. They all became my friends.

After Madison Square Garden in New York, we played Boston, Washington, D.C., Philadelphia . . . and ended up about a year later in Pittsburgh, where the union closed us down. It was the last time Ringling played under the big top.

I knew that I didn't really want to remain a porter, so when the train returned to Florida, I decided to get into an act.

Well, I heard that there was this guy named Tommy Paris who had a trampoline act. He'd let word get around that he was going to need a new partner for the act, because his partner and his wife had just run off together. Tommy was in town, getting drunk. I went into town and found Tommy. I said, "Hey, Tommy, I'd like to get into an act!" Well, he perked right up.

We started rehearsing out at the old trailer park where a lot of the performers stayed. He was a fantastic acrobat, and I was real strong. He taught me how to catch him on my shoulders, and in handstands. I knew a lot of tricks from my diving days, and I added a lot of comedy—falling through the trampoline springs, jumping rope—just to give him a breather.

Were you drawing or painting during your circus days?

During the Ringling year, I was busy all the time, so I only drew. I filled dozens of sketchbooks using my old Flowmaster pen . . . clowns, dwarfs, animals, almost everything around the circus. I still have all those drawings. While I was with Tommy, I was able to do a little painting, too.

Anyway, Tommy had always played the big-time—Ed Sullivan and Las Vegas—and he didn't want to break in a new act in this country, so we signed on with a Ringling Bros. unit that was playing Caracas, Venezuela.

After a while, that circus closed, and we joined a little local circus that went into the inte-

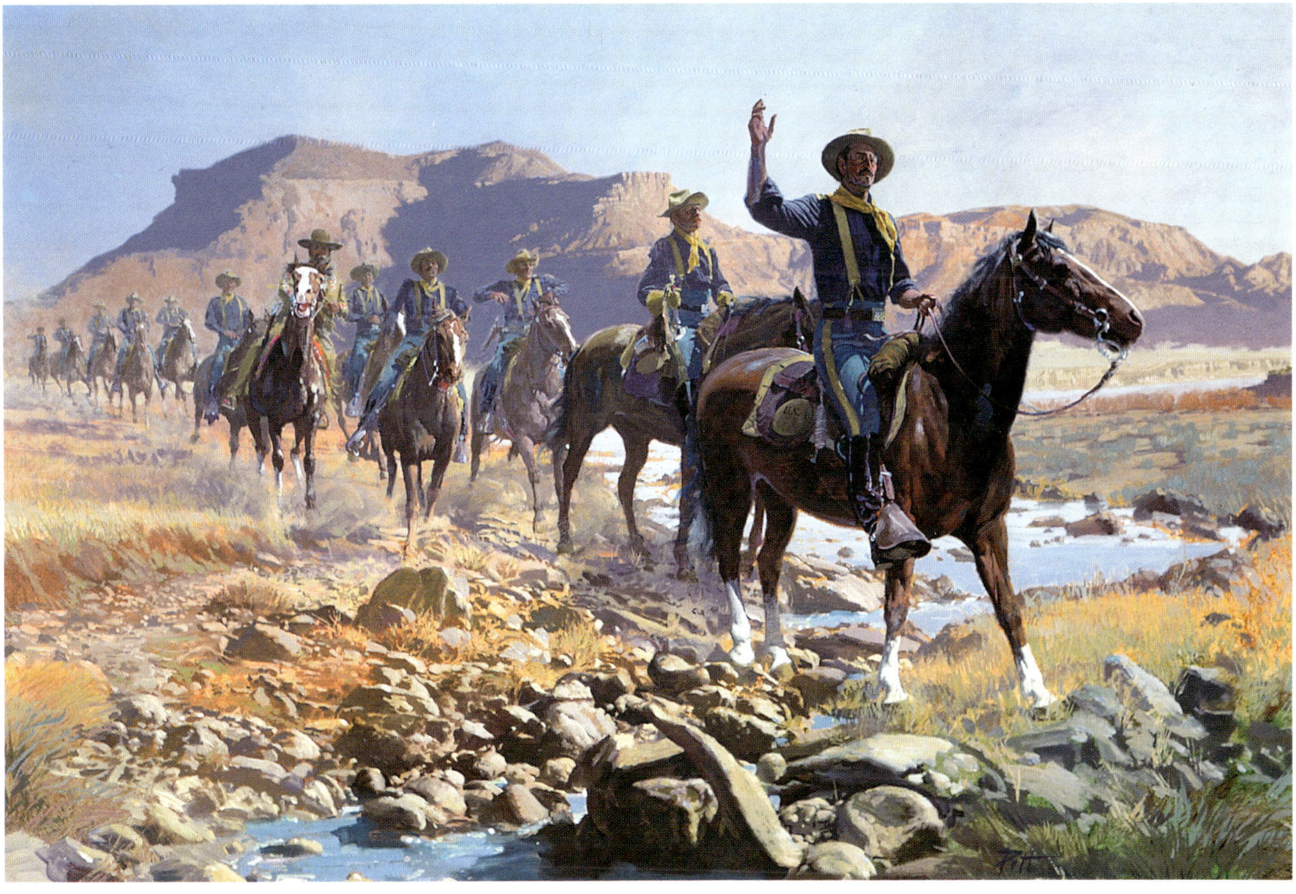

John Wayne
© 1970
Acrylic
40″ × 30″
Collection of
Bruce
Boxlightner

I placed "Big John" as the only figure interrupting the skyline, and not in the center of the picture. This is important because centering it would have frozen it and killed the movement. The most obvious way to create depth in a painting is to overlap elements.

White Run
1976
Acrylic
40″ × 30″
Collection of
Mr. Ed Kashain

In this painting, the snow becomes more yellow as it recedes, reflecting the yellow sky. I made the snow more violet (yellow's complement) as it comes forward. The feeling of speed is enhanced by having the horses go downhill, at the same time softening and losing detail on their back edges.

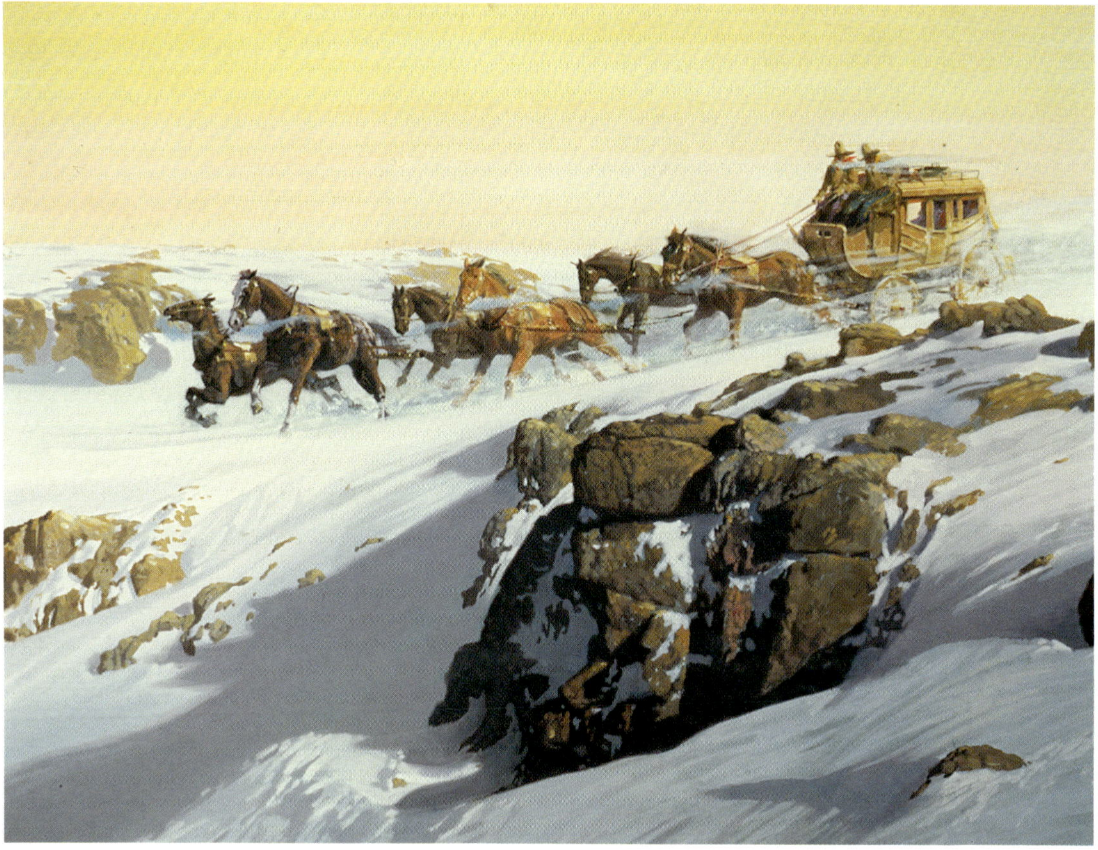

rior of Venezuela. We were really good by then, and we were the main act. We ended up in Barquisimeto, where that circus went bust. Everyone was so poor.

So there we were, stranded in Barquisimeto, practicing a second act where I'd get down flat and flip Tommy around on my feet. He had developed this lump on his arm, and it was bothering him to the point that he couldn't practice. The local doctor told him it was cancer.

We knew we had to get home to Florida, and we were practically broke. And just then I got the letter. Now, the way you get mail down there is to go to the post office and tell them you got a letter. They point you to a big pile of letters, and you have to find it.

Well, this letter was from the Circus Lounge in Sarasota. They had sold one of the paintings I had hanging there, and they enclosed two hundred dollars. What a break! That two hundred dollars was enough for air fare for the two of us, and we shipped the trampoline by boat. When we landed in Miami, we had two dollars left.

The doctors there told Tommy he only had a short time, and I took care of him for about a year, working at the Circus Hall of Fame, doing a little solo comedy act for the visitors. Eventually, the Ringling Bros. people heard about it, and they came over and watched me. At that time, Emmet Kelly, the famous clown, was leaving the circus to become independent, and they asked me if I'd take over his place.

I kind of weighed that. But by that time, I was already doing some murals in Florida and selling some paintings. I was really becoming more interested in my art, and didn't want to start traveling again. It had been a great experience, but I'd about had it. It's not a real easy life.

Was that the real beginning of your life in art?

I can't remember when I wasn't going to be an artist. As a young boy I'd say I was going to be a "commercial" artist, because everyone knew that artists starved. But even from the time I was very young, I drew constantly. When my mother dropped me off at kindergarten that first day, the only way they could get me to stop crying was to give me some crayons.

My folks were wheat farmers in Washington state. They moved to Los Angeles when the Depression came, and my father went to Texas to find work. He never came back. So my mom raised four boys. I was always the artist of the family.

I started off tracing the comics, using any kind of tissue paper I could find. Later I would copy them, and got pretty good at that. Started to do caricatures. Everyone would compliment me, and I got lots of attention, and got more and more into it. In school, I was always the one they called on to do the posters, or the cartoons for the annual. And I was great at sports.

I was drafted out of high school for World War II, because I was much older than my classmates. By the time I got out, my mother and new stepfather had moved to Grangeville, Idaho, and were tenant-farming there. I played football at Grangeville High, made All-State Idaho, and graduated in 1947.

After that I went to Fresno State, in California, with a football scholarship, taking art all the time to keep my average up and maintain my eligibility. I didn't do real well in college, as far as the academics, but I did great in art.

I never graduated from Fresno, but did get more serious about my art, and decided to go to Art Center College on the G.I. Bill. I worked in the cafeteria for food. And I cleaned studios for pocket money.

I didn't graduate from Art Center, either. They always wanted me to take lettering and layout, and those kind of courses. I said, "No way! I want to draw and paint!"

You knew right away that commercial art was not what you wanted?

Sure. Art Center was great because it woke me up . . . exposed me to all the art of the past.

In those days, I was an admirer of the great illustrators: Howard Pyle, Robert Fawcett, Harvey Dunn, the Famous Artists School artists. Still, I didn't want to be told what to paint. I wanted to paint for myself. The best training in the world for a painter was to take illustration in art school, because you had to learn how to draw and paint. If you took fine art, you didn't have to know either one. Just throw paint on the floor and run around on it, and put it up as art.

We were right next to all those "fine artists" in art school, and we could draw circles around them. They'd always pooh-pooh drawing ability. And that's really too bad. Because today, all the curators are graduates of universities that taught them that drawing and painting are not important. None of them can draw, and

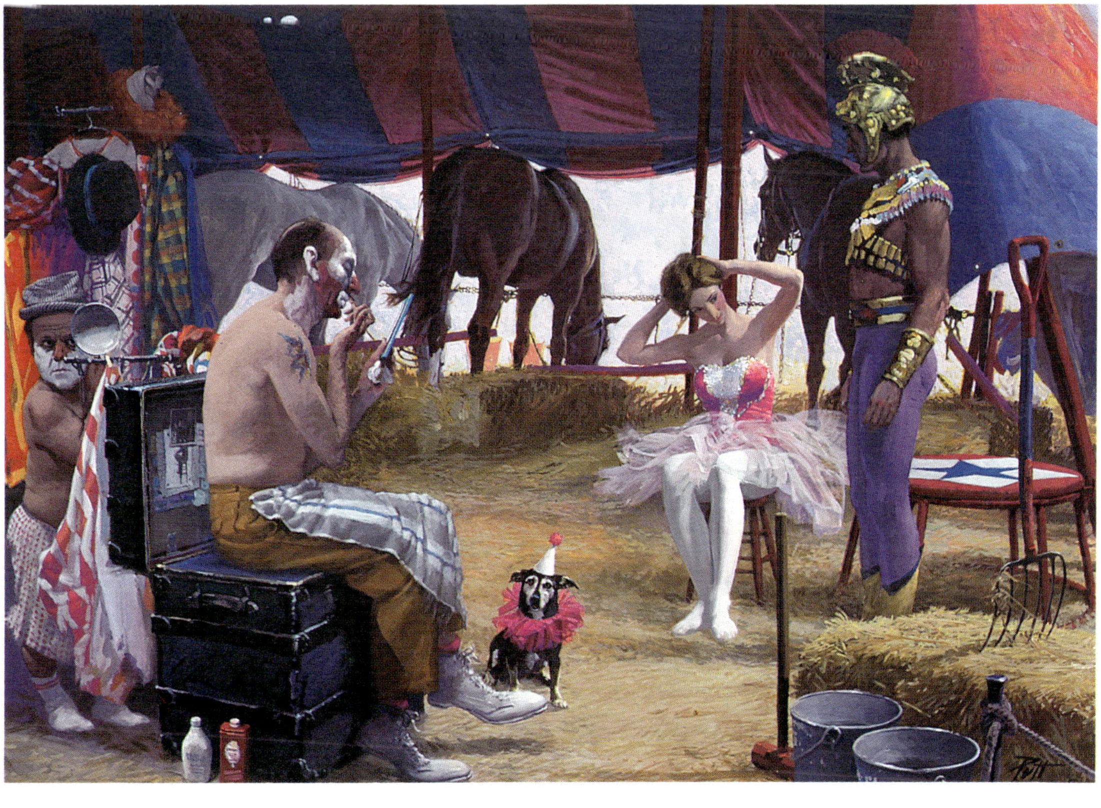

Man's Best Friend
1977
Acrylic
40″ × 30″

Back lighting, with negative shapes between canvas and horses, makes for an interesting backdrop. The strong man and his armor contrast with the girl bareback rider. Finally you discover the clown's dog—"man's best friend"—with his natural white face.

none of them can paint. And that's the only kind of art they respect. The really good painters that are still around can't get the recognition they deserve from the museums.

You can't compose music without knowing rhythm and harmony and all that. You can't write without knowing some grammar. But for some reason, that's not the way it is with art.

Let's go back to you. What happened next?

I went back to Florida, met Bobbie and got married. There wasn't much opportunity in Florida, so we decided to move to California, so I could be with serious artists. Almost immediately I got a job as a scenic artist.

How did you land that?

I went back to Art Center and learned that M.G.M. was hiring. A friend made an introduction call for me, and I got a job as a helper.

At M.G.M. I got to work with a magnificent group of artists, all older guys from Europe. They were trained in theater decoration, painting columns and gingerbread that look like the real thing. It was a great place to learn. I stayed about a year and a half before taking a teaching job at Art Center. We lived down at Redondo Beach. I stayed at Art Center all through the sixties, teaching, and painting on the side.

Eventually, I decided it was time to get into some galleries. That was a rude shock. I went to all those modern galleries that catered to the decorators, and to my surprise, they weren't interested in my stuff!

I was devastated. Finally I ran into Doug Jones, whom I had known at Art Center. I hadn't known it, but he was in the gallery business down in La Jolla. He looked at my work and said, "It's great! Let's put it up." It sold right away, and I've been a gallery painter ever since. Now I tell people, "When you go looking for a gallery, you'd better see what they've got in the window, and do some intelligent thinking about whether this gallery is right for you."

Let's talk about art in general. What do you think it is that makes some art seem to leap off the wall, while other work is essentially lifeless?

There are common denominators in art . . . things that have lasted over the ages.

The first is to know your subject, so you can paint truth. It doesn't matter what your subject is. If you care about it, that will show through in your painting. Degas may not have been a great aficionado of ballet, but he loved that subject matter. He understood it, and he did it right. Remington and Russell knew the West. They traveled it, and felt strongly about it. And that showed up in their work. It's important that you don't paint what you *think* the public might want. That will show, too.

The other common denominator in good painting is design. That hasn't changed over the ages. And it's strong in all the arts, even literature, dance, music, theater. The great ones know how to build to a climax, and how the end of the story should have something to do with the beginning.

You know, when you start a painting, the first thing you put on the canvas is the fifth thing. Because you've already got a top, a bottom and two sides. So the next thing is the fifth thing, and you don't want to stick it in the center, and you don't want it going in the same direction as the bottom or the sides. That's boring. The minute you start on something, the design principles have to be there.

In painting, I think it's very important to have variety of color combinations that are intentional, not accidental. I'd say 80 percent of the art you see looks the way it does because the artist couldn't do it any better.

Another thing that's common to all really good paintings is that the artist made it look easy. We know it wasn't, but it looks like it was as easy as falling off a log. Like the way Bing Crosby used to sing. It sounds like he wasn't even trying. There's no effort to it. If the singer has to strain his voice to get someplace, it hurts your ear. It's the same in a painting. It hurts your eye. You need to be able to render, and paint, well enough to make it look like there's nothing to it. We know it's very difficult, but the true artist makes it look easy.

With all your teaching, you must have met students with tremendous talent, who, five years later, have achieved nothing. Yet others, who may have had less talent and had to work harder, are on their way to success. What do

you think makes the difference?

Tenacity, probably. There's something to be said for longevity. Like Willie Nelson. If you can stay with something long enough, they finally catch on to you. Willie never changed. He just kept singing the way he did when he was young.

I remember, in art school, those guys who were pretty good, even as freshmen. They had a flair, but they never listened, never worked hard. They'd just do their flair. This other guy, he'd be struggling. He'd ask a thousand questions, and work all night. And he'd pass the first guy with no problem at all. It's that desire, the tenacity that's really important.

What advice would you give to an artist who wants to turn professional?

Draw. That's the most important thing. If you draw constantly, you'll get better and better. This doesn't mean that being a great draftsman makes you a great artist. It's what you put in and what you leave out, and how you interpret it. You really can't render it as exactly as a camera. What's important is to make it *better* than the camera. You cheat. You elongate some things, leave others out. Put other things in. Soften edges or lose them entirely.

Start looking at good art and see what artists do with edges. Usually you'll say, "Gee, she's beautiful!" or "That's a great ship!" You don't even realize how your eye is being manipulated. You're seeing the subject matter, not how the artist painted it.

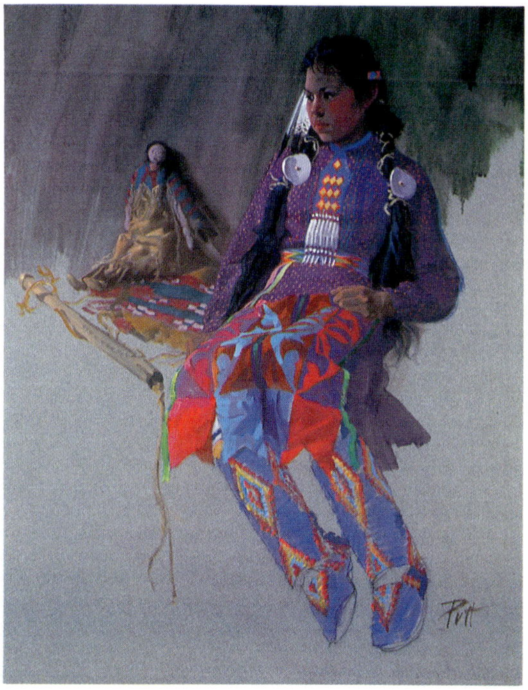

CROW MAIDEN
1980
ACRYLIC
20″ × 24″
COLLECTION OF
OKLAHOMA CITY
BANK

This is a demonstration painting in ink and acrylic on Canson paper for a workshop in Agusta, Montana. This little Indian girl from the Crow Reservation posed for the class. To keep her complexion dark, I surrounded her face with white eagle feathers and beading.

Technique aside, what would you tell the person who's in a non-art job, who's always wanted to paint but is scared to take that step?

I've run into a lot of them over the years. The first thing is to get a little working space so you can leave your stuff out. Then when you come home from work, you can pick right up and paint. If you have to get everything out at the beginning, and put it all away when you're through, forget it! I don't care where the space is: a garage, an old bedroom, a lean-to. Anything. Just so you can pick it up on the moment. Once you do, you won't let go. You'll paint the evening away.

Have good light to work with, so your eyes don't get tired. That's very important. And use good materials. Even if you have to save up longer. You can't be happy working if you use cheap paints and fight your brushes. Buy good equipment, and take care of it.

Any final thoughts?

There's one thing I've gone by over the years: "Becoming a good technician won't keep you from being a genius." I read that somewhere and it stuck with me. Because there's so much phony stuff going around – artists who don't want their naive talents "ruined" by learning how to draw and paint. That doesn't make sense to me.

If you had it to do over again, would you do anything differently?

I really don't think so. I probably would have drawn more. Or had a camera with me at the circus. I've been in places, seen things happen with the circus that you just wouldn't believe.

You know, there was one point where I could have gone into acting. I could have been a pretty good character actor. Not a leading man, but in slapstick comedy, that kind of thing. I'm thankful now that I didn't, because there are so many people involved – producers, directors, money and all that. Here I do a painting, and I sign it. If it's good I get the credit, and if it's not, I take the lumps. But I'm in it all by myself, which is much better.

MARILYN SIMANDLE
Always Have Your Stuff Out There

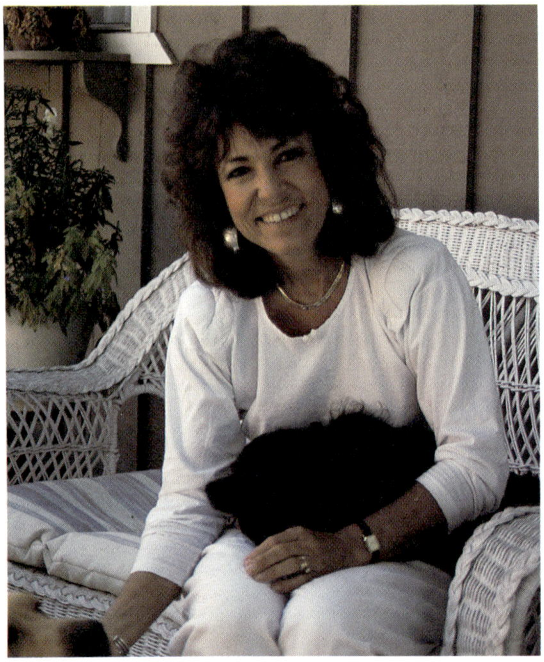

Marilyn Simandle at home.

I KNOW MARILYN SIMANDLE PRINCIPALLY THROUGH SEEING HER splashy, vibrant watercolors in the art magazines, and at O'Brien's Gallery in Scottsdale, Arizona. In a world of countless watercolorists striving for individuality, she has achieved it to an impressive degree. There is no mistaking a Marilyn Simandle watercolor, even from across the room.

I spoke with Marilyn at her home and studio in Santa Ynez, California, which she shares with her well-known artist-husband, Ted Goerschner, and their son, Nathan.

We spent some time discussing her beginnings in art, and her feelings about art in general. I found that her enthusiasm and spirit were as evident in her voice and her outlook as they were in her watercolors.

I began by asking her how she had become a professional artist.

I was born in 1946 and grew up in the Bay Area of San Francisco. Both my parents were very cultured, very music-minded. My mother was a wonderful musician. She started playing the organ at seven years old, and she played five hours a day, all the years I was growing up. She's been a concert pianist, has taught piano, and plays the organ in church to this day.

When I was six or seven, she took up painting, and she'd drag me along to shows and classes. I was always interested in drawing. It was her encouragement that gave me my start.

All through school, I took any art classes that were available. I had some pretty good teachers in high school.

I majored in commercial art at San Jose State University. It was a fantastic art school then, in terms of getting those fundamentals that are so hard to find these days: color, composition, value. I minored in illustration, so I learned a lot of technique. I didn't know at the time that I wanted to be a watercolorist, but I did know I wanted to paint. I had four years of design courses, life drawing and painting, classes that were not always fun but that laid the foundation for what I'm doing now.

When I graduated, I took my little portfolio, went for an interview at I. Magnin in San Francisco, looked around their studio and asked myself, "Okay, how far can I get here?" I saw the art director sitting behind his desk doing what everyone else wanted him to do, not what he wanted to do. I decided then and there that this was not what I wanted. So I put away the portfolio it had taken me four years to put together, and got a stewardess job with World Airways.

Whoa! That was certainly a sideways jump. How did that happen?

I wasn't married, didn't have kids, and this seemed like the perfect time to take a break from art. So that's what I did. I put my whole career on hold, but it was sort of a visual intake time. I had always had this passion for traveling.

Not the easiest way to make a living. Did you paint or sketch at all during that time?

I had jet lag for two solid years! I was in uniform

a minimum of eighteen hours every time I went to work. So as for sketching, I did very little. It was the only time in my life that I really didn't do much art.

By the time I'd put in those two years and was domiciled in Hawaii, I'd had enough. I liked Hawaii so much that when I quit World I remained in Honolulu. I started painting again, met a guy who had a gallery, and started hanging my work there. I was doing acrylics . . . and "water putties," of all things!

Water putties?

A technique I learned in one of my design classes. I've never seen them done anywhere. You know the water putty you use to fill holes in the wall? You can sculpt the stuff on masonite and make bas-reliefs. I had a ball with it! I'd paint over it and collage it with rope and rocks. (I was into textures and collage.)

Were you working elsewhere to support yourself?

I had a part-time job, not art-related, at first. I just painted on weekends, and when I had the chance. I'm prolific, and I had no problem keeping the gallery supplied with work. Painting outside, I had learned to paint pretty fast. I had to!

Anyway, that was short-lived, because I moved back to San Francisco and married my first husband. Started selling at the Artists' Co-op Gallery on Union Street, and soon became one of their top ten sellers. That was my first real gallery in San Francisco.

What kind of work were you doing for Artists' Co-op?

Watercolors. Plein-air paintings mostly. When I was in college, they took us outside a lot to paint, which they don't seem to do today. It's such an important part of learning, and I just developed a passion for it. John F. Carlson says that you should paint outside for at least ten years before you paint from a photograph. (To this day, I can usually tell when something has been painted from a photograph.)

Eventually we moved to Santa Barbara, and that's how I got to this area. I've been here for the last sixteen years.

Based on your own experience, then, what do you tell your own students about starting on an art career?

I advise anybody just starting out to hang wher-

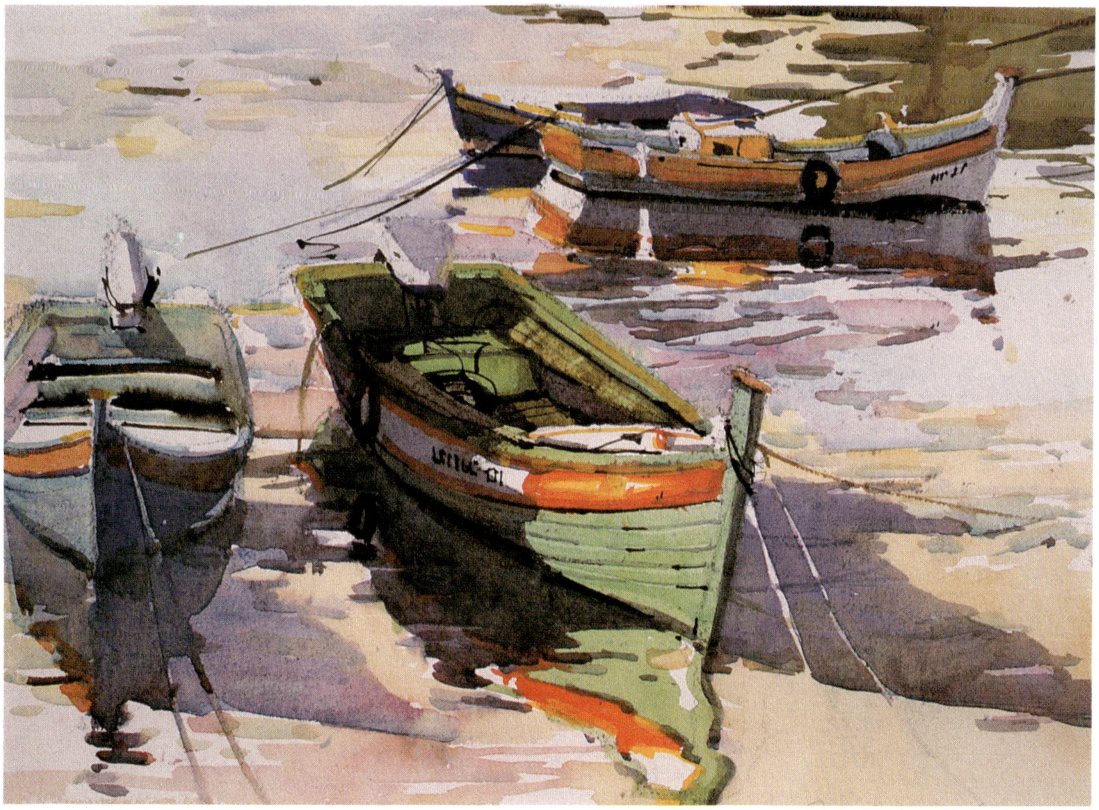

PORTUGUESE BOATS
1990
WATERCOLOR
16″ × 12″
COLLECTION OF ZANTMAN GALLERIES

This was one of those perfect six-in-the-morning golden hour paintings I did on location in Portugal. It's really a pain to get up so early, but what results! The light and shadows are most dramatic early in the morning or late in the day.

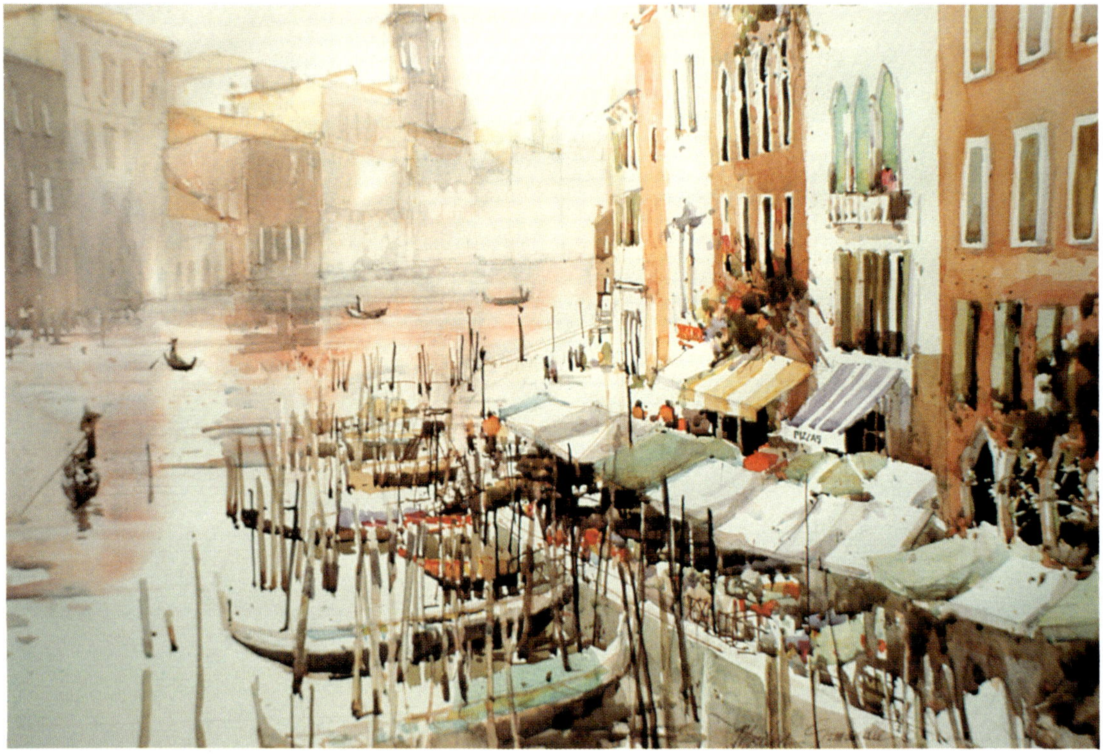

VENICE
1988
WATERCOLOR
36″ × 24″
COLLECTION OF
BURT REYNOLDS

Venice is the most colorful and wonderfully paintable city in Europe. Color, reflections, boats, romance . . . plus the best food in the world! It is by far my favorite painting spot. So, I will always paint Venice.

ever they can. Just like an actor has to act wherever possible. Get on stage. Be seen. Always have your stuff out there. Get feedback.

Artists' co-ops are a good place to start. Art associations, art groups, practically every town has them. Join. Try to win some awards to get recognition. That's something to put in your résumé. Hang in banks. Hang in restaurants. Wherever! Just get it up there for feedback. It will start happening. Then if you start selling, ask yourself, "What did I do right? Why did this one sell and not that one?"

On the other hand, if your work doesn't sell, you can't have so much pride that you become discouraged. You have to look at this as a business. I've taken a lot of downs, and a lot of no's, and a lot of rejections. You've got to become real thick skinned about this stuff. Even when your feelings get hurt, you just move on.

Do you think discouragement is a factor that keeps many artists from succeeding?

I think they're not willing to see themselves as part of the bigger world we live in. You have to find where your art fits in. And find out what will sell. But number one: You have to get good first. Get a good education. Too many artists today forget that. Which is why you see such bad art everywhere.

And the key to a good education?

Fundamentals. Forget the universities. They're academic. Professors will tell you, "Do eight paintings. I'll be in my office." That's not the kind of teaching you need. You want the kind of artist-instructor who will say, "It's not like this, it's like *this*!"

You need three years of life drawing. That's absolute, primo, necessary for learning how to draw. That's how you train your eye to see. Even if you want to eventually become an abstract painter, you still have to go through these preliminaries. Otherwise how do you know what you're throwing away?

It's really hard to find a good art education today. Too many abstract painters only paint that way because they don't know how to draw. That's one of my pet peeves.

How do you feel about workshops?

There are some really fine workshops, though you have to be careful, because some artists don't teach very well. However, at worst it's just a week out of your life, not a whole semester.

It's hard to learn very much in just one week, too. Someone just starting out needs a three- or four-year concentration. The degree is not as important as the instructors. Follow the instructor, not the school. Forget the degree. You just need a good education.

At what point should an artist consider breaking loose and trying to fly on his or her own?

Only you, the individual, can answer that.

That breakaway point is when you have had some sort of experience with sales. You have painted some paintings that are very good. Your work is hanging in a gallery. You show some sort of continuity in selling your work. And you know you can produce. Having a business sense helps, too. Being able to deal with the public, being somewhat organized with paperwork helps. As an artist you have to be your own boss. You have to set goals for yourself, then break them down to tiny steps so you can develop a daily routine.

What sort of goals are you suggesting? And what kind of steps?

Say you want to be in a good gallery within two years. To find that gallery, set yourself a goal of calling one a day. Or writing to one gallery. Or going to visit one gallery a day. In order to get into a gallery, you've got to see it first. Then you have to find out about it by talking to its artists. I have a whole set of criteria about how to get into a gallery.

What are they?

Number one: Make sure the gallery has been in business for *at least five years*. Galleries go in and out of business quickly. When they go out of business and they have your paintings, chances are you won't get them back. That's happened to me a couple of times. Or they owe you money and won't pay you, which amounts to the same thing.

Number two: Visit galleries. If you're a representational painter, you won't do well in an avant-garde gallery. When you walk into a gallery, if you like the work there, chances are they will like your work, too.

Number three: Before you go, take slides of six or eight of the best paintings you've ever done. Send them to the gallery with a letter saying you'll be following up with a phone call in a

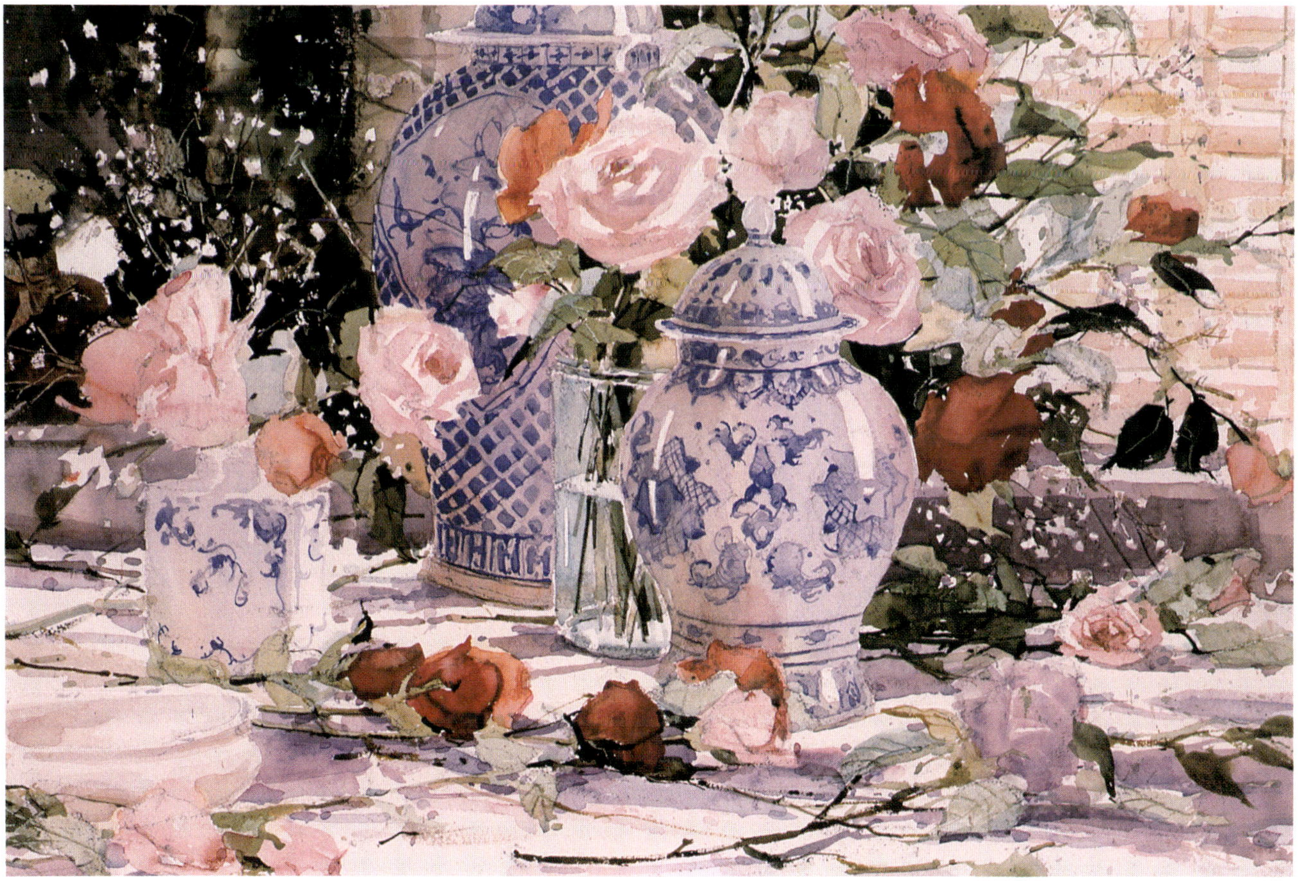

ROSE RHAPSODY
WATERCOLOR
30″ × 22″
COLLECTION OF THE ARTIST

When I paint still life, I actually turn my studio into a still life. Then I will take a section that excites me most, and paint that. With still life, you actually paint indoor landscape. These roses are from my own garden, grown with my luke-green thumb.

OCTOBER
WATERCOLOR
36" × 24"

Fall colors are always the most exciting. The best time to paint autumn trees is when two-thirds of the leaves have dropped off. Vermont in the fall, as this shows, can be the best place to be in October.

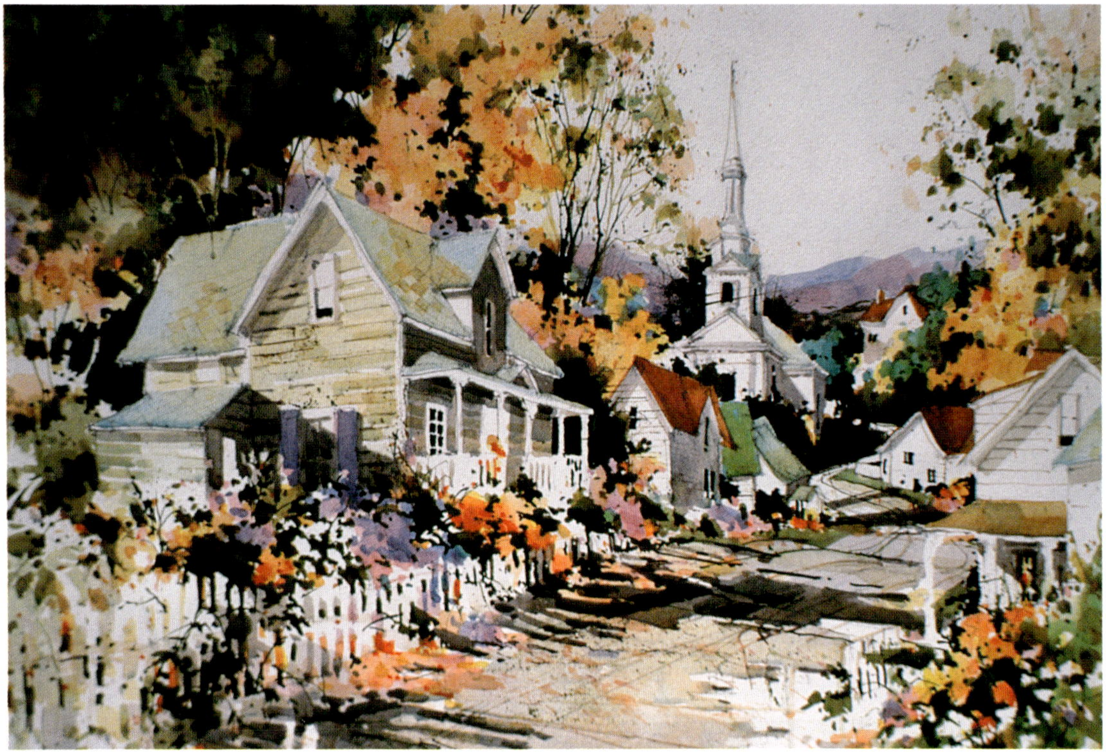

couple of weeks. Then call them. (Galleries don't want to be bothered with people walking in off the street.) If they like your work, chances are they'll want to see the originals.

Number four: Now you're at the gallery with your work. If they like it, they'll want to keep it. If they don't, make sure you find out why. Get as much feedback as you can. "Why isn't this good?" or "Can you give me any suggestions who else I might see?" You may not agree with what they say, but absorb it and keep in mind that galleries are in business for the *business* end of things, and not the *art* end of things. Don't take the comments personally.

And fifth: Any time you're thinking of doing business with a gallery or a publisher, ask for phone numbers of the other artists they do business with. Then call and talk to those artists. If the gallery won't give you the address of any artist they represent, they have something to hide. Forget them and move on! I think a lot of artists put these gallery people way up in the sky where they don't belong. A gallery is just a business. That's all it is. Very rarely will you find gallery owners in it just because they're passionate about art and artists.

Another thing: Spare no expense in framing your work. Your painting is usually as good as the frame around it.

Do you do your own framing?

I used to. I cut all my own mats, all my own glass. I remember looking forward to the day I could take all my paintings into the frame shop. Now I do. It costs a fortune, but I do it anyway, because I would rather spend the time painting. Or gardening.

Why do you think some art makes such direct contact with the viewer, while so much other art just hangs there?

I believe it's sincerity, honesty, and the intent of the artist in making the painting. By sincerity, I mean the artist's passion, her feeling toward her subject matter. Is the artist painting this child because she loves her and loves how the light is coming down on her face, or because she knows the painting will sell? It comes through, no matter what the subject is.

I think the general public can pick this up in a painting, even though they don't know much about art. It's like an electric bulb. You're not sure how it works, but you know when it does. You can always tell what's wrong in a painting, but when you see something right, you just sit there and admire it.

What other advice do you offer your students who ask about making a career of art?

Just work as hard as you can, every day, whether you feel like it or not. Go in and paint. Commit yourself to a certain amount of time every day. No shortcuts. Discipline is number one in terms of getting good. No one is more successful than the person who perseveres.

Work towards developing consistency in your art. That's another thing galleries look for. If you change your medium every two months, or your subject matter, or you haven't found your style, galleries don't like that. They want to see continuity, so don't go off on any tangents. If you do, the galleries won't take you on.

At the same time, don't get locked into painting just one thing because that's what sells. A lot of artists do, you know, paint the same thing over and over and over again. I don't know how they can do it. And once the artist is bored, the audience is going to be bored, too.

Every gallery will try to get you into that rut. It's a constant battle, especially when you're in five or six galleries and they all do well. It's hard for me to be true to my art when they're all asking for European themes or florals!

SAN FRANCISCO ORIENT
1990
WATERCOLOR
24″ × 36″
COLLECTION OF THE ARTIST

I used to paint outside as much as possible. To deal with the crowds that gathered, I'd put on my Walkman headphones and pretend I couldn't hear anyone talking. I love painting architecture. This probably stems from living in southern France in 1965, among all the old buildings and good architecture.

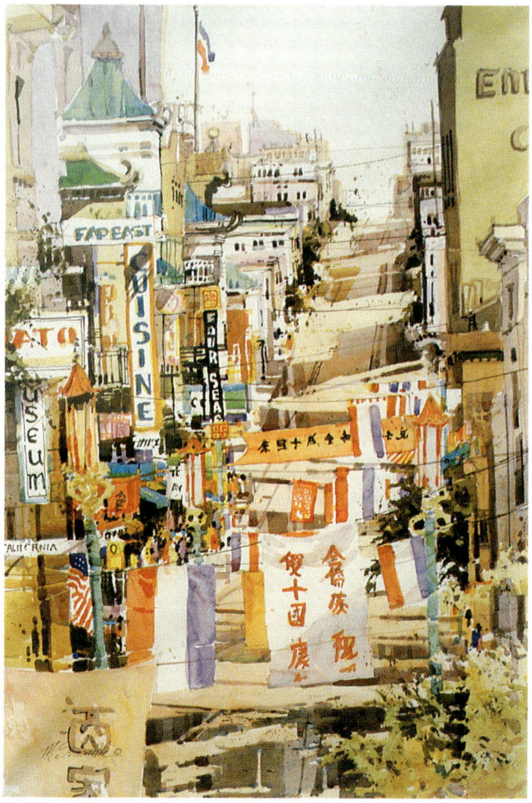

Let's talk about your work. Are you a disciplined painter?

Yes. My studio is in our home, and I'm there at least five hours every day. Even weekends. I paint outdoors, locally, and get up to the Sierras when I can. Ted and Nathan complain about all the time I spend painting, but I love it so much I could paint all the time!

Of course, I have other commitments. I'm a mother and wife, and I try to balance everything. It's good for artists to have kids. They keep your feet firmly planted on the ground. If it weren't for Nathan, I might be living somewhere in Europe, sending paintings back here for shows. I still have a Gypsy travel bug in me. Still love it. I'm always planning a trip to Europe.

Give me your own definition of success.

Fulfilling your dreams, whatever they are. I'm doing exactly what I want, and I'm making a living at it. Every now and then I have to pinch myself. All my life I have been so thankful I was given this gift, this talent, which I was born with but also had to cultivate.

How much of your success is talent, and how much is perseverance?

I'd like to think it's a little bit of both. The talent can get you started, but you've got to put in the hard work to develop it. Success, also, is having a balanced life in other ways. Having children, and a husband that I love, all of that goes together. When I'm successful, I want to share that success with my family.

It shows in your work.

I hope so. People always tell me that my work is uplifting. My philosophy is, as Sorolla said, "There should be nothing in art that is either sad or ugly." Art should be uplifting, not downgrading, demoralizing or demeaning. Otherwise why put it on the wall? In his book, Richard Schmid said, and I'm paraphrasing, "I want to be a part of the solution, rather than a part of the problem." To me, that says it all.

PAUL STRISIK
Be Good, Not Different

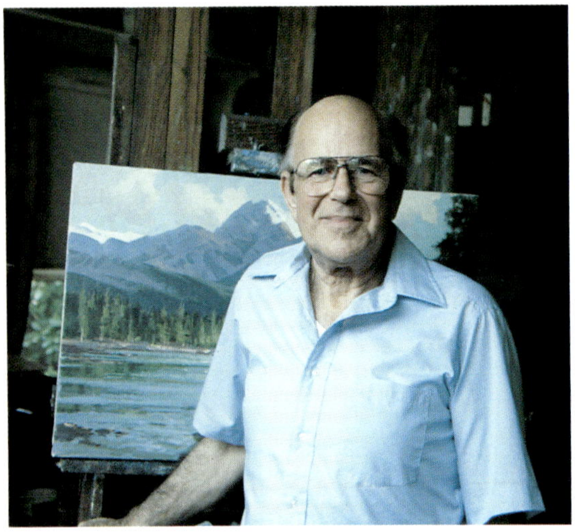

Paul Strisik, photographed in his light-filled Rockport studio. Photo by Lew Lehrman.

ARRIVING AT THE STRISIKS' ROCKPORT, MASSACHUSETTS ADDRESS, I AM welcomed into their spacious home. Perched on a low bluff overlooking the water, the house is filled with Paul and Nancy's impressive collection of antiques, as well as mementos of their extensive travels. The sun-sparkled living room, furnished in classic fine taste, glows in pastel tones of blue and beige; it contrasts with the rich colors of paintings, Paul's and others', that line the walls. Off the living room, down a short hallway, we enter his cathedral-ceilinged studio. Here I find the comfortable clutter and the pervasive aroma of turpentine and paint that one associates with the serious artist. Two easels dominate the room, between them a cherry-topped taboret/palette. Wide-mouth jars with well-used brushes in them stand ready. Overlooking the studio, the open storage loft is neatly stacked with canvases. Near the entry, as we leave, what looks like a mare's tail turns out to be countless prize ribbons, pinned together and hanging from the wall.

For our interview, we settle comfortably in the living room.

Paul, your work is sought after by a wide audience of collectors and dealers for its expression of traditional painting values. Where do you see your place in today's undisciplined, volatile, ever-changing art world?

There's so much nonsense in the art world today. It's the dealers who make these canvases a commodity. I remember watching the Andy Warhol estate auction. Some of his canvases went for two hundred to three hundred thousand dollars! One was a five-by-five canvas painted a solid flesh color. All over. Its title was *Flesh*. It went for almost two hundred thousand dollars!

Is it art? I just don't know. But throughout the ages, it has always been the new that's been noticed. Art, business, industry—everything would stand still without new ideas, new styles, new products. People get bored looking at the same old world. Picasso, for one, was a genius, if only with new ideas. There are no two ways about it, he influenced the look of design, art, advertising . . . you name it. Remember, not everything has to be lasting. Some things can be for now. Just for the moment. Ultimately, though, quality and good taste last. Beautiful design, even from hundreds of years ago, can still give people shivers.

As for my own work, I don't know whether or not my paintings will live. But I'm not interested in immortality. I tell young artists who want to paint for a living, "Be good, not different."

I like good painting. Not just my kind of painting. All types. All schools of painting are valid; any approach, if it's what the artist truly feels inside.

Taking the bad with the good, though, I don't think I could have chosen a finer profession. Art is one of the few things in history we can all be proud of. Look at all the others that have been so destructive.

I can see that art plays a very important role in your life. Did you always want to be an artist?

When I was a kid of nine or ten, you didn't find paintings in houses like you do today. If there were, that meant only one thing: The people were rich. I had two friends with wealthy fathers. There were paintings on the walls, and though my friends took no note of them at all, those paintings held a certain fascination for me. I can still see them in my mind's eye.

Then there was the time my father took me to the Brooklyn Museum. A wonderful place. I saw a man copying a painting. I saw that polished walnut box, all those tubes, and I said, "Oh, wouldn't it be fun to have something like that to play with." I still get a lot of pleasure out of the mechanics . . . the playthings of art.

But I had countless hobbies. I was always in the basement while the other kids were out playing. I was involved in a lot of creative things. I even dabbled in painting. Somebody gave me a little oil painting set for Christmas. I guess I was fifteen or sixteen. I copied some magazine covers. That was the extent of it.

Eventually, I went into business, but the war came, and I enlisted in the Navy as a photographer. That had been one of my hobbies, and I was knowledgeable. Eventually I made Chief Photographer's Mate.

When I got out of the Navy in 1945, I was twenty-seven, and got a job with an outfit that sold rope and cordage. I knew immediately that this was not the world I wanted, so I turned to art again. I bought a few materials and started to dabble. Then and there, I made the decision.

You had had no formal art training up to that point?

None. But that's what I wanted to do. It was tough on my family, of course. My father was brokenhearted that his son wanted to starve in a garret. That was the usual image of an artist in those days, especially to a business person.

I was newly married, and we rented a cold-water flat on Third Avenue and Ninety-fifth Street in New York. I started to study painting with a man named Nickolai Abracheff. He was Russian. A modernist. He held classes at night, in his uptown apartment, for about eight students. So I was painting now, but I was still unhappy. I knew that what he was teaching was not going to lead to the type of painting I was seeing and loving in the museums. But I was at a loss as to where to turn.

One of my classmates, who began to miss some of the classes, confided in me that he was

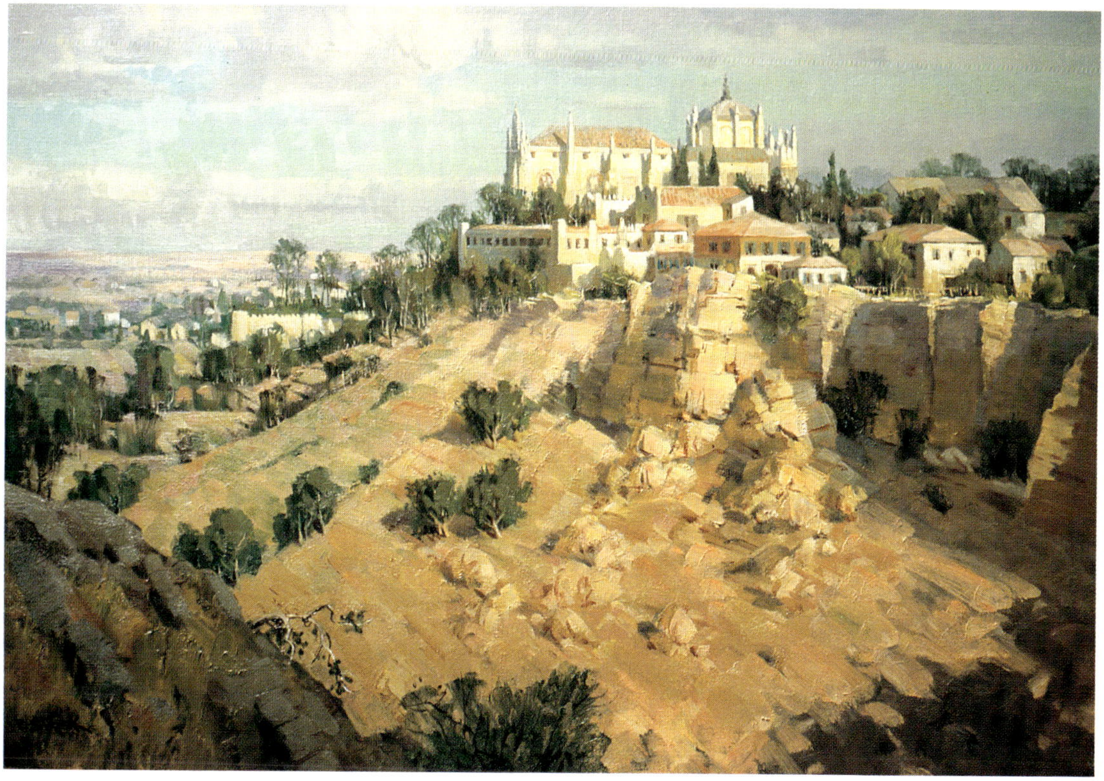

TOLEDO, SPAIN
1987
OIL
30″ × 20″
PRIVATE COLLECTION

When in Europe, or other locations reached by air, I do only 10″ × 14″ field sketches in oil, due to their easy portability. I spent eight days painting in Toledo, Spain, and since it is a city on a hill, surrounded by the Tajo River, there were many exciting vantage points from which to paint.

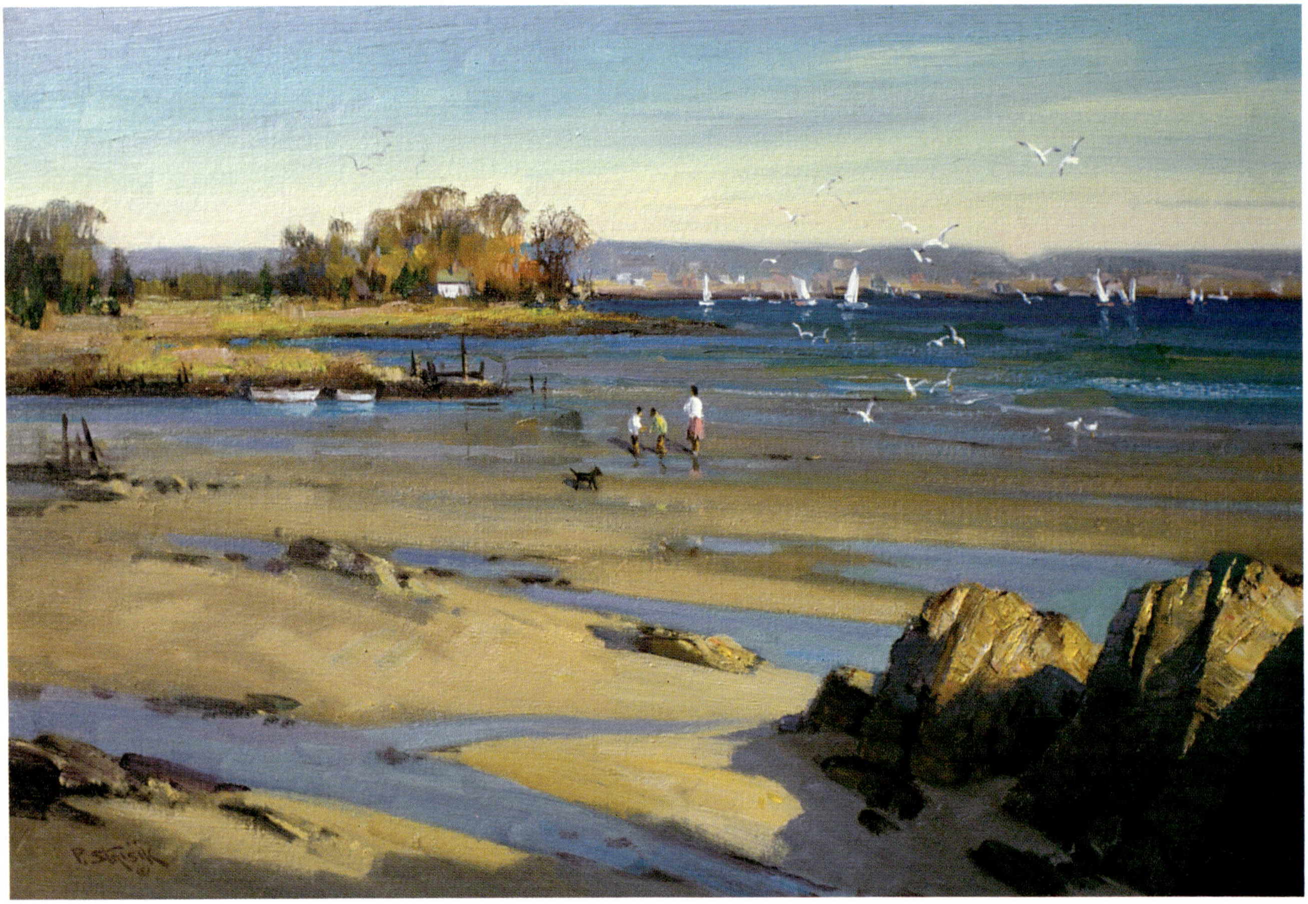

The Shell Collectors
1989
Oil
24″ × 16″
Private collection

This type of scene is common to my area. Low tide offers many possibilities for design in wet sand, rivulets of water, and tide pools. Of course, the figures add much to the center of interest and focal point of the painting. I tried to give the whole scene a lyrical summer mood.

attending Frank Vincent DuMond's painting classes at the Art Students' League on Fifty-seventh Street. He told me that DuMond taught summer classes in Vermont, and that he was going to attend those, too. I remember saying, "I'll go up there, but if he's going to take away my individuality and get me to paint like him, I can always leave and paint on my own." I didn't realize that it was the principles of painting I needed, and that individuality would come later when I understood the language of painting.

When I think back, I wonder how I could have been so ignorant about the things in painting I take for granted today! Based on my work, I was very ordinary. Nothing promising. I was a slow starter. I think I was filling my head with all the information, but I just couldn't put the pieces together. I'm still working on it, of course.

Anyway, I went to Vermont with DuMond. And the minute he started, I knew I had a rare teacher. I stayed with him for three and a half years. He was about eighty at the time. I studied with him in Vermont in the summer, and at the league the rest of the year.

How were you supporting yourself at the time?
My wife was working. And believe it or not, I was giving painting classes in our apartment at night. I always kept a few lessons ahead of my students. They were Sunday painters, but I understood the principles, and I kept them happy. It helped keep us afloat. My classroom was a cleared-out bedroom in our apartment where I could fit six students. I made lightweight easels I could fold up and put away. We slept on a pullout bed in the living room.

I was going to the league in the morning, painting in the afternoon, teaching in the evenings and some afternoons, and going to galleries and museums whenever I could.

Visiting the galleries, I discovered Frederick Waugh's seascapes. His surf scenes were wonderful. I had grown up in Brooklyn, out near the ocean, and I was familiar with it. I decided I wanted to live near the sea and paint marine subjects.

In about 1956, we made a trip up the coast,

The Peacock
1989
Oil
24″ × 30″
Private collection

I enjoy still life painting as a change of pace from landscape painting. In composing them, I usually try to favor a theme. In this case, I chose the peacock feathers, a Hiroshige print of a peacock, and these favorite richly textured Oriental objects.

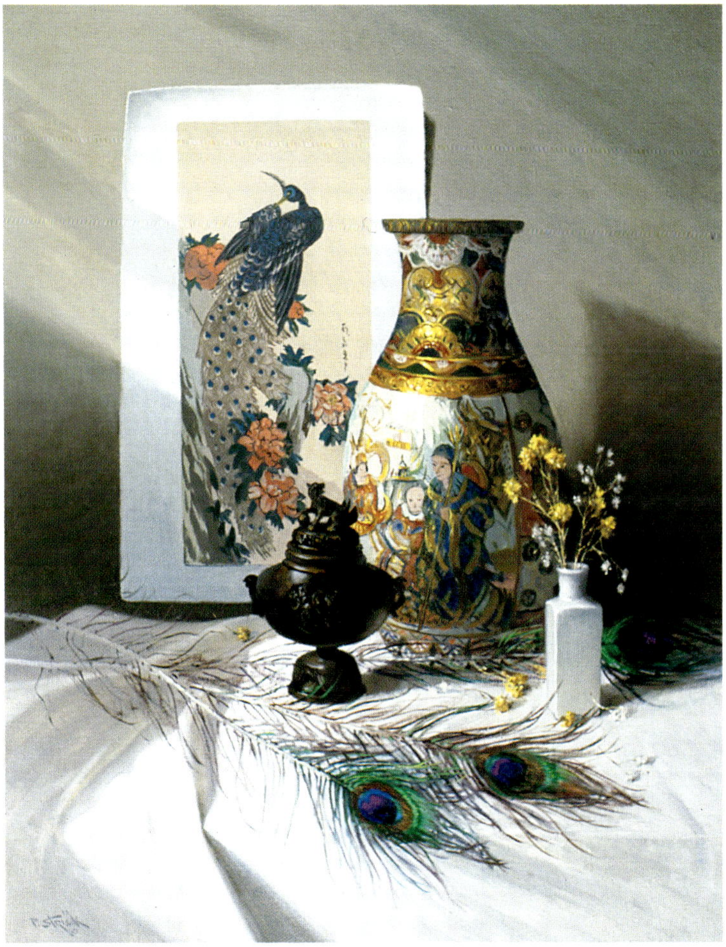

looking for a summer place, and discovered Rockport, Massachusetts. We bought a little summer house in Pigeon Cove, along the shore, for fifty-five hundred dollars. We'd come up here and I'd paint all summer, and take my work back to New York in the fall.

That first summer, I met Emil Gruppe, who was a well-known painter in nearby Gloucester. He was the greatest salesman. He loved to paint, but even more, he loved to sell. He visited us in Pigeon Cove one afternoon. Looking around, he asked, "Don't you have a gallery here?"

"No." I answered. "*Where* would I have a gallery?"

"Right here. In this living room. Get all the furniture out. Put plywood over the windows. Cut a door in your wall so the customers can come in that way. And put a sign out there that will stop 'em dead in their tracks!"

I did make a gallery out of the living room, and I did hang out a modest sign. And though there was not much traffic along our road, I got some visitors, and I sold some paintings.

About that time, things began to happen for me. I sent some paintings to Grand Central Galleries. I was accepted, and some sold. Finally, it dawned on me that the only reason I was staying in New York was that I'd been born there, and had family there. When I realized I had no real reason to stay, we moved here. We sold the Pigeon Cove house, and bought the building on Main Street where my gallery is now. I did a lot of the fixing up myself, and we moved into the apartment upstairs.

Having my own gallery was the answer for me. Rockport got lots of summer tourists. I painted the boats in Rockport Harbor, street scenes, coves, lighthouses, winter scenes and Cape Ann landmarks. Four out of five had surf in them. My work sold fairly well. I'd go out in the morning, paint some boats, and try to sell them in the afternoon.

Without the gallery, it would have been much more difficult. But the style here was for artists to have their own galleries. During the Depression, and even before, artists would come here, rent fish houses on Bearskin Neck, and put up their paintings. In the summer, the tourists always came, and the shacks grew into the galleries of today.

From the moment I got here in the fifties and sixties, I was teaching. I had summer classes for many years. Every Thursday night during the summer I gave demonstrations, in my gallery, and at art associations in the area during the winter. They were a good source of income. I'd get twenty-five dollars for the program. I would do a twenty-four-by-thirty-inch oil, a simple, bold subject that would move right along. I had a portable P.A., and I'd talk constantly while at the canvas so nobody would get bored. I'd sell the demo painting for one hundred or one hundred fifty dollars right there, so I wouldn't have to bring it home wet.

Between the demonstrations, which spread my name and got me more students, my classes, and my paintings, we managed to pay the mortgage every month.

Since we lived upstairs, I left the gallery hung all year 'round. In the summer, it was open from 10:00 A.M. until 10:00 P.M. If somebody rang the bell, day or night, year 'round, I just ran

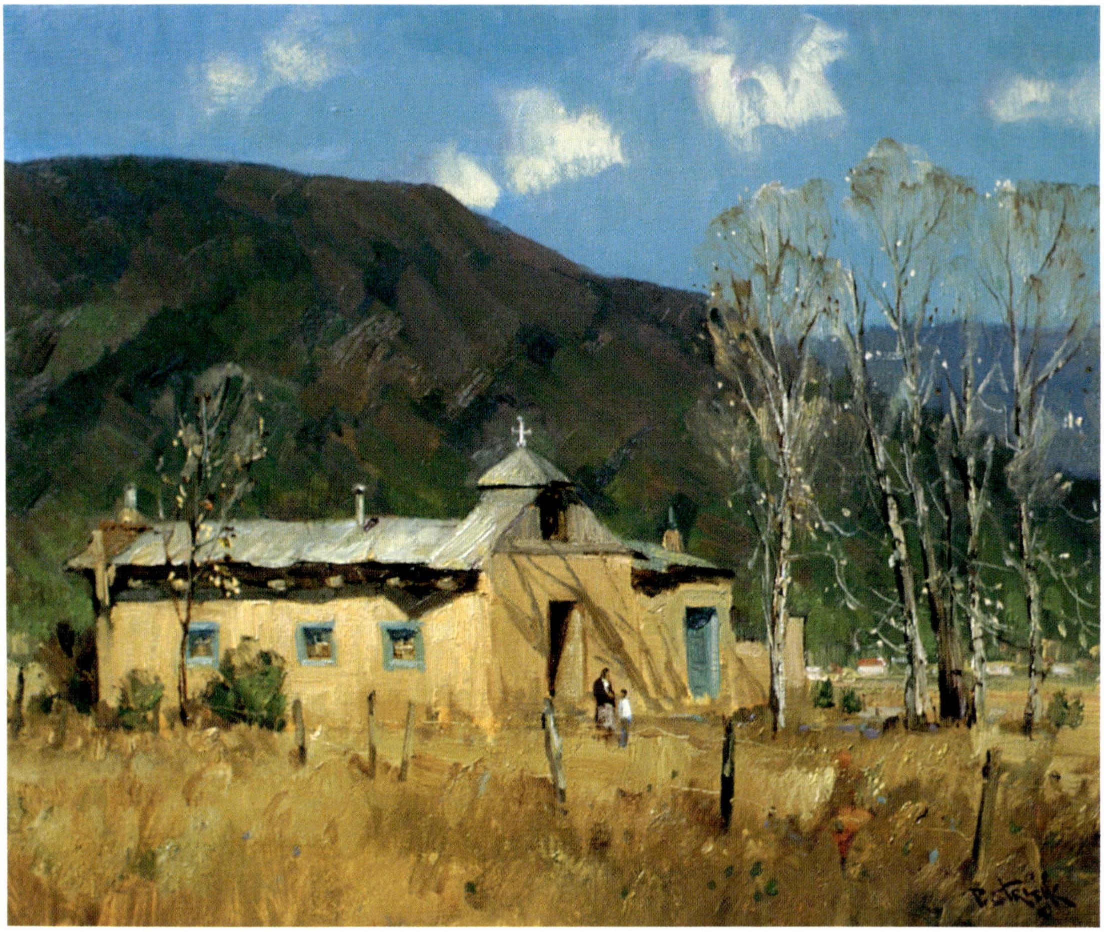

OLD CHURCH, NEW MEXICO
1989
OIL
20″ × 16″
PRIVATE COLLECTION

We have a home in Santa Fe, so part of each year is spent painting the Southwest. This is a typical small adobe village church in New Mexico. I was struck by the strong sunlight effect on the brilliant church, framed by the rich mountain—very much northern New Mexico as I have always felt it.

down and opened up. Today, the apartment is rented, and we're just open July and August, from noon to five.

Every October, I would go up to Maine and Vermont, and spend the month painting.

Then I started to travel, giving painting workshops around the country. I also joined up with Painting Holidays as an instructor. Tony Van Hasselt ran it just like a travel agency. He'd send along a director to take care of all the details, and I'd just teach. We went to Europe and all over. That went on for a number of years, until I realized that, with all the effort I was putting in, we could just travel on our own. I could paint just for myself, and come off better. So I began to taper off my traveling and my teaching, to put all my energies into painting. That was about eighteen years ago.

It sounds like you really had it made.

Well, I did, but my conscience started to bother me. Especially when good artists—artists I respected—came to the gallery. Finally I had to face the fact that I had gotten caught up in this Rockport way of painting saleable pictures. I began to wonder what had happened to my dream of becoming a *good* artist. I made the decision right then to paint more seriously. To be more committed to each canvas, instead of just painting what was popular.

I started to grow from there. There are still people who bought those old paintings, though, who say they like them better.

Did you have anyone who was a mentor or a role model for you?

I always regretted the fact that I didn't know any professional painters in the early days. I notice how fast artists accelerate when they're associated with professionals they can talk to. It held me back.

Were you ever worried that you didn't have the talent?

Talent is very overrated. It just makes things a little easier. Somebody quoted DaVinci as saying, "Talent is only the grease on the wheels of the wagon. Without it, you'll still get to town.

You'll just squeak a little more."

You just have to work harder. There are plenty of talented people who lack the other things that must go with it. They come to nothing. It's determination that counts. Plus that little voice down deep telling you others have done it, and you can, too. It reminds me of a saying I think is wonderful: "Geniuses at twenty are common. Show me one at fifty."

Certainly determination kept you going when you started, and it sustained you along the way. But a lot of years have gone by. How do you approach the discipline of work today?

Between interruptions!

An interviewer once asked Alex Haley, the author, about his work habits. He said, "A tramp steamer! When I have a project, I take it on an eight- to ten-week trip." I'm not so disciplined that I can go into my studio and close the door. The interruptions are trivial, but they're endless.

When I'm getting ready to start a new canvas, that blank canvas terrorizes me. For a week, I'm psyching myself and thinking about it. I'm mortally afraid that I'm going to make a mess. I dread making a bad canvas. I've talked to other artists about this. Many feel the same way. The first day, when I'm washing it in and laying out the idea, is very important. I live in fear that I'll be interrupted.

The ideal situation, for me, is to go away for two weeks.

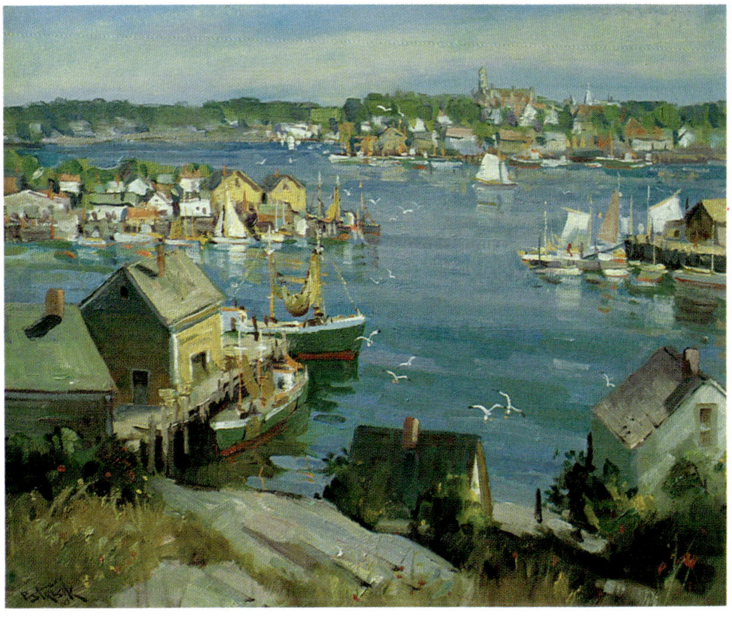

GLOUCESTER HARBOR
1989
OIL
20″ × 16″
PRIVATE COLLECTION

This view, from the heights in East Gloucester, has not changed all that much since Metcalf and Hassam painted it. I chose the time of day when the light was relatively flat, in order to have as much color as possible. Color was one of the factors that attracted me to this scene.

Do you really go? Where?

Vermont. Or Maine. I get a motel room somewhere. Alone. Then my paintings dictate when I eat, when I sleep, when I shave. I can make two efforts a day. No problem at all. I paint outdoors, rest at midday, have a snack, and go out again. I don't have to talk to anyone. I go to bed, wake up thinking painting, and never put those threads down. I develop a momentum that's fantastic. By the last four days, my brush moves by itself! Later, in the studio, I can judge them with a fresh eye and do further work.

I take it your wife has been a big help to you.

Oh yes. Nancy has relieved me of paperwork and all that. People think artists just paint pictures. But it's complicated. Books, records. Something all the time. It's just the nature of the profession.

About how many paintings are you doing a year now?

I guess forty or fifty. It varies greatly. Some are big and take a week or two. My still lifes, which tend to be Oriental arrangements, take five times as long as landscapes, because the textures and the drawing have to be just so. I can be much freer with my landscapes, because they're moving subjects.

Are you affected by the kind of critical reviews your exhibits receive?

No, I'm not. Somebody once said, regarding art critics, "Don't even ignore them."

What makes some pictures so exciting, and others so lifeless?

Conception. That's what makes Michelangelo great. His conception. A thousand artists have painted the descent from the cross, but very few are masterpieces.

And composition. You don't even start if that's not right.

And yet some paintings seem to transcend composition or pattern. When you see a really fine painting, it stops you and you know you're looking at something special. It goes beyond the surface. It has a magic. A soul. The rest are just descriptions.

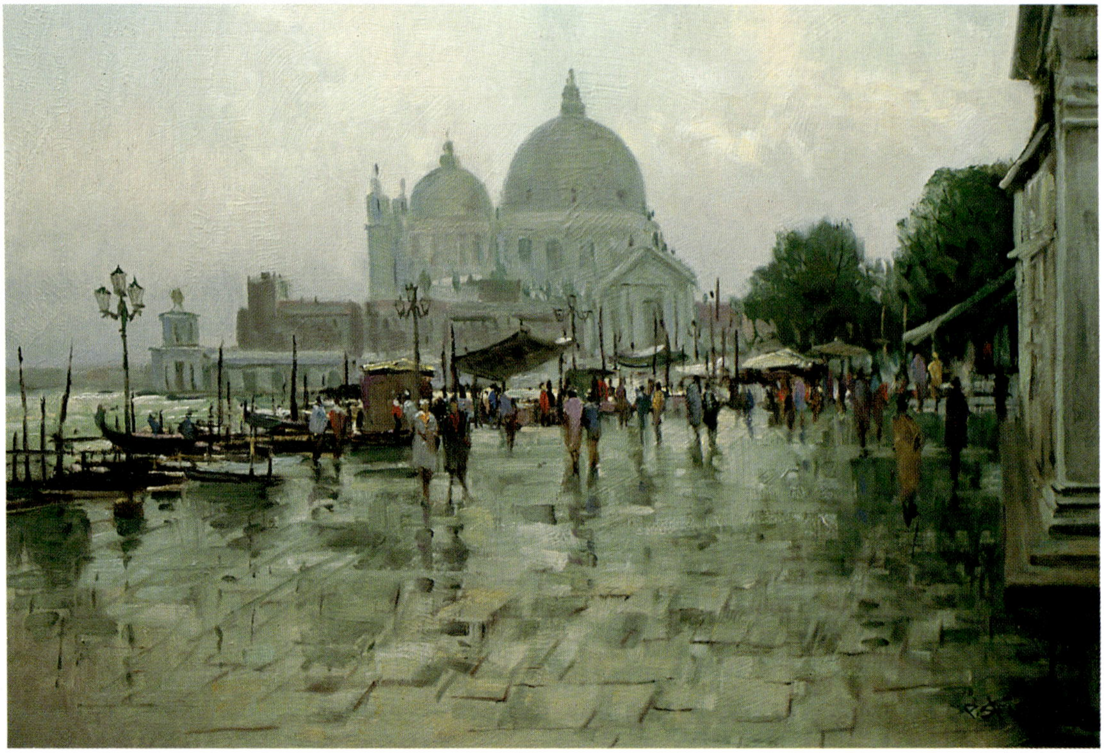

Clearing Skies, Venice
1990
Oil
24" × 16"
Private collection

Gray weather is not uncommon in northern Italy, especially in the off-season. I've always felt that gray sky in a waterfront scene adds to the mood. In this scene, the famous Della Salute church is in the background, and the ever-present tourists and wet reflections furnish a wonderful subject.

How can an artist achieve that magic?

If you're moved by a subject, and paint it, that painting will have something. On the other hand, if you paint boat pictures because people are buying boat pictures, that's not art. That kind of picture will never have any quality or magic to it. The technique may be slick. It may be painted perfectly, in the technical sense. It may be accepted into every show. But it will also be boring.

When we were students in Vermont, DuMond would tell us, "If you paint to sell, you'll grow to hate your profession and be bitter about it. But worse than that, you'll hate yourself." I've seen it happen.

Is entering competitions important?

For artists on the way up, I think it's very important to enter every show they can. It's important that their work be seen. People who count—collectors, dealers, gallery owners—start watching. One day they just may get in touch with you.

Is there anything else you'd like to say to artists just starting their careers?

First of all, go to museums as often as you can. Look at the best painting. Not just the best in your town. Don't aspire to paint like your teacher. Aspire to paint better! Find out why the best are so good. Read every book you possibly can. Not just the how-to books, but books on the history of art, and artists.

What'll make you a good artist is not just technique, and not just ability. You need to think like an artist, and aspire to do your craft in an artistic way. In the old days, artists really had to struggle. Because of that struggle, I think they painted better pictures.

Today, everybody buys art. Many artists make a lot of money with mediocre art. There's a big audience for what's corny or gimmicky. The more integrity you have, and the more artistic your work, the smaller your audience may be. But they'll be discerning people. You see, you have to look in the mirror every day and be able to say you're doing the best work you can.

Another thing: It's important, as an artist, to paint your own pictures. Stay away from "approved" subjects. Paint a red barn and you have three strikes against you. It's very difficult to give those overworked subjects a personal interpretation. But if you see a beautiful rock and some weeds . . . if something about the scene appeals to you and excites you . . . paint that. It's easier to get that kind of picture noticed, because it's *your* picture.

I tell my students, "When you're out looking for a scene to paint, and you get a tingle, and you stop, it's too easy to say, 'Now that I look at it, there are too many problems. Maybe down the road I'll find something better. . . .'

"No!" I say, "The minute you get that tingle, stop and ask yourself, 'What was it that made me stop?' Something made that scene appeal to you. That's what you've got to paint. Eliminate those elements that are common to all places. You're directing the scene. Place your principal players at center stage. It may be filled with other actors, but the audience has to get just one message. You have to distill that tingle you first felt, and you have to make your audience feel it, too."

J.C. Hawthorne, who wrote *Hawthorne on Painting*, said, "The artist is the high priest, in the sense that he sees things, and distills their essence, and puts it down so directly and so simply that people say, "Yes. That's exactly the way it looks. I've seen it that way so many times!" But they've never really seen it. They've only half suspected it. The artist has brought it into focus.

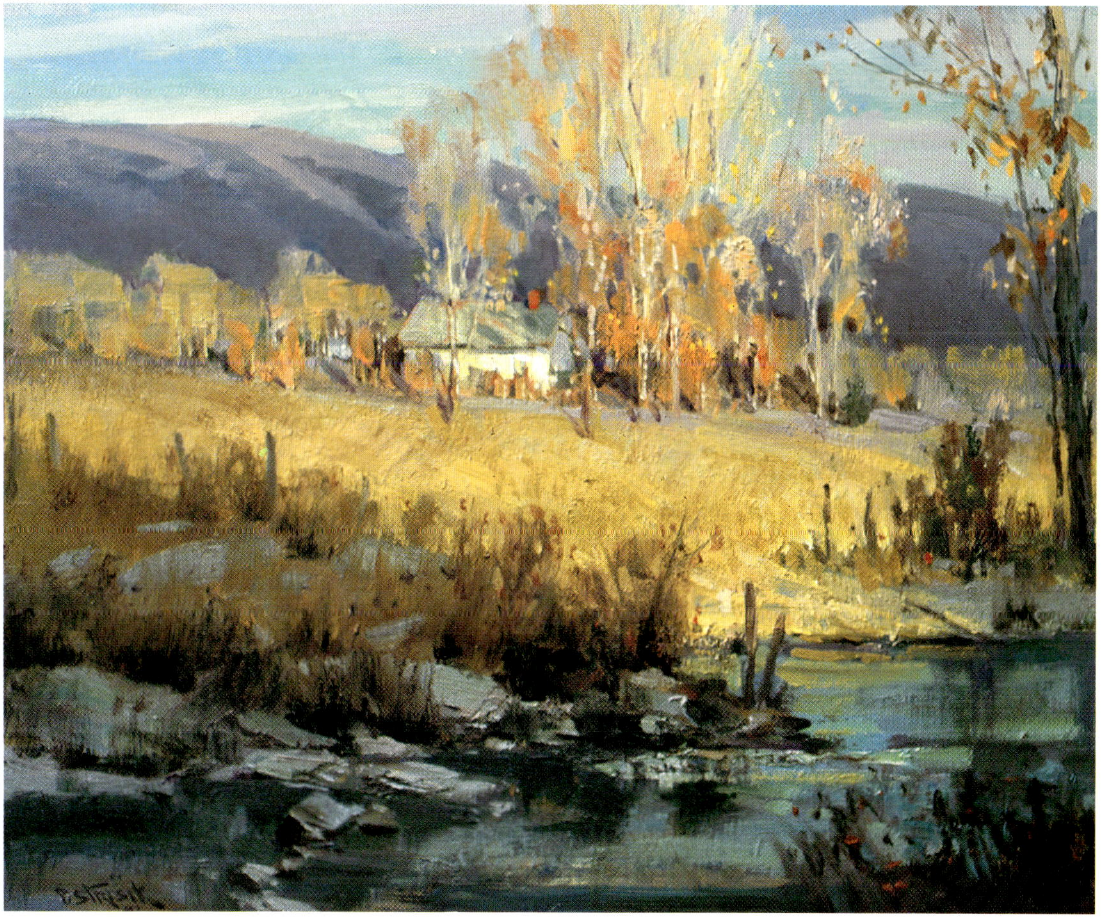

LAST LIGHT, NEW MEXICO
1989
OIL
20″ × 16″
PRIVATE COLLECTION

This is the time of day when the light becomes warm and glowing, set off by rich, dark shadows. The effect only lasts a short time, so fast sketching is necessary. A broadly painted eight- by ten-inch panel is covered without difficulty, which at least gives the color and values to build upon later in the studio.

INDEX

R

S

T

V

W

Y